WITHDRAWN

AMERICAN SCHOOLS OF ORIENTAL RESEARCH
BIBLICAL ARCHAEOLOGIST READER

Number 2

THE BIBLICAL ARCHAEOLOGIST READER
Volume II

edited by
Edward F. Campbell, Jr.
and
David Noel Freedman

SCHOLARS PRESS
Missoula, Montana

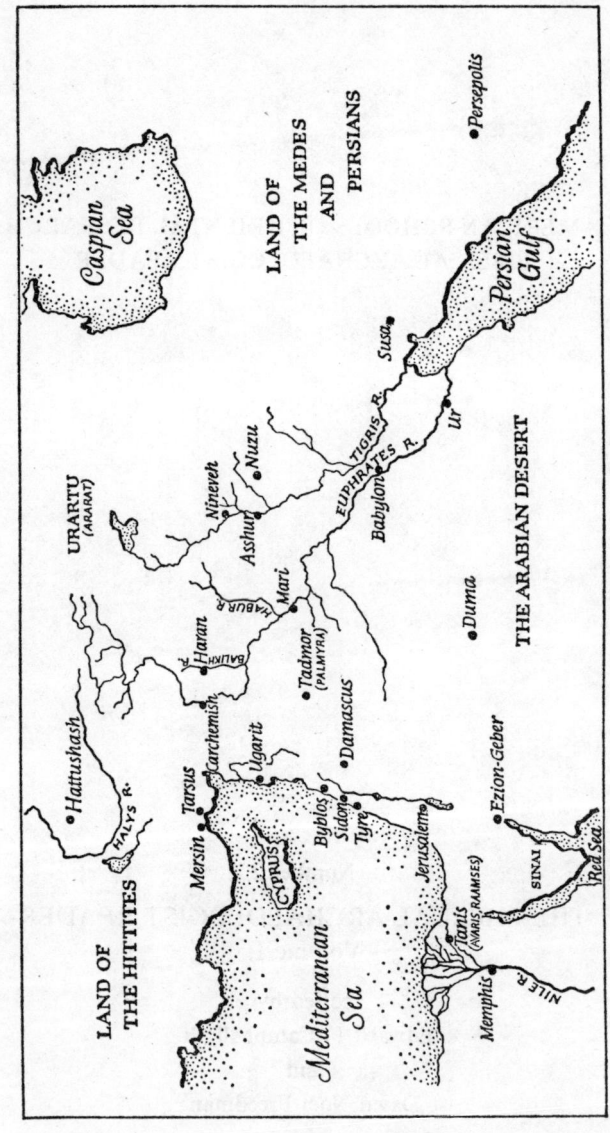

FIGURE 1. A map of the ancient Near East. Mari, Ugarit, Nuzu, and other cities discussed in this volume are indicated.

THE BIBLICAL ARCHAEOLOGIST READER
Volume II

edited by
Edward F. Campbell, Jr.
and
David Noel Freedman

Published by
SCHOLARS PRESS
for
The American Schools of Oriental Research

Distributed by
SCHOLARS PRESS
University of Montana
Missoula, Montana 59812

Copyright © 1957, 1958, 1959, 1960, 1961, 1962,
1963, 1964, 1975 by American Schools of Oriental Research

All Rights Reserved

Library of Congress Cataloging in Publication Data
Freedman, David Noel, 1922-   comp.
 The Biblical archaeologist reader.

 Vol. 2 edited by E. F. Campbell and D. N. Freedman.
 Reprint of the vols. 1 and 2 published in 1961 and
1964 respectively by Anchor Books, Garden City, N.Y.
 Includes bibliographical references.
 1. Bible—Antiquities—Addresses, essays, lectures.
I. Wright, George Ernest 1909-   joint comp.
II. Campbell, Edward Fay, joint comp.   III. The
Biblical archaeologist.   IV. Title.
BS621.F732   220.9'3   75-9592
ISBN 0-89130-002-3 (v. 2)

The articles in the volume are reprinted from

The Biblical Archaeologist

Maps for Figures 1, 3, 4, 5 by Stephen Kraft

Third Printing 1977

Printed in the United States of America

3 4 5 6

Edwards Brothers Printing
2500 South State Street
Ann Arbor, Michigan 48104

E. F. CAMPBELL, JR., is editor of *Biblical Archaeologist*. A graduate of Yale University, he received a Ph.D. in Ancient Near Eastern History from Johns Hopkins University, and a Bachelor of Divinity degree from McCormick Theological Seminary, where he is Associate Professor of Old Testament. Dr. Campbell served on the staff of the Archaeological Excavation at Shechem during the summers of 1957, 1960, and 1962.

DAVID NOEL FREEDMAN, who (with G. Ernest Wright) was editor of the first volume of *The Biblical Archaeologist Reader*, is Professor of Hebrew and Old Testament Literature at Pittsburgh Theological Seminary. Dr. Freedman was graduated from the University of California at Los Angeles (A.B.), Princeton Theological Seminary (Th.B.) and Johns Hopkins University (Ph.D. in Semitic Languages and Literature). He is general editor, with William Foxwell Albright, of The Anchor Bible.

PREFACE

The favorable reception accorded to *The Biblical Archaeologist Reader* (Doubleday Anchor Books, 1961) by reviewers and readers has encouraged the publisher and editors to undertake a companion work. It should be noted that there has been a change in editors—E. F. Campbell, Jr., of McCormick Theological Seminary has succeeded his former teacher, G. E. Wright, as editor of the *Biblical Archaeologist*, and as coeditor of the second *Reader*. As in the first volume, the articles have been selected from the files of the *B.A.* In most cases, the authors themselves have revised and brought their works up to date, though in a few instances the editors have made minimal changes in the light of more recent data.

The general purpose is still the same: to acquaint the interested reader with the results of archaeological activity in the lands of the Bible during the past decades, especially as these bear on the analysis and interpretation of the biblical materials. Reports of the principal excavations in Palestine and neighboring countries constitute a major part of the present volume, with the chief excavators themselves providing first-hand accounts.

There are three major divisions. The first consists of ten articles dealing with the cities and lands of Israel's neighbors. Following a roughly chronological sequence we begin with papers on the Mesopotamian sites of Mari and Nuzi (Nuzu) by G. E. Mendenhall and C. H. Gordon respectively. The sensational discovery of thousands of cuneiform tablets at both cities (only published in part to date) has proved of prime importance for the elucidation of the patriarchal age. The legal customs and practices of the patriarchs reflected in the narratives of Genesis are illuminated in these contemporary documents of their homeland.

Next in order are the Canaanites, the prior inhabitants of the holy land, and permanent enemies of the Israelites. Their language and culture, their literature and mythology are amply illustrated by the Ugaritic texts, discovered at the north Syrian mound of Ras Shamrah beginning in 1929. Comparison and contrast are the theme of H. L. Ginsberg's informative article on Ugaritic studies and the Bible.

Then the familiar names of other neighbors of Israel make their appearance; the Edomites, Philistines, and Ammonites who confronted, opposed, defeated the Israelites, and were, in turn, defeated by them. N. Glueck traces the tortuous course of the history of Edom and its involvement with the adjoining states of Israel and Judah from the time of the twin brothers Esau and Jacob until the disappearance of the separate states. G. E. Wright discusses the curious anthropoid sarcophagi found in 12th and 11th century B.C. tombs of Palestine and Egypt. These prove to be clues to the movements and activities of the elusive Philistines, who began as Egyptian mercenaries and came into their own as overlords of the land to which they gave their name. According to biblical tradition the Ammonites were distant relatives and persistent enemies of the Israelites throughout their history. G. M. Landes has gathered the available data from trial digs and surface explorations. On the basis of the scattered pieces of evidence he has reconstructed the story of the people of Ammon from the beginning of their state in the period of the Judges until its disappearance more than five centuries later.

During the great age of David and Solomon, there was rapid expansion of the territory of the kingdom of Israel, and extension of its political influence. Complex commercial and cultural relations with Israel's neighbors were developed—and are reflected in the material remains of their cities and countries. A detailed inquiry into the extensive trade in exotic spices—in particular frankincense and myrrh—by G. W. Van Beek results in a fascinating picture of vast commercial enterprises conducted along the shipping lanes and caravan routes of the Near East, involving enormous risks and great profits and losses, and shedding incidental light on the famous visit of the queen of Sheba to the court of King Solomon.

In a penetrating study of the political and diplomatic relations of the United Kingdom (of David and Solomon), A. Malamat probes for the historical reality obscured on the one hand by the legendary accounts of its power, fame, and wealth nurtured through centuries of pious elaboration, and on the other by more recent and fashionable scholarly skepticism. He examines specifically the contacts between Israel and its important neighbors, Egypt and Aram Naharaim, who alone remained when the buffer states between them had all been absorbed or subjugated. In the following article, B. Mazar traces the stormy history of the kingdoms of Israel and Aram, who fought together as allies, and with each other as foes, until both were swept away by the Assyrian tide in the 8th century B.C.

The Assyrians finally conquered the whole of the Near East, including in their empire the hapless kingdoms of Israel and Judah. W. W. Hallo has assembled the pertinent data from a multitude of sources and worked them into a comprehensive account of the relations between Assyria and Israel.

The second main section of the volume is devoted to a presentation of recent major excavations in Palestine. Two of the most important archaeological expeditions undertaken since the Second World War—at Hazor and Shechem—are reported in detail. Y. Yadin, the general director at Hazor, originally presented the work at the mound in a series of annual reports, thereby capturing some of the excitement and suspense of the campaign in progress. The present compilation provides a comprehensive survey of the results. He also has correlated the principal finds with other excavations in Palestine, indicating their importance for the history and culture of northern Palestine and their bearing on the biblical narratives.

There are several reports of the excavations at Shechem made by different members of the staff. W. Harrelson and B. W. Anderson discuss the literary sources, both biblical and nonbiblical for the reconstruction of the history of Shechem while E. F. Campbell and J. F. Ross deal with the excavations, centering attention on the stratigraphy of the site and pottery chronology. They set the details in the larger framework of the history of the country in biblical times.

The remaining articles in this section deal with other major excavations, and are in the nature of summary descriptions and critical evaluations derived from the principal published reports. Thus, Wright and Yadin discuss the great Megiddo undertaking sponsored by the Oriental Institute of the University of Chicago and argue for significant modifications of the conclusions reached by the excavators. Wright also reviews the work done at Samaria and Lachish, and recently published in the final official volumes of both excavations.

The final section of the volume is devoted to cities prominent in the New Testament period, and particularly those connected with that famous apostolic traveler, Paul. In each case a brief history of the city, drawn from ancient records and other sources, is offered, followed by a more detailed presentation of the evidence of modern topographical surveys and archaeological excavations, especially as these bear on the New Testament records and the emergence of the Christian Church in the first century A.D. Through the combined efforts of scholars in a dozen disciplines, the complex urban civilization of the eastern part of the Roman empire in this period has been recovered, making it possible to follow Paul and his colleagues from city to city, and see them at work propagating the gospel among the heterogeneous populations in the midst of whom they lived.

B. M. Metzger deals with Antioch-on-the-Orontes, next to Jerusalem the most important city in the story of the early spread of Christianity. Ephesus, another great center of church life in the early period, and Paul's headquarters for a time, is the subject of complementary articles by M. M. Parvis and F. V. Filson. S. E. Johnson discusses the cities of the Lycus valley in Asia Minor, which figure in the New Testament documents: Laodicea and its neighbors, Colossae and Hierapolis.

We continue in the company of the apostle to the European mainland and the famous Greek cities of Athens and Corinth. In his articles, O. Broneer has imaginatively reconstructed the visits of Paul and his companions to both cities. The setting and circumstances of Paul's address on Mars Hill in Athens are described in absorbing detail, while Paul's long stay in Corinth is plausibly connected with the famous Isthmian games celebrated biennially in this period of the Roman imperium.

The story of the Bible covers two millennia of human enterprise, centered in the eastern end of the Mediterranean and the countries bordering on it. The centuries from Abraham to Paul are marked by incessant movement of peoples, the emergence and subsidence of great urban centers. Biblical religion was in many ways a revolt against the civilization of the Near East and the sophisticated culture of its cities. At the same time, it is these long dead cities which have supplied the necessary artifacts for illuminating and interpreting the biblical materials. The destiny of biblical religion was to challenge the whole structure of pagan faith and practice in the same great cities which its prophets had so forcefully condemned.

The present volume traces the process of civilization from the age of Abraham to that of Paul—from Mari on the Euphrates to Corinth on the Isthmus. The considerable distance in space and time is bridged by a series of urban cultures which flourished in the intervening periods and area—and which have yielded through the painstaking efforts of archaeologists vast amounts of information bearing upon the history of peoples and places, arts and crafts, languages and laws— and in so doing have greatly illuminated the biblical record.

David Noel Freedman

CONTENTS

PREFACE, *David Noel Freedman* — vii

LIST OF ILLUSTRATIONS — xv

ABBREVIATIONS — xix

I. CITIES AND LANDS OF ISRAEL'S NEIGHBORS

1. MARI — 3
   George E. Mendenhall (The University of Michigan)
   XI.1 (Feb. 1948), 1–19.

2. BIBLICAL CUSTOMS AND THE NUZU TABLETS — 21
   Cyrus H. Gordon (Brandeis University)
   III.1 (Feb. 1940), 1–12.

3. UGARITIC STUDIES AND THE BIBLE — 34
   H. L. Ginsberg (The Jewish Theological Seminary of America)
   VIII.2 (May 1945), 41–58.

4. THE CIVILIZATION OF THE EDOMITES — 51
   Nelson Glueck (Hebrew Union College–Jewish Institute of Religion)
   X.4 (Dec. 1947), 77–84.

5. PHILISTINE COFFINS AND MERCENARIES — 59
   G. Ernest Wright (Harvard University)
   XXII.3 (Sept. 1959), 53–66.

6. THE MATERIAL CIVILIZATION OF THE AMMONITES — 69
   George M. Landes (Union Theological Seminary, New York)
   XXIV.3 (Sept. 1961), 65–86.

7. THE KINGDOM OF DAVID AND SOLOMON IN ITS CONTACT WITH EGYPT AND ARAM NAHARAIM — 89
   Abraham Malamat (Hebrew University, Jerusalem, Israel)
   XXI.4 (Dec. 1958), 96–102.

8. FRANKINCENSE AND MYRRH *Gus W. Van Beek* (The Smithsonian Institution) XXIII.3 (Sept. 1960), 69–95.	99
9. THE ARAMEAN EMPIRE AND ITS RELATIONS WITH ISRAEL *Benjamin Mazar* (Hebrew University, Jerusalem, Israel) XXV.4 (Dec. 1962), 97–120.	127
10. FROM QARQAR TO CARCHEMISH: ASSYRIA AND ISRAEL IN THE LIGHT OF NEW DISCOVERIES *William W. Hallo* (Yale University) XXIII.2 (May 1960), 33–61.	152

II. MAJOR EXCAVATED CITIES OF PALESTINE

11. EXCAVATIONS AT HAZOR, 1955–1958 *Yigael Yadin* (Hebrew University, Jerusalem, Israel) XIX.1 (Feb. 1956), 1–12; XX.2 (May 1957), 33–37; XXI.2 (May 1958), 29–47; XXII.1 (Feb. 1959), 1–20.	191
12. THE DISCOVERIES AT MEGIDDO, 1935–1939 *G. Ernest Wright* (Harvard University) XIII.2 (May 1950), 28–46.	225
NEW LIGHT ON SOLOMON'S MEGIDDO *Yigael Yadin* (Hebrew University, Jerusalem, Israel) XXIII.2 (May 1960), 62–68.	240
13. SAMARIA *G. Ernest Wright* (Harvard University) XXII.3 (Sept. 1959), 67–78.	248
14. SHECHEM IN EXTRA-BIBLICAL REFERENCES *Walter Harrelson* (Vanderbilt University) XX.1 (Feb. 1957), 2–10.	258
THE PLACE OF SHECHEM IN THE BIBLE *Bernhard W. Anderson* (Drew University) XX.1 (Feb. 1957), 10–19.	265

THE EXCAVATION OF SHECHEM AND THE BIBLICAL
TRADITION 275
Edward F. Campbell, Jr. (McCormick Theological Seminary) and *James F. Ross* (Drew University)
XXVI.1 (Feb. 1963), 1–27.

15. JUDEAN LACHISH 301
G. Ernest Wright (Harvard University)
XVIII.1 (Feb. 1955), 9–17.

III. PROMINENT CITIES OF THE NEW TESTAMENT PERIOD

16. ANTIOCH-ON-THE-ORONTES 313
Bruce M. Metzger (Princeton Theological Seminary)
XI.4 (Dec. 1948), 69–88.

17. EPHESUS IN THE EARLY CHRISTIAN ERA 331
Merrill M. Parvis (Emory University)
VIII.3 (Sept. 1945), 61–73.

EPHESUS AND THE NEW TESTAMENT 343
Floyd V. Filson (McCormick Theological Seminary)
VIII.3 (Sept. 1945), 73–80.

18. LAODICEA AND ITS NEIGHBORS 353
Sherman E. Johnson (The Church Divinity School of the Pacific)
XIII.1 (Feb. 1950), 1–18.

19. ATHENS, "CITY OF IDOL WORSHIP" 369
Oscar Broneer (Ancient Corinth, Greece)
XXI.1 (Feb. 1958), 1–28.

20. THE APOSTLE PAUL AND THE ISTHMIAN GAMES 393
Oscar Broneer (Ancient Corinth, Greece)
XXV.1 (Feb. 1962), 1–31.

LIST OF ILLUSTRATIONS

PLATES

1. Statue of Lamgi-mari, one of the kings of Mari in the early 3rd millennium. *From* Syria, *XVI* (*1935*), *Pl. VI, and* BA *XI.1* (*Feb. 1948*), *Fig. 2.*
2. A Nuzu "lion," from the Hurrian level. *Harvard Semitic Museum Photo.*
3. Inscribed adzes from Ugarit, showing Ugaritic alphabetic writing. *From C. F.-A. Schaeffer,* Ugaritica, *I* (*1939*), *Pl. XXIV, and* BA, *VIII.2* (*May 1945*), *Fig. 4.*
4. A bas-relief from Ugarit showing the Canaanite weather god Hadad. *Photo: C. F.-A. Schaeffer. From* Syria, *XIV* (*1933*), *Pl. XVI, and* BA, *VIII.2* (*May 1945*), *Fig. 6.*
5. Figurines from Edom, found near Buseirah. *From* AASOR, *XVIII–XIX* (*1940*), *Fig. XIX, and* BA *X.4* (*Dec. 1947*), *Fig. 7.*
6. A horse-and-rider pottery figurine from an Ammonite tomb. *From* QDAP, *XIV* (*1950*), *Pl. XIII, and* BA, *XXIV.3* (*Sept. 1961*), *Fig. 7.*
7. Statue of Yaraḥ ʿazar, from the vicinity of Amman, Jordan. *From* The Ancient Near East in Pictures, *ed. James B. Pritchard* (*1954*), *Fig. 64, courtesy of the Department of Antiquities of Jordan; and* BA, *XXIV.3* (*Sept. 1961*), *Fig. 1.*
8. A frankincense tree on the plain of Dhofar in southern Arabia. *Photo: Ray L. Cleveland. From* BA, *XXIII.3* (*Sept. 1960*), *Fig. 1.*
9. Tears of gum resin on the branch of a frankincense tree. *Photo: Ray L. Cleveland. From* BA, *XXIII.3* (*Sept. 1960*), *Fig. 4.*
10. The stele dedicated to Melqart by Bir-hadad, king of Aram. *Photo: James B. Pritchard.*
11. Part of Sefire stele IB containing a description of the boundaries of Aram in the mid-8th century. *From A. Dupont-Sommer,* Les inscriptions araméennes de Sfire (*1958*), *Pl. IX, and* BA, *XXV.4* (*Dec. 1962*), *Fig. 9.*

12. An ivory plaque inscribed in Aramaic and dedicated to "our lord Hazael," from Arslan-Tash. *From F. Thureau-Dangin, Arslan-Tash: Atlas (1931), Pl. XLVII, and BA, XXV.4 (Dec. 1962), Fig. 7.*

13. A statue of the Assyrian king Shalmaneser III, found at Nimrud. *From Iraq, XXI (1959), Pl. XL, courtesy of the British School of Archaeology in Iraq; and BA, XXIII.2 (May 1960), Fig. 1.*

14. A vassal treaty of Esarhaddon from the early 7th century, written on a cuneiform tablet. *From Iraq, XX (1958), Pl. I, courtesy of the British School of Archaeology in Iraq; and BA, XXIII.2 (May 1960), Fig. 5.*

15. An aerial view of the mound and lower city of Hazor. *Photo: the Israel Air Force, used by permission. From BA, XXII.1 (Feb. 1959), Fig. 2.*

16. The Holy of Holies in the Canaanite orthostat temple at Hazor. *From BA, XXII.1 (Feb. 1959), Fig. 3.*

17. A view of the furnishings in the Holy of Holies of the Hazor Canaanite temple, as they were found. *From BA, XXI.2 (May 1958), Fig. 6.*

18. An aerial view of Area A on the mound at Hazor, showing remains dating from Middle Bronze II through the 8th century B.C. *Photo: the Israel Air Force, used by permission. From BA, XXII.1 (Feb. 1959), Fig. 11.*

19. Plan of the Megiddo city gate from the time of Solomon. *Oriental Institute, University of Chicago Photo. From BA, XIII.2 (May 1950), Fig. 14.*

20. A proposed reconstruction of the Solomonic gateway at Megiddo. *Oriental Institute, University of Chicago Photo. From BA, XIII.2 (May 1950), Fig. 15.*

21. A Hellenistic round tower at Samaria, with a portion of the old Israelite wall coming up to it. *From J. W. Crowfoot et al., Samaria-Sebaste I, The Buildings (1942), Pl. XXXVI.2, and BA, XXII.3 (Sept. 1959), Fig. 16.*

22. Remains of the Fortress Temple at Shechem, viewed from before its front entrance. *Photo: Lee C. Ellenberger.*

23. A fine Assyrian adorant seal from the late 8th century ruins at Shechem. *Photo: Lee C. Ellenberger. From BA, XXVI.1 (Feb. 1963), Fig. 1.*

24. A cache of silver Ptolemaic tetradrachms from a Hellenistic level at Shechem. *Photo: Lee C. Ellenberger. From BA, XXIII.4 (Dec. 1960), Fig. 2.*

25. The siege of Lachish as depicted in the reliefs of Sen-

LIST OF ILLUSTRATIONS

nacherib at Nineveh. *From A. H. Layard, Monuments of Nineveh, II (1853), Pl. XXI, and BA, I.4 (Dec. 1938), Fig. 9.*

26. A reconstruction of the city of Lachish as it looked about 598 B.C. *From BA, I.4 (Dec. 1938), Fig. 12.*

27. Folio 4 of the Rabbula Gospels, a Syriac manuscript of A.D. 586. *From C. Nordenfalk, Die spätantiken Kanontafeln (1938), Pl. CXXXII, and BA, XI.4 (Dec. 1948), Fig. 9.*

28. The Chalice of Antioch, found in a well at Antioch in 1910. *Photo: The Metropolitan Museum of Art, the Cloisters Collection, Purchase 1950.*

29. A reconstruction of the west portico of the Artemis temple at Ephesus (6th century B.C.). *From F. Krischen, Die griechische Stadt (1938), Pl. XXXIII, and BA, VIII.3 (Sept. 1945), Fig. 3.*

30. A reconstruction of the center Harbor Gate at Ephesus. *From Forschungen in Ephesos, published by the Österreichischen Archaeologischen Institut, vol. III (1900), Pl. IV, and BA, VIII.3 (Sept. 1945), Fig. 6.*

31. The basilica in Hierapolis, which may possibly be a church dedicated to Philip. *Photo: Sherman E. Johnson.*

32. The Acropolis at Athens, with the Areopagus in the foreground. *Photo: Alison Frantz. From BA, XXI.1 (Feb. 1958), Fig. 2.*

33. The Areopagus in Athens, on which Paul spoke to the Athenians (Acts 17:22). *Photo: Eugene Vanderpool. From BA, XXI.1 (Feb. 1958), Fig. 13.*

34. A plan of the structures at Isthmia, site of the famous games. *Plan: W. B. Dinsmoor, Jr.*

35. The temple of Poseidon at Isthmia, indicated by foundation trenches cut in the rock. *Photo: Oscar Broneer, From BA, XXV.1 (Feb. 1962), Fig. 4.*

36. The starting line at the Early Stadium in Isthmia, showing starting devices. *Photo: Oscar Broneer.*

37. and 38. Two marble pieces from Isthmia: the head of a victorious athlete (37.) and the flame of a torch carried in the races (38.). *Photo: Oscar Broneer. From BA, XXV.1 (Feb. 1962), Fig. 12.*

38. Jumping weights found at Isthmia, with a vase painting to show how they were used. *Photo: Oscar Broneer.*

FIGURES

1. A map of the ancient Near East, showing the location of Mari, Ugarit, Nuzu, and other prominent cities. *Drawing by Stephen Kraft after* BA, *III.1 (Feb. 1940), p. 4.* — iv
2. Philistine artifacts from tombs and from Egyptian depictions at Medinet Habu. *From* Eretz Israel, V *(1958), 56; and* BA, *XXII.3 (Sept. 1959), p. 55.* — 60
3. Sketch map of Arabia and adjacent lands, showing probable locations of frankincense and myrrh forests, ancient ports, and caravan cities. *Drawing by G. W. Van Beek. From* BA, *XXIII.3 (Sept. 1960), p. 90, Fig. 5.* — 102
4. Plan of the site of Samaria. *From* Samaria-Sebaste I *(1942), Pl. I, courtesy of the Palestine Exploration Fund; and* BA, *XXII.3 (Sept. 1959), p. 68, Fig. 11.* — 251
5. Sketch map of Ephesus and its environs. *Drawing by R. C. Snyder. From* BA, *VIII.3 (Sept. 1945), p. 63, Fig. 2.* — 332
6. Plan of the Agora in Athens. *From* BA, *XXI.1 (Feb. 1958), p. 17, Fig. 9.* — 382
7. A drawing from a Panathenaic amphora from Isthmia recalling Paul's words in I Corinthians 9:24. *Courtesy of Oscar Broneer.* — 420

ABBREVIATIONS

AASOR	*Annual of the American Schools of Oriental Research*
ADAJ	*Annual of the Department of Antiquities of Jordan*
AfO	*Archiv für Orientforschung*
AJA	*American Journal of Archaeology*
AJSL	*American Journal of Semitic Languages and Literatures*
An. St.	*Anatolian Studies*
ANET	James B. Pritchard, ed., *Ancient Near Eastern Texts Relating to the Old Testament* (Princeton, 1950; 2nd ed. 1955)
APEF	*Annual of the Palestine Exploration Fund*
BA	*The Biblical Archaeologist*
BASOR	*Bulletin of the American Schools of Oriental Research*
BIES	*Bulletin of the Israel Exploration Society*
ca.	for *circa*, approximately
FSAC	William Foxwell Albright, *From the Stone Age to Christianity* (3rd ed., New York, 1957)
HUCA	*Hebrew Union College Annual*
IEJ	*Israel Exploration Journal*
ILN	*Illustrated London News*
JAOS	*Journal of the American Oriental Society*
JBL	*Journal of Biblical Literature*
JCS	*Journal of Cuneiform Studies*
JEA	*Journal of Egyptian Archaeology*
JNES	*Journal of Near Eastern Studies*
JPOS	*Journal of the Palestine Oriental Society*
JSS	*Journal of Semitic Studies*
JTS	*Journal of Theological Studies*
OLZ	*Orientalistische Literaturzeitung*
PEFQ	*Quarterly Statement of the Palestine Exploration Fund* (*Palestine Exploration Fund Quarterly*)

PJB	*Palästinajahrbuch*
QDAP	*Quarterly of the Department of Antiquities of Palestine*
RA	*Revue d'assyriologie*
RB	*Revue biblique*
VT	*Vetus Testamentum*
VTS	*Vetus Testamentum Supplement*
ZAW	*Zeitschrift für alttestamentliche Wissenschaft*
ZDMG	*Zeitschrift der deutschen morgenlandischen Gesellschaft*
ZDPV	*Zeitschrift des deutschen Palästina-Vereins*

Part I

CITIES AND LANDS OF
ISRAEL'S NEIGHBORS

1

MARI

GEORGE E. MENDENHALL

Until 1933, Mari was one of the innumerable ghost towns of the Near East which had been so completely buried under the sands of time and the middle Euphrates desert, that the very ghosts had nearly forgotten its location. To be sure, excavations at the sites of other ancient cities of Mesopotamia had yielded inscriptions of various kinds bearing references to the city of Mari. From these inscriptions it was possible to determine the general region of the Euphrates valley in which this city must have flourished. It was possible also very roughly to sketch the fortunes of the city in various periods of history. The old Sumerian King List preserved the tradition that Mari was the site of the 10th dynasty of Mesopotamia after the great flood, but of the six kings who reigned 136 years, we have the name of only one completely preserved.[1] It is a perplexing fact that after six campaigns of excavation, no reference to the name of a ruler of Mari mentioned in the King List has been found.

The identification of the ruin of Mari had been the subject of much study, but it was not until 1932 that W. F. Albright suggested with some confidence that Tell Hariri, near the Iraq-Syria boundary line, must have been ancient Mari. Confirmation could, of course, be gained only through excavation. That confirmation was soon to come, for in August of the following year, a group of Arabs came to the office of Lt. Cabane, Deputy-Inspector of the French military district, at Abu Kemal. They had been engaged in digging a grave for one of their defunct brethren and in searching for an appropriate gravestone to place over the grave. Their purpose in coming to Abu Kemal was to ask what they should do with the "man" they had dug up in the course of their search. Upon

[1] Thorkild Jacobsen, *The Sumerian King List* (1939), p. 102.

further questioning it became clear that they had discovered a heavy statue in a mound at Tell Hariri. Immediately Lt. Cabane went to the site to recover the statue, which, incidentally, weighed several hundred pounds. He then sent word of the discovery to Aleppo, whence the news was retransmitted to Paris. Several months later, the distinguished French archaeologist, André Parrot, arrived at Abu Kemal to begin excavation. The results were to become one of the most sensational discoveries in a generation of very important and interesting archaeological finds, and the task of assimilating and interpreting the new material made available will continue for many years to come. For the first time, we have considerable information concerning the civilization and political history of eastern Syria and western Mesopotamia in the time of Hammurabi of Babylon; and the Amorites, who play so important a part in the early history of Israel, are beginning to emerge into the full light of history.

Tell Hariri is composed of a group of low hillocks located about seven miles north-northeast of the frontier town of Abu Kemal, near the Iraq border. Though the tell is now over a mile from the Euphrates river, in antiquity the river flowed past the very edge of the city. The ruins lie several miles east of the main road which follows the river. For this reason and because of the relatively insignificant appearance of the site, Tell Hariri had almost escaped attention through the recent years of archaeological exploration. The mounds cover an area over half a mile long by less than a half mile wide. The highest of the hillocks is less than fifty feet high, quite insignificant in comparison to the huge mounds of the great cities in Mesopotamia proper.

Excavation of the site began in the middle of December, 1933. Each winter thereafter until 1938 several months were devoted to further excavation. Since the "Cabane statue" was found in the very center of the tell, excavations were started in that spot with the purpose of determining the stratification and dating of the debris of occupation, and also to break in the Arab laborers who were completely untrained and undisciplined at the outset. It was not long before unmistakable evidence came to light in the form of sculptures which showed a highly developed civilization dating before the time of Sargon of Akkad (*ca.* 24th century B.C.). This was followed by the discovery of tombs of the same period in which the corpse had been dismembered before interment, presumably to prevent the spirit of the deceased from coming back to trouble the living.

The work was then shifted to another of the low hillocks, this time to a location on the northwest edge of the tell where the archaeologist expected to find a city gate. Almost immediately the picks of the laborers began to unearth statues and fragments in great number: further digging showed that instead of the city gate or wall expected, they had discovered an ancient temple dedicated to Ishtar, for several of the statues bore dedicatory inscriptions to the goddess of love and war. One of these made possible the identification of the tell, for an imposing and cruel-looking character bore on his shoulder the lines: "Lamgi-mari, king of Mari, high priest of Enlil, dedicated his statue to Ishtar."

The first three seasons of work in the temple of Ishtar yielded eight complete statues, twenty-six headless statues (the heads had probably been removed and carried off as trophies of war), seventeen detached heads, thirty-six torsos, and many others parts and fragments. Ishtar was a popular goddess indeed, and well supplied with works of art to adorn her temple. The quality and material of these statues vary considerably, for not everyone could afford to dedicate a work of art in expensive stone. The workshops of the city accordingly seem to have turned out quantities of less expensive statues of standardized type, which enabled the pious pilgrims of less affluence to leave a gift to the goddess and ensure her benevolence. The majority of these sculptures represent the worshipers in the customary attitude of devotion, as pilgrims standing with the left foot forward and hands folded.

This temple, or rather, series of temples on the same site, was first built in the early 3rd millennium B.C. or earlier. It was repeatedly destroyed and rebuilt, sharing the fate of the city itself, until its final destruction at the hands of Hammurabi's soldiers. The form of the temple in pre-Sargonic times was very similar to the temples of the same period found at Asshur and Ur. It consisted primarily of a court approached through a long corridor, a holy place where the statue of the goddess was enthroned, and a third cult room, the purpose of which is not clear. The temple at Mari had a number of rooms to provide living quarters for the personnel attached to the goddess, and some of these rooms must have been occupied by priestesses, to judge from the jewels, necklaces, and amulets found on the floors.

Ishtar was not the only deity honored with a temple at Mari. In later excavations a ziggurat was laid bare, to which was adjoined a temple apparently of a completely new type. The most significant part of the temple furniture consisted of four raised platforms of mud brick placed against the walls. The excavator saw in these platforms not altars, but rather couches for the rite of sacred marriage.[2] The temple doors were guarded by two menacing lions of bronze, but further excavation uncovered some seventy eyes of stone set in bronze which seem to have belonged to similar animals. It is likely that the temple and ziggurat were protected by forty guardian lions, all but two of which were removed by the pillagers when the city was finally taken. The discovery of a foundation deposit revealed that this was a temple of Dagon, called "king of the land."

The Palace

In January 1935, a new sector of the mound was surveyed and laid out for excavation with the primary objective of determining the exact stratigraphy and origin of the site. Though many finds had been uncovered which pointed to very early occupation, the earliest settlement was still hidden under the debris of the cities of the third and second millennia. This time the first strokes of the pick revealed the thick mud brick walls of an important building. The building proved to be the palace of Mari, and its excavation required that a considerable portion of the time and effort be expended on the tell until the work had to be discontinued in December 1938. The palace is one of the finest, and certainly the best preserved of any so far found in the Near East. In extent and construction it is truly amazing. It boasts over 250 rooms, halls, courts and corridors, covering more than six acres. Though it was built of the only material available in quantity in Babylonia, mud brick, the care and skill with which it was constructed are indicated by the fact that after the destruction in war, and after the ravages of the elements for several thousand years, the walls are still standing here and there to a height of fifteen to

[2] André Parrot, *Syria*, XIX (1938), 23. For the rite of sacred marriage, see Herodotus *The Histories* i.181.

twenty feet. A further proof of the excellence of the architects and builders was vividly demonstrated on one occasion when a heavy downpour of rain occurred after a considerable part of the palace had been laid bare. The archaeologist, Parrot, feared lest the water undermine the walls and cause them to collapse, but to his surprise, when he arrived at the tell after the rain, there was not even a pool of water standing in the palace area! The ancient builders had constructed pottery drains which conducted the water far below the surface to protect the foundations, and after 3500 years the drains had worked perfectly.[3]

The palace seems to have had a second story extending over a part of the structure, and in one place were found stairs which seemed to lead to a basement, though that section of the mound was too badly eroded to be certain. The ceilings were very high, for good reason. It was determined that the ground floor, at least, had no windows, but light was assured for all parts of the palace by a very simple and effective arrangement of the ground plan. There were a number of large open courts, and grouped about each of these courts were a series of rooms interconnected by high doorways, the lintels of which were about sixteen feet above the floor. Thus light from the courts could easily penetrate to the innermost recesses. Since the walls were standing in places at practically their original height, it was easy to determine the effectiveness of this plan by covering the part of the palace where the walls were highest. The light was soft, but adequate for ordinary purposes. Wood was used only as beams for the ceilings, and occasionally for decorations. The floors were composed sometimes of flagstone or tile paving; often they were plastered; occasionally they were of beaten earth. The walls were plastered over the mud brick, and doubtless re-plastered from time to time. Some of the rooms had elaborate decorations in color on the walls. The royal palace must truly have been a magnificent sight in the days of its glory.

Since the palace was such a large and elaborate structure, it is only to be expected that it would include all sorts of accommodations and installations which would make it a small city in itself. In addition to the royal apartments, protected by tremendously thick walls on the outside and well shut off from the rest of the palace, there were lodgings for visiting

[3] Parrot, *Mari: une ville perdue* (1945), p. 161.

officials or couriers from other lands, and of course the storerooms and kitchens for preparing the considerable amount of food which must have been consumed daily by the personnel attached to the royal court. Near the kitchens were found a large number of platters with designs in intaglio on the bottom, evidently used as molds to decorate the dishes of the royal table. After the cheeses or whatever dish the king thought fashionable had set, the dish would be turned upside down, the mold removed, and the servant would bring to the king a delicacy decorated with a lion, a fish, a stag, or even a nude goddess.

Perhaps an even more convincing testimony to the civilized life led in the palace is the presence of well-designed bathroom facilities. Some of them still had two bathtubs in place—one for hot water and one for cold? The bathtubs were usually emptied into the floor drains by means of a long-handled dipper kept in a convenient niche in the wall nearby, but a few were equipped with outlets. The drains led sometimes as much as forty feet below the floor. The king's bathroom had an armchair where he could relax while having his massage. There were also toilets provided, of a simple type still in use in oriental lands.

Two of the rooms gave the immediate impression, even to inexperienced visitors, that they could be nothing but schoolrooms. The rows of benches, the pottery "writing-desks" in which the apprentice scribes held the moist clay tablets, and a few tablets scattered on the floor, perhaps discarded in haste when the enemy soldiers caused classes to be dismissed forever, all made it certain that this was indeed the place where the king's secretaries-to-be learned their *a b c*'s in the difficult but colorful cuneiform script of the day. Arithmetic had its place with reading and writing, for there were many small shells on the floor which doubtless had served to calculate numbers beyond the reach of fingers and toes.

In the very center of the palace, the king had his private chapel. It consisted of three open courts; the largest court was approached through a long corridor opening into the center of its long side. Upon entering, the worshiper could see through a portal into the second court where his eye would fall on a panel of wood hung over a podium. This panel was almost completely reduced to ashes, but it seems likely that it represented some sort of religious scene. The innermost court was the place where the king himself paid his respects to the goddess. It was over seventy-five feet long and the walls were thirty feet high. Along the walls an awning had projected six feet above the floor to serve as a protection from sun and rain. At one end of the court there was a base of stone set into the dirt floor where the royal throne stood during religious ceremonies. Above the throne a canopy had been spread. At the opposite end of the court the king could see into a little room ten steps above the court, and in this little room the statue of the god was presumably enthroned. But the little room was empty. There was nothing to indicate who the god was, but it was intriguing to find that the floor of the cella, the stairs, and the floor of the court below the stairs were all composed of burnt brick set in bitumen or pitch. This led to the conclusion that the cult of the deity must have been accompanied by very generous libations to require such careful provisions for protection against running water. When the other courts of the chapel were later excavated, there emerged the statue of a goddess holding a vase. The statue was in several pieces, with the head in one court and the rest in another. When the torso was recovered the interesting fact was noticed that the vase held by the goddess was hollow, and a hole in the bottom was connected with a channel leading through the middle of the statue to the base. It was literally a goddess with a flowing vase, for doubtless there was a reservoir at the proper height somewhere nearby, which supplied the "living water" for the goddess. It seems most likely that this was the figure which stood in the little room opposite the king. She was a goddess of fertility, the giver of the life-bestowing fresh water. Though many representations of a goddess or god with spouting vase have been found in cylinder seals[4] and in sculpture, this is the first example of a statue actually found which would act as a fountain.

Did Ezekiel see similar figures in Babylonia? In his prophecy (47:1) we read "Behold, waters issued out from under the threshold of the house eastward . . . and the waters came down from under, from the right side of the house, at the south side of the altar. . . . And by the river upon the bank thereof, on this side and on that side, shall grow all trees for meat, whose leaf shall not fade, neither shall the fruit thereof fail: it shall bring forth new fruit every month, be-

[4] W. H. Ward, *The Seal Cylinders of Western Asia* (1910), pp. 213 ff.

cause the waters thereof issue out of the sanctuary; and the fruit thereof shall be for food, and the leaf thereof for healing" (47:12). Possibly the same general idea is to be found in John 7:38, "He that believeth on me, as the scripture hath said, from his belly shall flow rivers of living water." Compare also Revelation 22:1.

The Royal Archives

Mari's most valuable bequest to us is doubtless the royal archives. More than 20,000 tablets have been recovered from various rooms of the palace, of which several hundred have already been published in facsimile or transcription and translation. In addition to the royal correspondence from many kingdoms of western Asia, there are a great number of business records, nearly three-fourths of the tablets coming under this category. There are scattered documents of various types, such as a few tablets in the old Hurrian language, a ritual belonging to the cult of Ishtar, and a few historical inscriptions. The letters are written in a very beautiful and clear cuneiform script, indicating that the very best scribes of the day were used in the king's offices, and that they took pride in their calligraphy. The form of the characters indicates Mari's close relationship to, and dependence on, the 3rd dynasty of Ur. The archives had originally been filed carefully by date, but the pillaging soldiers, not interested in the enemy documents, smashed and scattered the tablets so badly that only the smallest are generally well preserved.

Though it will take years completely to exhaust the mine of information to be gained from the Mari archives, much has already been done. With the publication of a volume of letters by C.-F. Jean in 1941, and another volume by G. Dossin in 1946, in addition to many abstracts and individual documents published in various journals, the history and international relations of eastern Syria during the period of Hammurabi are emerging into the light of day. The greatest importance of these archives for the biblical scholar lies in the information we may confidently expect to obtain concerning the still somewhat shadowy Amorites, who were the ancestors of the Israelites according to biblical tradition.

The first great contribution of the Mari letters to our historical knowledge was the proof that Shamshi-adad I of Assyria and Hammurabi of Babylon were for a time contemporaries. This fact, combined with the chronology preserved in the Khorsabad King List[5] made necessary a new revision of the chronology of the Old Babylonian and preceding periods.[6] Hammurabi is now to be dated approximately 1728–1686, and the 3rd dynasty of Ur consequently must be brought down to *ca.* 2070–1960.

The History of Mari

Though the origin of the city is still hidden under the sand, it is certain that Mari was occupied from very early times. The Sumerian Early Dynastic is well represented in the finds, and other objects may date to the preceding Jemdet Nasr period, to the beginning of the 3rd millennium B.C. Further excavation will be necessary to determine whether the city was occupied in even earlier periods. The temple of Ishtar was first built in the Early Dynastic period, but later stages of the same temple yielded the inscribed statues of Ebikh-il, Idi-narum, Lamgi-mari—all good Semitic names dating some 200 years before the time of Sargon of Akkad. This gives us additional evidence of the wide distribution of the Semites long before the time of Sargon, though it can hardly be used as evidence that the middle Euphrates was the original home of the Semites. This early Semitic dynasty was probably the one overthrown by Eannatum (*ca.* 2500), who mentions the capture of Mari in his inscriptions.

Sargon of Akkad in his turn took Mari, and from this time the city entered a period of eclipse, apparently ending in total ruin, for nothing was discovered which dated from the period between the fall of the dynasty of Akkad and the founding of the 3rd dynasty of Ur. It is during the following phase that Mari reached the zenith of its power and glory. Ur-nammu rebuilt the city, the palace was begun, and Mari gradually grew in strength. Under a long series of governors, not many of whom seem to have taken their subordination to Ur very seriously, Mari must have become more and more powerful till the city finally kicked the mother that fed it, by contributing to the fall of Ur in alliance with the Elamites.

The Amorites who had prepared the way for the fall of Ur by their persistent encroachments in search of fertile land and

[5] Arno Poebel, *JNES*, I (1942), 247 ff., 460 ff.; II (1943), 56 ff.
[6] W. F. Albright, *BASOR*, No. 88 (Dec. 1942), pp. 28–33.

booty made their influence felt likewise at Mari. The population of the city must have become increasingly Amorite during the 19th century B.C., and soon the city was in the hands of an Amorite dynasty founded by Iagit-lim. From then until the final destruction of the city, Mari was ruled by this dynasty except for a period of about sixteen years, during which time the Amorite king of Assyria succeeded in usurping the throne for his son Iasmakh-adad. Zimri-lim succeeded in ousting the Assyrian to regain the throne of his father, Iakhdun-lim, and ruled for about thirty years until the final destruction.

The reign of Zimri-lim is the source of most of the documentary material found at Mari. It is thus well illuminated by the great number of economic and epistolary tablets. Thanks to them, it is possible to place ourselves in his shoes as he hears his secretaries read the reports, diplomatic correspondence, and other letters from his own officials and from kings of neighboring lands. His correspondence is wide, and his reputation has spread afar. From Susa in Elam to Kanish in Asia Minor his fame has spread, but he still has difficulties with the various tribes within his own boundaries. His military attachés at the court of his powerful rival, Hammurabi, send him regular intelligence reports of the troop movements around Babylon and dispatches concerning the secret diplomacy of the day.

The territory actually ruled by Zimri-lim is still not defined in detail because of the difficulty in identifying many of the new place names encountered. It seems likely that he had control of the relatively rich region in the upper reaches of the Balikh and Khabur rivers, as well as a long stretch of territory on both sides of the middle Euphrates river. Thus he had control over the trade routes from the Mediterranean to Mesopotamia, from which he doubtless derived a considerable portion of his wealth. The active international trade of his time is illustrated by expensive importations from Crete and Cyprus; an inventory lists a "Cretan weapon whose head and base are coated with gold, and whose head is set with lapis-lazuli."

For a number of years, Zimri-lim and Hammurabi of Babylon were on the best of terms. In one letter, Ibal-pi-el, Zimri-lim's ambassador to Hammurabi, writes as follows: "When Hammurabi is occupied with any affair, he writes to me, and I go to him wherever he may be. Whatever the affair may be, he tells it to me."⁷ The two kings cooperate in military ventures, sending each other auxiliary troops when they are faced by a common enemy; but the lack of political acumen showed by Zimri-lim is well illustrated by one letter in which Hammurabi says that he is about to wage war against Rim-sin, king of Larsa. The king of Eshnunna has joined him, and he invites Zimri-lim also to send troops, in order to "realize the object of your desire."⁸ Zimri-lim did not realize that once Hammurabi's other rivals were put out of the way, he himself would follow in the way of those he helped destroy. An intelligence report from one of Zimri-lim's foreign service officials, Yarim-adad, gives the gist of correspondence between Hammurabi and Rim-sin, which shows that these two also were on good terms before Hammurabi felt strong enough to attack. Rim-sin said: "If the enemy comes against you, the troops will come to your aid; but if the enemy comes against me, let your troops come to help me."⁹ In the same letter we hear that Hammurabi sent word to Rim-sin saying "Do you not know that you are the person whom I love?"

As a wise father, Zimri-lim trained his sons in the responsibilities they expected some day to bear as the heirs of the kingdom. We have a letter from one son, Kabia, who tells of the state of affairs in the little kingdom of Kakhat which he ruled: "The camp of Khanu who are pasturing in my district are well. In the pasturage there is water, and in the tribunal there is impartial justice."¹⁰ Unfortunately, it was not always so peaceful and idyllic in the kingdom of Mari. The nomadic Khanu, who were one of the main sources of warriors for the armies of Zimri-lim were not always quite content and obedient. They objected to conscription, as we hear from one of the king's officials, who wanted permission for stern measures: "The Khanu have arrived from the pasturage, and are dwelling in the cities. Once, twice, I have written to the cities, and they have called them up, but they have not assembled, and they will not assemble for three days. Now if my lord permit, let them slay a criminal in the jail, and let them cut off his head, and let them circulate [it] among the

---

⁷ Charles-F. Jean, *Archives royales de Mari* (hereafter, *ARM*, 1950), Vol. II, letter 31:5–10.
⁸ *Ibid.*, letter 33:5–8.
⁹ *Ibid.*, letter 72:13–16.
¹⁰ *Ibid.*, letter 59.

various cities as far as Khutnum and Appan, that the troops may fear, and quickly assemble."[11]

We hear also of less weighty matters in the letters. Zimri-lim's interest in lions was not confined to the statues placed about the temple of Dagon, for he was much concerned to have live lions on display: "To my lord say: Thus Yakim-adad, thy servant. A little while ago I wrote to my lord as follows: 'One lion has been captured in the threshing floor of Bit-akkaka. Let my lord write to me, if that lion should remain in the threshing floor until I go; and if I should send it to my lord, let my lord write [thus].' Now I have awaited the tablet of my lord, and the lion has remained in the threshing floor for five days. They have thrown him a dog and a pig, and food . . . I feared lest he run amuck, so I have put that lion in a wooden cage, loaded it on a boat, and sent it to my lord."[12]

One of the most interesting of the letters is one sent by the king to the river god: "To the god River, my lord, say: Thus Zimri-lim, thy servant. Now I have brought a golden vase [?] to my lord. A little while ago I sent my message to my lord. My lord showed me a sign. Let my lord fulfill the sign which he showed me, and let my lord not be negligent in guarding my life. Let my lord not turn his face elsewhere. Let my lord desire none other than me."[13]

In the 32nd year of Hammurabi[14] Mari was taken and destroyed, never again to retain its former grandeur and splendor. The great Tukulti-ninurta I (1242–1206) of Assyria established a garrison there, and we hear of the bucolic life of Shamash-resh-usur, governor of the district, who engaged in acclimating date palms and honey bees in the region while guarding the frontiers for his Assyrian overlord. The final reference to Mari in antiquity is given by a Greek writer of the first century A.D., who lists the town as one of the stations on the caravan route between Syria and Mesopotamia. He calls Mari a "fortress" and a "village-town." It is likely that the Mari "fortress" of that day was not Tell Hariri, but the

[11] Jean, *ARM*, II, letter 48.
[12] *Ibid.*, letter 106.
[13] G. Dossin, *Syria*, XIX (1938), 126.
[14] F. Thureau-Dangin, *Symbolae Paulo Koschaker Dedicatae* (1939), pp. 11 ff.

striking ruin known as Tell Medkuk located about a mile west of the ancient Mari.[15]

The name of Mari seems to be derived from the name of the god Mer, or Mera,[16] which in turn is of Sumerian origin, meaning wind, or tempest. It indicates that Mer, like Hadad who became the Canaanite Baal, was a storm god. Mer was an important member in the pantheon of the middle Euphrates region for many centuries. At Mari we find one of the early governors of the city in the days of the 3rd dynasty of Ur bears the name of Niwar-mer. Zimri-lim tells us that it was at the command of this god (now known as Itur-mer) and of Dagon, that he defeated a troublesome enemy. These two gods often appear associated; in one letter the writer addressing an important member of the royal court prays: "May Dagon and Itur-mer for my sake cause thee to live for length of days."[17]

Mari and the Patriarchs

Since Abraham has for many years been associated with the general period of Hammurabi, and since the biblical account tells us that he migrated from Haran in Mesopotamia, it is only natural that information concerning the patriarchal period should be expected from the archives of Mari. We have already noted that the region about Haran was probably under the control of Mari. Parrot fancifully suggests it would not be too much of a surprise if among the archives there should appear a letter from Terah requesting permission to cross the royal territory to settle in Haran! This is assuredly too much to expect, but much very welcome information has come from these letters, and many perplexing puzzles as well.

It has long been known that the names of some of the patriarchs have been preserved as place names in the valley of the Balikh river south of Haran.[18] Serug, Peleg, and possibly Reu (Gen. 11:20 ff.) were known from inscriptions of later times as well as Haran itself. Nahor appears in the Mari letters quite frequently. One letter from Nahor is from

[15] Dossin, *Syria*, XXI (1940), 158.
[16] *Ibid.*, pp. 157–59.
[17] *Ibid.*, p. 155.
[18] Albright, *From the Stone Age to Christianity* (hereafter, *FSAC*, 3rd ed.; Doubleday Anchor Books, 1957), pp. 236–37.

a lady who writes to the king as follows: "To my lord say: Thus Inib-sharrim, thy maidservant. How long must I remain in Nahor? Peace is established, and the road is unobstructed. Let my lord write, and let me be brought, that I may see the face of my lord from whom I am separated. Further, let my lord send me an answer to my tablet."[19] Though as yet no evidence has been found of the patriarchs themselves, the names of Abraham, Jacob, and Joseph have been found elsewhere in extra-biblical sources,[20] indicating not only that they were names actually in use at the time traditionally assigned to the patriarchs, but also that they must have been relatively common.

The region which belonged to the kingdom of Mari was probably the scene in which the western Semites, or Amorites, heard and took over the old Sumerian and Babylonian material which eventually found its way into the Bible.[21]

The story of creation in its original form, the story of the flood, the tower of Babel, various Sumerian loan words, all most likely were brought to Palestine by the Amorite migrations associated with the name of Abraham from Mari, where the Amorites had taken over a civilization thoroughly Sumero-Akkadian in nature.[22] It is possible that some of Abraham's ancestors were among the Amorite mercenary troops which helped destroy Ur, or that fought in various battles of the troubled times preceding the triumph of Hammurabi. This is pure speculation, but one thing certain is that the more we know of the actual history of the patriarchal times, the more the traditions of Genesis fit into the general framework of that history. It must be admitted, however, that almost as many questions are raised as are solved, and in the former category belongs the problem of the Benjaminites.

One of the main sources of Zimri-lim's royal headaches must have been this fierce and turbulent tribe of nomads. The Banu-yamina, "sons of the right," were originally, to judge from their name, at home on the fringes of the desert south of the Euphrates, but had long since pushed their way into

[19] Jean, *ARM*, II, letter 112.
[20] Albright, *BASOR*, No. 88 (Dec. 1942), p. 36, n. 39. Jacob occurs as a personal name in texts from Chagar Bazar dating to *ca.* 1725 B.C., and as a place name in Palestine *ca.* 1740.
[21] For a detailed study of this problem, see Albright, *JBL*, LVIII (1939), 91–103.
[22] Albright, *FSAC*, pp. 155–56.

regions further north. Whether there is any connection at all between this Amorite tribe and the later Israelite tribe of Benjamin is a question that remains open. The nature of the Benjaminites is well indicated by the name of one of the years of the king: "The year in which Zimri-lim defeated[23] the Benjaminites at Sagaratum, and captured their princes."[24] Each year was named for the outstanding event of that year. Even more illuminating is a letter from the king himself: "Since the day when I . . . at the bank of the Euphrates, the Benjaminites have taken to raiding. Once they made a raid, and took many sheep. I sent auxiliary troops against them, who defeated them. Not one of them got away, and all the sheep which they had taken were returned. However, a second time they made a raid, and took sheep, and I sent auxiliary troops who caught them and defeated them, and brought back the sheep they had taken. Yet a third time they did likewise . . . none of the . . . which they had seized were left, and afterwards they did not dare any longer to carry out raids."[25] As Dossin points out, this picture of the Benjaminites agrees remarkably with the description of the tribe found in the blessing of Jacob (Gen. 49:27): "Benjamin is a marauding wolf; in the morning he devours the prey, and in the evening he divides the spoil." The warlike nature of this tribe is also mentioned in Judges 20:16 and I Chronicles 12:2, where Benjaminites are notable for their marksmanship.

The Benjaminites were by no means the only Amorite tribe mentioned in the archives. They had a counterpart in the Banu-sim'al, the "sons of the left," whose home originally was to the north of the Euphrates, and other tribes are mentioned as well. The movement of the Amorites which resulted in their spread from Babylon to Canaan is here illustrated in detail. Their search for more Lebensraum or simply for booty is a process which is taking place, to the discomfort of their already civilized brethren; we have in addition abundant testimony to the existence of already established Amorite

[23] The old translation "slew the chieftain," in which the word translated "chieftain" (*dawidum*) was thought to relate to David's name, has now been abandoned. See H. Tadmor, *JNES*, XVII (1958), 129–30.

[24] Georges Dossin, *Mélanges syriens offerts à Monsieur René Dussaud* (1939), II, 981.

[25] *Ibid.*, p. 988.

states all over the Asiatic section of the Fertile Crescent, whether it be Babylon under Hammurabi, Asshur under Shamshi-adad I, Eshnunna under Ibal-pi-el, Mari, Aleppo under Yarim-lim and another Hammurabi, or Byblus under Yantin-khamu.[26] Perhaps in the future it will be possible more closely to determine the place of Abraham and the ancestors of the Israelites among the numerous Amorite tribes of the 2nd millennium B.C.

There remain to be discussed several interesting details bearing on Old Testament matters. One is the phrase used repeatedly in the letters to designate the establishment of a peace treaty between two peoples or nations. This idiom, *khayaram qatālum* is not Akkadian at all, but Amorite; in fact, both words occur in Hebrew. The literal meaning, "to kill an ass," indicates the sacrifice which accompanied an oath of alliance. An official writes as follows to Zimri-lim: "I sent that message to Bina-ishtar, [and] Bina-ishtar replied as follows: 'I have killed the ass with Qarni-lim, and thus I spoke to Qarni-lim under the oath of the gods: if you despise [?] Zimri-lim and his armies, I will turn to the side of your adversary.'"[27] The connection between the ass and a covenant seems to be preserved by the Shechemites who are called the Bene-hamor, "sons of the ass" in Joshua 24:32, and their god was Baal-berith, "Lord of the covenant."[28]

An important element in the daily life of the people of Mari was divination. This technique or rather series of techniques for predicting future events was reduced to an empirical system by collecting and preserving in various ways the omens which preceded great events of the past, so that future diviners might know what to expect if they found similar omens. One of the favorite techniques of divination consisted of hepatoscopy, the inspection of the livers of sacrificial animals. Since the liver itself with its peculiar configurations could not be preserved, accurate clay models were made and an inscription was added which gave the information concerning the event which followed. At Mari there were found thirty-two of these clay models dating to the beginning of the 2nd millennium B.C.; they bear references to events which

[26] This by no means exhausts the list. See Dossin, *Syria*, XX (1939), 109.
[27] Dossin, *Syria*, XIX (1938), 108.
[28] Pointed out by Albright, *FSAC*, p. 279.

took place during the dynasties of Akkad, Ur, and Isin. One reads: "Omen of Shulgi, who discarded his tiara."[29]

Divination was particularly important for military enterprises. The care taken to assure the proper conditions for warfare is illustrated by another letter from Zimri-lim's ambassador to Hammurabi. Three hundred Babylonian soldiers and 300 from Mari have gone on a campaign to attack and destroy an unnamed enemy caravan. Each section of troops has its own diviner, and "the diviner is assembling the omens. When the omens appear favorable, 150 troops go forth, and 150 troops retire."[30] Another official has difficulty with his omens: "I and Ibbi-amurru have been preparing for the campaign of Warad-ilishu at Agdamatim, but our omens are not favorable. Those omens I have sent my lord. May my lord pay very close attention to those omens."[31]

Finally, there are references to the Khapiru, though not enough material so far to throw any additional light on the problem.[32] A letter from an officer notifies the king that an Amorite by the name of "Yapakh-adad has built the city of Zallul on this side of the Euphrates, and is dwelling in that city with 2000 troops of the Khapiru of the land."[33] When the field officer hastily threw up a fortified camp against Zallul, Yapakh-adad sent up fire signals, and all the cities on the opposite bank answered. The method of signaling by fire is well known, anticipating by more than a thousand years the fire signals to be used in the siege of Lachish.

All these scattered but valuable similarities of custom, onomastica, and even of language, serve to give us far more assurance as to the reliability of early biblical traditions than

[29] The liver models were published in *RA*, XXXV, 36-70, by Mlle. Rutten. Also see Albright, *BASOR*, No. 77 (Feb. 1940), 21-22.

[30] Jean, *ARM*, II, letter 22:28-31.

[31] *Ibid.*, letter 134:3-8.

[32] See *FSAC*, pp. 239-40, for the best summary of the relationship between the Khapiru and the Hebrews, and nn. 54 and 55 for recent treatments of the subject; in addition, see H. L. Ginsberg, "Ugaritic Studies and the Bible," *BA*, VIII (1945), 48 (reprinted in this volume, pp. 39 f.). Two excellent new studies of the subject should be noted: J. Bottéro, *Le problème des Ḫabiru* (*Cahiers de la Societe Asiatique*, XII [1954]); and M. Greenberg, *The Ḫab/piru* (*American Oriental Series*, XXXIX [1955]).

[33] Jean, *ARM*, II, letter 131:10-15.

has hitherto been possible. Indeed, now that more of these fascinating letters have been published,[34] the revision of this article for publication in this volume might easily have run to double its length, and we may look for yet more insight into the life and faith of the patriarchal period.

[34] Publication has reached nine volumes of the *ARM* series, with an additional volume, numbered XV, containing analytic studies of the first five volumes of texts.

2

BIBLICAL CUSTOMS AND THE NUZU TABLETS

CYRUS H. GORDON

One of the main reasons that Scripture is often misunderstood is the fact that its readers are generally unfamiliar with the ways of mankind in Bible lands and Bible times. If the scribes had prepared an edition of Holy Writ for us of the 20th century A.D., they would have taken far less for granted about many everyday matters that their contemporaries understood without difficulty.

Fortunately, we may overcome some of our ignorance by studying the many groups of documents unearthed by the biblical archaeologist. Among the most interesting of these are the thousands of Babylonian clay tablets of the 15th century B.C. found at Nuzu (or Nuzi), in northeast Iraq. Excavations were begun at this city in 1925 by the American School of Oriental Research in Baghdad under the direction of Professor Edward Chiera. Hardly had the work commenced when the villa of one of the city's nobles was encountered. Later on other villas were uncovered, as was also the palace of the local ruler. Fortunately, several of the families had been very careful to preserve records of their social and business transactions, which were stored away in archive rooms, awaiting their modern resurrection. Thus by 1931 when the excavations were completed by the American School in cooperation with Harvard University and the University Museum of Philadelphia, a very good picture of the life of this ancient city was at hand.

A point of interest which these discoveries have for the biblical student is that the Nuzians were Hurrians, the long lost Horites of the Old Testament. Even more significant is the fact that the archives of the Horite city of Nuzu reflect ways of living that are relatively close in time and place to those of the Patriarchs. Consequently, they clear up some of our misunderstandings regarding the lives of Abraham, Isaac and Jacob, who wandered between Mesopotamia and Egypt after the middle of the 2nd millennium B.C.

The Patriarchal Age

It may seem strange to us that at first Abraham's heir was a slave by the name of Eliezer (Gen. 15:2–3). The adoption of slaves is known in the tablets from the archives of Nuzu (H IX 22, for example),[1] and some of these documents make clear the reason for, and nature of, this relationship between Abraham and his adopted son, Eliezer.[2] It was a custom at Nuzu for childless people to adopt a son to serve them as long as they lived and to bury and mourn for them when they died. In exchange for these services the adopted son was designated as heir. If, however, the adopter should beget a son after the adoption, the adopted must yield to the real son the right of being the chief heir (H V 7, 60, 67). Once we know of this proviso, we have the legal meaning of God's reply in Genesis 15:4: "This [slave] shall not inherit thee, but he that shall come out of thine inwards shall inherit thee."

Since the purpose of marriage was procreation rather than companionship, it is not surprising that Nuzu marriage contracts may go so far as to oblige the wife who fails to bear children to provide her husband with a handmaid who will bear them: for example, "If Gilimninu [the bride] will not bear children, Gilimninu shall take a woman of N/Lullu-land [whence the choicest slaves were obtained] as a wife for Shennima [the bridegroom]."[3] This enables us to grasp the viewpoint of Sarah, who says to Abraham: "The Lord has kept me from bearing. Go in, I pray, unto my handmaid [Hagar]! Perhaps I shall be built from her" (Gen. 16:2). No

[1] I hope the reader will pardon such queer numbers and letters as these scattered throughout the text of this article, and also the numerous footnotes. The reason they are included is to give those who are interested a chance to go deeper into the matter. The abbreviations refer to the cuneiform originals, and the key is given in the journal *Orientalia*, VII (1938), 32.

[2] W. F. Albright, *The Archaeology of Palestine and the Bible* (3rd ed.; 1935), pp. 137–39.

[3] From tablet no. H V 67:19–21.

matter how unnatural it may seem to us in the light of our present point of view, Sarah's action fits into the social pattern of her environment, and, two generations later, Rachel gives Bilhah to Jacob for the same reason (Gen. 30:3).

After Hagar had borne Ishmael, Sarah was blessed with a son, Isaac. Resentful of Hagar and with misgivings that Ishmael's presence might be detrimental to Isaac's future, Sarah tells Abraham: "Drive out this handmaid and her son, for the son of this handmaid shall not inherit along with my son, Isaac" (Gen. 21:10). Under these circumstances the Nuzu wife was expressly forbidden to expel the handmaid's offspring: for example, "Gilimninu shall not send the [handmaid's] offspring away" (H V 67:22). Doubtless Sarah was not acting within her rights, for a divine dispensation is required to permit the unwilling Abraham to comply: "And the thing was quite bad in the eyes of Abraham on account of his son [Ishmael]. But God said to Abraham: 'Let it not be bad in thine eyes because of the lad and thy handmaid. [In] all that Sarah saith to thee hearken unto her voice, for in Isaac shall seed be called for thee'" (Gen. 21:11–12).[4]

Few incidents in family life seem more peculiar to us than Esau's sale of his birthright to his twin brother, Jacob. It has been pointed out that one of the tablets (H V 99) portrays a similar event.[5] The resemblance is not as striking as it might be, however, because the document is an agreement whereby one man makes over the right to inherit the major portion of his father's estate to another man's son. There is a better example in tablet N 204 in which a man by the name of Tupkitilla transfers his inheritance rights regarding a grove to his brother Kurpazah in exchange for three sheep. Students of the Nuzu tablets are well acquainted with the wretched lack of fraternal love among Hilbishuh's sons whose names were Kurpazah, Tupkitilla and Matteshub. In one of the documents (N 331) Kurpazah hales Matteshub to court on a charge of having committed assault and battery on Kurpazah's wife. In another[6] there is the record of the scandal in which Matteshub swears in court that Kurpazah stole eight sheep from the groves in Tupkitilla's inheritance por-

[4] E. A. Speiser, *AASOR*, XIII (1933), 44, and the subsequent discussion by the writer, *RB*, XLIV (1935), 35.
[5] Speiser, *AASOR*, XIII (1933), 44.
[6] *JAOS*, LI (1927), 36–60, text 18.

tion. As if it were not enough for one brother to rob another's estate, a third brother must play the informer! Tablet N 204, ironically enough, was labeled "a document of brotherhood." "Brotherhood" is here one of the technical terms used by the Nuzians to get around the law against selling land. In other words, the sale of a birthright is here kept within the law by being quite obviously disguised as an adoption into brotherhood, even though the parties are already brothers by birth. However complicated and perverse this may seem, it is nevertheless true. The main part of the text reads as follows:

> On the day they divide the grove [that lies] on the road of the town of Lumti . . . [there follow the dimensions and the exact location], Tupkitilla shall give it to Kurpazah as his inheritance share. And Kurpazah has taken three sheep to Tupkitilla in exchange for his inheritance share.

It is hard to imagine that any reason other than dire lack of food induced Tupkitilla to sell his patrimony for three sheep. But just as Kurpazah exploited Tupkitilla's hunger, so did Jacob take advantage of the famished Esau:

> And Jacob said: "Sell me thy birthright now!" And Esau said: "What with me about to die [of hunger], what good is the birthright to me?" And Jacob said: "Swear to me now!" And he swore to him and sold his birthright to Jacob. And Jacob gave Esau bread and a mess of lentils and [Esau] ate and drank (Gen. 25:31–34).

Jacob's dealings with Laban have been particularly illuminated by the Nuzu records. One tablet (G 51) is so important that we translate all of it except the names of the seven witnesses at the end:

> The adoption tablet of Nashwi son of Arshenni. He adopted Wullu son of Puhishenni. As long as Nashwi lives, Wullu shall give [him] food and clothing. When Nashwi dies, Wullu shall be the heir. Should Nashwi beget a son, [the latter] shall divide equally with Wullu but [only] Nashwi's son shall take Nashwi's gods. But if there be no son of Nashwi's then Wullu shall take Nashwi's gods. And [Nashwi] has given his daughter

Nuhuya as wife to Wullu. And if Wullu takes another wife, he forfeits Nashwi's land and buildings. Whoever breaks the contract shall pay one mina of silver [and] one mina of gold.

To bring out the more clearly the bearing of this text on the Hebrew episode we summarize the tablet, substituting "Laban" for "Nashwi," and "Jacob" for "Wullu": "Laban," who has no son of his own, adopts "Jacob" and makes him heir. If "Laban" should beget a son in the future, that son and "Jacob" are to share the inheritance, but only the begotten son is to take "Laban's" gods. If "Laban" does not beget a son, then alone may "Jacob" take "Laban's" gods (compare N 89:10–12). As a condition, "Jacob" is to marry "Laban's" daughter. "Jacob" is forbidden to marry any other woman under the penalty of forfeiting "Laban's" property.

Let us now examine the biblical account to see if and to what extent it coincides with the tablet. There is no indication that Laban had sons when Jacob first appears on the scene (Gen. 29). Laban's sons were apparently born between that time and twenty years later (Gen. 31:41), when they are first mentioned (Gen. 31:1). Laban agrees to give a daughter in marriage to Jacob when he makes him a member of the household: "It is better that I give her to thee than that I give her to another man. Dwell with me!" (Gen. 29:19). Our thesis that Jacob's joining Laban's household approximates Wullu's adoption is borne out by other remarkable resemblances with the Nuzu document.

Laban's insistence that Jacob take no wife in addition to his daughters (Gen. 31:50) is interesting but without other evidence would prove nothing because the prohibition against the bridegroom's taking another wife is rather widespread (compare also N 435:10). More significant, though by itself inconclusive, is Laban's gift of a handmaid to each of his daughters upon their marriage to Jacob (Gen. 29:24, 29). This is done under similar circumstances according to another tablet (H V 67:35–36). Rachel's theft of Laban's gods (Gen. 31:19, 30–35), however, is unmistakably paralleled in the tablet translated above.[7] While they are called *teraphim* in verses 19, 34 and 35, they are called "gods" in verses 30 and 32, as in the Nuzu tablets. There is no doubt, therefore, that

[7] S. Smith, *JTS*, XXXIII (1932), 33–36.

the *teraphim* were simply idols.[8] The possession of these gods was important for, along with their religious significance, they carried with them leadership of the family on the ancestral estate. Because Laban had begotten sons, none but the latter had any right to the gods and hence Laban's indignation is justified: "Why hast thou stolen my gods?" (Gen. 31:30). Jacob, on the other hand, had not bargained for so secondary a position. His hopes had been frustrated by the birth of Laban's sons.

The following words of Laban are quite intelligible if understood as being addressed to Jacob in the latter's capacity of Laban's adopted son (not son-in-law!): "The daughters are my daughters and the sons are my sons and the flocks are my flocks and whatever thou seest is mine" (Gen. 31:43). Laban was to exercise patriarchal authority over all his children and grandchildren as long as he lived. Jacob, as Laban's adopted son, and Jacob's wives, children and flocks belonged to Laban. Laban had every right to punish Jacob for running away and stealing members of Laban's household, but "the God of Jacob's father" had appeared to Laban in a dream and commanded him to deal gently with Jacob (Gen. 31:24, 29). Furthermore, even the heart of a crafty Aramean like Laban was not devoid of parental tenderness: "And as for my daughters, what can I do to them now—or to their children that they have borne" (Gen. 31:43).

That Rachel and Leah were not free to leave their father's household was not merely because they were his daughters (for under ordinary circumstances married women belonged to their husbands). They still belonged to Laban on account of their husband's status as an adopted son. They were as guilty as Jacob in agreeing to run off (Gen. 31:14–16).[9]

That Laban had been roguish in more ways than one is also evident from the biblical account. The most shameful occasion of which we know is the way he "palmed off" the wrong bride on the unsuspecting Jacob (Gen. 29:22–27). Furthermore, that he had not been an ideal father can be

[8] [This fact should be kept in mind to offset some of the wild speculations concerning the teraphim. A good example is to be found in the *Religious Digest*, IX (1939), 19–22, where a writer indicates to his own satisfaction that the teraphim were the original tablets which Moses used when he composed the Pentateuch. (Editor's note—G. Ernest Wright.)]

[9] Gordon, *BASOR*, No. 66 (April 1937), pp. 25–27.

gathered from the complaint of his daughters: "Are we not reckoned as foreign women unto him?" (Gen. 31:15).[10] The Nuzu tablets make a sharp distinction between native women (called "daughters of Arrapkha," the local capital), who cannot be subjected to mistreatment, and foreign women, who are regularly found to occupy inferior social positions.[11] This clarifies the terminology used by Rachel and Leah. They felt that Laban had treated them as foreign women, whatever be the precise financial significance of their reason: "For he has sold us and indeed eats our money" (Gen. 31:15).

A tablet published by Lacheman (N 661) records that a man by the name of Shamash-qarrad becomes Tehiptilla's slave on condition that Tehiptilla will provide him with a wife. This is an interesting parallel to Jacob's working for his brides (Gen. 29:18, 30). We may safely assume, however, that Tehiptilla did not give a daughter to Shamash-qarrad; he probably gave him a slave girl. Jacob, however, was not Laban's slave. The relationship between Jacob and Laban is paralleled far more closely in the tablet discussed above (G 51) than in this one.

The blessings of biblical characters, as, for example, those of the Patriarchs, were taken quite seriously for they amounted to irrevocable last wills and testaments. Even after Esau's blessing had been extorted from Isaac by Jacob under false pretenses, Isaac, distressed as he was and knowing that he had been tricked, could not go back on his word: "And Isaac trembled much with great trembling and said: 'Whoever it was that hunted game and brought [it] to me and I ate of all [of it] before thou camest and I blessed him—even he shall be blessed'" (Gen. 27:33). Be it noted that patriarchal standards require Isaac to keep his word even under these extenuating circumstances, and he is prepared to do so even though a stranger inherit him; for he does not yet know that his blessing has been given to Jacob, and not to an impostor outside the family.

However much the blessings themselves may have been shaped to fit subsequent history, their original function as testamentary wills is still preserved. Thus Isaac appoints his son to follow him as family chief: "Be a lord to thy brothers!" (Gen. 27:29), while Jacob designates Judah as his successor:

[10] M. Burrows, *JAOS*, LXI (1937), 261.
[11] Gordon, *Zeitschrift für Assyriologie*, XLIII (1937), 149.

"Judah, may thy brothers pay thee homage . . . may thy father's sons bow down to thee!" (Gen. 49:8).

It should also be observed that impending death provides the occasion for the blessings. Upon choosing the time to give his blessing, Isaac says: "I have grown old and I know not the day of my death" (Gen. 27:2). Jacob was actually on his deathbed and after blessing and instructing his sons, "he gathered his feet unto the bed and died and was gathered unto his people" (Gen. 49:33).

One of the Nuzu tablets (PS 56) is a document recording the lawsuit of a certain Tarmiya against his two brothers, who contested his right to take a woman by the name of Zululishtar as wife. Tarmiya wins the case and is awarded his bride because the court recognizes the validity of his father's "blessing," which Tarmiya reports as follows: "My father, Huya, was sick and lying in bed and my father seized my hand and spoke thus to me: 'My other older sons have taken wives but thou hast not taken a wife and I give Zululishtar to thee as wife.'" This text conforms to biblical blessings like those of the Patriarchs in that it is (a) an oral will, (b) with legal validity, (c) made to a son by a dying father.

The Pentateuch provides us with more data on oral last wills and testaments than do the Nuzu tablets. What is strange is that in a settled community like Nuzu, where even trivial transactions were carefully documented, the oral "blessing" should be upheld in court. Regarding these "blessings," then, the Bible throws more light on Nuzu than vice versa. In such studies as these it is well to remember that the Bible, aside from its great inner worth, remains our leading source for the ancient Near East. The historian does not use inscriptions and archaeology to "prove" (or "disprove") the Bible, but rather does he use the Bible to illuminate the antiquity in which our cultural heritage is rooted.

Lack of space prevents us from entering into all the minor Nuzu sidelights on patriarchal days. We shall limit ourselves to Jacob's claim that he had been a faithful herdsman for Laban. He says, among other things: "I did not eat the rams of thy flocks" (Gen. 31:38). It is interesting to compare the lawsuits brought by Nuzu cattle owners against their herdsmen for slaughtering animals without permission. For example, the Nuzu plutocrat Tehiptilla filed and won two suits against his herdsman Tilliya for illegal slaughtering (N 326 and 353). However much Jacob may have sinned against

Laban, he had at least refrained from feasting clandestinely on mutton at Laban's expense.

The Nuzu parallels show that the picture of patriarchal society was not distorted during any process of oral transmission before the account was first committed to writing. Thanks to the Nuzu texts we may feel confident that the social institutions have come down to us authentically.

Parallels to Other Biblical Laws and Customs

A number of writers have pointed out many other Nuzu parallels to the Bible; not all of these have stood the tests of further investigation and additional evidence. In reviewing what I consider some of the more probable parallels it will be noted that they do not cluster around a single period as those above do around the Patriarchal Age. The resemblances are due sometimes to common origins, sometimes to borrowing and sometimes to chance. In several cases there are still more analogies in other documents of the ancient Near East. Not included here are the purely linguistic or terminological parallels, of which there are many interesting examples.

While Hebrew society was essentially patriarchal, with the father ruling the family, it had certain fratriarchal aspects, whereby a man is singled out to exert authority over his brothers. Another brother may be appointed vice-fratriarch (I Sam. 8:2, 17:13; I Chron. 5:12). In Hebrew the terms designating "fratriarch" are quite distinct from "first-born": for example, "Shimri was the fratriarch, though not the first-born, for his father made him fratriarch" (I Chron. 26:10). Fratriarchy is detectable in the Nuzu tablets as well as in the cuneiform records of the Hittites and Elamites.[12]

While the right of daughters to inherit is quite familiar to us, it is not recognized in all states of society. Numbers 27:8 decrees thus: "If a man die, and he have no son, ye shall transfer his estate to his daughter." Under similar circumstances a daughter is to get a share of the parental estate in one of the Nuzu tablets (H V 67:27–29).[13]

Levirate marriage (to cite one of its variant forms) designates the institution whereby the widow of a man who dies without having begotten a son is to marry the deceased's

[12] I have discussed the question from the biblical angle in *JBL*, LV (1935), 223–31.
[13] *RB*, XLIV (1935), 38.

brother and the first son of this union is legally the son of the dead husband. Such is the essence of the law according to Deuteronomy 25:5–7 (compare also Gen. 38 and Ruth). Though the institution came to be interpreted as a measure to preserve the deceased's name in Israel (Deut. 25:6), it seems to have originated in purchase marriage, according to which a girl is bought by and belongs to her husband's family. This, at any rate, is the case in a Nuzu tablet (N 441) wherein a father, when obtaining a bride for his son, specifies that if the son dies, she is to be married to another of his sons.[14]

Hosea 2:4–5 refers to the custom of having a reprehensible wife expelled naked by her own children: "Take action against your mother, take action, for she is not my wife nor am I her husband [i.e., I herewith divorce her] . . . lest I have her stripped naked and set her as on the day she was born" (compare also Ezek. 16:39; 23:26). In a Nuzu tablet (N 444:19–23) a husband wills: "If [my wife] Wishirwi goes to another husband [i.e., I herewith divorce her] . . . lest I have her clothes of my wife and drive [her] out of my house." Another tablet (H V 71:34–36) contains the same injunction. This custom finds a parallel in a cuneiform tablet from Hana, in Aramaic magical bowls from a very much later time in Babylonia, and, oddly enough, among the ancient Germans.[15]

Frequently the Nuzians sold their daughters or sisters into what are called adoptions, with the proviso that the adopters shall marry the girls off. Exodus 21:7–11 shows that a similar custom existed in Israel, whereby a man could sell his daughter as a slave and the purchaser was to see that she was married. One of the possibilities mentioned is that his son should marry her.[16]

Exodus 22:6–8 reads as follows:

> If a man give silver or vessels to another for keeping and it is stolen from the latter's house; if the thief be found, he shall pay double. If the thief be not found, the owner of the house shall draw nigh unto the gods [to

[14] *RB*, XLIV (1935), 37.

[15] C. Kuhl, *ZAW*, LII (1934), 102–9; and Gordon, *ZAW*, LIV (1936), 277–80; LV (1937), 176.

[16] As is the case in tablet H V 79:17–18. See I. Mendelsohn, *JAOS*, LIX (1935), 190–95. Cf. Burrows, *The Basis of Israelite Marriage* (1938), pp. 22–23.

swear] that he did not put his hand upon the other's goods. As for every transgression regarding an ox, an ass, a head of small cattle, a garment—regarding any lost article about which [someone] says that: "This is it," the case of both of them [the litigants] shall come before the gods. Whom the gods declare guilty shall pay double to the other party.

Though we do not know the technical details, divine images were used in deciding cases where contradictory claims led to a deadlock. Of course, in later times the word here translated "gods" was translated by "judges," "rulers," or by "God," but there is no doubt that *originally* the sense of the passage was as given above. The ordeal-oath before the gods is a common feature of Nuzu trials, and translations of the Bible which alter the sense are unjustified.[17] In later Hebrew law the use of these idols was eliminated.

From ancient times to the present the town nearest the spot of an unsolved crime is often held responsible in the Near East. Thus, in tablet N 125 from Nuzu the inhabitants of the town of Purilli collectively face a charge of burglary and larceny. Community responsibility is reflected in Deuteronomy 21:1 ff., where the elders of the nearest city must make a sacrifice, wash their hands and declare: "Our hands have not shed this blood and our eyes have not seen [the murder]."[18]

The institution of the release is well known in the ancient Near East.[19] Hebrew law reckoned with two releases:

1. The "Sabbatical Year," in which Hebrew slaves were freed, debts canceled and the soil left lying fallow; and
2. The "Jubilee Year," when real estate reverted to its original owner.

Oriental rulers of former days occasionally proclaimed releases and perhaps such a one is referred to in Esther 2:18. Many Nuzu tablets are dated "after the release." Further study of them is necessary, however, before the resemblances with the biblical releases can be established. An identity in detail seems to be out of the question.[20]

[17] Gordon, *JBL*, LIV (1935), 139–44.
[18] For fuller treatment, see the writer, *RA*, LII (1936), 1–6, and *ZAW*, LIV (1936), 278, n. 1.
[19] J. B. Alexander, *JBL*, LVII (1938), 75–79.
[20] *RB*, XLIV (1935), 38–41.

Hebrews and Horites

Most scholars accept the identification of a people called *Khapiru* in the cuneiform inscriptions with the Hebrews. That is, they maintain the words are identical and referred originally to the same type of people. According to this view, "Hebrew" did not originally denote a nation, a religion or a language, but instead a social status. The Nuzu tablets are a leading source of information on this subject. It is quite normal in Nuzu for the Khapiru (Hebrews) to enter voluntarily into permanent slavery: e.g., "Sin-balti, a Khapiru woman, entered into servitude in the household of Tehiptilla. If Sin-balti breaks the contract and goes into another house, Tehiptilla may pluck out Sin-balti's eyes and sell her for a price" (N 425). Another tablet reads, "As for Silli-kubi, the Khapiru, his [own] mouth and tongue caused him to enter [into servitude in the house of] Tehiptilla, son of Puhishenni" (N 454). This institution had a practical economic reason. Instead of facing the poverty which was virtually certain to cling to them all of their days, the Khapiru acquired security by joining wealthy households as slaves. In a home like Tehiptilla's there would be no dearth of food, clothing and shelter.

In Exodus 21:2 ff. are laws pertaining to the "Hebrew slave," where "Hebrew" retains the social connotation it has in Nuzu. It is especially interesting to note verses 5 and 6 where the "Hebrew slave" enters voluntarily into permanent servitude.[21] It is too soon to say what bearing the Khapiru data may have on the study of the enslavement of the Hebrews in Egypt.

While the Nuzu tablets were written in the Babylonian language, the native population was Horite. The scribes now and then use Horite words, whose meanings are often fixed by the Babylonian context. These loan words are adding considerably to our growing knowledge of the language which these people spoke. The Horites were formerly known only from a few obscure references in the Old Testament. Now we know them to have been a dominant ethnic element in the Near East throughout the 2nd millennium B.C. Unscientific

[21] With frequent reference to Nuzu, Lewy discusses the Khapiru question in *HUCA*, XIV (1939), 587–623.

etymologists had misconstrued their name to mean "cave dwellers." Of course, they were nothing of the kind and their own inscriptions from Egypt, Canaan, Asia Minor and Mesopotamia have helped to restore them to their proper place in history. The Nuzu tablets have made life in the Horite town probably the best known of any community in remote antiquity.

3

UGARITIC STUDIES AND THE BIBLE

H. L. GINSBERG

The name Ugarit is not new to readers of the *Biblical Archaeologist*. A special article was devoted to the sensational discoveries associated with that name in one of the earliest numbers of this periodical (Vol. II. 1), and data from Ugarit have been cited in various connections in subsequent numbers. A new, and more extensive, special article at the present time is warranted by the importance of the subject, which can hardly be exaggerated, and by the considerable quantity of new data which has become available despite the war and the interruption of excavations.

I. *Geographical and Chronological Definition of Ugarit*

Near the northern end of the Syrian coast, only about twenty-five miles south of the present Turkish frontier, there is a cove called Minet el-Beida ("the white harbor," "Whiteport"), into which flows a small stream. Today Minet el-Beida is neither a large nor a safe harbor, and is only used by a few fishermen; and the nearest town of any size is Latakia, some seven or eight miles to the south. However, when archaeologists became interested in it seventeen years ago, they discovered clear evidence that it had once been both larger and safer. At its seaward end, the white chalk cliffs from which it gets its name have been undermined by the waves and have tumbled into the sea, forming dangerous breakwaters; while at its landward end, as a result of the accumulation of sand and gravel thrown up by the boisterous winter sea and of soil and stones swept down by the swollen winter stream, the shoreline has advanced about 400 feet during the 3000 odd years that have elapsed since it ceased to be the busy waterfront of the prosperous city of Ugarit. Of course, it should also be remembered that the ships of those times did not require nearly such large and deep harbors as ours do.

That there was once a very rich city half a mile to the southeast of the harbor has always been known to the people of the neighborhood. For here is the northwestern corner of a mound known as Ras esh-Shamrah (its ancient name was Ugarit), in and around which they had often discovered valuable antiquities—including gold objects—both by chance and by treasure hunting. The attention of the scholarly world, however, was only attracted to this rather lonely spot in the spring of the year 1928, when, in the vicinity of the harbor, a peasant's plow struck what proved to be one of the stone slabs of the convex roof of a sepulcher. It was full of silt and valuables, and the peasants lost no time in removing most of the latter. However, the discovery came to the notice of the police, who in turn apprised the Department of Antiquities in Beirut; and when the representatives of the Department arrived they were still able to recover some beautiful Cypro-Mycenean pottery of the 13th century B.C. from the rubbish. As a result, both the harbor and, more especially, the aforementioned mound were excavated by a French expedition headed by M. Claude F.-A. Schaeffer for about three months every year from 1929 through 1939. After the Second World War, excavations were resumed. They have yielded valuable finds, but not such sensational ones as the pre-war operations.

A few exploratory shafts have revealed that the mound is the grave of not one but five cities lying one on top of the other. The lowest one is, of course, the most ancient. It flourished in the 5th, and perhaps even as early as the 6th millennium B.C. Of greatest interest to us, however, are the second and first strata, representing respectively the first and second halves of the 2nd millennium B.C. Both these cities were known as Ugarit. Obviously no stratum can be investigated methodically before those above it have been cleared away; and at present only the top one, or the younger Ugarit (*ca.* 1500–1200 B.C.), is at all well known. It is primarily with this Ugarit that we are concerned here. Roughly speaking, its history begins with the establishment—which may have been a re-establishment—of Egyptian sovereignty over this remote corner of Syria and ends with the irruption of the Sea Peoples whom we also encounter in Palestine from the 12th century on under the name of Philistines. The abandonment of Ugarit around 1200 B.C. was no doubt due to just this invasion of the Sea Peoples.

II. Writing in Western Asia in General and at Ugarit in Particular

Within the above period, the most interesting phase, not only in the history of Ugarit but in that of the Ancient Orient as a whole, is the first half of the 14th century. This is what is known as the Amarna Age, from the circumstance that the first insight into its character was afforded by the archives of Amenophis IV, better known as Akhnaten, discovered at Tell el-Amarna (in Egypt). These documents revealed that both this pharaoh and his predecessor Amenophis III cultivated diplomatic relations with practically all the independent kings of western Asia and married their daughters. Secondly, their correspondence not only with Babylonia and Assyria but also with the other independent states of western Asia, and even with the Egyptian dependencies in Syria, was conducted in the script and (with very few exceptions to which I shall refer immediately) in the language of the Babylonians and Assyrians. The name of that language is Akkadian, and for the sake of convenience I shall also refer to its script as Akkadian.

It was subsequently discovered that the peoples in question had been doing their writing in the Akkadian script long before the Amarna Age. However, the leading non-Semitic nations had adapted it to the notation of their own languages at an early date, so that already in the Amarna Age the kings of Arzawa (in Asia Minor) and Mitanni (in northern Mesopotamia) were disregarding the privileges of Akkadian as the diplomatic medium and the convenience of the Egyptian Foreign Office by corresponding with it in their own respective idioms. But with regard to the western Semites, it was believed up to the year 1929 that their written language, even in purely domestic matters, remained Akkadian until not long before the end of the 2nd millennium, when writing in the vernacular became common among them simultaneously with the use of the Phoenician alphabet.

Then came the first season of digging at Ugarit (spring 1929), which brought to light a number of inscribed clay tablets from the Amarna Age; and behold, the great majority of them employed not the very complicated Akkadian script but a previously unknown one. Upon examination the new system was found to consist of only some thirty simple signs, which obviously represented single sounds rather than syllables or ideograms (signs representing single words or ideas). We shall call it *the Ugaritic alphabet*. I may say here that to date no specimens of it have turned up at any other site, with two exceptions:

1. In 1933 a clay plaque inscribed with Ugaritic writing *in reverse* was unearthed at Beth-shemesh, Palestine. Unfortunately, too much of it is missing for any coherent reading. Is it a local product or did some much-traveled person bring it to Beth-shemesh from Ugarit?

2. In 1944 a bronze dagger with an inscription in this alphabet was discovered near Mt. Tabor, Palestine, and an article on it by Mr. S. Yeivin has appeared in *Kedem*, a periodical publication of the Museum of Jewish Antiquities of the Hebrew University, Jerusalem.[1]

Provided the language is known and the material not too limited, and provided that the words are separated from each other—in our texts they are fortunately marked off from each other, as a rule, by a special sign which we call a "word divider"—such alphabetic writing is relatively easy to decipher. By adopting the working hypothesis that the language, in view of the location of the find and of the brevity of the words, was akin to Phoenician (which in turn, as is well known, is closely related to biblical Hebrew), the German scholar Hans Bauer succeeded in an astonishingly short time in identifying half of the letters correctly. That meant that every word which contained only letters from that half was transliterated by him in a manner which we now know to be correct. Then, with the help of a newspaper article in which Bauer gave a popular presentation of his results, the French savant, Ed. Dhorme, corrected Bauer's identifications of most of the remaining characters, so that he (Dhorme) read nearly every complete word correctly.

All this was accomplished despite the fact that the texts on which the decipherers had to work were, unlike some of those discovered in later campaigns, rather crudely written and very fragmentary and for the most part contained only lists.[2]

[1] *Kedem*, II (1945), 32–41.
[2] The scholar who, by publishing very careful copies of these first texts, made Bauer and Dhorme's contributions to their de-

How was it done? In the observations which the French scholar, Virolleaud, prefaced to his copies of the first texts, he noted that in the first line of one of the tablets a line which is marked off from the following lines by a horizontal stroke (in the manner in which the headings are frequently marked off from the bodies of letters in Akkadian writing), a sign which we shall represent by x is followed by a sequence of six signs which also appears on five bronze adzes. From this Virolleaud rightly concluded that the tablet in question is a letter, that its initial sign, x, means "to," and that the sequence of six signs designates in the letter the addressee, and on the adzes the owner. Now, in Hebrew and Phoenician the single letter that means "to" is l and is written together with the following word, so that a large proportion of words in a Hebrew or Phoenician text begin with l. Bauer observed that similarly a large proportion of words in these new texts began with our x; so apparently x had the value of l, and the language really was (as he had tentatively assumed) related to Phoenician.

In another text was found a word consisting of x flanked on either side by a sign which we shall call y. If x really $= l$, then $y = sh$, for the only Hebrew and Phoenician word consisting of l flanked by two identical consonants is the numeral *sh(a)-l(o)-sh* 'three.' These identifications were confirmed by the presence in the neighborhood of the word read *sh-l-sh* of a word *sh-sh*, evidently equivalent to Hebrew *sh(e)-sh* 'six.' A four-letter word in the same vicinity was tentatively read *'-r-b-'* 'four,' and it was noted that the last two letters of it frequently combined with l to produce what was evidently the name of the great Phoenician god *b-'-l* 'Baal.' Further, the first two letters of the word tentatively read *'-r-b-'* 'four' frequently occurred along with the letter identified above as *sh* in the combination *'-sh-r-z*, where z represents still another letter whose value had not yet been determined. This combination proved to be the name of the goddess *'-sh-r-t*, Phoenician *'Ashirt* (biblical *Asherah*); so that $z = t$. The five-letter

---

cipherment possible was the French Assyriologist Ch. Virolleaud. As we shall see in a moment, Virolleaud also discovered the first clue to the decipherment, of which Bauer made grateful use. It was also Virolleaud who was charged with editing most of the texts discovered in subsequent campaigns, with the help of which he isolated and determined the values of most of the letters which Bauer and Dhorme had failed either to distinguish from others which they resembled or to interpret correctly.

combination ʿ-*sh-t-r-t* could now be identified without further ado as the name of the goddess Astarte, Phoenician ʿ*Ashtart* (biblical *Ashtoreth*). And so on. The working hypothesis that the texts were composed in a language similar to Phoenician soon became an established fact.

We shall call the Phoenician-like language which was written at Ugarit in the Ugaritic alphabet *the Ugaritic language*.

However, not long after the alphabet had been deciphered it was discovered that it was also employed for writing the language of at least one non-Semitic minority of the population of Ugarit; but the material of this nature that has come to light is limited in quantity and still very imperfectly understood. On the other hand, the writings in the Ugaritic language published to date (for a certain amount of material still awaits publication) consist of thousands of lines. Large sections of them are now quite well understood, and at every turn comparison with the Bible is suggested.

III. *Materials for Comparative Biblical and Ugaritic Studies*

While, however, it is primarily the Ugaritic texts that are of interest to the student of the Bible, it should be noted that, for obvious reasons, the Ugaritians still employed Akkadian in diplomatic correspondence and, maybe out of sheer conservatism, often preferred it as the language of legal documents, business accounts, and seals. Most surprising of all, perhaps, are a few Akkadian (?) hymns to Mesopotamian deities transcribed in Ugaritic characters and provided with rubrics in the Ugaritic language. The biblical scholar has much to learn from all these writings too. I shall cite only two cases in point.

1. The Khabiru of the Tell el-Amarna correspondence, who act in cooperation with rebels against the pharaoh's authority, used to be regularly identified with the Hebrews and adduced as proof that the Israelite conquest of Palestine took place in the 14th or even in the 15th century. Particularly since the First World War, however, evidence has accumulated to the effect that the word in question

a. is rather to be read *Khapiru,*

b. was in use all over the Orient in the 2nd millennium B.C., and

c. designated men *of any and every nationality.*

What all the people so designated have in common is that

they are economically rootless or broken, just like those who gathered around the outlaws Jephthah (Judg. 11:3) and David (I Sam. 22:2) or hired their swords to the usurper Abimelech (Judg. 9:4). It is obviously this circumstance, and not racial kinship, that accounts for the analogous roles played by *Khapiru* in Amarna Age Palestine on the one hand and "vain and light fellows" in early Israel on the other. But the severest blow of all was dealt to the identification of *Khapiru* with *Hebrews* by the discovery at Ugarit of partly parallel Akkadian and Ugaritic lists of towns of the kingdom of Ugarit. For the town which is called "Khalb of the Khapiru" in Akkadian is called "Khalb of the *'apirim'* (not *'ibriyyim* [= 'Hebrews'] or the like) in Ugaritic.[3]

2. That the system of weights in use at Ugarit was not the Babylonian one but the one which the Israelites employed is proved not by a Ugaritic document but by a business account in the Akkadian language and by a series of uninscribed balance-weights. The document reckons 3000 shekels to the talent in agreement with Exodus 38:25–26 and as against the Babylonian system, which (consistently sexagesimal) reckoned 3600 shekels. The common balance-weights of Ugarit[4] tell the same story. The largest is evidently a mina (one-sixtieth of a talent) and the others equal one-fiftieth of this mina or multiples or fractions of one-fiftieth. Evidently, therefore, the Ugarit mina was divided into fifty shekels (not into sixty like the Babylonian), so that again a shekel comes to (1/50 × 1/60 =) 1/3000 of a talent. Interestingly enough the

[3] To the negative result that the Israelites are not identical with the Khapiru of the Amarna Age, may be added the positive observation that both archaeological and literary indications point rather definitely to the third quarter of the 13th century as the date of the Israelite conquest of Palestine. Most of the Ugaritic documents, on the other hand, were copied in the second quarter of the 14th century; and in the case of literary works, that will usually mean that they were composed considerably earlier. When, therefore, a comparative study of Ugaritic and biblical literature reveals resemblances which can hardly be accounted for otherwise than by borrowing, it must be the Israelites who borrowed from the Canaanites and not vice versa.

[4] In addition to the native mina of 470 grams, the Ugaritians made occasional use of the Egyptian mina of 440 grams and of the Babylonian mina of 490 grams.

mutual relationships of the uninscribed weights of Judah similarly confirm Exodus 38:25–26.[5]

IV. *The Ugaritic Writings and the Bible*

While letters, records of various sorts, a manual on the treatment of horse ailments,[6] and even a schoolboy's exercise are not wanting, the bulk of the Ugaritic writings are literature—or rather, unfortunately, fragments of literature—in the strict sense of the word. This literature is exclusively poetical, and it is for the most part epic.[7] There are parts of two epics embodying legends about kings and parts of what was probably one great epic embodying myths about gods. There is also one smaller writing which seems to be a ritual text embodying a myth about gods.[8]

Obviously, such writings are not likely to furnish exact data on history or geography—least of all, in view of the place where they were found, on Palestinian history and geography. Yet that is precisely what was claimed for them by some European scholars during the 1930's. Some readers of the *Biblical Archaeologist* have doubtless heard of the "Negebite hypothesis." It asserted that some of the Ugaritic texts preserve the memory of the expulsion of the Phoenicians from their alleged original homes in an allegedly thriving southern part of Judah. Their supplanters were said to be a people bearing the name of Terah, which in the Bible is the

[5] See most recently Albright, *AASOR*, XXI–XXII (1943), 76 ff. The Palestinian units were heavier than the Ugaritian (11.4 grams to the shekel as against 9.5 grams), but their inner relationships were the same (50 shekels to the mina).

[6] The *materia medica* includes "old fig-cakes," with which cf. II Kings 20:7; Isa. 38:21.

[7] Except for a few fragments, the literary texts all turned up in the campaigns of 1930, 1931 and 1933. The post-war excavations have continued to swell the mass of records (mostly "economic") and added to the letters and exercises (including *a b c*'s), but have yielded only a few literary fragments.

[8] This text is of special interest to Bible students for two reasons. Firstly, a feature of the ritual was the boiling of a kid in milk, so that Maimonides was apparently right in attributing the prohibition of this very practice in Exod. 23:19; 34:26; Deut. 14:21 to its pagan associations. Secondly, apart from Ps. 29:8, this is the only text in or out of the Bible in which "the wilderness of Kadesh" is named. On this, see below.

name of Abraham's father. The events in question were consequently connected with the Abrahamic migration from Mesopotamia to Palestine. South Palestinian localities like Ashdod, Sharuhen, and the wilderness of Kadesh were also said to be named in the texts. However, some of the words in question (e.g., the alleged "Terah" in some of its occurrences) are in reality verbs, and others are common nouns. A probable exception is "the wilderness of Kadesh," but we shall see presently that the region thus designated is at least as close to Phoenicia as to Palestine. No, the startlingly prosperous and populous Negeb (south) of the Ugarit texts belongs in the same limbo as the important state of Musri flourishing in the dreary wastes of Sinai and Midian which Hugo Winckler claimed to have discovered in the annals of the kings of Assyria forty-odd years ago, and which he proposed substituting for "Egypt" (Hebrew *Misrayim*) in large segments of the Bible! What one can expect to learn from the poetical myths and legends of the Ugaritians is something about

1. their ideas and ideals and
2. the technique and quality of their poetry.

Then, since in the Amarna Age the Semites of Palestine and the Syrian coast constituted a cultural continuum which may be called "the sphere of Canaanite culture," we may, with due caution, generalize our findings so as to cover the Canaanites of Palestine as well.

1. *Ideas and Ideals.* To put it tritely, their ideas about men are distinctly more edifying than those about gods. The piety, the loves, and the family life of the human heroes are (always allowing for human frailty) appealing. A good monarch like *King Daniel* "judges the cause of the widow, adjudicates the case of the fatherless"—a phrase which is familiar to every reader of the Bible. On the other hand *King Keret,* who is convalescing after a very serious illness, is admonished by his scapegrace son Yassib approximately[9] as follows:

> Hearken, I pray thee, O Keret the noble! List, and let thine ear be attentive. . . . Thou shouldst judge the cause of the widow, adjudicate the case of him that is in anguish of spirit. Thou shouldst deliver the poor man from his oppressors, shouldst feed the fatherless before thee and the widow behind thy back. How long hast

[9] The passage in question, II K 6:41–54, was published in *Syria,* XXIII (1942–43), 12.

thou been a brother of the bed of sickness, a friend of
the lofty couch? Descend from the king's throne! Let me
be king. Upon the seat of thy dominion let me sit.

No doubt the monarchic reality often contrasted luridly
with this ideal among the Canaanites, as it notoriously did at
times in the Israelite monarchy. But the ideal was there, and
when the Israelites, late in the 11th century B.C., took over
from their neighbors the millennia-old institution of monarchy, they evidently also took over the ideal connected with
it.[10] For one thing, they almost certainly knew about the
legend of King Daniel, the ruler who was not remiss in "judging the cause of the widow, adjudicating the case of the fatherless." The prophet Ezekiel enunciates the doctrine that,
when God visits upon a sinful land a nationwide calamity,
the righteousness of an individual dweller of that land can
save the life of that individual but not the lives of any of his
fellow-citizens, not even those of his own children (14:12 ff.).
To bring his point home, he keeps reiterating that under such
circumstances not even Noah, Daniel, and Job would save
either a son or a daughter. There can be no doubt that in
naming these men, Ezekiel is citing three classical saints of
yore. The antiquity of Noah requires no proof. That Job was
thought to have lived "in the days of the patriarchs" is evident from certain well-known indications in our book of Job.
Between these two, the Daniel of the book of Daniel, at best
Ezekiel's own younger contemporary, is out of place; especially as Ezekiel is obviously illustrating a *general* proposition, which is applicable to *any* land, with types of pious
men that might conceivably be found in any nation. Obviously his Daniel, to whom, by the way, he refers again in
another passage (Ezek. 28:3), is like Noah and Job, a saint
of hoary antiquity, and consequently belongs to mankind as
a whole. His identity with the Daniel of the Canaanite epic
is highly probable.

But the Bible also contains a striking parallel to the son's
rebuke of Keret, the king who allegedly did not "judge the
cause of the widow, decide the case of the fatherless." The
opening paragraph of Jeremiah 22, the famous chapter on
kings of Judah, reads as follows:

[10] That ideal is the origin of the concept of the Messiah, the ideal
ruler of "the latter days."

Thus saith the Lord, go down unto the house [palace] of the king of Judah and speak there this word. Say, Hearken unto the word of the Lord, O king of Judah that sittest upon the throne of David, thou and all thy servants that enter in by these gates [of the palace]. Thus saith the Lord, Execute ye justice and righteousness, and deliver the spoiled out of the hand of the oppressor; and do no wrong, do no violence, to the stranger, nor the fatherless, nor the widow, neither shed innocent blood in this place. For if ye do this thing indeed, then shall there [continue to] enter in by the gates of this house kings sitting upon the throne of David. . . . But if ye will not hear these words, I swear by myself, saith the Lord, that this house shall become a desolation.

The resemblance of this admonition to the Ugaritic admonition to King Keret is of course not due to imitation, but it is due to the common premise that a king's job is to execute justice. At the same time, the difference between the two cases should not be overlooked. The story of Keret is legend, that of Jeremiah history. Keret's son was demanding the throne for himself, and his high-sounding sermon was only a hypocritical pretext. But Jeremiah was motivated solely by the intense religious and moral earnestness of a Hebrew prophet. Even if it is granted (though it is very improbable) that the fate of the royal house, and even of the temple, was a matter of indifference to him, that of the nation was surely not; yet in another passage he makes the fulfillment of the same requirements an indispensable condition for the continued existence of both the temple and the nation (chap. 7).

Indeed, the Ugaritic texts themselves make it difficult to conceive of a Nathan, an Elijah, an Amos, or a Jeremiah arising in Ugarit, or Byblus, or Tyre, to denounce the failure of their princes to live up to the ideal of the legendary King Daniel. For the example of the human characters of Canaanite literature was heavily offset by that of the divine ones. The gods of the Ugaritic epics are not only anthropomorphic (in human form) and anthropopathic (with human emotions), but morally sometimes inferior to the genus homo at its best.

One of the most shocking examples, and the one most germane to our subject, is that of the ferocious warrior-goddess Anath. King Daniel's son Aqhat possesses a cunningly wrought bow, a gift of the craftsman-god Kothar. Anath coaxes him to give it to her in exchange for wealth or immortality, but Aqhat will on no account part with his bow. Thereupon Anath commissions an assassin to dispatch Aqhat. I do not pretend to be certain that the Phoenician princess Jezebel, who found the same happy solution for the problem of Naboth's unwillingness to sell his vineyard to her husband, the Israelite king Ahab (I Kings 21), had read this particular story of Aqhat's bow or been told it by her nurse. But it does seem obvious that, other things being equal, a sovereign who had been brought up, like Ahab, in the sternly ethical religion of the Lord of Hosts would be less likely to get such bright ideas, and less ready to act upon them if he did, than one who had been brought up in a milieu where the notions of divinity prevailed which we find in the Canaanite literature. And a monarch who did resort to such practices was infinitely more likely to meet with an Elijah in a society which harbored the Israelite concept of deity than in one that harbored the Canaanite concept.

It is fortunate that the Israelites did not borrow any fundamental ideas about God from the Canaanites! On the other hand, they did borrow, with profit, some subsidiary ones. An example is the notion of his successful combat, long long ago, with a hydra-headed sea-dragon (Ps. 74:14), known as Leviathan and by several other names and epithets, and with other enemies. The seven-headed dragon, the very name Leviathan, and most of the other names and epithets, recur in the Ugarit texts, according to which the same beings were vanquished by Baal (with the aid of trusty allies). Similarly, the Hebrew poets described Jehovah, just as the Canaanite poets described Baal, as a storm god riding in a cloud-enveloped chariot, uttering peals of thunder and sending out darts of lightning; and they even borrowed Baal's epithet of the "Cloudrider" and transferred it to Jehovah.

We also have a complete composition, namely Psalm 29, which is full of echoes of Canaanite poetry and whose geographical standpoint is not Palestine but Phoenicia, or at least the Syro-Palestinian "sphere of Canaanite culture."

It is well known that all of the rainstorms of Syria and Palestine originate in the Mediterranean Sea and proceed in a landward direction (cf. I Kings 18:43-45). Our Psalm 29 speaks of such a storm as if it were a ride across the skies by a thundering God. Naturally, his voice is first heard roaring over the "mighty waters" (vs. 3). Next, it shatters the cedars of Lebanon (vs. 5). Still further inland, it shakes the Anti-Lebanon range (vs. 6). Finally, far to the east, it causes the Syrian desert to tremble (vs. 8).

1. Now, while the Lebanon and the Anti-Lebanon do lie within the ideal boundaries of the Promised Land (Deut. 11: 24; Josh. 1:4), they do not lie within the historic boundaries of Israel.

2. Furthermore, the name by which the Anti-Lebanon is designated here, namely Sirion (vs. 6), is not the usual one. Apart from I Chronicles 5:16, where Sirion is perhaps to be read for Sharon, the name only occurs again in the Scriptures in Deuteronomy 3:9, which verse states that it is the Sidonian, i.e. Phoenician, name of the range which is otherwise know as Hermon or Senir. And in effect, it is the name employed by Ugaritians and other northern peoples.

3. So, too, the great desert to the east of the Anti-Lebanon range, the Syrian desert, is called in our Psalm "the wilderness of Kadesh,"—a name found nowhere else in the Bible[11] but mentioned in a ritual text of Ugarit, where only preconceived notions could have led anybody to take it to refer to a very circumscribed area on the border between the Palestinian Negeb (southland) and the Sinai Peninsula.

4. The climactic ("staircase") parallelism which is so characteristic of our Psalm (vss. 1, 4, 5, 8) is exceedingly common in the Ugaritic poems.

5. As I have already pointed out, the very notion of the storm-riding thunder-god is a Canaanite borrowing.

The cumulative evidence for the ultimately Canaanite origin of Psalm 29 is therefore overwhelming, and examples of some shorter pieces of Canaanite verse adapted by the Hebrew poets will be cited presently. However, the procedure of the Israelites with these borrowings was the opposite of that which we observed in connection with the king-ideal;

[11] Contrary to an impression which is not confined to adherents of the Negebite hypothesis, none of the wildernesses in the vicinity of Kadesh, or Kadesh-barnea, which admittedly plays an important part in the account of Israel's wanderings prior to her entry into the Promised Land, shares with that oasis the name of Kadesh. That oasis lies between the wilderness of Zin and the wilderness of Paran (see Wright-Filson, *Westminster Historical Atlas to the Bible* [2nd ed.; 1956], Pls. V, X). Indeed, in view of Gen. 14:7 it is doubtful whether even the oasis was called Kadesh at the time when the Ugarit texts were written.

that is to say, they took them *less* seriously than the Canaanites, more as poetic ornamentation than as fact. (Compare the Puritan Milton's use of Greek mythology even in poems of a specifically theological nature.) For Israelite monotheism leaves no room for any powers which are not subject to the sovereign will of God. Consequently it leaves no room for mythology; that is why the Bible contains only a few fossils or erratic boulders of mythology. And it is incompatible with the notion of God's needing to fight; that is why such combats are only introduced for rhetorical or poetic effect, and why "God's enemies" becomes merely a figure of speech for "evildoers." Not only do the two expressions alternate with each other (Ps. 68:1–2), but—very characteristically—they alternate with each other in a verse which is unquestionably adapted from a passage in a Canaanite epic that speaks *only*, and literally, *of an enemy*. In a Ugaritic text, an ally of Baal encourages him in preparation for an encounter with another god with the words: "Lo, thine enemy O Baal, lo, thine enemy wilt thou smite; lo, thou wilt cut off thine adversary." The Psalmist, on the other hand (Ps. 92:9), expresses his confidence in the ultimate triumph of righteousness as follows: "For lo, thine enemies, O Jehovah, lo, thine enemies shall perish; all they that work iniquity shall be scattered."

2. *The Form and Quality of Canaanite Poetry*. This example, however, illustrates not only the ideas of the Canaanites as revealed by the Ugaritic texts and Israel's reaction to them, but also the form and quality of Canaanite poetry and its influence upon Israelite poetry. And indeed, the most important and assured results of comparative biblical and Ugaritic studies come under this heading. The formal elements of Hebrew poetry are largely borrowed from the Canaanites. I have already mentioned that climactic parallelism is a favorite device of Canaanite poets. The Ugaritic passage I have just translated is an example—as is also, of course, its biblical modification. That the same kind of climactic parallelism also occurs in early Akkadian poetry is beside the point. The Canaanites, whose written language, as we have seen, was originally Akkadian, doubtless adopted this and other techniques from Akkadian poetry. But that was long before the Israelites appeared upon the scene, and the latter could only have borrowed those techniques from the Canaanites. Moreover, for the determination of mutual relationships, the frequency of a feature is at least as important as its mere presence. The well

known parallelism of clauses is present in a certain measure in the poetry of many ancient and modern peoples. (It is very prominent, for example, in the national epic of the Finns!) But in the ancient Orient, it is only in Canaanite poetry that its use attains the same, sometimes monotonous, regularity as in Hebrew. In order to meet the exigencies of such a prosody, the Canaanite and Hebrew poets have some fixed pairs of synonymous words or phrases for certain concepts which poets have frequent occasion to express (e.g.: head, eternity, to fear, to rejoice). Many such fixed pairs are common to Ugaritic and biblical poetry (though of course the words were not pronounced exactly alike in the two languages). Moreover, the members of such a pair are—with apparently no exceptions in Ugaritic poetry and with very few in Hebrew—always employed in the same order, and that order is also nearly always the same in both literatures. Common to both is the rule that it is the more usual expression that comes first, the second in some cases being hardly used at all except precisely for the purpose of balancing the first. For example, the ordinary Hebrew word for "eternity" is *'olam* (or *'olamim*), and if the poet wishes to express this concept a second time in a parallel clause he uses "generation and generation," *dor wa-dor* (or *dor dor,* or *dor dorim*). And except for the pronunciation, it is the same in Ugaritic. Thus, the continuation of the encouragement of Baal which I quoted above is, literally:

Thou wilt win thy kingdom of eternity [*'lm* = Heb. *'olam*],
 thy dominion of all generations [*dr dr* = Heb. *dor dor*];

with which compare (Ps. 145:13):

Thy kingdom is a kingdom of all eternity [*'olamim*],
 and thy dominion endureth through all generations [*dor wa-dor*].

I need not point out that the importance of this illustration is not limited to the use, in the same sequence, of the same pair of synonyms for "eternity"! Our verse, like Psalm 92:9 which I quoted above, is obviously borrowed and adapted from its Canaanite parallel.

But to return to the identical use of fixed pairs of parallel synonyms, such agreement goes beyond a mere agreement of form and results in a considerable similarity of diction. So great, in fact, is the agreement in poetic diction that the Ugarit texts have become—in absolute terms to a very modest extent, but in relation to their limited bulk to a surprisingly large extent—an aid to the textual criticism of poetical passages in the Hebrew Bible; sometimes they confirm emendations previously proposed, sometimes they suggest convincing new ones. For example, Psalm 42:1 is rendered in both the Authorized and the Revised Version: "As a hart panteth after the water brooks." However, "hart" is masculine, whereas the verb rendered "panteth" is feminine in form in the Hebrew. Now, all that is necessary for changing the Hebrew word for "hart" into the word for "hind" is the addition of a final *t;* and as the following word begins with a *t*, scholars have long suspected that, as frequently happens, our "hart" is simply due to the failure of a scribe to write the *t* twice (at the end of the noun as well as at the beginning of the following verb) instead of only once. It so happens that the same figure of speech occurs in a Ugaritic passage, and there the feminine form of our substantive (i.e., with final *t*) is employed, thus confirming the proposed emendation in the Psalms passage. So, too, a Ugaritic parallel to II Samuel 1:21 shows that instead of *u-sde terumot* 'nor fields of offerings'—which no serious exegete regards otherwise than as a makeshift translation —*we-shera' tehomot* 'nor upwelling of the deeps' (i.e., flowing of springs) is to be read. Again, in Job 37:3 the rendering "He sendeth it under the whole heaven, and his lightning unto the ends of the earth" is unsatisfactory for three reasons: firstly, because a mere pronoun "it" stands in parallelism to a substantive "lightning"; secondly, because "it" does not mean "lightning" but refers back to the "sound" (i.e., "thunder") of the preceding verse; and thirdly, because the verb rendered "sendeth" does not have that meaning anywhere else in Hebrew or in the related idioms. However, the observation that a noun from the same root means in Ugaritic "a flash of lightning" suggests that we have here an example of the opposite error from that which we have just noted in Psalm 42:1; i.e., the scribe has repeated at the end of the verb the *w* with which the following word begins. With this final *w* omitted, the word reads instead of *yishrehu* 'he sendeth(?) it'—*yisre(h)* 'he flasheth'; and in a flash, all three of our difficulties are solved. (Probably *Sarai*, the original name of Abraham's wife Sarah, is from the same root and means "brilliance.")

A fourth example is Proverbs 26:23, in which a person with smooth lips but a bitter heart is compared, as our text now reads, to "an earthen vessel overlaid with silver dross." Apart from the question as to what exactly "silver dross" is, the Hebrew expression means rather "dross silver"—which is not much easier to define. Moreover, neither "silver dross" nor "dross silver" is used for plating earthenware in real life and, what is more serious, neither would form a particularly attractive exterior. However, if the two Hebrew words in question (*ksp sygym*) are written together, i.e., as *kspsygym*, the initial *k* can be taken as the particle meaning "like," while the rest of the word can be identified with Ugaritic *spsg* 'quartz, glaze.' And "an earthen vessel overlaid with glaze" is exactly what the context requires.[12]

The last three examples illustrate, besides the value of Ugaritic literature for the textual criticism of the Hebrew Scriptures, its contribution to Hebrew lexicography. Under this heading may also be included the confirmation which it affords for the surmise, previously made by an American scholar on the basis of the Arabic, that the verb rendered "to be dismayed" in Isaiah 41:10, 23 is not the hithpael of *shaʿah* 'to look' but an independent verb *shataʿ* 'to be dismayed,' as also its testimony that the Hebrew word for "table" does *not* mean properly "a skin mat," nor the word for "window," "a hollow." In general, the number of Hebrew words whose meanings have been correctly understood but whose etymologies will have to be revised in view of their Ugaritic correspondences is surprisingly high.

I have yet to say a word about the quality of Ugaritic poetry. After what I have already hinted about the crudity of the Canaanite concept of divinity, it will come as no surprise that some of the passages are quite crude, and that few display real power or profundity. However, some—especially those about men!—are not without delicacy and grace. But there can be no two opinions about it: the Israelite pupils far outstripped their Canaanite masters.

I would add, however, that the purpose of comparative studies is not invidious comparison, but better understanding. The literature, archaeology, history, and individuality of Israel, the world it lived in, and its place in that world and in history, have all been clarified in varying degrees by the discoveries made at Ugarit, and will undoubtedly be further clarified by further study and discovery.

[12] For further examples, see *JBL*, LXII (1943), 109 ff.

4

THE CIVILIZATION OF THE EDOMITES

NELSON GLUECK

At the beginning of the 13th century B.C. a new agricultural civilization appeared in Transjordan belonging to the Edomites, Moabites, Ammonites and Amorites. They belonged to the Semitic groups that took possession of Transjordan perhaps in the 14th or early 13th century B.C., and probably partly absorbed and partly drove out the Bedouins, who since about 1900 B.C. had been the masters of most of the land. Prior to the 20th century B.C., the arable lands of Transjordan had been occupied by sedentary inhabitants. During successive periods of more or less intensive development, going back at least as far as 4000 B.C. certainly, their agricultural civilizations had risen and fallen and superseded each other, leaving ancient sites and indestructible artifacts behind to testify to their former presence. Some Chalcolithic settlements of the late 4th millennium B.C. have been found. Then again, archaeological discoveries may have confirmed the account in Genesis 14:5–7 of how the eastern kings led by Chedorlaomer conquered all of Transjordan, by subduing and destroying one after another all the fortified sites which lay in their path, from Ashtaroth and Ham at the northern end to el-Paran at the southern end of the territory which later on became known as Edom. This civilization, destroyed about 1900 B.C., never again recovered from the blow, as a long line of ancient sites testify, most of which were never again occupied, or at least not until after the lapse of approximately 600 years.

In the interval, particularly in the areas later designated as Moab and Edom, sedentary civilization of the Middle Bronze and Late Bronze periods, extending between the 20th and 14th centuries B.C., did not flourish, as it did to a larger degree in northern Transjordan, in the Jordan valley and particularly in Cisjordan. It is significant in this connection, that neither the Egyptian lists of towns nor the Tell el-Amarna tablets refer to eastern Palestine in the period extending from the 20th to the 14th centuries B.C. Edom and Seir are first mentioned in the records of Merniptah (*ca.* 1235–1227 B.C.) and Rameses III (*ca.* 1198–1167 B.C.). It may further be mentioned in this connection, that there are no archaeological traces of Horites in either the hill country of Edom or in the Wadi Arabah or in southernmost Palestine, unless under Horites are to be understood purely nomadic groups, such as the Edomites must have found and conquered when they entered southern Transjordan (Gen. 14:6; 36:21, 22; Deut. 2:12).

The Semites who occupied Transjordan about the 14th century B.C. soon broke up into natural divisions. This was conditioned partly by the fact that they represented originally separate tribes or tribal groups, however closely related in general they may have been to each other. Fully as important, however, for the partition of eastern Palestine into the kingdoms of Edom, Moab, Ammon, and the two Amorite kingdoms of Gilead, were the natural land divisions of the entire country. It is bounded on the west by the Wadi Arabah, the Dead Sea and the Jordan river valley, on the east and south by the desert, on the north by the wide and deep and precipitous Wadi Yarmuk, which separates it from Syria. These kingdoms were marked off in the main from each other, traveling from the south to the north, by the wide and deep natural boundaries of the Wadi Hesa (the river Zered), the Wadi Mojib (the river Arnon), the Wadi Zerqa (the river Jabboq), and the Wadi Yarmuk.

The main period of the development of these kingdoms during the Iron Age extended between the 13th and 8th centuries B.C., after which a period of deterioration set in, culminating in complete destruction in the 6th century B.C. These were highly advanced, strongly organized, internally well-integrated kingdoms. The land was dotted with well-built stone villages and towns. The borders of these kingdoms, which can now be accurately fixed, were fortified by strong fortresses, built usually on eminences and commanding a view of each other. The agriculture of these kingdoms was intensive, their pottery well made, their commerce sensibly ordered, their literature in all probability of no mean order, if one may draw inferences from the inscription of Mesha or the background of the book of Job. The wealth of these kingdoms, even under Assyrian domination, may be judged from the tribute paid to Esarhaddon. Edom paid 12 minas of silver, in comparison with 10 minas of silver paid by Judah; Ammon paid 2 minas of gold; Moab paid 1 mina of gold. The development and wealth of the countries of Transjordan, which existed contemporaneously with those of Israel and Judah, were very real, however scanty the literary remains and memory of their existence have chanced to be.

The archaeological survey of Edom revealed why it was that a foreign group could not enter the territory of Edom without permission. The permission refused, the applicants for entry must perforce turn aside as the Israelites were compelled to do (Num. 20:17; 21:22). Strong fortresses barred the way on all the frontiers of Edom and of Moab north of it. The high, comparatively fertile and well-watered Edomite plateau ends suddenly in the south, with sheer or precipitous walls and slopes marking the abrupt fall to the desert of the Wadi Hismeh, which stretches to the Red Sea and Arabia. Edomite armed escorts probably guarded caravans which traveled through the Wadi Hismeh and the Wadi Yitm to the Wadi Arabah and to Ezion-geber:Elath on the north shore of the eastern arm of the Red Sea. The main line of defense, and for all practical purposes the southern border of the Iron Age kingdom of Edom, was marked by a line of fortresses along the southern edge of the plateau, dominating the Jebel Shera.

The eastern border of the Edomite kingdom was even more strongly protected than the southern, its defenses being marked by a long line of fortresses situated on the highest hills in the arid, uncultivated region between the desert and the sown. From one end of the country to the other, it would have been possible to transmit fire or smoke signals in a very short time. This line of fortresses continued northward and marked also the eastern boundary of Iron Age Moab.

The north boundary of Edom was marked by the Nahal Zered (Wadi Hesa), and the west by the Wadi Arabah, both of them clear, natural geographical limitations. These northern and western boundaries were no less strongly protected than the eastern and southern, although there were not actually as many fortresses and police-posts. In the first place, the danger of Bedouin invasion was not great from the west, and was non-existent from the north. In the second place, the deep canyon of the Wadi Hesa and the inhospitable rift of the Wadi Arabah were in themselves formidable barriers to would-be invaders. Nevertheless, strong posts protected these fronts also. The possibility that Edomite power once extended into parts of southern Palestine is suggested by a number of biblical verses which definitely locate Edom-Seir on the west side of the Arabah. These verses, however, reflect the Idumèan settlement in southern Palestine, where many Edomites settled after being expelled from Edom proper by the Nabateans, who in time took over their former territory. These Edomites became known as Idumeans, when their name was Grecized. From their midst stemmed Herod the Great. His son, Herod Antipas took as his first wife the daughter of the Nabatean king, Aretas IV, thus completing a cycle of history. Many of the Edomites who remained in their original territory were absorbed in time by the Nabateans, just as those who found a new home in southern Palestine became Judaized. It is this Idumean settlement in southern Palestine that the author of Deuteronomy 23:8 probably had in mind when he said: "You shall not abominate [consider as outside the pale of the community] an Edomite, because he is your brother," meaning those Idumeans who had been Judaized and had become Yahweh worshipers.

Within its main boundaries, Edom in the Iron Age was a thriving, prosperous, civilized kingdom, filled with cities and towns and villages, with its economy based on intensive agriculture, trade, and, to a certain extent, industry. The passage in Amos 1:12 referring to Bozrah and Teiman as being evidently in the northern and southern parts of Edom, respectively, suggests the relative positions of Buseirah in the north, which is to be identified with Bozrah, and Tawilan near Petra in the south, which is to be identified with the Teiman of that verse. The Edomites were devoted to the gods and goddesses of fertility. Townspeople and peasants had in their houses crude pottery figurines, representing the deities whose good will they sought. Thus, near Buseirah (Bozrah) was found a 9th–8th century B.C. pottery figurine of a fertility goddess, wearing a lamp as a crown, and holding in her hands what seems to be a sacred loaf of bread—or is it a tambourine?

The Edomite and other Transjordanian pottery of the 13th–6th centuries B.C. in itself bespeaks a highly developed civilization. Much of the ware is similar to contemporary ware in Palestine. However, there are differences, sufficiently large, to compel an individual classification. The distinctiveness of some of the Iron Age pottery of Edom and Moab may perhaps be ascribed to influences emanating from Syria via the trade route that followed the "king's highway" (Num. 20:17; 21:22), which has been marked by the same line throughout all the historical periods of Transjordan. The orientation of Edom, Moab, Ammon, and Gilead, for cultural as well as topographical and geographical reasons, may be said to be directed more to the north and south than to the west, that is, mainly to Syria and Arabia rather than to Palestine.

It may be emphasized with regard to the Iron Age pottery of Edom and Moab, that its beginnings go back not later than the first part of the 13th century B.C. Thus do archaeological facts bear out the validity of details, or of the background, of biblical accounts. The precedence of the beginnings of Edomite and Moabite pottery, for instance, over those of Israelite pottery, has a direct relationship to the account in Genesis 31:31–39, which lists eight Edomite "kings," who reigned in the land of Edom before the Israelites had a king.

It becomes impossible, therefore, in the light of all this new archaeological evidence, particularly when studied in connection with the deposits of historical memory contained in the Bible, to escape the conclusion that the particular Exodus of the Israelites through southern Transjordan could not have taken place before the 13th century B.C. It will be recalled that the Israelites begged the Edomites and Moabites in vain for permission to travel through these kingdoms on their way to the Promised Land. The Israelites were compelled to go around these kingdoms, and finally force their way westward to the Jordan via the north side of the Nahal Arnon (Wadi Mojib), which at that time was the southern part of the territory of Sihon, king of the Amorites. Had the Exodus through southern Transjordan taken place before the 13th century B.C., the Israelites would have found neither Edomite nor Moabite kingdoms, well organized and well fortified, whose rulers could have given or withheld permission to go through their territories.

The relationship between Israel and Edom throughout much of their history was a stormy one, characterized by unremitting enmity and almost continuous warfare. The main causes of the discord between them were the struggle for the control of the strategically important trade route down the Wadi Arabah, the possession of the rich copper and iron mines which abounded in it, and mastery of the seaport and industrial center of Ezion-geber:Elath at the head of the gulf of Aqabah.

Long before the advent of the Israelites, the presence of the mineral deposits in the Wadi Arabah was known and the mines exploited in all probability by the Qenites and the Edomites, to whom they were related through the Qenizzites (Gen. 15:19; 36:10, 11, 42). It was the Qenites, who were native to this region and whose very name indicates that they were smiths, and the related Qenizzites, many of whom were also smiths by profession, who probably first imparted to the Israelites and Edomites information about the ore deposits in the Wadi Arabah; and who introduced the Israelites and the Edomites to the arts of mining and metallurgy. The Bible tells us (Gen. 4:22) that Tubal-cain (a Qenite) was the first forger of copper and iron instruments. That the Qenites were at home in Edom is indicated by Balaam's punning proverb with regard to them in Numbers 24:21: "Everlasting is thy habitation and set in the Rock [Sela] is thy nest [Qen]." The pun on Qen and Qenite is obvious.

There was also an ancient trade route that led from Sela or Petra to the Wadi Arabah, then south to Ezion-geber:Elath (or Aila as the Nabatean-Roman-Byzantine site which took its place farther to the east, nearer modern Aqabah, became known later on), and westward via Qurnub to Gaza and Ascalon. This trade route from Sela or Petra to Gaza and Ascalon assumed particular importance during the Nabatean period. However, it was undoubtedly of large importance also during the times of the Edomite kingdom and the United and Divided Kingdoms of Israel and Judah. This was probably the route used for slave traffic between Gaza and Edom, mentioned, for instance, in Amos 2:6.

The prosperous periods in the history of the United Kingdom of Israel and Judah and then of the kingdom of Judah have a direct relationship to the periods during which they controlled the Arabah and a port on the Red Sea. The Arabah was equally important for the Edomites and the Nabateans who succeeded them.

It is possible that David began the exploitation of the mines in the Wadi Arabah after he had subjugated and enslaved the Edomites (II Sam. 8:13–15; I Kings 11:15–16). The pottery in Edom which was used during this and all the remaining parts of the Iron Age, continued to be Edomite, just as

Nabatean pottery continued to be used after the Romans had occupied the Nabatean sites in it. The exploitation of the mines in the Wadi Arabah was undoubtedly intensified during the reign of Solomon. Indeed, it may be said that he was the first one who placed the mining industry in the Wadi Arabah upon a really important industrial scale. Solomon, to be sure, had to contend with the guerilla warfare waged against him by Hadad, prince of Edom, who had returned to Edom from Egypt, whither he had fled from David when the latter conquered Edom (I Kings 11:17–19, 25). When we next hear of Edom, it was ruled by Jehoshaphat through a deputy-governor (I Kings 22:47). One may assume, therefore, that Judah had retained control over Edom from the time of Solomon on. It was probably towards the end of the reign of Jehoshaphat that the Edomites made a raid on En-gedi (II Chron. 20:1 ff.). During the reign of his son, Joram, Edom revolted and set up a king in place of the former Judean deputy (II Kings 8:20–22). At this time the nation probably regained control of the Wadi Arabah and seized the port-city and industrial center of Ezion-geber:Elath, identified with Tell el-Kheleifeh on the north shore of the gulf of Aqabah, the eastern arm of the Red Sea.

For about a century, Judah was unable to push forward again into Edom, which during this period evidently worked the mines in the Wadi Arabah. Edom, however, was not long to enjoy its independence. Amaziah of Judah waged successful war against it, capturing Sela, whose name he changed to Joktheel (II Kings 14:7; II Chron. 25:11, 12). It is to be identified with the great, sheer, flat-topped hill of Umm el-Biyara in Petra, where we have found Iron II Edomite pottery. His capable son Uzziah completed the conquest of Edom begun by his father, it being recorded that he recovered Elath from Edom (II Chron. 26:1, 2; II Kings 14:22). Edom then remained subject to Judah till the time of Ahaz, when it regained possession of Elath (II Kings 16:6). After that Judah was never again strong enough to dispute Edom's control over the Wadi Arabah, though Edom itself became progressively less able to hold and exploit it. Elath continued to be occupied by the Edomites till the downfall of their kingdom in the 6th century B.C.

It is to this final period of Edomite independence, before succumbing, like Judah, to Babylonian conquest, that we assign the Edomite stamped jars found in Period IV of the excavations of Tell el-Kheleifeh (Ezion-geber:Elath). These jars were stamped with a royal seal in ancient Edomite-Hebrew characters reading: "Belonging to Qosanal, the servant of the king" (see *BA*, I [1938], 15–16). Qosanal is a typical Edomite name, the first part of which, Qos, is the name of a well-known Edomite and then Nabatean deity. It seems likely that this Qosanal, who was probably an Edomite, was the officer commanding the district of Elath, and was the representative (servant) of the Edomite king of that time.[1]

[1] *BASOR*, No. 79 (Oct. 1940), p. 13; No. 82 (April 1941), pp. 3–16; *Annual Report of the Smithsonian Institution* (1941), p. 474. Additional bibliography on the entire Edomite question: Glueck, *The Other Side of the Jordan* (1940); *AASOR*, XIV (1934), XV (1935), XVIII–XIX (1939), XXV–XXVIII (1951); *Rivers in the Desert* (1959).

5

PHILISTINE COFFINS AND MERCENARIES

G. ERNEST WRIGHT

During the last seventy-five years a number of curious clay coffins have been turning up, a few at a time, in Palestine and Egypt. They are now dated between the 13th and 10th centuries B.C., and most of them are probably to be fixed in the 12th century. The relevant examples found in Egypt can be shown to belong to people from Palestine, and all but three of those found in Palestine seem clearly to have held the bodies of Philistine men and women of the 12th century B.C. Hence it can be plausibly argued that those in Egypt were also made and used by Philistines who were hired mercenaries employed to protect the Egyptian borders.

We may begin our story with the summer of 1922 when Clarence S. Fisher of the American School of Oriental Research in Jerusalem discovered nearly a dozen of the clay sarcophagi in the northern cemetery of Beth-shan, a major Palestinian city south of the sea of Galilee in the Jordan valley. The excavation of Beth-shan by Philadelphia's University Museum was the first major archaeological undertaking in Palestine after the First World War, and Fisher was the first director of the work. In 1926 Alan Rowe, who succeeded Fisher as director, found three more of the coffins in a single tomb of the same cemetery. Father H. Vincent of the Dominican École Biblique in Jerusalem wrote a brief study of them in 1923,[1] but they have never been completely published together with all of the objects found in the tombs with them.[2]

The coffins were cylinders of baked clay, just large enough for a body. At the point where the head and shoulders would

[1] *RB*, XXXII (1923), 435–41.
[2] Rowe, *The Topography and History of Beth-shan* (1930), pp. 39–40 and Pls. XXXVII–XL. Cf. G. M. Fitzgerald, *PEFQ*, 1931, p. 60.

be, a lid was cut out. On it the head, hands, and sometimes arms of the deceased were formed in high relief, either by molding the clay before the coffin was baked or by applying and working bands of clay. Where the upper arms are shown, they begin near the top of the head and bend at the elbows just below the ears (Fig. 2). While this is a purposive styliza-

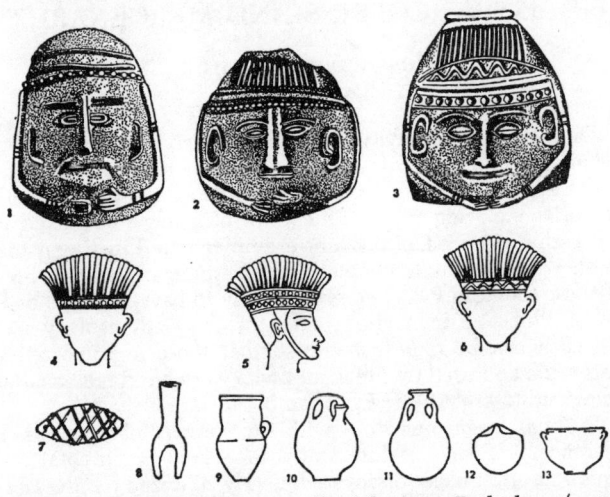

FIGURE 2. Three Philistine coffin lids from Beth-shan (1-3), and items found in tombs with them (7-13). Items 4-6 show the feather headdress worn by one group of Sea Peoples as depicted by an artist of Pharaoh Rameses III at Medinet Habu in Egypt.

tion, there can be no denial of the fact that the figures are not great works of art! Furthermore, considering the coffins from the various places as a group, it is clear that they do not come from one workshop, nor is there one artist whose work has influenced the production. The idea for the coffin was present, but those who translated the idea into clay were people who had had no artistic training.

The Beth-shan coffins were found in rectangular tombs, the contents of which were dated by Vincent in the 12th century and by Fisher in the same period. By contrast Canaanite tombs of the preceding Late Bronze Age tended to be more round in shape. While the pottery in the tombs was locally made, a number of scarabs showed that the deceased had been influenced by Egyptian customs. A lozenge-shaped mouth-plate of gold foil was found in one tomb. It had a hole in each end and originally had been tied over the mouth of a corpse. This reminded the archaeologists studying the finds of comparable discoveries at Mycene in Greece.

Between 1927 and 1937 Sir Flinders Petrie concluded a long and productive archaeological career by working mainly at three tells in southern Palestine, Tell Jemmeh, Tell el-Far'ah and Tell el-'Ajjul. At the second site in 1928–29 he found a cemetery which contained a quantity of Philistine pottery ("Cemetery 500"). In tombs 552 and 562, which he dated 1240 and 1050 B.C. respectively, he found two clay coffins of the type here in review. The tombs were square with a wide bench or ledge running around the sides and back, an early example of the bench tomb which became so popular in later Israelite times. A staircase hewn down into the rock gave access to the room, and an additional small square chamber had been added at the rear. In 552 the coffin was found in the rear chamber; in 562 the coffin had originally been placed on the left bench.[3] Petrie dated 552 in the 13th century because it contained an Egyptian scarab which bore the name of the pharaoh, Rameses II (*ca.* 1290–1224 B.C.). Yet more than one Palestinian archaeologist has gotten into difficulty in trying to date discoveries by royal scarabs from Egypt. The reason is that scarabs were often preserved for generations as heirlooms. In addition, certain examples at least appear to have been regarded as possessing magical properties, so that they were locally imitated, sometimes for centuries, after the pharaoh in question had died. Consequently, the presence of a scarab of Rameses II does not date a tomb except to indicate that it is probably not earlier than his reign.

In 1932 W. F. Albright published an important survey of the evidence for the sarcophagi in an article entitled, "An Anthropoid Clay Coffin from Sahab in Transjordan."[4] He was publishing the headpiece of a coffin obtained in 1929 by the Transjordan Department of Antiquities from a village some twelve kilometers southeast of Amman. The people of the village while looking for old cisterns had found a tomb,

[3] Petrie, *Beth-pelet*, I (1930), 6–9 and Pls. XIX–XX, XXIII–XXV.
[4] *AJA*, XXXVI (1932), 295–306.

roughly two meters square. In it they said there had been a "barrel" which they promptly smashed in order to get the treasure presumed to be within. The date of the coffin could not be proved because Albright was unable to examine the pottery found with it. A few pieces around the tomb's mouth dated from the 10th–9th centuries, but that they were precisely the same as what had once been with the coffin was impossible to tell. Nevertheless, Albright related the find to those at Beth-shan and Tell el-Far'ah, correcting Petrie's dating to the 12th–11th centuries B.C. Furthermore, he made two additional observations.

First, he recalled that Petrie and Naville had found similar coffins at Tell Nebesheh and Tell el-Yehudiyeh in the northeastern part of the Egyptian Delta between 1885 and 1888,[5] as other scholars who had studied the question also had pointed out. At Nebesheh the sarcophagi were found in rectangular tombs which Petrie called "Cypriote" and dated between the 7th and 5th centuries. Albright was able to date them between the 12th and 10th centuries because of the parallels to Palestinian pottery found in them. The Yehudiyeh coffins came from eight stone and sand burial-tumuli found in the desert about one and one-half miles from the ancient town. Here again Albright was able to show that the tombs contained Palestinian pottery and were to be dated about the 12th century. One piece of iron was found at each site along with a considerable quantity of copper implements. A number of the Yehudiyeh coffins were painted with very badly executed hieroglyphs, surely not written by native Egyptians. They could not be read, except for one which appears to have part of a feminine name, [?]-*tirsunaya*, written in imitation of the classic style of writing (before the 10th century). Two scarabs of Rameses III (*ca.* 1175–1144 B.C.), one of his father Set-nakht, and another with the prenomen of Rameses VI (*ca.* 1130 B.C.) were also found.

Albright's second observation was that these coffins of foreign people in Egypt must have been made in imitation of native Egyptian pottery sarcophagi. Many coffins with molded lids, belonging to the poor, have been found in Lower

[5] Petrie, Murray, and Griffith, *Tanis*, Part II, *Nebesheh and Defenneh* (1888), pp. 20 f. and Pls. I, III, XVI; and Naville and Griffith, *The Mound of the Jew* (1890), pp. 15–17, 42–48 and Pls. XII–XV.

Egypt, dating from the 18th and 19th dynasties (*ca.* 1575–1200 B.C.) and from the 9th and 8th centuries B.C. Furthermore, the Egyptian use of anthropoid coffins was later imitated also by the Phoenicians in the Persian period, and the custom spread widely. One example is the Ford Collection of marble sarcophagi from Sidon, which represents one of the first archaeological discoveries of the newly formed American School of Oriental Research in Jerusalem in 1900. These beautiful coffins were excavated by the late C. C. Torrey, who was the School's first director, and they were published in the first volume of the *Annual* of the School.

During the twenty-five years following Albright's article little new appears to have been added to the discussion except for J. L. Starkey's discovery in 1938 at Lachish in Palestine of a tomb (No. 570) with two of the clay coffins.[6] Olga Tufnell in publishing them seems to prefer a date for the tomb in the 20th Egyptian dynasty (that is, in the early 12th century).[7] In studying the pottery found in the tomb, however, I would venture the opinion that her date may be too late. The ceramic forms of Tomb 570 are difficult to date much later than the end of the 13th century, because they are typical Late Bronze pottery and quite different from that appearing with the coffins at Tell el-Farʻah, Beth-shan, Nebesheh and Yehudiyeh. In any case, even if the Lachish tomb stands at the very beginning of the 12th century, it is definitely earlier than the coffin tombs at the other four sites.[8] Hence according to the evidence presently known I would not hesitate in considering the Lachish tomb the earliest of our particular series.

In 1957 and 1958 Trude Dothan, Field Supervisor of Area

[6] L. Hennequin, in *Mélanges syriens offerts à Monsieur René Dussaud* (1939), II, 965–74, speaks of three sarcophagi found at Lachish, but in the final publication (Olga Tufnell, *Lachish IV: The Bronze Age* [1958], pp. 36, 131–32, 248–49 and Pls. XLV–XLVI) only two are mentioned and illustrated.

[7] In *Lachish IV*, p. 248, Miss Tufnell dates the tomb "1225–1175 B.C." On p. 36, however, she definitely suggests "the XXth dynasty during the reign of Rameses III," evidently because of the other Palestinian and Egyptian examples of that period.

[8] Too tight a generalization is difficult because of the failure of the Beth-shan expedition to publish all of its evidence. Such ceramic information as we have from the site, however, points to a definitely Iron Age horizon, though very early in the period.

C in the great Hazor Expedition and wife of Israel's Assistant Director of Antiquities, published two important articles on the coffin tombs, surveying the whole problem afresh and contributing new information.[9] Her first important observation was that the molded features on the Beth-shan coffin lids fall into two types. One with stylized arms and hands has such clear feminine characteristics that it must be assumed to depict women. Exact parallels, are found in graves at Aniba, Nubia (modern Sudan). The other type is more grotesque with arms framing the face. In Fig. 2:2-3 are two examples with a feathered headdress only to be understood as that worn by one group of Sea Peoples whom an Egyptian artist of Rameses III shows the pharaoh defeating on land and sea, in a famous battle sketched on the walls of the Medinet Habu temple in Upper Egypt (Nos. 4-6 in Fig. 2). No. 1 lacks the feathers but he has the beaded circlet around the forehead worn by the Sea People. There can be no doubt, therefore, that these men in 12th century Beth-shan were Philistines.[10]

After this illuminating discovery Mrs. Dothan turned to an analysis of the contents of the tombs. Certain pottery vessels at Beth-shan, the scarabs, amulets and figurines certainly possess an Egyptian background. A forked spearbutt (Fig. 2:8) is precisely like a number found in the Nebesheh tombs. Other pottery forms (Fig. 2:10 and 13) certainly have a background in the Greek world, from which the Philistines came.

The tombs at Tell el-Far'ah have a representative collection of Philistine pottery, the only type of pottery in Palestine that can definitely be associated with a specific people. It occurs in quantity in the southern coastal plain where the Philistines settled, at precisely the time when it should be found in the archaeological contexts, if it did belong to the Sea Peoples.[11] Furthermore, the most characteristic elements of

[9] Her main article with scholarly footnotes is in Hebrew, in *Eretz Israel*, V (1958; the Mazar Volume), 55-66. Her conclusions are summarized without footnotes but with fresh material added in her English article, *Antiquity and Survival*, II:2/3 (1957), 151-64.

[10] Originally this term (from the English Bible) designated only one group of the Sea Peoples, but the Hebrew word behind it was used by the Israelites for them all, perhaps because the Philistines were the dominant group in Palestine.

[11] That is, during that 12th and 11th centuries B.C., Israel's period of the Judges. The best made and best decorated forms occur

the pottery, while locally made in Palestine, were derived from late Mycenean traditions of the Greek world from which the Philistines came.[12] Included are the characteristic bird patterns, connected spirals and other decorative designs, together with certain forms of vessels, particularly the bowl with horizontal handles (crater) and a special jug called a "stirrup" vase. Other Philistine forms are native Palestinian, which in turn may go back to earlier traditions of the Canaanites in Syria who borrowed widely from various sources.

The coffin tombs at Tell el-Farʻah, Mrs. Dothan shows, are surely Philistine, and their pottery and objects have the eclectic background expected: Palestinian, Aegean and Egyptian influences mingling. Turning to the Yehudiyeh and Nebesheh tombs in the Egyptian Delta, and to comparable finds at Aniba in Lower Nubia (the Sudan),[13] Mrs. Dothan indicates the same mixture of pottery types. She concludes, therefore, that such features point to a common cultural background, "probably explicable by the service of foreign mercenary groups in the Egyptian armies. Only in Palestine can these be identified with a definite ethnic group, *i.e.*, the Philistines."

According to biblical traditions it seems clear that Israel understood her invasion of the Promised Land (during the

---

mostly in the 12th century. By the last quarter of the 11th century, when the Philistines attained the height of their power and controlled much of the country just before and again at the conclusion of the reign of King Saul, most of their special ceramic traditions had been forgotten or set aside, so that their pottery is similar to that in the hill country. This point was originally made by B. Mazar (Maisler) on the basis of his clear results at Tell Qasile on the northern outskirts of Tel-Aviv: see his Strata XII and XI in contrast to Stratum X, *IEJ*, I (1950–51), 61–76, 125–40, 194–218. It is confirmed at other sites, particularly at Megiddo where the best Philistine pottery occurs in Stratum VII A of the 12th century (unpublished, but I have observed it in the Oriental Institute collections), but has disappeared by the end of Stratum VI in the second half of the 11th century. Beth-shemesh III had a great amount of Philistine pottery. It was destroyed during the second half of the 11th century, and few special Philistine traditions remain by the time of Stratum IIa in the first half of the 10th century.

[12] A basic study that is still important is that of W. A. Heurtley, *QDAP*, V (1936), 90 ff. See also A. Furumark, *The Chronology of Mycenaean Pottery* (1941).

[13] Published by G. Steindorff, *Aniba* I–II (1937).

second half of the 13th century) to have occurred before that of the Philistines. The latter became so strong during the 12th and 11th centuries, however, that Israel was forced to adopt a monarchical system of government to gain both political and economic freedom. From Egyptian sources we know that Rameses III (*ca.* 1175–1144 B.C.)[14] defeated an invasion by sea and land of Sea Peoples, presumably displaced people from the Aegean world who are also credited with the destruction of such great Syrian cities as Alalakh, Ugarit, Sidon and Tyre. It has been assumed that as a result of this defeat one large group of them, the Pelast (Philistines) settled in the southern Palestinian coastal plain between Gaza and Joppa. There, according to biblical information, they were organized under five rulers, called by a foreign and non-Semitic title, *seren*, who were established in five city-states, Gaza, Ashkelon, Ashdod, Gath and Ekron (Josh. 13:3; Judg. 3:3; I Sam. 6:17), which formed a confederation. Hebrew tradition said they came from Crete (Caphtor: Deut. 2:23; Amos 9:7; though cf. Gen. 10:14), but, while their precise source and movements must be conjectured, they soon adapted themselves to their new Semitic environment, in the course of time learning the Canaanite-Hebrew language and adopting Canaanite gods. A temple of Dagon existed at Ashdod in the 11th century (I Sam. 5) and a temple of Baal-zebul (not Baal-zebub) at Ekron had such a reputation that a son of Ahab and Jezebel tried to send messengers there to secure information about his recovery from an injury, only to be prevented by Elijah (II Kings 1:2). The Egyptian tale of Wen-amun, dated about 1100 B.C., tells us that another group of the same people called Tjikal, perhaps people who gave their name to Sicily, called Sikel in Homer's *Odyssey*, were settled in Dor, chief city of the plain of Sharon south and west of Mt. Carmel.

Mrs. Dothan's archaeological analysis makes it possible to say something further about them. Philistines in 12th century Beth-shan were most probably there because they were or had been in the employ of Rameses III as mercenaries. Stra-

[14] The exact date of this king's reign is quite uncertain. The figures here given are those of Albright, *From the Stone Age to Christianity* (3rd ed.; Doubleday Anchor Books, 1957), p. 289. M. B. Rowton, *JEA*, XXXIV (1948), 72, suggests an even lower date, 1170–1139 B.C. Higher dates of older chronologies certainly appear too high.

tum VI of the city (misdated by Rowe who called it the "Seti I" stratum) was controlled, in all probability, by that pharaoh, just as his predecessors of the 19th Egyptian dynasty had been in control of the city represented by the preceding Stratum VII. An official of his left an inscription on a door lintel and a statue of the pharaoh in the city. Hence we can only conclude that after his defeat of the Sea Peoples early in his reign, he proceeded to hire them to protect his interests in Beth-shan. They were still in possession of the city at the time of the death of Saul, whose body and armor were there exhibited by the Philistines (I Sam. 31:10; I Chron. 10:10). Indeed, for a time in 12th century Palestine the Philistines and Sicilians (Tjikal-Tsikal) may have been permitted to live along the main Egyptian-Asian trade route only as the pharaoh's nominal vassals.[15]

As for the anthropoid coffin burials in the Egyptian Delta and in Nubia which we have here mentioned, it would appear proper to assume that they, too, belonged to Philistines (that is, Sea Peoples) who were guarding both the northern and southern frontiers of the Egyptian homeland for the pharaohs of the 20th dynasty (*ca.* 1175–1065 B.C.), or their immediate successors. It is agreed that the people who used the coffins had all been in Egypt, used Egyptian scarabs, amulets, and pottery, and also got the idea for the coffins from a native Egyptian custom. Yet the coffins were not made by native Egyptians, but by foreigners, who put Palestinian pottery in their tombs alongside Egyptian pottery. This can only mean that the foreigners were from Palestine, where we know that the coffin-people were Philistines. I might note one additional piece of evidence for this conclusion. Two pieces of iron appeared in the Nebesheh and Yehudiyeh tombs, one of them being an iron spearhead. While it is true that archaeologists begin the Iron Age in Western Asia about 1200 B.C., nevertheless iron implements in Egypt as early as the 12th century are not expected because the metal is said to have come into common use there much later than in Asia. In Palestine the evidence seems to indicate that it was the Philistines who first introduced the metal into the country for weapons, and jeal-

---

[15] For a reconstruction of the historical situation on the basis of present evidence, see especially W. F. Albright, *AJA*, LIV (1950), 162–76.

ously guarded its smelting process from Israel.[16] If so, then the identification of the Egyptian coffin-tombs in question as Philistine is further strengthened.

The coffins in Tomb 570 at Lachish may perhaps be interpreted as an earlier presence of the coffin-people, as already indicated. As was the case with a number of the Yehudiyeh coffins, one at Lachish was inscribed with crude Egyptian hieroglyphs which make no clear sense, and which were certainly not written by an Egyptian. While the pottery dates from the 13th century in my judgment, it may be that the bodies in Lachish Tomb 570 were Philistine. If so, they were newcomers in a Canaanite context, using native pottery before their own particular variety was made in the country. Indeed, since Pharaoh Merniptah (*ca.* 1224–1216 B.C.) claims to have defeated not only the people of Israel in Palestine, but to have beaten back the Sea Peoples also, and since Rameses II (*ca.* 1290–1224 B.C.) before him is known to have had a number of the same people in his employ, it would not be at all strange to find a few of them along the Palestinian coastal area before the Israelite conquest. On the other hand, there is no reason why those buried in the Lachish coffins were not Egyptians, or Canaanites influenced by Egyptian customs. Since coffins were in common use in Egypt, there is no reason why we must assign all Palestinian coffins to Philistines, unless the internal evidence in the tomb indicates otherwise.

The era around 1200 B.C. was marked by disturbances everywhere and a vast movement of peoples. The seminomads around the fringes of the Fertile Crescent were astir. The kingdoms of Sihon and Og, Moab and Edom were established during the 13th century. Then came the people of Israel during the second half of the century, while the great Aramean invasions occurred in the 12th. To the north and west, invaders inundated and ended the Hittite empire in Asia Minor and the great Mycenean civilization in Greece. These events are reflected in Homer's story of ancient Troy, and in the appearance of the Sea Peoples along the shores of Syria, Palestine and Egypt. An old age was ended and a new one born.

[16] Cf. I Sam. 13:19–22, and see the writer's remarks, *BA*, I (1938), 5–8; VI (1943), 33–36; *Biblical Archaeology* (1957), pp. 90–93; and his article which presents the archaeological evidence at the time of publication, *AJA*, XLIII (1939), 458–63.

6

THE MATERIAL CIVILIZATION OF THE AMMONITES

GEORGE M. LANDES

The results of archaeological activity in Transjordan since 1930 have provided the basis for tracing the course of sedentary settlement in this area from neolithic times (*ca.* 5000 B.C.) down through the Hellenistic and Roman ages. In spite of the fact that no comprehensive excavation of any major tell in Transjordan has been carried through to completion,[1] extensive surface explorations of the region and the analysis of several tomb-groups, combined with the relevant data from biblical tradition and from extra-biblical epigraphic sources have made possible the reconstruction of the territorial and political history of this region in general outline, while also shedding light on a number of details, both of a historical and cultural nature. In 1960, A. H. Van Zyl, Senior Lecturer of Semitic Languages at the University of Pretoria, South Africa, published the first comprehensive monograph on the Moabites,[2] drawing upon the wealth of source material recent research has provided. During the decade of the 1950's, several doctoral dissertations, dealing respectively with the political and cultural histories of the Edomites, Ammonites, and Moabites, were produced at Johns Hopkins University under the guidance of W. F. Albright, including the present writer's own *A History of the Ammonites* (1956), from which much of the material for this article has been drawn. Unfortunately, none of these dissertations has been published, though several ar-

[1] The most hopeful recent prospect has been the work begun at Dhiban in ancient Moabite territory, but after five seasons of excavation, 1950–56, the project has not been resumed, nor have the results of work already done been published in detail.

[2] *The Moabites* (1960).

ticles based upon their research have appeared in the *Interpreter's Dictionary of the Bible* (1962).

Sources

Mention of the Ammonites in biblical literature—the principal and fullest source of our knowledge of these peoples—occurs more than one hundred times in contexts spanning the major course of pre-exilic Israelite history from the time of the Exodus to the fall of Jerusalem in 587 B.C. The question of their origin and ethnic affiliation remains unanswered. We can add very little to the legendary biblical tradition in Genesis 19:36–38 that the progenitor of the Ammonites was the son of Lot, Abraham's nephew; this shows that, in Israelite memory, Ammonite origins were traced back to the early Patriarchal Age, i.e. the first half of the 2nd millennium B.C., and that they were in some way related to the earliest Hebrews. This is also suggested by the name of "the father of the Ammonites," Ben 'Ammi, which means literally, "son of my people," or more originally, "son of my paternal clan." This name is now clearly attested in the guild lists found among the Ugaritic archives dating from the 14th century B.C., and also seems to occur among personal names from the city of Alalakh in northern Syria and from south Semitic sources of later periods. There is a widespread use of this name, then, from the mid-2nd millennium on. And it follows that Ben 'Ammi is not to be explained simply as a popular etymology indicating the origin and meaning of *Bnē 'Ammon* 'the sons of Ammon' (the regular designation of the descendants of Ben 'Ammi), but also preserves remembrance of an actual clan and personal name whose origin could well lie in the early 2nd millennium B.C. The biblical tradition that the Ammonites, along with their brothers the Moabites, originated in southern Transjordan (near Zoar, cf. Gen. 19:30) can probably never be demonstrated historically, since in all probability they began as nomadic clans who would leave behind little or no evidence of their existence.

One of the most important results of Nelson Glueck's surface explorations in Transjordan was the discovery of the almost complete break in sedentary occupation of the territory south of the Jabbok river (Wadi Zerqa) between the end of Middle Bronze I (*ca.* 1900 B.C.) and the beginning of the 13th century B.C.[3] Despite some opinions to the contrary, this picture need not be significantly modified in light of more recent discoveries, one at Amman, where several Middle Bronze tombs have been uncovered whose pottery fits best a Middle Bronze IIB (Hyksos) milieu (17th–16th century B.C.),[4] and another two miles outside of Amman, where a small shrine or temple, curiously isolated from any building complex has been found containing huge quantities of pottery dating to the Late Bronze period.[5] The location of the shrine, together with the richness of the finds within it, suggest that it was built and used by a nomadic or seminomadic people who had control of caravan trade in contact with emporia supplied from the west, particularly the Aegean region. In connection with his studies of the Israelite tribal league and its ancient Near Eastern parallels, Prof. Frank Cross has pointed out that this shrine may well be an amphictyonic sanctuary. This seems a sound conclusion, and this by no means forces us to understand it as evidence of a (semi-)sedentary occupation; rather the opposite is the case. Moreover, the discovery of the Middle Bronze IIB tombs also does not necessarily imply a settled population, since nomads and seminomads of this time are known to have buried their dead in tombs (cf. e.g. the story of Abraham and the cave of Machpelah in Gen. 23).

That there was a vigorous resurgence in permanent settlement throughout the southern half of eastern Palestine at the beginning of the Iron Age appears to have been demonstrated by Glueck's surface explorations. One of the earliest and most

[3] N. Glueck, *AASOR*, XXV–XXVIII (1951), 423.

[4] G. L. Harding, *APEF*, VI (1953), 14. See now F. S. Ma'ayeh, *ADAJ*, IV–V (1960), 114. It should be noted that the discovery of several Middle Bronze tombs on the Amman citadel hill and a general survey of their contents is merely reported here, and the finds have not as yet been published and analyzed in detail. Ma'ayeh reports in the same article the discovery of a "sloping plastered 'glacis' revetment, resting on natural rock, and crowned by a wall," which was revealed when the north end of Tell Safut was destroyed in connection with construction of the new Jerash-Na'ur highway. He appears certain that the fortification uncovered is of a definite Middle Bronze-Hyksos type, and points to permanent settlement at Tell Safut during MB II. However, no photographs or other details are published with this notice, and until these are forthcoming, it would appear best to reserve judgment.

[5] Harding, *PEFQ*, XC (1958), 10–12. See also *BA*, XVIII (1955), 80.

significant witnesses to the organized political authority and vitality of the early Ammonite state is the strong line of border fortresses forming a well-integrated defensive system protecting the western approaches to the Ammonite capital at Rabbath-ammon (located at modern Amman, capital of Jordan). Glueck defined the course of this boundary from el-Mumani, *ca.* ten miles north-northwest of Amman at the eastern edge of the rich el-Beqah region to Qasr es-Sar, some five miles directly west of Amman. H. Gese[6] and R. Hentschke[7] have more recently traced the line of Ammonite border fortresses from Qasr et-Tabaqe, to a site known as Shadsharat Bil'as. Thus it is now possible to define rather precisely the entire western border of the Ammonite kingdom. It is of course difficult to date any particular fortress complex with exactitude, since pottery evidence found both in and around various buildings has not been dated more closely than to the general periods Iron I–II (Iron I: 1200–900 B.C.; Iron II: 900–600 B.C.).[8] However, Glueck has assigned the construction of the strongly built circular tower Ammonite fortresses to early Iron I (although their use extends into Iron II), since at several sites where this architectural type occurs, the ceramic evidence points to heaviest occupation during Iron I.[9] We learn from the biblical record that the first political expansion of the Ammonites took place during the period of the Judges, initially involving probably a small scale action in the time of Jephthah (cf. Judg. 11:4–33), followed some time later by a more serious military threat in the days of Saul (cf. I Sam. 11:1–11). In either case the setting would seem to be the last half of the 11th century B.C. (Iron IB). In all probability, by the end of that century, the Ammonites had begun to build their circular tower fortresses and to establish their well-organized border defense system.

Ammonite Architecture

Architecturally, the Ammonites built in what has been generally called the "megalithic" style, owing to the tremendous

[6] H. Gese, *ZDPV*, LXXIV (1958), 55–64.

[7] R. Hentschke, *ZDPV*, LXXVI (1960), 103–23.

[8] There is a great need to excavate several of these fortresses in order to check and refine the conclusions based so far only on surface finds; in many cases, surface evidence is no longer visible on these sites.

[9] Glueck, *BASOR*, No. 68 (1937), p. 19.

size of stones used (some as large as ten feet by three feet by three feet). The style may represent an adaptation of the much older megalithic construction from neolithic Ammon, when the so-called "dolmen-builders" developed a quasi-sedentary agricultural society in Transjordan as early as the 6th millennium B.C. In any case, the Ammonites of the Iron Age probably found a number of the ruined dwellings of their ancient precursors still standing, providing ready stone for their own new structures or for the rehabilitation of older ones. Usually the large, roughly hewn, rectangular flint (or limestone) blocks were not dressed or smoothed beyond their initially hewn state. One of the still puzzling questions is how the Ammonite builders moved these large, heavy stones into position after they had been prepared for use. If earthen ramps were used, no traces of such have ever been reported. Typical wall construction technique consisted of laying blocks at the corners in headers and stretchers, while between the corners stones were placed in rude courses with smaller stones interspersed to make the rows fairly even. The average thickness of walls was from four to seven feet, showing their relative strength. In his survey of Ammonite sites Glueck found little evidence of outer circumvallating walls, and concluded that the independent strength of individual buildings apparently rendered such enclosing walls unnecessary.[10] More recent German exploration has turned up traces of outer surrounding walls at several sites, though whether these walls were of primary or secondary character in relation to the first settlement is not always clear. Glueck's original conclusion would still seem to hold.

Ammonite architects planned most of their buildings with a square to rectangular form, the circular towers being the major exception. A typical installation consisted of several flint blockhouses together with one or more towers. The number of towers associated with a settlement varied from only one to as many as three. Both the square-rectangular and circular forms could appear in the same building group, though this was somewhat unusual. Generally the towers were closely situated with other buildings in a settlement, but on occasion they have been found more or less removed

[10] *Ibid.* This is in striking contrast to Ammon's most immediate southern neighbor, Moab, where fortified settlements surrounded by strong enclosing walls were frequently attested. Cf. *AASOR*, XXV–XXVIII (1951), 62, 94–95, 118–21, 123, 126.

from such. The number of other buildings adjoining or associated with a tower-fortress depended upon the size of the original agricultural settlement. At Khirbet Morbat Bedran, no less than twelve separate buildings were counted, including a circular tower with a square compound in front of it.[11] Probably the Ammonite tower fortresses, blockhouses, and other groups of buildings housed the principal military installations in the land throughout the Iron Age. Agrarian families would then have dwelt in tents during most of the year, resorting to the stone dwellings mainly in times of trouble or invasion. Cross-walls were frequently constructed within these stone houses, dividing each structure into several rooms. Sometimes courtyards, possibly for the keeping of small cattle, were built up against them, or walled garden areas were adjoined. However, not every fortified group had the sole purpose of housing and guarding an agricultural settlement; some, as for example Khirbet Mafraq situated on the desert trade route to Syria,[12] must have also protected the caravans as they passed through Ammon en route to centers of trade. In no case could these Ammonite settlements be called anything more than villages. Outside of Rabbathammon, city or town life did not flourish in Ammon, and in contrast to western Palestine, there developed no major tells covering a long history of urban settlement, either before or after the beginning of the Iron Age. This of course is in keeping with the predominantly rural agricultural life in which a significant portion of the Ammonite populace participated.

The most striking architectural feature of Ammonite building enterprise was their fortress-towers, which in arrangement, design, composition, strength, and number remain unparalleled by any similar phenomenon in western Palestine. In form, the towers could be circular, square, or rectangular. The circular form is unique to Transjordan during the Iron Age, and much more typical of Ammon than of either Moab or Edom.[13] The largest and best preserved circular tower

[11] *AASOR*, XXV–XXVIII (1951), 186–90.
[12] Glueck, *BASOR*, No. 86 (1942), p. 14.
[13] In describing the forms of Ammonite buildings, Glueck distinguishes two types, the *malfuf* or circular form and the *qasr* or square-rectangular form. He does not further refine the latter category by distinguishing square or rectangular fortress-dwellings from the same shaped fortress-towers. Admittedly this is not always easy in view of the ruined state of many of these buildings, yet a dis-

south of the Jabbok is at Khirbet el-Kursi, where it guards the fertile fields east of Wadi Dabuq; around it are the remains of a small number of flint blockhouses. It possessed an inner diameter of about fifty-two feet, and had walls ten feet thick. The best preserved section of the tower wall was on the northeast where it stands almost twenty feet high. Though no complete Ammonite building has ever been found, from foundation and wall ruins still observable it is estimated that no structure exceeded two stories in height, and the tallest were certainly the fortress-towers, the lookout posts in the Ammonite defensive system. The towers were presumably entered at ground level. Glueck has noted traces of an outside entrance on several of the towers he examined,[14] and in the region southwest of Amman at the site of Rujm Naʻur, Hentschke found a quadratic building from which a passageway led to a small square tower entered through an opening at the ground level.[15] Some of the circular towers, however, have apparently left no trace of a ground-level entrance, leading one observer to suggest that for these, access "was probably at least ten feet up and reached by a ladder."[16] This is problematic, since no tower wall has yet been found completely preserved above ten feet in height. Unlike the Sardinian *nuraghi* (massive stone towers peculiar to the island of Sardinia), no clear remains of a stone staircase, either within or without an Ammonite tower, has ever been observed.[17] In the southern half of the small oblong tower at el-Hemraniyeh near Amman, Pape mentions what he took to be a series of inclined ramps leading to an upper floor (or floors), but the structure was in such a ruined state that it was difficult to say which stones were still in their original po-

---

tinction would seem to be possible on the basis of ground plan measurements where these are ascertainable. Thus the large dimensioned (fifty feet or more on a side) square-rectangular structures probably functioned as fortified residences, whereas the smaller quadratic buildings served primarily as tower observation posts.

[14] *AASOR*, XXV–XXVIII (1951), 156, 165, 167, 172.

[15] Hentschke, *ZDPV*, LXXVI (1960), 113–14, and his Fig. 9.

[16] C. Pape, in *The City of Shepherd Kings*, by Petrie *et al.* (1950), p. 42.

[17] Though Glueck thought there was possible evidence of a staircase giving access to the top of the tower at Khirbet el-Kursi; cf. *AASOR*, XXV–XXVIII (1951), 162.

sitions.[18] Some kind of floor, either midway or higher on the wall, would be expected, but to judge from external appearance, the former existence of an upper story is impossible to ascertain. The only Ammonite building so far discovered which has its roof still intact is at Qasr et-Tabaqe, where Gese reports an original significant heightening of the outer wall above the roof for the protection of a defender stationed there. Moreover, at the southeast end of the building was found a hole in the roof through which the dweller must have ascended to assume his defensive position.[19] Though this building was not a tower, it suggests that the tower roofs were probably reached from within by means of a ladder.

The location and placement of these towers show a conscious plan geared to the unusual topographic character of the Ammonite landscape, where frequent valleys cut sharply through upland flats. Without such strategically placed observation posts, a hostile force could have easily moved along the valley floors and taken the Ammonites by surprise attack. Within the boundaries of ancient Ammon numerous fortresses were erected on high isolated hills within easy vision of one another, permitting rapid communication of distress or warning throughout most of the settled portions of Ammon. The strategy of this system can still be observed in the Amman region,[20] and along the northwest-southeast line of border fortresses in the country stretching between Wadi es-Sir and Na'ur.

Ammonite architecture is not characterized by any notable artistic features or striking decorative motifs. The Ammonites built primarily for shelter and protection. But the number and strength of their fortress dwellings, together with the conscious plan manifest in their arrangement and system, point to a dynamic civilization with a well-organized center of political authority. And the effectiveness of their defensive setup is attested by the fact that, as far as we know, only once in some six centuries of Ammonite history was the ring of defenses around their capital at Rabbath-ammon ever breached, and the capital itself besieged and taken: in the 10th century B.C., when Israelite military power was at its height, under the leadership of David and his commander Joab (cf. II Sam. 11:26–31).

[18] Pape, *The City of Shepherd Kings*, p. 40.
[19] Gese, ZDPV, LXXIV (1958), 61.
[20] *AASOR*, XXV–XXVIII (1951), 173.

Tombs and Their Tale of Prosperity

The 7th century B.C. witnessed a significant rise in the fortunes of Ammon. Historical conditions were peculiarly favorable. Throughout most of the 7th century, Ammon was a nominal Assyrian vassal, but it was permitted to have its own native ruler without the presence of an Assyrian provincial governor, thus enjoying internal administrative freedom. Moreover, Assyrian protection meant a lessening of the threat from external enemies.

A striking literary documentation of Ammonite prosperity at this time occurs in one of the letters found at ancient Nineveh, apparently written to King Esarhaddon. From it we learn that the Ammonites, Moabites, and people of Judah (among others) paid specified amounts of tribute to the Assyrian monarch.[21] Of the amounts given, the Ammonites were assigned the largest figure, two minas of gold (= one-thirtieth of a talent, equivalent to about twenty minas of silver). Though not an impressive sum, yet when compared with that assigned to Moab (one mina of gold) and that exacted from Judah (ten minas of silver, or about the same as that of Moab) it shows the relatively more affluent position of the Ammonite state in this period. Under beneficent Assyrian protection, the Ammonites were able to keep control of the lucrative caravan trade from the desert, thereby enhancing their prosperity.

Our knowledge of the flourishing Ammonite material culture during Iron II is based primarily upon evidence which comes from tombs discovered either at Amman itself, or in the vicinity of the ancient Ammonite capital. Of four tombs found at Amman, two were located on the north side of Jebel Jofeh overlooking the Roman theater (these will be referred to as Tombs A and B),[22] while two others were situated close by on the south slope of the citadel.[23] One of these (or both?) was the tomb of an Ammonite high official by the name of

[21] A translation of the text appears in L. Waterman's *Royal Correspondence of the Assyrian Empire* (1930), Part I, pp. 440 f., with his notes in Part III, p. 208. Though Esarhaddon's name is not mentioned in the letter, the historical situation implied by the text would seem to fit his reign best.

[22] Harding, *QDAP*, XI (1944), 67–74.

[23] Harding, *APEF*, VI (1953), 48–65.

Adoni-nur.[24] Outside of Amman, two Ammonite tombs have been uncovered at the village of Sahab (*ca.* eight miles by road southeast of Amman), one (hereafter designated as Sahab A) lying on the gently sloping hillside opposite the village,[25] the other (Sahab B) on the northwest edge of the site,[26] while at the small settlement of Meqabelein, *ca.* three miles south-southwest of Amman, still another Ammonite tomb has been identified.[27] Judging from the deposits, principally pottery, the oldest of the tombs was Sahab A, dating to *ca.* 900 B.C. though several examples of pre-7th century types in the pottery corpus of Amman tombs A and B may indicate that they were first constructed as early as the 10th–9th century B.C. Harding has dated the original construction of Sahab B to the 9th–8th century B.C., though many of its pottery forms were identical with the 7th–6th century types found in the Amman tombs. Clearly all the Ammonite tombs so far examined, with the exception of Sahab A, show heaviest use in the late Iron II era.

Before turning to a detailed discussion of the cultural remains found in these tombs, it is of interest to consider the light they shed on Ammonite burial practices, of which hitherto nothing has been known. All the tombs were cave tombs, roughly hewn out of the natural rock, either below the ground surface or in the side of a hill. With respect to layout, no two were exactly alike. Outside of Sahab A, most appear to have been built for more than one person, and several probably functioned as family burial vaults. The largest of the presently known Ammonite tombs is Sahab B, which measures approximately twenty-five feet on each of four sides. Most of the tombs appear to have been of the bench variety, either featuring a single bench on one side, as in Tomb A at Amman, and at Sahab B, or benches on three sides, as in the Meqabelein tomb. The first examples of the bench tomb were discovered by Sir Flinders Petrie in Philistine tombs at Tell

[24] The identification is based upon his seal ring which was found among the tomb deposits, and of which more will be said later. The fact that these deposits had been removed from the tombs and laid indiscriminately along the ledge below the tomb openings makes it difficult to say which tomb belonged to Adoni-nur. It is not unlikely, however, that both constituted his family vault.

[25] Cf. W. F. Albright, *AJA*, XXXVI (1932), 295–306.
[26] Harding, *QDAP*, XIII (1948), 92–102.
[27] Harding, *QDAP*, XIV (1950), 44–48.

el-Farʿah, and it became the characteristic type of tomb throughout the Iron Age down to the Greek period, when new Hellenistic types replaced it.[28] Structurally unique features of the Ammonite tombs include cupboard-like recesses at the east end of Amman Tomb A, and a curious chimney-like construction in the middle of the southwest side of Sahab B. Presumably the chimney reached up to the original land surface, which has led Harding to suggest that the cave may have been used for a dwelling before it was converted into a sepulcher. It is also possible that a fire was built somewhere along the bench beneath the chimney, the fire perhaps being connected with some kind of burial rite. Be that as it may, the chimney-like construction has no parallel in any of the tombs thus far cleared in Palestine, unless it is the Chalcolithic cave 2.I at Gezer, which was a crematorium.[29]

All the tombs contained bone remains, with the exception of Adoni-nur's tomb-group at Amman, which had been anciently robbed and burnt, and the tomb at Meqabelein, in which no bones are reported. The burials, where evidence of such existed, had almost all been disturbed anciently, presumably, by tomb robbers, so no complete skeletons were found and little could be ascertained concerning the way the dead were prepared for burial, or in what position they were laid. In Sahab B, the fragments of seven skulls were distinguished, and though they could not be removed intact, they still may yield some information concerning the cranial measurements of the ancient Ammonites. An intriguing feature of this tomb is that it had apparently never been disturbed or robbed, yet its skeletal remains were fragmentary, while also much of the pottery was in a very broken state. Harding thinks this tomb may actually have been an ossuary, i.e., a place of secondary rather than primary interment. By way of parallel he cites a tomb excavated by Miss Caton Thompson at Hureidha in the Hadhramaut (South Arabia), in which

[28] Cf. Albright, *AJA*, XXXVI, 298, n. 4. Glueck (*AASOR*, XXV–XXVIII [1951], 192) reports some single bench tombs at Tell Safut near Suweileh, first described by de Vaux (*RB*, XLVII [1938], 418–19). All had been robbed in antiquity, and were completely empty of material remains. This, coupled with the dolmenic style of building, makes it uncertain whether they were Ammonite in origin, or even used by the Ammonites.

[29] R. Macalister, *The Excavation of Gezer*, I (1912), 74 f. (fig. 20), 285–88.

there were conditions strikingly similar to those in Sahab B. However, Miss Caton Thompson herself has admitted that she encountered some difficulty in interpreting the data which she found, and with regard to the nature of the two tombs she investigated, she was forced to conclude: "Identity of function, as an ossuary pure and simple, is, however, not so sure; much remains speculative owing to the (presumably) rifled condition of the contents and the large area unexcavated."[30] A similar statement would perhaps not be inapplicable to our Ammonite tomb, for here likewise it is not clear that we are dealing with an ossuary (which would be the first of its kind known in Iron Age Palestine). However, the fact still remains that there is a striking similarity in the general situation of the tombs at Hureidha and Sahab B. Whether this is merely coincidental or whether some sort of relationship (however indirect) should be sought, is an open question. It is true, as Harding has pointed out, that on the whole, Transjordan was ethnologically closer to Arabia than Palestine, and it is very likely that commercial relations between Ammon and South Arabia existed from the time of great commercial expansion in the ancient Near East (10th–9th century B.C.).

Of special interest in Amman Tomb A was a mass of broken animal bones, too splintered to be assigned to specific animals. They were deposited in a cupboard-like recess cut into the south wall of the east end of the tomb. A similar cupboard-like recess was cut into the north wall directly opposite at the same end of the tomb, but it contained nothing. Many knuckle bones, clearly separate from the animal bones, were also found in this tomb mixed up with some pottery inside the entrance. The meaning of the animal bones is not certain. Harding's suggestion that they represent the remains of offerings, presumably for the dead, is plausible, but not demonstrable. The curious isolation of the knuckle bones from the other animal bones defies explanation. This phenomenon in tombs is so far unparalleled, though knuckle bones have been found in houses and dwellings excavated in Palestine where they have been interpreted as gaming pieces.

From the Adoni-nur tomb at Amman, we learn that the Ammonites sometimes buried their dead in clay coffins, of

[30] G. Caton Thompson, *The Tombs and Moon Temple of Hureidha (Hadhramaut)* (1944), p. 90.

which three large specimens (all broken) of well-known Assyrian type were found. In Sahab A, moreover, was recovered the headpiece of a pottery anthropoid coffin, a crude adaptation of a type of clay coffin known from Egyptian models of the 18th–19th dynasties. Anthropoid coffins of this type which have been turned up in Palestine (particularly at Beth-shan and Tell el-Far'ah) belong to Iron I (especially to the 12th century B.C.).[31] It would thus seem that the Ammonites used clay pottery coffins in some burials from the end of Iron I through Iron II, and of striking interest is the earlier period, when unexpected Egypto-Philistine influence is shown.

Art Objects of Ammon

In the realm of plastic art, we have few specimens, but what has come to light is both interesting and revealing. We have already mentioned the Egyptianizing headpiece of a pottery anthropoid coffin found at Sahab A, which was rather crudely wrought. This represents the earliest example of Ammonite plastic art so far discovered. In addition, three small pottery horse-and-rider figurines have been found, one in Tomb A at Amman, two others in the Meqabelein tomb. The first was the most crudely made. The horse's body had been formed on a wheel, while its head, neck, legs, and tail had been applied afterward. The rider, whose head was missing (probably anciently broken), was also placed upon the body of the horse after it had been wheel-shaped. Traces of red and cream slip are noticeable, together with some black paint on the horse's mane and chest and on the rider's right arm. The horse-and-rider figurines from Meqabelein were both complete. Moreover, the bodies of the two horses and riders give evidence of having been individually formed, with very fine modeling of the features. The riders carry what seem to be whips in their right hands. Both figurines were painted in black and white, although one had a red wash which had since flaked off, taking most of the surface paint with it. Of special interest is the rider's pointed cap, which in one figurine is out-

---

[31] For the most recent discussion of these coffins (with bibliography) and the very plausible suggestion that they were originally made and used by Philistine mercenaries employed to protect the Egyptian borders, see G. E. Wright, *BA*, XXII (1959), 54–66, republished in this volume, pp. 59–68.

lined in black and white, with a white band between black across the rider's forehead below a black "splodge" that was clearly intended to represent some kind of decoration. This conical cap is best paralleled by Assyrian warrior's dress from the 7th century B.C.[32] The possible historical significance of these horse-and-rider figurines will be mentioned below in another context.

Undoubtedly the most significant examples of Ammonite plastic art are two statues found outside the Amman city wall at the north end of the citadel. They stand among the few complete specimens of native sculpture yet to be found in either Transjordan or western Palestine for the early periods (Iron Age or before). With the complete statues have been found three other parts of sculptured figures, one the head of a small limestone figurine, the others the broken torsos of almost life-size limestone statues, to which the head had been attached separately.[33] All the figures had originally been painted, one of the limestone torsos in red, the others in black or dark blue, faint traces of which still remained on the smaller of the two complete statues. The style of dress represented was reminiscent of Syria in the Assyrian period. It is the small statue, wrought in soft limestone and displaying beautifully detailed workmanship, that is especially noteworthy, for engraved on the front side of its square base is an inscription in Old Aramaic characters pointing paleographically to a 7th century date.[34] Although the last two words are hard to make out, the inscription probably read Y-R-CH-'-Z-R R-B R-K-SH-N 'Yarah'azar, chief of the horse.' In all probability, the unusual name Yarah'azar (meaning, "The moon-god has helped") identifies the personage represented by the statue. The statue shows him holding a lotus blossom in his left hand, which clearly signifies that he was a person with some kind of official status.[35] Since the inscription upon his

[32] Cf. the reliefs of Ashurbanipal depicting the capture of Egyptians and a conflict with the Arabs, *The Ancient Near East in Pictures*, ed. J. B. Pritchard (1954), Nos. 10 and 63. Note especially in No. 63 that the Assyrian horsemen are wearing conical caps.

[33] Cf. Harding, *ILN*, CCXVI (1950), 266–67; R. D. Barnett, *ADAJ*, I (1957), 34–36; and Ma'ayeh, *ADAJ*, IV–V (1960), 114 and Pl. IV.1.

[34] Cf. Albright, *Miscellanea Biblica B. Ubach* (1954), p. 135.

[35] Cf. R. T. O'Callaghan, *Orientalia*, XXI (1952), 187 f., 192,

(mortuary?) statue gives him a specific title, it is unlikely that he was an Ammonite king. If the above rendering of the title is correct, it would seem that Yaraḥʿazar performed an important military function as chief of the cavalry. Through Assyrian influence it is conceivable that the Ammonites had an organized cavalry division in their army during the 7th century. Such a military arm was an essential unit to any effective fighting force at this time. The pottery horse-and-rider figurines mentioned above should certainly be cited in this connection, for they would suggest the existence of Assyro-Ammonite cavalry. And it is interesting to note that perhaps the most common single object of plastic art to be found in typically Iron II deposits in Palestine are these horse-and-rider figurines, which certainly are to be connected with the introduction of cavalry into western Asia by the Assyrians.

Ammonite Written Materials

The short inscription on the Yaraḥʿazar statue is so far the longest to be turned up in ancient Ammon,[36] and even this is not written in the native Ammonite tongue, but in Aramaic. Unhappily for our knowledge of the Ammonite language we still do not have anything as extensive or helpful as the Mesha stele, which has done so much to illumine ancient Moabite. Our knowledge of the Ammonite dialect is thus solely dependent upon a few words, mostly personal names, found inscribed on a small collection of Ammonite seals. The first of these was brought to light as long ago as the late 19th century, when it was published by Morris Jastrow, whose misreading of the inscription was subsequently corrected by Clermont-Ganneau.[37] Presumably the seal came from Amman, but already in Jastrow's time its original provenance was no longer known. Its identification as Ammonite is verified by

---

where he shows that in Asia whenever the lotus was placed in human hands it was a sign either of royalty or of high authority, and that the Canaanites employed the lotus flower as a symbol of royal power or kingship from the Late Bronze Age to the neo-Assyrian period.

[36] A longer inscription which was turned up in Amman in 1962 has, as of this writing, not been published.

[37] M. Jastrow, *Hebraica*, VII (1891), 257–67; C. Clermont-Ganneau, *Études d'archéologie orientale*, I (1895), 85–90. See also C. C. Torrey, *AASOR*, II–III (1923), 103–5.

the inscription, which reads: "Adoni-pillet, servant of Ammi-nadab." Ammi-nadab's name appears elsewhere in the so-called Cylinder C inscription of Asshurbanapal in which it is identified with the Ammonite ruler who, together with "twenty-two kings of the seacoast," paid tribute to the Assyrian king in the course of the latter's Egyptian campaign (*ca.* 667 B.C.). The seal inscription manifests the formula familiar from many northwest Semitic seals designating a royal officer in the service of the king. The scene engraved on the face of the seal displays strong Assyrianizing characteristics especially typical of the late Assyrian period. Moreover, the winged demon with tightly curled tail and holding a short dagger in its left hand distinctly suggests an artistic motif current in the time of Asshurbanapal. Ammi-nadab's name occurs again on another Ammonite seal, this one found among the contents of the tomb assigned to Adoni-nur. The inscription reads, "Adoni-nur, servant of Ammi-nadab." Two other inscribed seals come from this same tomb-group, one of black and white stone on which have been carved winged Assyrian genii, and the name *SH-B-'-L* (biblical Shebu'el or Shuba'el), the other a brown stone seal divided into three sections, the middle of which contained the Egyptian emblem of the four-winged scarab with the ball before it, the upper and lower registers displaying an inscription in partly-worn Hebrew-Phoenician characters: "Belonging to Menahem, the son of Yinham (or Yanham)."[38] From the nature of this last seal, it would appear that Menahem was also an important personage, possibly from the family of Adoni-nur. Two of the uninscribed seals from Adoni-nur's tomb are also of interest, one a carnelian seal of Assyrian type, mounted in a silver suspension engraved on two sides, the base showing several Assyrian deities; the other a chalcedony seal bearing the figure of a priest standing before an altar on which rests a standard with a crescent above it. Another chalcedony seal, this one from the Meqabelein tomb, also depicts a priest (or worshiper?) wearing a long skirt down to the ground and a round headdress with either a lock of hair or fillet hanging down

---

[38] These seals were first published by Harding, *ILN*, CCXV (1949), 351. For interpretive comments, see Albright, *Miscellanea Biblica B. Ubach*, p. 133, and N. Avigad, *IEJ*, II (1952), 63–64.

behind. The same motif occurs again on an octagonal conical seal from the tomb of Adoni-nur. These seals give us interesting clues as to the nature of Ammonite native dress. Moreover, the last mentioned seal is the first one so far discovered for this period which could be worn on the clothes as an item of adornment. The figure on this seal also wore a beard, which may have been typical of Ammonite men. To date we have no illustrations of Ammonite women's dress or hair style.

Two more Ammonite inscribed seals[39] are of special significance, not only for the personal name types, but also because the inscriptions reflect an interesting political practice in operation in Ammon near the beginning of the 6th century B.C. The first inscription reads, "Belonging to 'Alyah, maidservant of Hanan'el," the second, "Belonging to 'NMWT, maidservant of DBLKS." As Albright has shown,[40] the feminine name 'Alyah is to be associated with the eastern desert fringe of Palestine, and is attested biblically in the alternative names of an Edomite clan (cf. Gen. 36:40 = I Chron. 1:51) and in the name 'LYT in an early Thamudic inscription from the 6th–5th century B.C. 'NMWT is related to an early Thamudic name from the same period, actually constituting the Ammonite form of the common early north Arabic name group Ghanim, Ghanimat. DBLKS, though so far unattested as such in the south Semitic onomasticon, can be explained on the basis of personal name elements known from early Thamudic and Edomite. The name Hanan'el is quite old (cf. its shortened form in Hanun, king of Ammon in the 10th century B.C.), and probably identifies a hitherto unknown king of Ammon who was either a close successor to Ammi-nadab in the latter half of the 7th century, or possibly one of the last kings of Ammon during the early 6th century. The legal formula, "A, maidservant of B," is parallel to "A, servant of B" already noted on the seals of Adoni-pillet and Adoni-nur; we find the latter commonly employed to specify the relationship between a reigning prince (second name) and a particular official in his service (first name). Consequently, the formula "A, maidservant of B" on these seals most probably indicates that they belonged to officials who were women, just as in the case of the corresponding formula on Akkadian

[39] A. Reifenberg, *Ancient Hebrew Seals* (1950), p. 39 (No. 27); p. 43 (No. 36).
[40] *Miscellanea Biblica B. Ubach*, p. 134, esp. nn. 16, 18–19.

seals. Here is an illustration of the superior relative position of women in the land of Ammon, in agreement with nomadic practice. Women as queens of Arab states or tribes in the 8th–7th century B.C. are well attested in the Assyrian records, and, for a somewhat earlier period (10th century B.C.), it is strongly suggested by the biblical account of the visit of the queen of Sheba to Solomon (I Kings 10).

The most recently published Ammonite seal,[41] which was found during the course of excavations on Jebel Jofeh in Amman, is a stamp seal, the first of its kind so far turned up in the Ammonite group. Stylistically and epigraphically, it can be assigned an early 7th century date. The two-line inscription reads: "Belonging to 'W', son of MR'L [Mar'il]." The first name gives us not only a new Ammonite personal name, but also the first witness to this name in the extra-biblical onomasticon. The closest biblical parallel is that of Evi, the name of one of the Midianite kings cited in Numbers 31:8. The second name is related to several Lihyanite and Thamudic personal names occurring in the early north Arabic inscriptions dating between the 4th century B.C., and the 2nd–3rd century A.D. As may have already been gathered, the existence of Ammonite names, or name-elements, showing a north Arabic provenance is now clearly recognized, and fits well with what we know of Ammon's long-standing close relationship with the desert and of Ammonite political custom reflecting nomadic practice. For throughout their organized political history the Ammonites maintained a more intimate contact with the desert than did either of their southern neighbors, Moab or Edom, and even as late as the 7th century B.C. they retained a social structure of essentially nomadic type. Moreover, the persistent reference in biblical literature to the Ammonites as *Bnē 'Ammon* suggests their perennial recognition as descendants of a tribal ancestor; apparently they never completely lost their identification with some form of tribal organization.

From the rather meager epigraphic evidence presented above, very few conclusions can be drawn about the Ammonite language. However, it was definitely related to Hebrew, and written in the Old Canaanite-Phoenician script which could, in all probability, be read and understood by the Israelites. But it would certainly be rash to suggest that the

[41] P. Hammond, *BASOR*, No. 160 (1960), pp. 38–41.

Ammonites may have been literary artists as gifted as their contemporaries on the other side of the Jordan river.

Summary

Our survey of Ammonite material culture illustrates not only the dynamic vigor and comparative wealth of this Iron Age civilization, but also the many diverse streams of cultural influence that affected these people during the course of their history. Throughout the latter half of Iron II, as would be expected, Assyrian influence was predominant, evidenced in pottery and seal motifs, as well as in the statuary. Earlier, some traces of mediated Egyptian influence were noted, particularly in the anthropoid clay coffin lid, and possibly also in the ceramic imitation alabastron ointment jars found in several of the Ammonite tombs, which if not directly inspired by Egyptian models, were certainly parallel to such forms, securely dated to the 7th–6th century B.C. The winged scarab on the Menahem seal also is ultimately traceable to Egyptian influence. From western Palestine, some influence can be detected in the Ammonite saucer lamps, which share the tradition of Palestinian development, whereas the Ammonite trefoil-mouth jugs, although possibly local products, show close affinity to a form which was fairly common at sites on the Mediterranean, and which generally has been assigned to an imported class in the Cypriote corpus of Red Slip I (III) ware. There seems to be some question, however, as to whether these jugs should be attributed to a Cypriote milieu, and Miss Tufnell has expressed the opinion that they owe their origin to Phoenicia, from whence they were diffused and locally imitated.[42] Phoenician influence is very probable in a type of two-handled vessel illustrated in the pottery repertory of the Adoni-nur tomb, while the suggested Cypriote origin for the bull-vase from Amman Tomb B should possibly be assigned a penultimate Phoenician setting. In any case, during this period of the Ammonite state's ascendancy, the cultural streams which surged through Ammon were of varied origin, and many undoubtedly followed along the various caravan routes, which in Transjordan were dominated by Ammonite commercial interests for several centuries.

Archaeological explorations have shown that sedentary oc-

[42] O. Tufnell, *APEF*, VI (1953), 68.

cupation in the land of Ammon virtually ceased before the middle of the 6th century B.C., and did not return until the 3rd century B.C. Into the vacuum created by the destructive advances of the Babylonians poured once again the Bnē Qedem, the "sons of the East," the bedouin hordes from the desert, who now destroyed all formally organized political activity in this area, and brought to an end the semi-autonomous Ammonite state. Though succeeding centuries would witness more or less brief political revivals in what had been Ammonite territory—the curious and rather enigmatic Tobiad "dynasty" (5th–2nd centuries B.C.), the coming of the Nabateans (1st century B.C.) and the Romans (1st century B.C.–3rd century A.D.)—not until our own day (after 1948) was this region to see again the re-creation of such a well-organized seminomadic state, composed of an advanced people capable of establishing a vigorous and dynamic civilization, as once flourished between the 12th and 6th centuries B.C.

THE KINGDOM OF DAVID AND SOLOMON IN ITS CONTACT WITH EGYPT AND ARAM NAHARAIM

ABRAHAM MALAMAT

While there is a wealth of biblical material concerning the kingdom of David and Solomon, there are no contemporary external sources pertaining to this kingdom. Consequently, research in this period is confined to an internal historical approach. Yet the rule of Israel at that time, extending far beyond the borders of the national state, was a political phenomenon without parallel in the history of the ancient Near East, the kingdom becoming an intermediate power between Mesopotamia and Egypt. The position of the kingdom of David and Solomon deserves, therefore, to be investigated in a wider historical perspective, in its interaction with the history of the ancient Near East.[1]

The scanty information scattered in various biblical passages bearing on points of contact between the history of Israel and that of the Near East, especially of the two great centers, Egypt and Aram Naharaim, may serve as a starting point. Three incidents of the time of David and Solomon bear upon the political relations between Israel and Egypt:

1. The flight of Hadad, "of the king's seed in Edom," to Egypt, after David had conquered his country at the beginning of the 10th century B.C.;

2. Solomon's marriage to a daughter of the pharaoh and the annexation of the city of Gezer as his dowry;

3. The flight of Jeroboam, charged with the administra-

[1] A. Alt, in his paper "Das Grossreich Davids," *Kleine Schriften zur Geschichte des Volkes Israel* (hereafter, *KS*), II (1953), 66–75, has already put forward this demand. Some points in the present article have been elaborated in the author's recent study, *JNES*, XXII (1963), 1–17.

tion of forced labor in Ephraim, to Shishak, king of Egypt.

The first two occurrences should be placed in the context of events during the 21st Egyptian dynasty which reigned approximately 1085–945 B.C.[2] Its last kings ruled at the time of David and during the first half of Solomon's reign. Under this dynasty Egyptian power declined, after having lost its sway in Asia already in the middle of the 12th century. Egypt now broke up into two separate units, the Theban theocracy in the south and the kingdom of Tanis in the north. Most likely only the latter came into contact with Palestine. Hadad's reception at the pharaoh's court and Solomon's marriage reflect Egypt's renewed interest in Palestine during the first half of the 10th century, a trend for which the archaeological discoveries at San-el-Hagar, the ancient Tanis and biblical Zoan, may perhaps provide additional evidence.

The biblical narrative concerning Hadad (I Kings 11:14–22) reflects the political hopes which the Egyptians pinned on the Edomite heir. Not only was he offered political asylum, but was received with great honors at the court and given the sister of Lady Tahpenes, wife of the pharaoh, as his spouse, while his son was brought up "among the sons of the pharaoh."[3] It is interesting to note that the biblical narrative mentions the pharaoh's wife by name, while that of the pharaoh himself remains undisclosed. The fact that the biblical historiographer was familiar with the lady's name or, at least, mentions her Egyptian title,[4] accords with the high position

---

[2] For this dynasty see in particular E. Meyer, *Sitzungsberichte Preussischer Akademie der Wissenschaft* (Phil.-Hist. Kl.), XXVIII (1928), 495–532. Cf. also recently E. Drioton and J. Vandier, *L'Égypte* (3rd ed.; Paris, 1952), pp. 511–22.

[3] On the literary structure of the biblical story, see Meyer, *Die Israeliten und ihre Nachbarstämme* (Halle, 1906), pp. 359 ff. See there also for the tradition incorporated in the Septuagint concerning the marriage of Jeroboam to Pharaoh Shishak's sister-in-law, a tradition which is modeled after the story of Hadad; cf. J. A. Montgomery, *A Critical and Exegetical Commentary on the Books of Kings* (Edinburgh, 1951), pp. 236 ff.

[4] The name Tahpenes has not been identified in the few existing contemporary Egyptian sources. Yet P. Montet is inclined to relate it to a name of a princess appearing on a statue attributed to the 21st dynasty; see his *Le drame d'Avaris* (Paris, 1940), pp. 197–98. It has also been asserted, on the basis of the version of the name in the Septuagint, *Thekemeina* (*Thechemeina*), that this is not a proper name at all, but an Egyptian title for "king's wife" ($t\beta\ ḥm.t$

and political influence wielded by the wives of the pharaohs of the 21st dynasty. There is a record of the wife of one of the pharaohs of this dynasty receiving the title of "The King's son of Kush, Governor of the Southern Lands." A woman was thus appointed viceroy of Nubia, an exceptional event in Egyptian history.[5]

Passing now to Solomon's marriage with the daughter of the pharaoh (I Kings 3:1), it is to be noted that, strangely enough, this matter has not been given the consideration it deserves. Yet here we have a political occurrence without parallel not only in Israelite, but also in Egyptian history. As far as we know, there is no other real example of a pharaoh's daughter given in marriage to a foreign royal house, although the pharaohs quite frequently married daughters of foreign rulers. The case of Tutankhamen's widow, who wished to marry one of the sons of Shuppiluliuma, the Hittite king, is in fact a political marriage of the sort contracted by the pharaohs, as stated explicitly in the sources.[6] The hypothesis that the four nobles from Syria, called "king's son" (*mār sharri*) in the Amarna letters, of the 14th century, were in reality the pharaoh's sons-in-law, is quite unsubstantiated.[7] Equally doubtful is the contention that the mother of Queen Tiy, wife of Amenhotep (Amenophis) III, was a pharaoh's daughter and married to a Syrian prince.[8] The only example of the marriage of an Egyptian princess to a foreign

---

nsw.t); see Grdseloff, *Revue histoire juive Égypte*, I (1947), 89 ff. If so, the word *gᵉbirā* 'grande dame' in I Kings 11:19 is a gloss for the Egyptian title.

[5] H. Kees, *Das Priestertum im ägyptischen Staat* (Leipzig, 1953), 162 ff.

[6] A. Goetze, in *Ancient Near Eastern Texts*, ed. J. B. Pritchard (1950), p. 319.

[7] As against Weber in J. A. Knudtzon, *Die El-Amarna-Tafeln*, II (1915), 1097.

[8] Weber (see previous note) relies on this example, following W. M. F. Petrie, *A History of Egypt*, II (4th ed.; 1904), 182–83, in order to substantiate his interpretation of the Amarna letters. However, many scholars believe that both parents of Queen Tiy were foreigners; according to others, both were Egyptians, thus for instance R. Engelbach, *Introduction to Egyptian Archaeology* (1946), p. 90 (I owe this reference to Mr. J. Leibovitch). Most likely, however, they were not of royal blood at all since their ancestry is not mentioned in the sources. Cf. also recently C. Aldred, *JEA*, XLIII (1957), 30 ff.

ruler comes from Ugarit. There, on sherds of a vase dating from about the middle of the 14th century B.C., a marriage ceremony is depicted. But even here, in all probability, the woman concerned, given in marriage to Nikmad, king of Ugarit, was a member of the royal harem and not a real daughter of the pharaoh.[9] On the other hand, as we know from the Amarna documents, the king of Babylon, Kadashmanenlil I, did actually ask for the hand of Amenhotep III's daughter, and was refused in the following terms: "From of old, a daughter of the king of Egypt has not been given to anyone."[10] Herodotus also implies that the marriage of a daughter of the pharaoh to a foreign king would be contrary to Egyptian tradition. According to the Greek historian, Amasis, king of Egypt, refused to give his daughter to Cambyses, king of Persia, in marriage.[11] From what can be gleaned from the few contemporary Egyptian documents, political marriages in the 21st dynasty took place only between the two ruling houses of Egypt proper, i.e. in Tanis and Thebes.[12] So too Shishak, the founder of the 22nd dynasty, married his son, Osorkon I, to the daughter of the last king of the 21st dynasty, in order to give an air of legality to the new dynasty.

In the light of the foregoing, Solomon's marriage into the Egyptian royal house acquires extraordinary political significance. This step can perhaps be explained by the fact that, up till that time, no power comparable to the kingdom of

[9] See the discussion of Ch. Desroches-Noblecourt in *Ugaritica*, III (1956), 179–220 and Fig. 118 on p. 165. The Egyptian princess is wearing a head ornament which is worn only by wives of pharaohs or their daughters who entered the royal harem. The author argues that if this description applies to a pharaoh's daughter at all, it can only be a child previously married to the pharaoh himself (see especially pp. 198 ff.).

[10] Amarna letter 4, lines 6–7 and further on; cf. S. A. B. Mercer, *The Tell el-Amarna Tablets*, I (1939), 12–13.

[11] Herodotus iii.1. The fact that Cambyses' offer was prompted by the advice given him by an Egyptian physician who wanted to avenge himself on the pharaoh, shows that the Egyptians knew that the marriage of a pharaoh's daughter to a foreigner was unacceptable. In order to prevent an armed conflict with the Persians, Amasis sent the daughter of the former deposed Egyptian king to Persia; but this deception was discovered.

[12] Pinodjem I, high priest of Thebes, married two Tanite princesses, namely Makare and Henuttaui, both, apparently, daughters of Psusennes I, king of Tanis.

David and Solomon had risen on Egypt's frontiers—a power greater than the northern Egyptian kingdom itself.[13] The dowry given to Solomon in the form of the city of Gezer (I Kings 9:16), no less than the marriage itself, should be interpreted as a sign of the supremacy of the kingdom of Solomon.

The problem of the identity of Solomon's father-in-law has puzzled many scholars. The archaeological evidence discovered in Tanis perhaps provides a clue to this long debated question. Here a bas-relief of King Siamon, the predecessor of Psusennes II, the last king of the 21st dynasty, was discovered, representing the king in the act of slaying an enemy, most likely from among the Sea Peoples. On this evidence Montet, the excavator of Tanis, put forward the theory that this pharaoh made a military expedition against the Philistines in the course of which he conquered the city of Gezer on the frontier between Philistia and Israel, a conquest which the Bible ascribes to Solomon's father-in-law.[14] Even if this does not constitute incontrovertible proof of the identity of Solomon's father-in-law, chronologically only the last two kings of the 21st dynasty fit the identification. It is true that we do not know exactly how long each one of the Tanite kings had ruled, but even taking the minimum estimate of twenty-eight years as the period of the reign of the last two kings, Siamon must have ascended the throne shortly before Solomon and thus could easily have been his father-in-law. If, however, we follow the chronology based on Eusebius' recension of Manetho, according to which Psusennes II ruled thirty-five years, then this pharaoh must have been Solomon's father-in-law.[15]

[13] Indeed, in biblical sources pharaoh's daughter occupies a special place among Solomon's "one thousand" wives, who included other foreign princesses (I Kings 11:1), and only in her case do they mention the building of a palace (I Kings 7:8–9; 9:24; II Chron. 8:11).

[14] See P. Montet, *Le drame d'Avaris* (1940), pp. 195 f. Of particular interest in this connection is the discovery of a scarab of King Siamon at Tell el-Far'ah in the western Negeb, one of the gateways to the Philistine region as one comes from Egypt; cf. W. M. F. Petrie, *Beth Pelet*, I (1930), 10, Pl. 29:259.

[15] According to Africanus' version Psusennes II reigned fourteen years only. Note that Drioton and Vandier, who in the last edition of their book (see n. 2) accept the identification of Siamon with Solomon's father-in-law, still adhere to a chronology of the 21st

As to the third point of contact between Israel and Egypt, namely Jeroboam's flight to Shishak, the explicit mention of the pharaoh's name in the Bible (I Kings 11:40) may serve as a criterion for the validity of biblical chronology. By taking into account the various chronological data in the books of Kings one arrives at the conclusion that Jeroboam's revolt took place not prior to the 24th year of Solomon's reign. The revolt occurred as Solomon was engaged in the building of Millo, begun, according to the Bible, after the construction of the temple and palace, i.e. in his 24th year (cf. I Kings 6:4, 38; 7:1; 9:10, 24). At this time Shishak was already reigning in Egypt, as can be deduced from the synchronism between Rehoboam's 5th year and Shishak's expedition to Israel, which was undertaken not long before the pharaoh's death.[16] The reliability of the biblical chronology concerning Solomon's career up to the revolt of Jeroboam is thus established. Moreover, it is entirely plausible that Jeroboam's rebellion is connected with the accession of Shishak, who renewed Egypt's traditional militant foreign policy.

The course of events after Solomon's death proves that Egypt miscalculated by pinning hopes of political expansion on Hadad the Edomite, and Jeroboam the Ephraimite. The military expedition of Shishak to Palestine in the 5th year of Rehoboam's reign was directed particularly against Edom in the south and the kingdom of Jeroboam in the north, as may be deduced from the new reading of Shishak's geographical list from Karnak,[17] while Judah escaped by paying a heavy tribute.

Turning now to the other side of the kingdom of Israel, we see that the extensive conquests made by David in the north established his kingdom as a political factor in the region of Aram Naharaim and brought it within the sphere of traditional Assyrian influence. Owing to these conquests, the kingdom of Israel began to assume proportions exceeding those of any independent political organization ever before established

---

dynasty which contradicts the chronological basis for this identification, placing the ascent of Psusennes at 984 B.C.

[16] For this synchronism see most recently W. F. Albright, *BASOR*, No. 130 (1953), pp. 4 ff. The above chronological computations are independent of the determination of absolute dates concerning Solomon's reign (*ca.* 961–922 according to Albright, or *ca.* 970–930 according to the widely accepted higher chronology).

[17] Cf. B. Mazar, *VTS*, IV (1957), 57–66.

within the borders of Syria and Palestine, including "all the kingdoms from the river [Euphrates] . . . unto the border of Egypt" (I Kings 4:21; II Chron. 9:26). This unprecedented territorial expansion may be explained by assuming that David's kingdom based itself on comprehensive political organizations which had existed before and which, through David's victories over their rulers, passed into his hands with their complex systems intact.

Alt has probably correctly interpreted the manner of transmitting political rule in Palestine during David's time: the Philistines considered themselves the legitimate heirs of the Egyptian rule in Palestine and their defeat by David implied the passage of the Egyptian province of Canaan into the hands of the Israelites.[18] But the growth of the kingdom of Israel did not halt here. It now had to confront another political bloc, namely, the kingdom of Aram Zobah, which, like David's kingdom, extended its sway over country after country.

This political entity, whose strength is difficult to estimate from the fragmentary evidence found in the Bible, expanded during the reign of its king Hadadezer, a contemporary of David, over vast territories. In the south it apparently reached the frontier of Ammon, as can be deduced from the intervention of Aramean troops on the side of the Ammonites in their war with David (II Sam. 10:6 ff.). In the northeast the kingdom of Zobah extended to the river Euphrates and even to territories beyond it (II Sam. 8:3; 10:16; I Chron. 19:16).[19] In the east it touched the Syrian desert and in the west it included Coele-Syria. These boundaries roughly correspond to the expansion of the kingdom of Amurru which still flourished in the 13th century.[20] We have no information on the political organization in this area in the 12th century after Amurru was destroyed by the Sea Peoples, or in the 11th century during the period of the Aramean settlement until the consolidation of the Aramean states on the eve of David's period. The question is whether Hadadezer's kingdom, like that of

[18] Alt, *KS*, II, 68–69.

[19] The geographical term "beyond the river" refers here to the eastern bank of the Euphrates.

[20] On the boundaries of the kingdom of Amurru and its expansion towards the area of Damascus in the south at the beginning of the 13th century see B. Maisler (Mazar), *Encyclopaedia Biblica* (in Hebrew), I (1950), 445 (*s. v.* Amorite).

David, was not based, in one way or another, on a previously existing political organization. It is to be pointed out, however, that in the case of Aram Zobah, there was apparently no continuity in the transmission of political rule as in the case of Israel, and the influence of the political tradition reaching back to the days of the kingdom of Amurru could only be indirect.[21]

The main issue of David's era was the contest between Zobah and Israel, each of which had gradually expanded until no independent territories were left between them. The outcome of this conflict was to lead directly to the political hegemony over the area between Mesopotamia and Egypt. Probably even the kingdom of Hamath in central Syria came under the domination of the king of Israel following his victory over Hadadezer. This may be inferred from the sending of an embassy from Toi, the king of Hamath, to David (II Sam. 8:9–10; I Chron. 18:9–10). The fact that the embassy was headed by Joram, the son of the king of Hamath, and that it brought David expensive gifts, seems to imply that it was not simply a show of courtesy nor even an act for concluding a parity treaty.[22] If we are correct in assuming that Hamath was in fact dependent on Israel, then the kingdom

[21] For the foundation of the various Aramean states in Syria on ancient centers dating from the Bronze Age, cf. also M. Noth, *Beiträge zur biblischen Landes- und Altertumskunde*, LXVIII (1949), 24 ff.

[22] The Bible, too, mentions side by side the precious gifts which David received from the king of Hamath, the tribute he exacted from the conquered countries and the booty he took from Hadadezer (II Sam. 8:9–12; I Chron. 18:1–11). There might also be a historical kernel in the allusions preserved in Chronicles concerning David's and Solomon's wars on the border or even inside the country of Hamath (I Chron. 18:3; II Chron. 8:3), as well as Solomon's building activities in the cities of Hamath (II Chron. 8:4). The geographical term Hamath-Zobah mentioned in connection with Solomon's military expeditions, is not quite clear, but it may be doubted whether we have here a mere anachronistic usage. The name Sbh, in Aramean script, on bricks excavated in Hamath in level E (10th–8th centuries) testifies, probably, to an ancient connection between Zobah and Hamath. Compare A. Dupont-Sommer, *Les Araméens* (1949), p. 30, n. 13. Cf. also the obscure biblical reference concerning Jeroboam II's conquests, "who *recovered* Damascus and Hamath, which belonged to Judah, for Israel" (II Kings 14:28).

of Israel extended its sway to an area in which the tradition of the Hittite empire was still alive.[23]

The question arises whether there is no indication in external sources of the above-mentioned events in Syria and in Aram Naharaim. Since no contemporary Assyrian annalistic sources have been preserved, later Assyrian inscriptions should be examined for details pertaining to the era discussed in this paper. And, indeed, Ashurdan II (934–912 B.C.) as well as Shalmaneser III (858–824) mention in the annals relating their victories that during the reign of Ashurrabi II (1012–972), a contemporary of David, the king of Aram conquered various Assyrian districts. The name of the Aramean king is not given in the sources. The area conquered by the Arameans according to Shalmaneser can be approximately located, since Pitru (biblical Pethor) and Mutkinu are specifically mentioned in this connection. These cities were situated opposite each other on the two banks of the Euphrates some twelve miles south of Carchemish.[24] It is possible that Ashurdan's annals, too, mention the area of the Euphrates south of Carchemish, but the names of the places conquered by the Arameans are mutilated in the inscription and cannot be positively identified.[25]

The attacks of the Arameans in the Euphrates region apparently came from the west side of the river since the kingdom of Assyria was then in a process of retreat towards the east. The main power among the Arameans in Syria at that

[23] The country of Hamath, of course, was not really annexed to Israel, and therefore it is often mentioned in the biblical literature in connection with the northern frontier of the Israelite kingdom. For the northern frontier of David's kingdom, cf. B. Maisler, *BJPES* (in Hebrew), XII (1945/6), 91 ff.; K. Elliger, *PJB*, XXXII (1936), 34–73; M. Noth, *PJB*, XXXIII (1937), 36 ff.

[24] Cf. D. D. Luckenbill, *Ancient Records of Assyria* I (1926), § 603. According to the biblical tradition the Pethor of Balaam belonged to Aramean territory (Num. 22:5; 23:7; cf. Deut. 23:5). This may be an anachronistic conception which came into being in the 10th, or at the beginning of the 9th century when Pethor was actually in Aramean hands.

[25] See *Annals*, obverse, lines 23–32. The document was published by E. Weidner, *AfO*, III (1926), 156–57. For the identification of the place names mentioned in this document and the various opinions concerning them compare A. Malamat, *The Aramaeans in Aram Naharaim and the Rise of their States* (in Hebrew; 1952), pp. 20, 46–47.

time was the kingdom of Zobah. In the light of the great expansion achieved by this kingdom, from Transjordan in the south to the Euphrates in the north, it can be assumed with a fair degree of probability that it acquired additional territories to the north of the bend of the Euphrates, which are mentioned in the Assyrian sources. The information given in Shalmaneser's inscription accords well with the biblical tradition concerning the rule of Hadadezer on both sides of the Euphrates (II Sam. 10:16; I Chron. 19:16).[26] If the Aramean king mentioned in the Assyrian sources is really to be identified with Hadadezer, we arrive here at an Aramean-Assyrian synchronism which leads us at the same time to an indirect synchronization of Israelite, Aramean, and Assyrian history.[27]

[26] This has already been alluded to by E. Forrer in *Reallexikon der Assyriologie* I, (1928), 135; and cf. E. Cavaignac, *Revue de l'histoire des religions*, CVII (1933), 134–36; A. Malamat, *The Aramaeans in Aram Naharaim*, p. 60; and *Encyclopaedia Biblica*, II (1954), 791 f. (*s. v.* Hadadezer).

[27] It would thus appear that Hadadezer conquered the Euphrates area in the period between the beginning of Ashurrabi's reign in 1012 and David's wars with the Arameans in the 90's of the 10th century; cf. S. Yeivin, *Encyclopaedia Biblica*, II, 640 (*s. v.* David).

8

FRANKINCENSE AND MYRRH

GUS W. VAN BEEK

Now when Jesus was born in Bethlehem of Judea . . . behold, wise men from the East came . . . and going into the house they saw the child with Mary his mother, and they fell down and worshipped him. Then, opening their treasures, they offered him gifts, gold and frankincense and myrrh.

Matthew 2:1, 11.

Gold, frankincense, and myrrh, gifts worthy of a king! That gold was a treasured gift in antiquity is easily understood by us, because its value today is no less than it was then. But what about frankincense and myrrh? Where the ancients ranked them in value with gold, there is in our time virtually no market for these substances. So great has been their fall from favor that most of us know nothing about them, apart from the words of the Gospel narrative, which do nothing to remove the veil of mystery surrounding them.

But what are these substances which were so widely used and highly prized by ancient man? How and where were they produced? How were they distributed? What uses were made of them in antiquity? What were the cultural, economic, and political effects of the demand for these substances? Not all of these questions can be answered as definitively as we would like; in fact no more than partial answers can be given to any of them at this time. Such answers as we are able to give are based on reports of Egyptian, Palestinian, Mesopotamian, Greek, and Roman authors, accounts of modern travelers and explorers, archaeological research, and studies by a number of scholars, chiefly Adolph Grohmann and the writer.[1]

---

[1] Much of this study is based on two earlier articles by the writer, which appeared as Appendix II in Richard LeBaron

Description and Geographical Distribution of Incense Trees

Frankincense and myrrh are fragrant gum-resins. The former varies from pale yellow or green to yellowish-brown in color; it is translucent when gathered and in freshly cut sections, but becomes semiopaque when pieces rub against one another in transport, producing a fine white dust which covers its surface. It burns readily, giving off a sooty, slightly scented, black smoke; when the flame is extinguished, it smolders for a considerable time and yields a white, delicately aromatic smoke. Myrrh, on the other hand, is reddish-brown in color; it burns readily giving off little smoke and no soot; when smoldering, it gives off a white, slightly pungent smoke, not nearly as aromatic as that of frankincense.

Both of these gum-resins are obtained from trees. Frankincense of commercial value is produced by two species of the genus *Boswellia*, *B. Carterii* and *B. Frereana*, and possibly by a third *Bhua Dajiana*. The former lacks a central trunk; its branches spring from near the ground, giving it the appearance of a shrub.[2] Normally it attains a height of only seven

---

Bowen, Jr., and Frank P. Albright, *Archaeological Discoveries in South Arabia* (hereafter, *ADSA;* 1958), pp. 139–42; and *JAOS*, LXVIII (1958), 141–52; the reader is referred to these articles for additional details. The writer also recommends two studies by Adolf Grohmann, *Südarabien als Wirtschaftsgebiet I*, in *Osten und Orient* (Vienna, 1922); and *II*, in *Schriften der Philosophischen Fakultät der Deutschen Universität in Prag*, XIII (Brünn, 1933), 101–31. Unless otherwise noted, the following abbreviations of classical works are used throughout: Theophrastus, for Theophrastus, *Enquiry into Plants; Periplus*, for *The Periplus of the Erythraean Sea* (trans. and anno. by W. H. Schoff [1912]); Pliny, for Pliny, *Natural History;* Strabo, for *The Geography of Strabo;* Diodorus, for *Diodorus Siculus;* Claudius Ptolemy, for *The Geography of Claudius Ptolemy* (trans. by E. L. Stevenson [1932]); and Celsus, for Celsus, *De Medicina*. With the exception of the *Periplus* and Claudius Ptolemy, the Loeb Edition has been used for classical sources. The writer wishes to express his appreciation to Mr. George Robert Lewis of the Department of Anthropology, Smithsonian Institution, for his assistance in preparing the map which appears in this article.

[2] Bertram Thomas, *Arabia Felix* (1932), p. 122; and R. E. Drake-Brockman, *British Somaliland* (1912), pp. 256–60, 305–6.

or eight feet, but under very favorable conditions, it sometimes reaches a height of about fifteen feet. I have not been able to find an accurate description or to obtain photographs of *B. Frereana;* the reports which I have seen on this species suggest that it has a central trunk and grows to a height of about twenty feet.[3] Lucas states that another kind of frankincense is obtained from the tree *Commiphora Pedunculata* of eastern Sudan and neighboring Ethiopia.[4]

Myrrh is obtained from *Balsamodendron Myrrh,* Nees, a tree with a central trunk, whose diameter is sometimes as much as one foot, and whose branches circumscribe an area with a maximum diameter of about twenty feet. Its height ranges from about four to fifteen feet, depending on the climate of the area in which it grows. The myrrh tree is in foliage for only a short time after the rainy season, i.e., about the end of August or the beginning of September, and when its serrated dark green leaves decay, long thorns appear on the branches.[5] Reasonably faithful representations of myrrh trees by an ancient Egyptian artist are preserved in the Temple of Hatshepsut at Deir el-Baḥari,[6] about which we will have more to say later. Among classical authors, the descriptions of these trees given by Pliny the Elder (XII. xxxi, xxxiv) and Theophrastus (IX. iv. 2–3) most nearly correspond to those of modern explorers.

Frankincense and myrrh are obtained from the trees by tapping, that is by cutting and peeling the bark for a distance of about five inches in several places, which permits the gum-resin to exude. The substance hardens upon contact with the air, and forms globules and irregular lumps of varying size, which are sometimes referred to as "tears." The trees are tapped in the hot season, usually in May,[7] but during the Roman period, when frankincense was in great demand, the trees were also tapped early in the spring to obtain a second crop. In the autumn, the tears are collected and stored. Storage buildings were especially designed for this purpose and were strategically placed in the frankincense country. One of

[3] *Ibid.,* p. 258.
[4] A. Lucas, *Ancient Egyptian Materials and Industries* (1934), p. 92.
[5] Drake-Brockman, *British Somaliland,* pp. 243–50.
[6] E. Naville, *The Temple of Deir el-Bahari* III, Pls. LXXVIII, LXXIX; see also A. Lucas, *JEA,* XXIII (1937), 29.
[7] Thomas, *Arabia Felix,* p. 122.

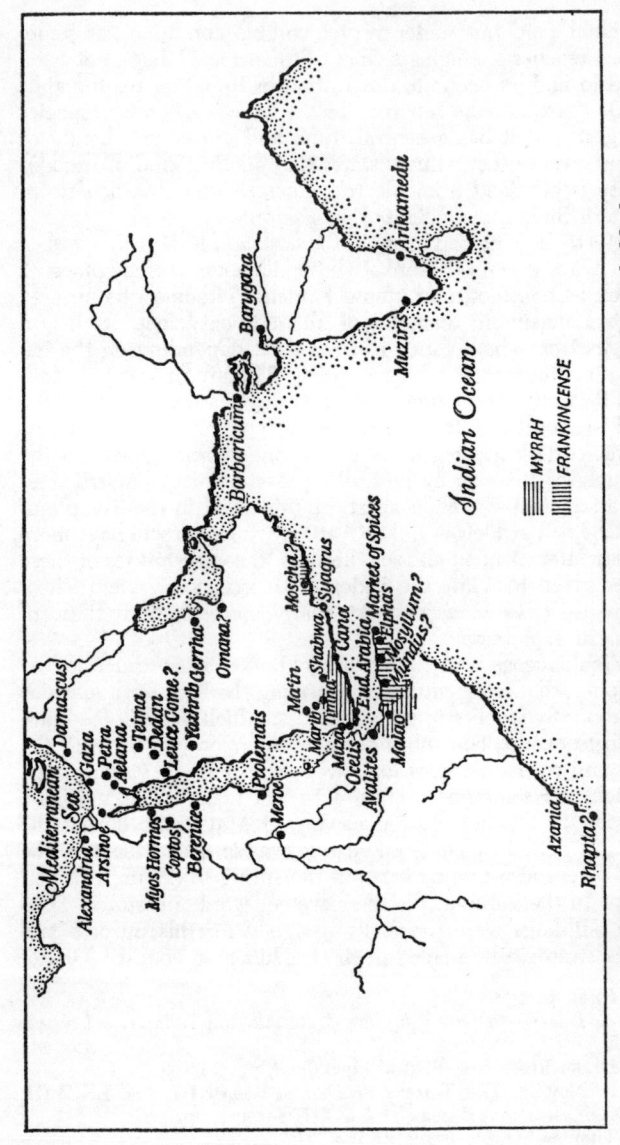

FIGURE 3. Sketch map of Arabia and adjacent lands, showing the probable locations of frankincense and myrrh forests, ancient ports, and caravan cities.

these installations, located in the heart of a frankincense forest at Hanun, approximately thirty air miles north of Salalah, has recently been investigated by Ray Cleveland for the American Foundation for the Study of Man.[8] It consists of a series of nine storage rooms and a larger room on one side, the latter presumably serving as a temporary dwelling for workmen and guards. By winter, the harvest is complete, and the gum-resin is put in bags and shipped. According to Pliny (XII. xxxii. 58–60), this schedule was also followed in antiquity.

Frankincense and myrrh trees are native to only two parts of the world, southern Arabia and northern Somaliland; their restricted distribution seems to be conditioned by the particular combination of moisture (resulting from the southwest monsoon), temperature, and soil which is found only in these regions. Specifically, the frankincense tree of southern Arabia grows only in the province of Dhofar, between longitude 53° 00' and 55° 21' on the coastal plain and the slopes of the Qara mountains.[9] This description agrees almost exactly with that of Pliny the Elder (XII. xxx. 52), the anonymous author of the *Periplus* (pars. 27–30), and Claudius Ptolemy (Book I, XVII; and the 6th map of Asia). The *Periplus*, for example, states that the frankincense country is located in a deep bay called Sachalites, and that frankincense was stored at Syagrus (modern Ras Fartak) and shipped from a port known as Moscha. In his geography, Claudius Ptolemy is even more explicit regarding the location of this region. In referring to Marinus' mistakes, he notes, "In addition to these mistakes, he gives us some further assignments of localities with which the knowledge of our times does not agree. For example, he places the Bay of Sachalita [*sic*] on the western shore of the promontory of Syagros, but all who navigate these parts unanimously agree with us that it is toward the east from Syagros and that Sachalita is a region of Arabia and from it the Bay of Sachalita takes its name" (Book I, XVII). Strabo, on the other hand, apparently disagrees with other classical authors by stating (16.4.4): "Cattabania [Qataban] produces frankincense, and Chatramotitis [Hadhramaut] produces myrrh." In view of modern exploration, it is clear that either Strabo or his sources are wrong, or that his text has become corrupt in

[8] I should like to thank Dr. Cleveland for permission to include this material from a letter to me dated January 22, 1960.
[9] Thomas, *Arabia Felix*, p. 123.

transmission. The products have simply been reversed, so that we must read, "Qataban produces myrrh, and Hadhramaut produces frankincense." Here however, Hadhramaut does not refer to the wadi of that name, but to the ancient kingdom known as Hadhramaut, which included the region of Dhofar—the frankincense region—as shown by several inscriptions found during the excavations at Khor Rori by Frank P. Albright for the American Foundation for the Study of Man in 1952–1953.[10] These inscriptions also prove that the name of this region given by both the *Periplus* and Claudius Ptolemy, is correct. In these inscriptions, the land is called S'KL (Sa'kal).

Across the Gulf of Aden in Somaliland, frankincense trees grow in the central and eastern portion of the coastal range of mountains, making their first appearance in the west at a point about eight miles east of Berbera (ancient Malao), and inland on the plateau.[11] This same general region is described by both the author of the *Periplus* and by Strabo. The *Periplus* tells us that frankincense was exported from the following ports: Malao, Mundus, Mosyllum, and the Market of Spices (pars. 8–12). Strabo states that frankincense trees first appear at Pytholäus (probably Ras Khanzira) in an area where myrrh trees also grow, but that they grow exclusively in the river lands to the east (16.4.14).

The myrrh tree is apparently restricted to the west-central portion of South Arabia, although there has been so little modern exploration of this region that we are not certain of the limits of the myrrh-producing country. Some authors have reported myrrh trees in the region of Wadi Hadhramaut and as far east as the Qara mountains of Dhofar,[12] but none of these accounts has been confirmed. Van der Muelen photographed a myrrh tree growing near modern Niṣab,[13] which is located approximately 155 air miles northeast of Aden. In the course of his study of the ancient irrigation installations in Wadi Beiḥan, Bowen discovered a series of discolored cir-

[10] See W. F. Albright's review of J. Ryckmans, *L'institution monarchique en Arabie méridionale avant l'Islam*, in *JAOS*, LXXIII (1953), 39, n. 7; and Van Beek, *ADSA*, p. 141.

[11] Drake-Brockman, *British Somaliland*, pp. 240, 256, 258.

[12] Theodore Bent, *Southern Arabia* (1900), p. 253; Doreen Ingrams, *Geographical Journal*, XCVIII (1941), 131 ff.

[13] D. van der Meulen, *Aden to the Hadhramaut* (1947), Pl. XXII.

cles laid out in straight rows on the ancient fields composed of silt deposited by irrigation. After studying the modern flora of the region and the relevant classical sources, Bowen reached the tentative conclusion that these circles marked the location of groves of ancient myrrh trees.[14] He also saw a tree in the mountains bordering Wadi Beiḥan, which he tentatively identified as myrrh.[15] But although modern sources tell us little about the exact location of the myrrh region, classical authors enable us to define it more precisely. Pliny (XII. xxxv. 69) lists several kinds of myrrh, each of which is named after the region in which it grew: Minean in ancient Maʿin, Astramitic in Hadhramaut, Gebbanitic in Qataban, Ausaritic in Ausan, Sambracene in southern Tihama, and two other varieties from areas as yet unidentified. All of these areas are located in the western and west-central portion of South Arabia. The author of the *Periplus* tells us (par. 24) that the only South Arabian port which exported myrrh was Muza (modern Mocha), suggesting that the myrrh-producing region was located not far from this town, since products of the hinterland were customarily sent to the nearest port. Claudius Ptolemy in his sixth map of Asia places the myrrh-producing regions (*Smyrnophoros Interior* and *Smyrnophoros Exterior*) to the north and northwest of Arabian Emporium (modern Aden).

The myrrh-producing region of Somaliland is confined to the western and central portion of that country. Specifically it grows in the coastal region between Zeila and Heis, and on the inland plateau as far east as the Nogal valley.[16] The same distribution is described by Strabo (16.4.14) and the author of the *Periplus*. The *Periplus*, for example, states that myrrh was exported from Avalites, Malao, Mundus, and Mosyllum, but that only small quantities were shipped from Avalites and Mosyllum (pars. 7–10). This suggests that the chief myrrh-producing region of Somaliland was located in the center of the region bounded by these ports. Thus, in Somaliland, frankincense was largely confined to the central and eastern portion of the country, while myrrh was restricted to the central and western portion. Modern exploration and classical authors agree that the myrrh and frankincense re-

[14] R. LeBaron Bowen, Jr., *ADSA*, pp. 60 f.
[15] *ADSA*, p. 41.
[16] Drake-Brockman, *British Somaliland*, pp. 241–45.

gions overlap in the center of the country along the coastal plain and the inland plateau.

Land and Sea Trade Routes

Frankincense and myrrh were in great demand in antiquity, because of the many uses to which they were put by the peoples of the Fertile Crescent and the Mediterranean world. To satisfy this demand, the South Arabs developed a well-organized system of distribution. They were aided in this effort by the geographical position of the Arabian peninsula, which is connected by land with Sinai, Syro-Palestine, and Mesopotamia, and is surrounded by navigable waters on the west, south, and east. Thus by both land and sea, the South Arabs were in contact with the great centers of civilization to the north and west, Mesopotamia, Syro-Palestine, Egypt and classical lands, and by sea only with Africa and India.

It should be noted that at no time was there one single incense route, as most of the explorers of Arabia have assumed.[17] We must reckon in all periods with the use of several routes on both land and sea. The importance of these routes probably varied considerably with political and economic conditions in Arabia and Africa. For example, severe losses resulting from piracy on the high seas (e.g., Pliny VI. xxvi. 101; *Periplus* par. 20) might cause a shipper to turn to land caravans to convey his merchandise, or, on the other hand, heavy taxation by tribes through whose territory caravans passed might force a merchant to use seagoing vessels to transport his commodities.

Let us consider some of the more important routes which linked the regions of production with the consumer world. In both Somaliland and Arabia, frankincense and myrrh were transported over a number of short feeder routes from the forests to major ports and caravan centers. In Somaliland, these routes led to the ports on the northern coast, from which frankincense and myrrh were shipped by sea (Strabo 16.4.19; Pliny XII. xxxiii. 66). From the frankincense forests in Dhofar, routes led to Moscha and Syagrus on the south coast (*Periplus* pars. 30, 32). During the winter, part of the frankincense was shipped by native boats and rafts from Moscha and Syagrus to Cana (South Arabic Qana, modern Bir 'Ali),

[17] Bowen, *ADSA*, pp. 35-42.

the principal Hadhrami port on the southern coast; the remainder was loaded on ships bound for Egypt. From Cana, some of the frankincense was transported overland to Shabwa, the capital of the kingdom of Hadhramaut, and some was stored until the following summer when it was carried to India on east-bound ships (see below). Other routes led overland from the collecting stations in the forests of Dhofar to Shabwa.[18]

The myrrh groves in the west central portion of southern Arabia were linked by routes to Eudaemon Arabia (Aden), Ocelis, and Muza, the principal South Arabian myrrh ports, and to Shabwa and Timna', the capital of the kingdom of Qataban. The principal overland route to the north began at Shabwa and included stops at Timna', Marib, Ma'in, Yathrib (Medina), Dedan (el-'Ola), and Gaza. This journey, according to Pliny, was made in sixty-five stages (XII. xxxii. 63–64). At the northern end of this route were several branches leading to different destinations. One branch passed through Aelana (Elath) (Strabo 16.4.4), and another went by way of Leuce Come, Petra, and Rhinocolura (el-'Arish; Strabo 16.4.24; *Periplus* par. 19). Although not specifically mentioned in the literature, one branch must have followed the "king's highway" through Transjordan, and another route probably branched off at Teima, en route to Mesopotamia.

Several lines of evidence point to the existence of an overland route across the middle of the Arabian peninsula from Wadi Hadhramaut to the Persian Gulf. Strabo (16.4.4) tells us that a journey from Hadhramaut to Gerrha required forty days, and that from Gerrha, frankincense was shipped to Mesopotamia and Palestine. Now the fact that Gerrha was inhabited by Chaldean exiles from Babylon in the 3rd century B.C. according to Strabo (16.3.3), and probably somewhat earlier, and the fact that the Chaldean script probably had its origin in southeast Arabia, as shown by Albright,[19] strongly suggest a link between Dhofar, Hadhramaut, and Gerrha, reaching across the Empty Quarter, and tend to support Strabo's statement. The date of the origin of the major route from South Arabia to Syro-Palestine can be determined with

[18] For routes in medieval times, see Grohmann, *Sudarabien als Wirtschaftsgebiet*, II, 126 ff., and Freya Stark, *The Southern Gates of Arabia* (1936), pp. 310 ff. For modern routes, see W. Thesiger, *Geographical Journal*, CVIII (1946), 139, n. 1.

[19] W. F. Albright, *BASOR*, No. 128 (1952), pp. 44 f.

some certainty. The journey of the unnamed queen of Sheba to the court of Solomon, which was presumably made for the purpose of obtaining a favorable agreement covering the distribution of products of Arabia, almost certainly followed the Marib-Yathrib-Dedan route. This event took place about the middle of the 10th century B.C., proving that this route was in use at that early date. Furthermore, since travel across Arabia would have been impossible without the use of the camel, and since the effective domestication of the camel seems to have occurred in the 13th or 12th century B.C.,[20] this route must have come into use between the 12th and the 10th centuries B.C.

In addition to these land routes, a vast complex of sea routes linked the incense ports of southern Arabia and Somaliland with the east and the west. As early as the 11th dynasty, at the end of the 3rd millennium B.C., Egyptian boats were sailing the length of the Red Sea to obtain incense and distinctly African products from Punt (Somaliland).[21] On the return voyage from Punt, these vessels sailed to Quseir where cargoes were conveyed overland to Coptos and then transported by boats northward on the Nile. Although this route seems to have been used for centuries, several alternate ports at the north end were used in the second half of the first millennium B.C., according to classical authors. One was Myos Hormos (Strabo 16.4.24), another was Berenice (Pliny VI. xxvi. 102-3), and still another was Arsinoe, from which goods were transported to Alexandria over one of three different land routes (Pliny VI. xxxiii. 166-67). By the first century A.D., Greco-Roman merchant fleets based in Egypt were making annual trips to the ports of Somaliland and East Africa. On these voyages, ships called at ports along the west coast of the Red Sea and the northern coast of Somaliland, and some rounded the horn of Africa, sailing as far south as Azania, which was perhaps in the region of Zanzibar (*Periplus* pars. 2-18). Other vessels, after calling at the Somaliland incense ports, sailed directly from the Market of Spices to India (*Periplus* par. 57). On the return voyage, some ships sailed from

[20] Albright, *From the Stone Age to Christianity* (3rd ed.; Doubleday Anchor Books, 1957), pp. 149, 164; Reinhard Walz, *ZDMG*, CI (1951), 29-51; CIV (1954), 47-50; *Actes du IVe congrès international des sciences anthropologiques et ethnologiques*, Vienna 1952, III (1956), 190-204.

[21] Grohmann, *Sudarabien als Wirtschaftsgebiet*, II, 101-4.

India to Dioscorida (Socotra) and the Somali coast (*Periplus* pars. 14, 31). Arab merchantmen also participated in the Somali coast trade, according to the *Periplus* (pars. 7, 27). It is quite likely that in early times, as well as in the Greco-Roman period, a portion of Somaliland frankincense and myrrh was brought to the South Arabian ports or carried northward and eastward by Arab merchantmen.

A portion of the Greco-Roman fleet seems to have specialized in incense, and these ships visited only the incense ports of Somaliland and Arabia, sailing no farther east than Cana before returning to Egypt (Pliny VI. xxvi. 104). According to the *Periplus* (pars. 6, 24), vessels engaged in this trade sailed from Egyptian ports no later than September.

The greater portion of the Greco-Roman fleet, however, was used in the lucrative Arabia-India trade. These ships sailed from Egypt no later than July and called at the South Arabian myrrh ports, Muza, Ocelis, or Eudaemon Arabia, and then at Cana, the principal Arabian frankincense port (*Periplus* pars. 24, 27–28; Pliny VI. xxvi. 104). At Cana, this sea route divided into three branches:

1. One branch led to the Persian Gulf, and vessels using this route followed the Arabian shore from Cana eastward. According to the *Periplus*, one of the Persian Gulf ports, Omana, imported frankincense, and along this entire coast ships traded for pearls, the principal commodity of this region (pars. 30, 32–37).

2. Another route led to northwest India, with calls at Barbaricum, which also imported frankincense, and Barygaza. Ships using this route hugged the coast of Arabia for three days after departing from Cana—which took them to about Syagrus (Ras Fartak)—and then headed into the open sea (*Periplus* pars. 39, 41–49, 57).

3. The destination of the third branch was southwest India, where the fleet called at a number of ports, including Muziris. Ships bound for this region set out for the open sea immediately after leaving Cana, heading off wind (*Periplus* pars. 54, 57; Pliny VI. xxvi. 100–101).

The return voyage from India was begun in December or January with the northeast monsoon (Pliny VI. xxvi. 106). If the winds were favorable, ships from both northwest and southwest India sailed directly to Ocelis (*Periplus* par. 25). If their departure from India was delayed, they sailed to Moscha, where they wintered and traded merchandise for frankincense, which they took to Egypt when fair weather returned (*Periplus* par. 32).

Even though none of our sources specifically describes the use of the Somaliland and Arabia-India route in earlier times, it must have been used by Arab and Indian merchant vessels for centuries before the Greco-Roman period.[22] It is the most direct and easiest route linking Arabia and Somaliland with India, because it makes use of the annual alternation of the southwest and northeast monsoon wind systems. Arabs and Indians, who had been engaged in fishing and coastal trading, and had experienced the annual alternation of these wind systems on the high seas for centuries and perhaps millennia, must have discovered quite early the technique of sailing with these winds to reach their desired destination. Although it has been argued that the sea is too rough during the southwest monsoon to be weathered by the type of vessels which the Arabs probably had, a study of insurance rates on Indian coastal vessels[23] and of reports prepared by the India Meteorological Department[24] proves that it is treacherous only along the coast of India and only there for three of the six months of this prevailing wind system. Elsewhere in the Indian Ocean, craft as small as a thirty-foot *jalbut* are able to sail with this wind in comparative safety.[25]

Evidence of early trade in the Indian Ocean and Arabian Sea is slowly accumulating. We know, for example, that cinnamon, which is native to Ceylon, was being brought to the ports of South Arabia, Somaliland, and perhaps Ethiopia, as early as the 15th century B.C. and perhaps somewhat earlier. Reliefs in the temple of Hatshepsut at Deir el-Baḥari list cinnamon among the commodities which were brought by the ships of her expedition to Punt.[26] The Papyrus Harris, which was prepared by Rameses IV for the tomb of his father Rameses III soon after the latter's death, several times mentions cinnamon among the offerings which Rameses III gave

[22] For details, see the writer's paper, *JAOS*, LXXX (1960), 136–39.
[23] K. B. Vaidya, *Sailing Vessel Traffic on the West Coast of India* (1945), p. 136.
[24] S. Basu, *Winds, Weather and Currents on the Coasts of India and the Laws of Storms* (1931), especially pp. 3–10.
[25] A. Villiers, *Monsoon Seas* (1952), pp. 86 f.
[26] J. H. Breasted, *Ancient Records of Egypt*, II (1906), 109.

to the Egyptian gods.[27] By the 4th century B.C., cinnamon was being imported into South Arabia, Somaliland, and Ethiopia in such quantities that all classical authors before Pliny (Theophrastus IX. iv. 2; Strabo 16.4.4, 14, 19; Diodorus III. 46. 3) assumed that it was native to these lands. How can we account for the great quantities of cinnamon and other distinctly eastern products in Arab and Somali ports in this early period, long before Greek sailing vessels had begun to participate in the Indian trade? The only possible explanation is that Arab and Indian merchant fleets were bringing them to this area for transshipment to the north and west. In all probability, they used much the same route that was used by Greco-Roman vessels at a later time.

Arab vessels also carried on local trade over a number of coastal routes. The *Periplus* tells us that Leuce Come, a Nabatean town on the eastern shore of the Red Sea, was primarily an Arab merchant town (par. 19); that Dioscorida (Socotra) belonged to the kingdom of Hadhramaut and was settled in part by Arab traders from Muza (pars. 30–31); and that ships from Cana *regularly* called at Moscha, at Sarapis Island (Masira Island), at Omana and the coast of Persia in the Persian Gulf, and at Scythia, Barygaza, and Muziris in India (pars. 27, 32–33, 54, 57). In addition, Arab vessels regularly visited the ports on the north coast of Somaliland as we have seen above, and carried on trade at a number of ports on the East African coast as far south as Rhapta, according to the *Periplus* (pars. 7, 15, 16, 27). These relations with the coast of East Africa are specifically described by the author of the *Periplus* as ancient, and must go back to at least the middle of the first millennium B.C., as we have shown elsewhere.[28]

The picture which emerges from this recital of the land and sea routes mentioned in the classical sources is one of considerable complexity. It could hardly have developed overnight, but presupposes a long tradition of commercial relations with the east and the west. The basis of this trade was the universal demand for frankincense and myrrh, in which the Arabs and their associates held a complete monopoly, and the transfer of goods from east and west.

That Arabs were actively engaged in trade with other lands is proven by several discoveries. (We are not including here

[27] *Ibid.*, IV, 132–97 *passim.*
[28] Van Beek, *JAOS*, LXXVIII (1958), 146, n. 37.

the South Arabian finds in Ethiopia; since Ethiopia was a Sabean colony, the South Arabian objects discovered there belong to a different category of relationship from those from areas not under the political or economic control of the South Arabs.) The earliest of these is a large fragment of a South Arabian clay stamp, which was discovered by James L. Kelso at Beitin (biblical Bethel) in 1957.[29] The stamp, which is made of typically South Arabian straw-tempered clay, originally contained three lines of text; unfortunately the first and half of the second lines are broken away. Preserved on the second line are the letters *my* . . . and the lower portion of the strokes of two letters, and on the third line, *fdn*. Jamme reconstructs the text to read: line 1 [. . . *ḥ*], line 2 *my* ⌈*n*⌉, line 3 *fdn*, which he tentatively translates ". . . Hamiyan, the delegate." Now this stamp is clear evidence of trade between South Arabia and the Northern Kingdom of Israel. More specifically, the fact that Bethel was one of the two temple cities of the Northern Kingdom (I Kings 12:25–33; Amos 7:13), and that frankincense was used in connection with religious rites in Israel (see below) enables us to conclude that the chief commodity of this trade was frankincense. Even though the stamp was found in debris outside the city wall in an undatable context, several lines of evidence indicate that it was brought to Bethel between the late 10th and the fourth quarter of the 8th centuries B.C. These limits are provided by I Kings 12:29, which states that the Bethel temple was built by Jeroboam I, probably not long after 922 B.C., and by I Kings 17:5, which suggests that it was destroyed by the Assyrians before *ca.* 722–721 B.C. After the latter date, there was, of course, no need for frankincense at Bethel. Considerations of paleography, based on a comparative study of certain letters of this stamp with those of a number of graffiti in Wadi Beiḥan and Mukeiras in South Arabia, also suggest a date in this period.

Two other South Arabian inscriptions have been found in areas outside of South Arabia. One appears on a sarcophagus discovered at Gizeh (RÉS 3427), which describes financial

[29] G. W. Van Beek and A. Jamme, *BASOR*, No. 151 (Oct. 1958), pp. 9–16. A fragment of an identical stamp found at a pre-Islamic site near Meshhed in Wadi Du'an proves that the stamp found at Bethel is Hadhrami and that Hadhramaut was the point of origin of the Bethel frankincense; see Jamme and Van Beek, *BASOR*, No. 163 (Oct. 1961), pp. 15–18.

obligations of the deceased and mentions trade in aromatics. The second (RÉS 3570), found on the island of Delos, is a bilingual inscription in the Minean dialect of South Arabic and in Greek. It dedicates an altar of sacrifice to Wad and the divinities of Ma'in. Both of these inscriptions belong to the 3rd century B.C. These finds from Egypt, Palestine, and Delos, ranging in date from about the 9th to the 3rd centuries B.C., bear witness to the geographical extent and time span of South Arabian trade in the first millennium B.C.

Uses of Frankincense and Myrrh

Having alluded in several places to the demand for frankincense and myrrh in antiquity, let us now examine the basis of this demand, namely the uses to which these substances were put by peoples of the Fertile Crescent and the Mediterranean world. Owing to limits of space, we shall describe only the major uses of frankincense and myrrh and give a few examples of each; the fact is that both of these gum-resins were used in so many different ways that a monograph would be required to treat their usage in detail.

Frankincense (Heb. *lebōnāh;* Akkad. *labanatu;*[30] Arab. *lubān;* Greek *libanos, libanotos;* Lat. *tūs*) was chiefly used as incense, i.e., to produce a fragrance when burned, in religious rites of most ancient peoples. This was its major function in ancient Israel, and its use as incense is attested in numerous passages in the Old Testament. It was one of the ingredients of the special blend of incense, which was considered holy to and reserved for Yahweh, and was placed in the Tent of Meeting (Exod. 3:34). It was also placed on meal offerings of first fruits (Lev. 2:15-16), and on the Bread of the Sanctuary, which was set before Yahweh each Sabbath (Lev. 24:7). In the first two of these offerings, the whole quantity of frankincense was consumed by fire on the altar; in the last, it was apparently eaten by Aaron and his sons in the Sanctuary. It continued to be used in offerings as late as the first century A.D., as shown by a number of passages in the *Mishnah* (see, for example, tractates Zebahim, Menahoth, Shekalim, Yoma, and Sotah). It may have been similarly used by individuals

[30] I am indebted to Professor Julius Lewy, who called my attention to Ebeling's discussion of this word, *Orientalia,* XVII (1948), 137.

and families in their homes, in view of the fairly large number of small incense burners which have been found in archaeological excavations at several Palestinian sites. Although specific references to the use of frankincense as incense in Akkadian and Egyptian literature are comparatively rare, it is virtually certain that it was employed for this purpose in both regions. There are, for example, numerous references in worship; if Assyrian texts to the use of incense offerings in worship; if these offerings were similar to those of their neighbors to the west, we can assume that frankincense was also used. The same is true of Egyptian references to incense. In both regions, incense burners have been found, which may have been used for burning frankincense. The balls of incense found in the tomb of Tutankhamen, which were analyzed and tentatively identified by Lucas as frankincense,[31] were perhaps also meant to be burned as incense in the afterlife. Frankincense was also burned as incense by Greeks and Romans (for example, see respectively Theophrastus IX. iv. 9 and Pliny XII. xxxii. 62). In XII. xli. 83, Pliny also tells us that a whole year's production of Arabian frankincense was consumed at the obsequies for Poppea, the wife of Nero, and that this was commonly done to cover the odor of burning bodies. While this may have been a practical consequence of using frankincense at cremations, the custom was originally intended to propitiate the gods, to whom frankincense was most dear, according to Diodorus (II. 49. 2).

Frankincense seems to have been little used in the manufacture of cosmetics and perfumes. The Song of Solomon (3:6), which states that it was one of the substances used to scent the couch of Solomon, indicates that it sometimes functioned as a perfume in ancient Israel, and it is possible that it was similarly used elsewhere.

Frankincense was also prominent in Greco-Roman *materia medica*. Its properties rendered it efficacious for stopping bleeding, healing wounds, promoting suppuration, and cleansing, according to Celsus (V. 1–8). Of the many prescriptions in which frankincense was an ingredient, we have selected a few to illustrate the wide variety of application. It was used in antidotes for hemlock and other poisons (Theophrastus IX. xx. 1 and Celsus V. 23) and in prescriptions for pains in the

[31] A. Lucas, *Ancient Egyptian Materials and Industries*, pp. 93–94.

side (Celsus V. 18. 6) and chest (Celsus V. 4B. 8), hemorrhoids (Celsus V. 20. 5), hemorrhages from the mouth and throat (Celsus IV. 11. 6), wounds and broken heads (Celsus V. 19. 11), paralysed limbs (Celsus III. 27. 1D), bruises (Celsus V. 18. 24), ulcerations (Celsus VI. 6. 13), and abscesses (Celsus V. 3). Although it is not commonly mentioned in the literature of other ancient peoples in this connection, it is probable that it was also used in the Fertile Crescent, since medications prescribed by the Greeks and Romans were in many cases similar to those used by the physicians of the ancient Near East.

Myrrh (Heb. *mor;* Akkad. *murru;* Arab. *murru;* Greek *murra, smyrna, stakte;* Lat. *murra, myrrha, stacta*) was also used as incense in antiquity, but to a lesser extent than frankincense, judging from the dearth of specific references in the literature. The inscriptions of Hatshepsut at Deir el-Baḥari refer to the use of myrrh in the temple for its fragrance,[32] which suggests that it was burned as incense. Plutarch tells us that myrrh was used as incense by the Egyptians in classical times.[33] In Assyria, it was burned in a censer, which was placed at the head of a patient's bed, perhaps to fumigate the bed chamber.[34] The Greeks are also reported to have burned myrrh as incense (Theophrastus *Concerning Odors* 12).

More important was its use in ancient cosmetics and perfumes. In Israel, flowing myrrh—presumably a neutral oil containing myrrh—was mixed with a number of spices to make a fragrant, holy, anointing oil (Exod. 30:23). On a profane level, it was used to perfume royal garments (Ps. 45:8), beds (Prov. 7:17; Song of Solomon 3:6), and the human body (Song of Solomon 1:13; 5:5). According to Esther 2:12, it was considered to have other beneficial cosmetic effects, since a six-month series of beauty treatments employing oil of myrrh was given candidates for queenship in the Persian court. We learn from the Amarna letters that myrrh and oil of myrrh were included among the gifts of Tushratta, the king of Mit-

[32] Breasted, *Ancient Records of Egypt,* II, 118.

[33] According to Lucas, *Ancient Egyptian Materials and Industries,* p. 94, n. 12, where he cites *Isis and Osiris,* which I have not seen.

[34] R. Campbell Thompson, *A Dictionary of Assyrian Botany* (1949), p. 340, and references.

anni, to Amenhotep III and perhaps to Akhnaton of Egypt,[35] and, in both instances, these preparations were probably intended for use as perfumes or ointments. Turning to Egypt, the Deir el-Bahari inscriptions state that Hatshepsut rubbed myrrh on her legs,[36] in order to impart fragrance. Theophrastus (*Concerning Odors* 28) states that "Egyptian" perfume was made of myrrh and cinnamon among other substances, and Pliny (XIII. 2. 6) tells us that myrrh was one of the ingredients in Mendesian ointment, a famous preparation which was named after the city of Mendes in the Delta where it was manufactured. The Greeks also used myrrh in making perfumes. It is mentioned in the formula of a renowned perfume known as *Megaleion* (Theophrastus *Concerning Odors* 17, 29), and Theophrastus lists stacte (myrrh-oil), *Megaleion*, and "Egyptian" among the perfumes which were considered best for women because of ". . . their strength and substantial character [which] do not easily evaporate and are not easily made to disperse, and a lasting perfume is what women require" (*Concerning Odors* 42). These references, together with the reference from the Gospel of Matthew cited at the beginning of this article, show that myrrh and myrrh products were associated with gracious living—to borrow a current phrase—in ancient times.

Myrrh was also widely used in the practice of medicine in antiquity. There is no unequivocal evidence that myrrh formed part of the *materia medica* of ancient Palestine, although this can be reasonably assumed in view of its extensive use in medicine elsewhere, especially in Mesopotamia and the Greco-Roman world. It is possible that the mixture of wine and myrrh, which was offered to Jesus just before the crucifixion (Mark 15:23), was an analgesic or painkiller. In Mesopotamia, it had a number of applications in the practice of medicine.[37] It was used in making poultices for the head, and for blains and chilblains; it was prescribed for ear, eye, and nose ailments; it was mixed with alum for a mouth wash; it was prescribed for strangury; it was used as an anal ointment, presumably for hemorrhoids, and in enemas. Myrrh also figured in a number of remedies used by Greco-Roman physicians, according to Celsus. For example, it was used internally

[35] J. A. Knudtzon, *Die El-Amarna-Tafeln*, I (1915), 22.III.29 and 25.IV.51.

[36] Breasted, *Ancient Records of Egypt*, II, 113.

[37] See R. Campbell Thompson's excellent summary, *A Dictionary of Assyrian Botany*, pp. 339–40.

in prescriptions for quartan fever (III. 16. 2), dropsy (III. 21. 6), and as an antidote to prevent poisoning (V. 23. 3). Externally, it was an ingredient in prescriptions for the relief of pain in the side (V. 18. 7B) and the liver (V. 18. 3); for relief of inflammation of the ears and earache (VI. 7. 1–2), and for treating eye diseases (VI. 6. 1); for hemorrhoids (V. 20. 5), bladder stones (V. 20. 6), inflammation of the uvula and genitals (V. 20. 4); to induce menstruation (V. 21. B); for abscesses (V. 18. 16), and to promote healing (V. 2); and in plasters for broken heads (V. 19. 7).

One of the better known applications of myrrh was in connection with preparing corpses for burial. The Gospel of John (19:39–40) states that Joseph of Arimathea brought a mixture of myrrh and aloes, which was wrapped with the body of Jesus in linen. In Egypt, myrrh was commonly used in the process of mummification.[38] According to Herodotus, it was one of the substances which were used to fill the eviscerated and cleansed body cavity in the most expensive embalming technique. Diodorus, on the other hand, states that myrrh was rubbed on the eviscerated and cleansed body for the purpose of preserving and perfuming it (I. 7). Both uses are considered probable by Lucas, who also states that he found a substance, which is probably myrrh, in mummies of royal and priestly persons, ranging in date from the 18th dynasty through the Ptolemaic period.

Thus frankincense and myrrh touched many phases of life in antiquity, with applications in religious rites, in the home, in the area of personal comfort and adornment, in medicine, and in embalming. This brief summary includes by no means all of the known uses of these substances, and, in addition to those that are known, there were undoubtedly many other applications which are still unknown, owing both to the loss of literature and to the failure of ancient man to put in writing full descriptions of his techniques and formulae. Enough is known, however, to establish the importance, indeed the necessity, of these substances in the cultures of the ancient Near East and Mediterranean world. The many uses of frankincense and myrrh created a universal clamor and demand for these substances, which the South Arabian producers and distributors sought to supply.

[38] See Lucas' discussion, *Ancient Egyptian Materials and Industries*, pp. 230–34, 263–65.

Economic Effects of the Incense Trade

This demand for frankincense and myrrh, together with the limited supply of these commodities, resulting from the restrictions of production and the difficulties of transportation imposed by nature and the prevailing level of technology, made incense very costly in the ancient world. Our most complete information on the value of gum-resins is obtained from classical authors. Pliny tells us that in order to prevent theft "at Alexandria . . . where the frankincense is worked up for sale, good heavens! no vigilance is sufficient to guard the factories. A seal is put upon the workmen's aprons, they have to wear a mask or a net with a close mesh on their heads, and before they are allowed to leave the premises they have to take off all their clothes . . ." (XII. xxxii. 59). He also states that before a frankincense caravan has reached the Mediterranean, the expenses per camel amounted to 688 denarii, owing largely to taxation en route (XII. xxxii. 65). Whether this figure includes the original purchase price of the gum-resin in Dhofar, we are unfortunately not told. If a camel could carry 300–400 pounds of frankincense—today caravan camels in Wadi Beihan carry about this amount of salt[39]—the transportation of each pound of incense cost from 1.72 to 2.29 denarii. When we add to this the caravaneer's profit, the overhead and profit of the factory where it was processed, and of those who transported and sold the final product, it is no wonder that the best frankincense sold for six denarii, the second best for five denarii, and third quality for three denarii per pound (Pliny XII. xxxii. 65).

But what do these figures mean in terms of the average Roman's wages and cost of living? And is it possible to translate these costs in terms of our modern-day wages and cost of living? Such estimates are, of course, difficult to make, owing to our incomplete data on the economy of the ancient world, and comparisons between ancient and modern price structures are much more uncertain. Of the data available, perhaps the most reliable are those dealing with the relationship of prices to cost of living, although these varied somewhat from region to region and from time to time. Thus, it is possible to compare the cost of a commodity with the minimum, annual, urban cost of living, and to express this comparison

[39] Bowen, *ADSA*, p. 35.

as a percentage. Similarly, we can estimate the minimum cost of living in our time, and calculate the approximate value of an ancient product today by applying the same percentage figure. Such comparisons cannot be pressed closely, and are of value only for making the roughest estimates of costs; they do provide a basis for a better understanding of ancient prices, if used with great caution. We know that in the 2nd century A.D., 100–140 imperial denarii per year were required for the basic necessities of life in Roman Syro-Palestine.[40] If we use the mean figure, 120 denarii, the above-mentioned prices of a pound of frankincense would represent 2.5–5.0% of the amount required to maintain a minimum standard of living for a year. This percentage is rather high, and establishes the relative costliness of frankincense in the Roman empire in that period. If we assume that frankincense were equally valued in our time, and that the cost of its production and distribution were the same today, we can roughly compute the value of a pound of frankincense in our economy by applying the same figure, 2.5–5.0%, to our minimum urban cost of living. As of March, 1960, the average factory worker in the United States was earning about $4715.00 per year,[41] of which perhaps $3500.00 was spent on basic necessities (this includes food, shelter, clothing, and a small amount for miscellaneous expenses, but excludes transportation, recreation, etc.). Using $3500.00 as an average figure and multiplying it by the above percentages, we find that a pound of frankincense would cost between $87.50 and $175.00 today depending on its quality. In other words, under similar circumstances, a factory worker would have to work one week to purchase a pound of poor quality frankincense, or two weeks to buy a pound of the best quality. Frankincense is, of course, not worth a fraction of this sum now, but this figure gives us a better appreciation of its value to the Romans of the first and 2nd centuries A.D.

The widespread demand for costly incense, the monopoly of centers of incense production, and the control of distribution systems brought great wealth to the South Arabian states, according to classical sources. In the first century A.D., Pliny described the South Arabs as the wealthiest race in the world (VI. xxxii. 162). Elsewhere (XII. xli. 84; VI. xxvi. 101),

[40] For details, see F. M. Heichelheim, in *An Economic Survey of Ancient Rome*, ed. T. Frank (6 vols.; 1933–40), IV (1938), 178–81.

[41] *U. S. Department of Labor News* 4078 (April 25, 1960).

he conservatively estimated that of the 100 million sesterces which were expended by the Roman empire for goods from the East—that is Arabia, India, and China—approximately half of this sum was spent for Arabian merchandise alone. While a portion of these funds was used for the purchase of pearls at Persian Gulf ports, the bulk was used to buy incense in South Arabia. Diodorus picturesquely describes the prosperity of the Sabeans as follows:

> This tribe [the Sabeans] surpasses not only the neighbouring Arabs but also all other men in wealth and in their several extravagancies besides. For in the exchange and sale of their wares they, of all men who carry on trade for the sake of the silver they receive in exchange, obtain the highest price in return for things of the smallest weight. Consequently, since they have never for ages suffered the ravages of war because of their secluded position, and since an abundance of both gold and silver abounds in the country, . . . they have embossed goblets of every description, made of silver and gold, couches and tripods with silver feet, and every other furnishing of incredible costliness, and halls encircled by large columns, some of them gilded, and others having silver figures on the capitals. Their ceilings and doors they have partitioned by means of panels and coffers made of gold, set with precious stones and placed close together, and have thus made the structure of their houses in every part marvellous for its costliness; for some parts they have constructed of silver and gold, others of ivory and the most showy precious stones or of whatever else men esteem most highly. For the fact is that these people have enjoyed their felicity unshaken since ages past because they have been entire strangers to those whose own covetousness leads them to feel that another man's wealth is their own godsend (III. 47. 5–8).

We are also told by Strabo that Augustus' purpose in sending Aelius Gallus on the Arabian campaign in 24 B.C. was to win wealthy friends or to conquer wealthy enemies (16.4.22). Although these descriptions of the wealth of South Arabia date from the first century B.C. and the first century A.D., we can reasonably assume that the level of prosperity was much the same in earlier times, that is throughout most of the first millennium B.C. The great demand for aromatics, the visit of the queen of Sheba to Solomon, the Sabean colonization of Ethiopia, trade with the coast of East Africa, and the role of South Arabian ports as intermediaries in the transshipment of eastern and western goods indicate a prosperous economy in South Arabia during this period.

This flow of wealth into the country made possible the importation of a wide range of *objets d'art*, minor objects, and techniques, as well as the construction of large splendid cities (on the latter, see below). Here we will briefly mention a few of the imports, local imitations of foreign works of art, and techniques which have been brought to light by recent archaeological excavations. The earliest are two stelae, which were discovered by the expeditions of the American Foundation for the Study of Man at Hajar Bin Ḥumeid, a village site located about nine miles south of Timna', and at Ḥeid Bin 'Aqil, the Timna' Cemetery. These stelae—in alabaster—are the work of local craftsmen, who imitated northern prototypes of the first half of the first millennium B.C.; the former goes back to a Syro-Phoenician prototype, dating between the 12th and the middle of the 8th centuries B.C.,[42] and the latter is an Arabian adaptation of a combination of Syro-Hittite motifs of about the 6th century B.C.[43] We also have evidence of the influence of Syro-Palestinian and Mesopotamian ceramic forms and finishing techniques on several types of South Arabian pottery; this borrowing goes back to the early centuries of the first millennium B.C., and in some instances perhaps slightly earlier.[44] In the Marib excavations, a bronze statue of a youth wearing a lion skin was discovered, which reflects a syncretism of chiefly Syro-Phoenician and Egyptian features, ranging in date from the end of the 2nd millennium to about the end of the 7th century B.C.[45] Marginally drafted, pecked masonry, which was used in major structures at a number of sites in South Arabia, has been shown to have been borrowed probably from Assyria in the 8th century B.C.[46]

In Hellenistic times, a number of bronze statues were imported—or cast locally from imported molds—from a northern

[42] B. Segall, *Ars Orientalis*, II (1957), 38–41.
[43] Segall, *AJA*, LX (1956), 169–70.
[44] See the writer's forthcoming volume entitled *Hajar Bin Ḥumeid*.
[45] Segall, *AJA*, LX (1956), 165–70.
[46] Van Beek, *ADSA*, pp. 287–96.

center, such as Alexandria. The most important of these is the pair of Hellenistic bronze lions with infant riders, which were discovered near the South Gate of Timna', and have been studied by Dr. Berta Segall.[47] To this period also belong fragments of an alabaster statuette of Isis,[48] which closely imitates a Greek prototype. A number of pieces of imported pottery, including fragments of a net lekythos, glazed ring-handled skyphoi, Rhodian type amphorae, and especially fragments of Italian and Near Eastern Sigillata and ACO ware have been found at Timna', at Hajar Bin Ḥumeid in Wadi Beihan,[49] and more recently at Khor Rori in Dhofar.[50] South Arabian coinage was also locally adapted from well-known coin types of the Greco-Roman world. As yet we have only one import from the east, a small bronze statuette of a dancing girl of Indian origin and dating from about the 2nd century A.D. This statuette from Khor Rori is our first proof of trade between South Arabia and India;[51] it gives us cause to hope that other evidence of trade from the east will be found in future excavations in southern Arabia.

These objects attest a surplus of wealth in ancient South Arabia that made it possible for the states to import works of art of considerable value from the great civilizations of the west, north, and east. While they do not necessarily support Pliny's statement that the South Arabs were the wealthiest people in the world, they strikingly confirm the view generally held by classical authors that South Arabia was a truly prosperous land.

South Arabian Culture in the Light of Incense Trade

The description of South Arabian production and distribution of frankincense and myrrh in the preceding pages presents some, but by no means all, of the complex problems of this aspect of South Arabian economy. We are in the dark, for example, regarding the measures taken by the South Arabian states to guard their frankincense and myrrh forests

[47] Van Beek, *ADSA*, pp. 155–64.
[48] Segall, *AJA*, LIX (1955), 213–14.
[49] Howard Comfort, *ADSA*, pp. 199–207.
[50] Mentioned in a letter dated February 29, 1960 from Dr. Ray Cleveland, to whom I wish to express gratitude for permission to use this material.
[51] F. P. Albright, *Archaeology*, VII (1954), 254.

from people of other lands, who coveted and sought to plunder them. It is clear from the classical sources that until the beginning of the Christian Era and for some decades afterward, there was considerable confusion about the nature of the frankincense and myrrh trees and the exact location of the forests (see, for example, Theophrastus IX. iv. 5, Diodorus III. 46. 1–3, and Strabo 16.4.19), a confusion which seems to have been deliberately fostered by South Arabian traders and diplomats, if we can believe the words of Pliny (XII. xxxi). We have also said nothing about the organization of the caravans and merchant fleets which distributed these commodities to the various markets. We do not know what arrangements were made among the various South Arabian states to assure the flow of frankincense and myrrh from the groves in Arabia and possibly Somaliland to ports and caravan collecting points. It is certain that some arrangements were made, owing to the fact that no single state controlled both centers of production and distribution for very long, if at all. This is also true of details of the negotiations for treaties with other tribes and states along the routes of transport, whose unfriendly actions, in the form of piracy on the seas or the robbery of caravans, could jeopardize this trade, and in turn seriously handicap, if not destroy, the economic basis of the South Arabian states. We know that overland caravans were permitted to pass through tribal and state territories by paying taxes en route about the beginning of the Christian Era and presumably earlier, but we do not know how these agreements were negotiated or the details of their terms. In spite of these lacunae in our data, there can be no doubt that the production and distribution of frankincense and myrrh was a big business in the South Arabian states, much as the production and distribution of petroleum products is a major industry in our time.

Success in the production and distribution of frankincense and myrrh, as in any comparable industry, was only possible in a highly organized society. Negotiations with other tribes and the maintenance of security presupposed a strong and relatively stable government; the production of incense and the development of trade routes, ports, and port facilities, which were sufficiently large to serve as major points of transshipment, required a sound economic and political structure. Thus the fact that the South Arabs were successful in the incense trade is excellent evidence of the high level of social, economic, and political organization achieved by the various states.

That the culture of South Arabia was highly developed is further supported by the material remains which have been brought to light by the few explorers of southern Arabia during the last 150 years, and by the small group of amateur and professional archaeologists who have excavated in this region during the past thirty years or so. The remains of efficient irrigation systems in most, and probably all, of the valleys north of the watershed of the east-west range of mountains paralleling the southern coast point to planned community effort. Bowen has successfully explained the principles of the irrigation system in Wadi Beihan, the center of the ancient kingdom of Qataban, and of the system in Wadi 'Amd, which was investigated by Elinor Gardner and Gertrude Caton Thompson in 1938.[52] Briefly, the system utilized the *seil* or flash-flood, which suddenly fills the wadies during the rains of the spring and autumn. In antiquity, the silt-laden water rushing down the sides of the mountains was caught by a large primary channel which ran along the base of the mountains. As the water flowed down this channel, it was diverted by stone-built sluices into secondary channels, and from the secondary channels it flowed through a network of tertiary channels to the fields, on which it deposited its load of silt. In other valleys large dams were constructed, such as the famous dam at Marib, for the purpose not of storing water but of diverting it into channels, which in turn distributed it over the fields. The construction and maintenance of the many irrigation installations in this region required community action, and effective community action at this level was only possible under strong government.

Although archaeological investigation of the area is still in its infancy, we know from several excavations that the South Arabian cities were equal in size and grandeur to those of the Fertile Crescent.[53] The mound of Timna', for example, has a surface area of approximately fifty-two acres, which is about four times as large as that of Megiddo. The larger cities were well planned and well built. Some of the buildings were constructed of blocks, the cutting and dressing of which are

[52] *ADSA*, pp. 43–88.
[53] Pending completion of the final publications, see F. P. Albright, *ADSA*, pp. 215–86; Wendell Phillips, *Qataban and Sheba* (1955); and G. W. Van Beek, *BA*, XV (1952), 2–18.

equal to the finest masonry in Egypt and Palestine in any period, and many structures were lavishly decorated with plaster and recessed panels of marble and limestone. Locally cast bronzes, including tools, utensils, and sculpture, attest the high level of technology and craftsmanship. A number of temples, the best known of which is Awwam (Maḥram Bilqis, the precincts of Sheba) at Marib, which rivals in magnificence the great temples of the north in Mesopotamia, Syro-Palestine, and Egypt, are evidence of a well-developed and highly organized cult. Taken together, these few examples indicate that the social, political, and economic organization of the ancient states of South Arabia was quite complex and advanced.

This means, of course, that we can no longer think of the Mineans, Sabeans, Qatabanians, and Hadhramis as nomadic tribes, drifting from oasis to oasis in the Arabian peninsula during the first millennium B.C. As early as the middle of the 10th century, Saba (biblical Sheba) was sufficiently well organized and powerful that its queen and a richly laden caravan could safely journey to Palestine, nearly 1500 miles to the north, and that a century or two later, or perhaps about the same time, it could establish colonies in Ethiopia. The archaeological evidence from Wadi Beiḥan proves that the South Arabs had already achieved a developed sedentary culture in this period and even a few centuries earlier, since the first of a series of towns at Hajar Bin Ḥumeid was built about 1000 B.C. on silt which had been deposited by an earlier irrigation system.[54] Although nothing is known of the cultures of Hadhramaut and of the region which later became the center of the kingdom of Ma'in in the first half of the first millennium B.C., we are probably justified in assuming that these territories also enjoyed comparably high cultures. It is therefore certain that if the ancient South Arabs were ever nomadic, the period of their nomadism goes back to about the middle of the 2nd millennium B.C., and possibly even earlier. Perhaps further excavation in southern Arabia will bring to light material that will enable us to trace the development of sedentary occupation and patterns of settlement in this region.

As yet we do not have sufficient data to write a reasonably complete political history of any one of the South Arabian states, and the farther back we go beyond about 500 B.C., the

[54] Bowen, *ADSA*, p. 67.

more obscure historical details become.[55] Annalistic and historical texts in South Arabic are few, and the states are seldom mentioned in the historical documents of the great nations of the north, owing to their peripheral location. Notwithstanding our lack of data at this time, it is reasonable to assume that frankincense and myrrh played an important role in shaping the course of the political history of South Arabia. The fact that the frankincense and myrrh forests were separated by several hundred miles of difficult terrain, and that there were a great number of sea and land routes, over which the gum-resins were transported, meant that it was extremely difficult—though not impossible—for any one state to control both the sources of production and the means of distribution. Thus Ma'in (centered in the Jauf, in northern Yemen), Saba (with its capital at Marib, and occupying much of central Yemen), Qataban (located in the Western Aden Protectorate, and sharing a common border with Saba), and Ausan (situated in the mountains between Qataban and Aden) were in a position to dominate the myrrh-producing region of Arabia and Somaliland, the ports in the southwest corner of Arabia, and the major overland route to the north and west. On the other hand, Hadhramaut (centered in the Eastern Aden Protectorate, with its capital at Shabwa) was favorably located to control the frankincense forests of Dhofar, the ports from Cana eastward, and the overland route to the Persian Gulf. In this situation, these states must have striven constantly with one another for control of the incense areas and the routes of distribution. It is therefore probable that frankincense and myrrh, with their promise of wealth and economic advantage, greatly affected the political history of South Arabia, and in a large part determined the rise and fall of the various South Arabian states.

This, then, is a brief and incomplete summary of the importance of frankincense and myrrh in antiquity. There is much that we do not know, and much of what we do know, we know only in part. While we cannot as yet restore the whole picture of the role of these substances in antiquity, enough has been assembled to show that they touched many areas of ancient life and in part shaped the destiny of ancient Arabia and its neighbors.

[55] See further, Van Beek, *The Bible and the Ancient Near East*, ed. G. E. Wright (1961), pp. 229–48; J. Ryckmans, *L'institution monarchique en Arabie méridionale avant l'Islam* (1951), pp. 134 ff.

9

THE ARAMEAN EMPIRE AND ITS RELATIONS WITH ISRAEL

BENJAMIN MAZAR

[*We are delighted to present this highly significant study by Professor Mazar; it first appeared in 1961 in the volume* The Kingdoms of Israel and Judah *published in Hebrew by the Israel Exploration Society. The translation has been made by Rabbi Ben-zion Gold of Cambridge, Massachusetts. Professor Mazar has agreed to let us remove some of the documentation of the original article, since it refers to materials in the Hebrew language; those who need these references will be able to use the original publication.*]

The Rise of Aram

Mutual relations between Aram and Israel in the course of many generations are vividly described in the Bible. These relations were not merely the result of political contact through prolonged periods of time, in war and peace, but in a great measure were also the product of related origins and language, and of common traditions from time immemorial. This fact is amply documented in biblical sources, primarily in ancient patriarchal traditions about Israelite and Aramean ancestors who roamed the extensive region between Naharaim and Canaan sustaining themselves mainly from small livestock breeding, and in the genealogical lists which emphasize consanguinity and common fate from patriarchal days down to division and settlement in separate and distant regions. An investigation of genealogies pertaining to Aram preserved in Genesis shows, first of all, that the genealogies are not of one piece and period; they reflect to some degree an historical development from which the wandering Aramean tribes emerged as an important factor in the political and economic life of the Near East. This development effected important changes in the relations between Aram and Israel and related ethnic groups.

The oldest genealogy is that of Nahor (Gen. 22:20–24), Abraham's brother. This genealogy affords us a glimpse of an ancient historical tradition about a cluster of nomadic and seminomadic tribes who had apparently reached the zenith of their strength in the 18th century B.C. The area of their expansion stretched from the political-religious center of Haran, where Nahor lived, to the valley of Lebanon (Tebah and Tahash) and to northern Transjordan (Maacah).[1] In this list Aram is the son of Kemuel,[2] one of Nahor's sons; that is, Aram, the eponym of the Arameans, a younger branch in the organization of the Nahor tribes, was the grandson of Nahor, just as Jacob, the eponym of the Israelites, was the grandson of Abraham, "the father of many nations."

Another tradition, prevalent in Israel, bestows a position of high importance on Laban,[3] the son of Bethuel and the father of Leah and Rachel. In the genealogy of Genesis 22, Bethuel appears as Nahor's younger son and brother of Kemuel the father of Aram (vs. 22), whereas in the cycle of stories about Jacob and Laban, Laban is described as an Aramean who lives in Aram Naharaim or Padan Aram,[4] that is, in Haran (Gen. 27:43 ff.) and in the neighboring town, Nahor (Gen. 24:10).[5] The Israelite folk tradition apparently ascribed to

[1] On several of the geographical conclusions here see *Zion*, XI (1946), 1 ff.; XXIII–XXIV (1958–59), 118 f.; *Eretz Israel*, III (1954), 18 ff. These references are all in Hebrew.

[2] Kemuel is not found in extra-biblical sources, but is an ancient west Semitic name mentioned in the Bible as the name of the leader of the tribe of Ephraim (Num. 34:24).

[3] On Laban as an epithet for the moon-god and his relation to Haran, the cultic center of the moon-god Sin, see J. Lewy, *HUCA*, XVIII (1944), 434, n. 39, and pp. 455 f. It is noteworthy that Laban appears as a component in west Semitic names and as a geographical name, for example in Mt. Lebanon.

[4] On Padan Aram (= "Field of Aram"), see R. T. O'Callaghan, *Aram Naharaim* (1948), *passim*.

[5] The town Nahor, which is in the vicinity of Haran, is known as an important city already from the Cappadocian tablets (19th cent. B.C.) and in particular from the Mari tablets (18th cent.). It is also mentioned in documents from the middle Assyrian empire (14th–12th cent.) see W. F. Albright, *BASOR*, No. 78 (April 1940), pp. 29 f. and *From the Stone Age to Christianity* (hereafter, *FSAC*; 3rd ed. Doubleday Anchor Books, 1957), pp.

Jacob's father-in-law Laban the position of eponym of the Aramean tribes, who spread from their center into the land of the "people of the East" (Bene Qedem) as far as eastern Transjordan, and there conspired against Israel (Gen. 29:1).[6] Surely the story in Genesis 31 deserves attention here. This story tells about the covenant between Laban the Aramean and Jacob at Mt. Gilead, where they fixed the boundaries of their territorial possessions; as a witness thereof, they built a stone heap, set up a pillar, and called on the names of their ancestral gods, the god of Nahor and the god of Abraham (vss. 44 ff.).

The latest genealogical list is given in the "Table of Nations" (Gen. 10:22–23), where Aram, Asshur, Arpachshad, and others are counted with Shem; Aram's firstborn is Uz, the eponym of the large tribe that appears in the older genealogy of Genesis 22:21 as the firstborn of Nahor. The Table of Nations evidently reflects the period of mighty expansion by the Arameans and their settlement throughout the countries of the Fertile Crescent, which began about the end of the 2nd millennium B.C. Therefore, in this author's time, Aram, the father of the Arameans, was considered to be the son of Shem and the grandson of Noah, and not, as in the older genealogy, the grandson of Nahor.

The cuneiform sources testify that the Arameans were but a relatively late ethnic group among the west Semitic nomadic tribes; they are designated Akhlamu in Assyrian documents from the 14th century B.C. Only towards the end of the 12th century are they mentioned explicitly in the combination *akhlami-'aramaya* as nomadic and seminomadic tribes. At that time they spread through the Syrian desert[7] and the border

236 f.; J. R. Kupper, *Les nomades en Mesopotamie* (1957), pp. 8 ff.

[6] In Genesis, Qedem is the name of the enormous area from the eastern borders of Palestine to the vicinity of Haran, including the Syrian desert (Gen. 25:6). Balak, king of Moab, called Balaam from Aram, from the mountains of Qedem (Num. 23:7), that is "from Pethor, which is near the River [Euphrates] in the land of Amu" (Num. 22:5; see Albright, *BASOR*, No. 118 [1950], p. 15), that is, Pethor of Aram Naharaim (Deut. 23:5). As early as the Middle Kingdom, the Egyptians used this name; this we know mainly from the Sinuhe story.

[7] Palmyra (Tadmor) certainly was an important center of wandering Arameans, mentioned in the inscriptions of Tiglath-pileser I

areas of Mesopotamia and Syria. The Assyrian king Tiglath-pileser I (1114–1076) fought them fiercely, mainly to weaken their pressure upon regions conquered by the Assyrians and to wrest from them the control over lines of communication to Syria and the Mediterranean shore.[8] However, in the course of time the Arameans not only gained enough strength to swallow up many west Semitic tribes, to gain control over vast regions in the Euphrates area and in northwest Mesopotamia (Aram Naharaim), and to break into southern and northern Syria, but also to impose their authority on Babylonia. This process initiated far-reaching changes in the ethnic and political scene of the Near East. Already in the second half of the 11th century the Arameans had attained great power in large areas on both sides of the Syrian desert and had even succeeded in settling and taking possession of them, in adjusting to living conditions in their adopted lands and in establishing ruling dynasties in the conquered countries. Having gained control over caravan routes, the lifelines of the Near East, leading from Mesopotamia to Anatolia and Syria (including the desert roads) and having gained a foothold in the large centers and important stations for merchant caravans and nomadic tribes with their enormous flocks, they secured for themselves a constantly growing position of importance in international trade. In their expansion southwest, the Arameans clashed with the Israelites who already in preceding generations had extended the borders of their settlement from its center in Palestine to the distant regions in northern Transjordan. This clash produced bloody and pro-

---

as Tadmar. On Palmyra, see Dhorme, *RB*, XXXIII (1924), 106. Here we find an explanation for the mention of Palmyra as one of the cities built by Solomon, that is Tadmor in the desert (I Kings 9:18, following the *qere;* II Chron. 8:4), because it served as the main station for the caravans from the banks of the Euphrates to Damascus. Palmyra was in existence already in the time of the Cappadocian and Mari tablets; cf. J. Lewy, *Symbolae Hrozný*, IV (1950), 369, n. 19.

[8] It appears that it is from this period that the term "Aramean"—meaning a nomad—was retained in the Israelite and Assyrian tradition: "A vagrant(?) Aramean was my father" of Deut. 26:5 and "the fugitive, wandering Aramean" in Sennacherib's Taylor Prism, Col. 5, ll. 22 f. For the origin of the name Aram and the Arameans, see in detail R. A. Bowman, *JNES*, VII (1948), 65 ff.; Kupper, *Les nomades en Mesopotamie* (1957), pp. 112 ff.; A. Dupont-Sommer, *VTS*, I (1953), 40 ff.; S. Moscati, *JSS*, I (1959), 303 ff.

tracted wars for domination and over boundary disputes; it also produced mutual influence and intermarriage in times of peace. Concerning this eventful period detailed information is preserved in the Bible.

Israel and Aram from the Bible

In the 11th century, the Arameans penetrated en masse the settled countries of the Fertile Crescent, countries with a rich material and spiritual culture, and an ancient royal tradition; gradually they widened their area of settlement and control. It ought to be noted that during this time the great empires suffered amazing decline. Already at the beginning of the 12th century, the Hittite empire was shattered into fragments. Its large districts in Syria were inherited mainly by comparatively small Hittite kingdoms such as Carchemish on the Euphrates and Hamath in middle Syria. The Egyptian empire fell from its mighty position during the second third of the 12th century and ceased to be a weighty political factor in Canaan in the 11th century. Babylon fell prey to its neighbors and to the Aramean tribes, while Assyria declined after Tiglath-pileser I and shrunk into narrow borders. At the same time, three west Semitic nations, the Arameans, the Israelites, and the Phoenicians, were rising. These nations attained a great measure of power at the beginning of the first millennium.

As far back as the end of the 11th and the beginning of the 10th century we encounter an important Aramean kingdom in southern Syria, Aram-zobah, ruled by the dynasty of Beth-rehob. This kingdom established a federation of Aramean and non-Aramean kingdoms in Syria and northern Transjordan, thus controlling the roads leading to Mesopotamia (see II Sam. 8:3, 10:16; I Chron. 19:10). The focal point of the Zobah kingdom, which included in its boundaries also Mt. Senir (Anti-Lebanon), was probably in the northern part of the Lebanon valley; that is where we ought to look for the three main cities of Hadadezer ben-Rehob, the king of Aram-zobah, namely Tebah, Cun, and Berothai, which were conquered by David in his decisive battle with Hadadezer.[9] The region of Damascus was one of the Aramean districts in the

[9] See A. Malamat, *BA*, XXI (1958), 82 ff.; M. F. Unger, *Israel and the Arameans of Damascus* (1957), pp. 42 ff. For the disputed explanation of Hamath-zobah, see Lewy, *HUCA*, XVIII (1944), 443 ff.

confederation under the leadership of Aram-zobah, whereas the kingdom of Maacah and the land of Tob in the northern part of eastern Transjordan were presumably not Aramean as yet, but along with the kingdom of Ammon, an ally of Hadadezer's, were among the satellites. It is my opinion that in his wars with David, and especially in his great military expedition to Transjordan which brought him as far as the valley of Madeba (I Chron. 19:7), Hadadezer sought to gain control over the "king's highway" (see Num. 20:17, 21:22), one of the essential caravan routes in international commerce, which led from Damascus along eastern Transjordan to Elath and Arabia. It is worthy of note that the kings of Aram-damascus[10] subsequently followed the same policies. However, these ambitions of Aram-zobah were frustrated by the young kingdom of Israel.

David, who firmly established the Israelite kingship founded by Saul, and around it consolidated the Israelite tribes in a permanent and lasting political-military and social regime, succeeded not only in conquering the countries bordering Israel but also in subjugating the confederacy of Aramean kings and their satellites up to the border of the Hittite kingdom of Hamath, the adversary of Aram-zobah. Hamath established intimate relations with David and apparently acknowledged his suzerainty (II Sam. 8:9–11, II Chron. 18:9–11) in southern Syria[11] and to the Euphrates in the northeast. Control over the wide spaces from the River of Egypt up to

[10] One ought to mention Hazael's military expedition to Gilead and the conquest thereof up to its southern border at the river Arnon (II Kings 10:33). It is not unlikely that he proceeded southward across Israel's border to Moab and Edom. This is borne out, indirectly, by a list of tribute-payers to Adad-nirari III after his expedition to Damascus in which Edom is mentioned (D. D. Luckenbill, *Ancient Records of Assyria and Babylonia* [hereafter *ARAB*] I [1926], § 739). That Rezin reached Elath is explicitly stated: "And he drove the man of Judah from Elath" (II Kings 16:6). After having conquered Damascus and incorporated it into their empire, the Assyrians continued the same policy. This accounts for the extreme importance of Damascus in Syria and its strong ties with Arabia under the Assyrians and in later periods. See the survey on trade with Arabia in Gus W. Van Beek (*BA*, XXIII [1960], 70 ff.) and W. F. Albright, *Eretz Israel*, V (1958), English section, pp. 7*–9*.

[11] See Mazar, *BIES*, XII (1946), 96 ff. (Hebrew), and Malamat, *BA*, XXI (1958), 101.

Lebo in the Lebanon valley (Lebo'-Hamath), and over the main caravan routes to Mesopotamia and Arabia, raised the young Israelite kingdom to the level of one of the important states in the Near East. David's treaty with Toi, king of Hamath, and with Hiram, king of Tyre (the Sidonian kingdom), as well as the friendly relations with the rulers of Arabia in the days of Solomon and the development of trade relations with them (I Kings 10:1–13, 15), added much to Israel's political stature and economic power. According to a source preserved in II Chronicles 8:3–6, Solomon even succeeded in strengthening and broadening his control over Syria.

The districts under Israelite rule in the days of David and Solomon can be divided into conquered countries in which David set up governors and states subject to Israel whose rulers were in the position of satellites. About Aram-damascus we are told: "Then David put governors in Aram of Damascus; and the Arameans became servants to David and brought tribute" (II Sam. 8:6), whereas the story about the defeat of the armies of Aram-zobah and its satellites under the leadership of Shobach, Hadadezer's general, concludes with the words: "And when all the kings who were servants of Hadadezer saw that they had been defeated by Israel they made peace with Israel and became subject to them" (II Sam. 10:19). Deserving particular attention is the fact that in dealing with the kingdom of Solomon, Israelite historiographers emphasize that "Solomon ruled over all the kingdoms from the river [Euphrates] to the land of the Philistines and to the border of Egypt" (I Kings 5:1; II Chron. 9:26).

It seems that late in Solomon's reign when his rule weakened and the state was disintegrating internally and externally, the position of several conquered nations and particularly that of the Arameans changed. In this period of weakness, when Egypt's power waxed under the leadership of Shishak, the founder of the 22nd dynasty, and a rebel movement was afoot in Israel, Aram-damascus took advantage of the opportunity, threw off the yoke of the house of David and built itself upon Israel's decline. The reigning dynasty in Damascus, founded by Hezion,[12] made Aram-

[12] Some time ago, in *Leshonenu*, XV (1944), 42 f., I expressed the opinion that Hezion ought to be taken as the proper name of

damascus the most important Aramean state in Syria. Hezion's grandson Ben-hadad I initiated aggressive policies against Israel. It is possible that he founded the coalition of Aramean states in Syria under the leadership of Aram-damascus which attained great power in the time of Ben-hadad II. This king of Damascus is mentioned in several interesting biblical historiographical sources. According to I Kings 15:18–20, and II Chronicles 16:2–4, Ben-hadad availed himself of the opportunity to interfere in a Judean-Israelite dispute and broke through the line of fortified cities in Naphtali, from Ijon and Dan to Chinneroth. This war most certainly took place in the 26th year of Asa's reign (886 B.C.; II Chron. 16:1 "the 36th year of the reign of Asa" is an error) which was Baasha's[13] last ruling year. It seems that one ought to attribute to the period of Israel's decline after Baasha's death the historical information interpolated in the genealogical list of Judah to the effect that Geshur and Aram took Havvothjair as well as Kenath and its settlements—"sixty towns" (I Chron. 2:23). Evidently Aram-damascus and its satellite Geshur wrested Bashan from Israel—to be exact, from the district of Ramoth-gilead founded by Solomon (I Kings 4:13)—and joined it to their states.[14] Undoubtedly the pressure of Aram-damascus on Israel did not slacken in the days of Omri. According to the testimony of I Kings 20:34, Ben-hadad II's father Ben-hadad I took cities from Ahab's father Omri and established bazaars in Samaria.[15] However, the assumption that Bir-hadad, the king of Aram,

---

the founder of the dynasty, and Rezon (cf. Prov. 14:28) as his royal title. Some scholars assume that, after Rezon, Hezion was the founder of a new dynasty in Damascus.

[13] See H. Tadmor in the Hebrew *Encyclopaedia Biblica*, I, cols. 469 f., against Albright, *BASOR*, No. 100 (Dec. 1945), p. 20. Albright accepts the Chronicler's date and proposes a new chronological method differing from the one accepted by most scholars, even identifying Ben-hadad of Baasha's time with Ben-hadad of Ahab's time.

[14] See *JBL*, LXXX (1961), 24. Recent trial-digging at Tell 'Ein-Gev on the eastern shore of the sea of Galilee gives evidence of the destruction of an Israelite city fortified by a casemate wall and its subsequent occupation by Arameans.

[15] I Kings 20:34; see G. Boström, *Proverbiastudien* (1935), pp. 91 ff., referring to the extra right given to the stronger ally to build business quarters for merchants in the large cities and especially in the capital of the state.

who dedicated to Melqart the stele found in the vicinity of Aleppo, is Ben-hadad I is problematic. This assumption was based on Albright's proposed restoration of a break in the text, but this restoration is not satisfactory. The inscription seems to refer to Ben-hadad II instead.[16]

Much information about Ben-hadad, Ahab's contemporary, apparently Ben-hadad II son of Ben-hadad I, has been preserved in the Bible. It stands to reason that this Ben-hadad is none other than Adad-idri (Hadadezer) king of Aram, known from the inscription of Shalmaneser III, king of Assyria. It is even likely that Ben-hadad (Bir-hadad) is not a personal name but a title common to kings of Aram-damascus; it means "son of the god Hadad" (Hadad-rimmon, the god of Damascus).[17] Under Ben-hadad II, wrangling between Israel and Aram-damascus turned into a protracted war which put Israel to a severe test. During the last years of Ahab's rule, when the kingdoms of Judah and Israel were enjoying some measure of political and economic prosperity, Ben-hadad II put Israel under extreme pressure in hopes of gaining control over the whole state. At that time Shalmaneser III (859–829 B.C.) was already terrorizing Syria with his military expeditions to the region of Sam'al (858) and his war with Betheden (857–855) which resulted in the conquest of this important Aramean kingdom in the Euphrates and Balikh regions and its annexation to Assyria. It is not unlikely that Ben-hadad's aggressive policy towards Israel and his attempt

[16] The inscription was published by Dunand in *Bulletin du Musée de Beyrouth*, III (1939), 65 ff. Albright wrote in *BASOR*, No. 87 (Oct. 1942), pp. 23 ff. See R. de Vaux in *Bulletin du Musée de Beyrouth*, V (1943), 9, n. 1; J. Starcky *apud* Dupont-Sommer, *Les inscriptions araméennes de Sfiré* (1958), p. 135, n. 1, and Mazar, *Leshonenu*, XIV (1946), 181.

[17] Albright, *BASOR*, No. 87 (Oct. 1942), p. 28, n. 16, is of the opinion that the kings of Damascus, like the kings of Israel, took on an additional name upon coronation. The parallel expression "the house of Hazael" and "the palaces of Ben-hadad" in Amos 1:4 in my opinion alludes to Hazael as the founder of a new Aramean dynasty which gives its name to the kingdom of Damascus in a later Assyrian document (the house of Hazael, like the house of Omri as the name of Israel; see D. J. Wiseman, *Iraq*, XIII [1951], 120–21); and alludes to Ben-hadad as the title of Aramean kings in general. Also worthy of note is the parallel in Jer. 49:27: "And I will kindle a fire in the wall of Damascus, and it shall devour the palaces of Ben-hadad."

to gain control over it were intended primarily to secure his rear by turning the strong and flourishing kingdom of Israel into one of Aram-damascus' satellites[18] before the Assyrian king began his decisive battle for the conquest of Syria.

From a highly interesting historiographical source in the book of Kings we draw enlightening information about the Aramean incursion into the center of Israel and about Ben-hadad's siege of Samaria, where Ahab had entrenched himself. This military expedition ended with defeat for Ben-hadad "and the thirty-two kings who helped him" (I Kings 20). The biblical story describes Ben-hadad as the head of the Aramean kingdoms: "Ben-hadad the king of Aram gathered all his army together; thirty-two kings were with him, and horses and chariots; and he went up and besieged Samaria and fought against it" (I Kings 20:1). There is no reason to assume that the number thirty-two was invented by the author. Among Ben-hadad's satellites were apparently not only the rulers of small states in southern Syria and Transjordan (as for instance Geshur and perhaps even Ammon), but also tribal princes from all over the Syrian desert as well as the Aramean kings of northern Syria. This view gains force if one accepts the proposition that Ben-hadad II set up the Melqart stele found near Aleppo.

The dramatic description of the Aramean defeat by "the servitors of the governors of the districts" who were besieged with Ahab in Samaria, contains several interesting details. According to this story, which is part of a cycle of prophetic tales of the period of the Omri dynasty, the attack surprised the Aramean kings while they were drinking in their booths: "And each killed his man and the Arameans fled" (I Kings 20:20). It is not unlikely that a bloody dispute broke out among Ben-hadad's followers, completely undermining the basis of the political alliance and precipitating its dissolution.

Another story in the above-mentioned cycle (I Kings 20:22 ff.) provides us with explicit information about basic changes in the structure of the kingdom of Aram-damascus. These changes resulted in the absorption of satellite kingdoms into Aram, following the defeat at the gates of Samaria. According to this source Ben-hadad with the advice of his min-

[18] It stands to reason that the Egyptians supported these policies of Ben-hadad. During the battle at Qarqar, the Egyptian army lined up with Ben-hadad.

isters instituted political and military reforms in order to renew with more vigor the war against Israel: "And do this: remove the kings, each from his post, and put governors (*pāhōt*) in their places: and muster an army like the army that you have lost, horse for horse and chariot for chariot" (I Kings 20:24–25). One is not to assume that these words are bereft of historical basis;[19] for not only does the Israelite historiographer report them in all innocence, but they also fit the events which occurred between the fall of Beth-eden in 855 (echoes of which were still reverberating strongly in a much later period: Amos 1:5), and the battle of Qarqar in the land of Hamath where a Syro-Palestinian coalition headed by the king of Damascus lined up against Shalmaneser III (853). The biblical story leads to the conclusion that the reform primarily accomplished the conversion of the loose coalition of Aramean kings under the leadership of Ben-hadad into the great united and sovereign Aramean empire, with Damascus as its capital. The satellite states were liquidated and turned into administrative districts headed by governors appointed by the king of Aram. Administrative reforms were followed by military reforms. Ben-hadad unified under his command the various armies of the satellite kings, and welded them into a mighty force. According to Shalmaneser III's testimony in his description of the battle of Qarqar, the army of Aram was composed of 1200 chariots, 1200 cavalry, and 20,000 infantry.

Results and Implications of Unification

The results of these military and political reforms, which for generations shaped the image of the Aramean regime, are clearly discernible in the subsequent period. It is important to note that biblical and Assyrian sources make no further mention of satellite kingdoms of Aram-damascus. In the battle of Qarqar, Hadadezer, who certainly is none other than Ben-hadad II, with a mighty army under his command heads the coalition of Syrians, Phoenicians, and Israelites. The list of the twelve allies mentions but one Aramean state—Damascus.

[19] See among others A. Alt in *Kleine Schriften*, III (1959), 223 f. Alt is not unaware of the fact that the author was acquainted with the life of the period, but he disqualifies the trustworthiness of the testimony concerning the establishment of a unified empire (*Einheitsstaat*).

Beginning with the 9th century, Aramean kingdoms in southern Syria as well as non-Aramean satellites of Damascus, simply disappear from the historical arena. What is more, names of Aramean administrative districts, unknown from previous sources, begin to receive mention. For example, the administrative unit Qarnaim does not appear in the sources before the 9th century; it is named after the new capital of the district which was located in Sheikh Sa'ad, not far from Ashtaroth, previously the capital of Bashan. Geshur, formerly an Aram-damascus satellite, was apparently absorbed into this district. It is not unlikely that Ben-hadad II not only founded the district Qarnaim (Assyrian *Qarnīni*) in Bashan but also the district capital Qarnaim, while Ashtaroth declined and became just one of the towns in the new district.[20] This, by the way, explains the name Ashtaroth-qarnaim in Genesis 14:5; Qarnaim here is used to locate the ancient city in the administrative division of later times. Presumably the foundation of the administrative districts of Hauran in east Bashan and Mansuate in the southern part of the Lebanon valley[21] dates back to this time. Hauran is first mentioned in an inscription of Shalmaneser III describing his campaign against Hazael, and Mansuate is known from Adad-nirari III's military expeditions. Both districts subsequently became Assyrian prefectures under Tiglath-pileser III. It is enlightening that when the Assyrian scribe depicts the conquest of Damascus by Tiglath-pileser III, he counts sixteen districts of the Aramean empire, despite the great changes in the political scene of Syria and after the truncation of the empire. The Assyrians obviously did not change the administrative division introduced by the Aramean kings which originated with Ben-hadad II as he centralized power in his own hands.

Ben-hadad's reform undoubtedly affected other areas of life. Damascus became the metropolis of a mighty empire, the seat of civil and military government, and it dominated major lines of communication, the life arteries of east Asia. It became *the* city of Aram,[22] first in national, religious, and

[20] Cf. F.-M. Abel, *Géographie de la Palestine*, II (1938), 413 f.
[21] Cf. M. Noth, *PJB*, XXXIII (1937), 42 f.
[22] It is likely that one of Damascus' names was *'ir 'arām* ("the city of Aram," to be compared with the designation of Jerusalem as "the city of Judah"). This is apparently the reading in Zech. 9:1 for *'yn 'dm* (Malamat, *IEJ*, I [1951], 82, n. 13). The variant reading *'yn/'yr* is frequent in the Bible (e.g., Josh. 19:29 and 41).

economic significance for the Arameans. It became "the famous city, the joyful city" (Jer. 49:25; cf. Ezek. 27:18), like Jerusalem, the city of Israel under David and Solomon. Not much is known about Damascus as a religious center. By inference from several sources, one can conclude that Hadad, worshiped in Damascus under the name Raman, (biblical Rimmon),[23] became prominent in the 9th century. His temple, the remains of which are now covered by the Omayyad Mosque, was famous for hundreds of years down to Roman times as that of "Jupiter Damascinus."[24] It is not at all unlikely that the use of the name Ben-hadad as the common title for Damascus kings originated in the cultic-religious relationship between the rulers of the locality and their god. We encounter the composite name of the god Hadad-rimmon in Zechariah 12:11, where reference is made to mourning for Hadad-rimmon in the valley of Megiddo. This certainly was a religious ceremony performed regularly in the sanctuary on the crossroads near Megiddo and derived from the cult practiced in the temple of Hadad-rimmon in Damascus,[25] the royal temple which is referred to as Beth-

[23] The epithet or divine title *Rāmān* known from Assyrian sources and personal names is undoubtedly of Aramaic origin. In the Bible, the vocalization has been adjusted to the Hebrew word *rimmon* (pomegranate), which is also the name of several places in Palestine. In my opinion, *rāmān* is an extended form of *rām* with the suffix *-ān;* at first it was a divine title like *Rām* or *'Elyōn* (in the Sefire treaty *'lyn*). It stands to reason that from time immemorial the deity of Damascus was Hadad, one of whose major cultic centers was in Aleppo; the Aramaic epithet *Rāmān* was attached to him after the Arameans took Damascus.

[24] For the place of Hadad's temple in Damascus, see Dussaud, *Syria*, III (1922), 219 ff.; worthy of note is the orthostat from Damascus' heyday as the capital of Aram, depicting a "cherub" in Syrian (Aramean) style, which was found out of place in one of the ancient walls on the grounds of the Omayyad Mosque (Djafar Abdel-Kadr, *Syria*, XXVI [1949], 191 ff.).

[25] According to Jerome in his commentary on Zechariah, Hadad-rimmon is the ancient name of Maximianopolis (Legio) that took the place of Megiddo; Jerome may have been influenced by a folk tradition which linked Hadad-rimmon with Gath-rimmon (Josh. 21:25). There was presumably a sanctuary of Hadad-rimmon on the crossroads of the Megiddo plain, not far from the Assyrian district capital of Megiddo. There may have been some connection between this sacred ground and the threshing floor (Adar, No. 28) and Yad Hammelek (No. 29) mentioned alongside Megiddo (No. 27) in the Shishak inscriptions. See *VTS*, IV (1957), 60, 62.

rimmon in Damascus (II Kings 5:18). It stands to reason that the priest Uriah patterned the altar in the temple of Jerusalem which he built by order of Ahaz, king of Judah (II Kings 16:10–13), after the altar in that temple. Furthermore, the story about Ahaz emphasizes the high esteem in which the Damascene cult was held in Jerusalem: "He sacrificed to the gods of Damascus which had defeated him and said: 'Because the gods of the kings of Aram helped them, I'll sacrifice to them that they may help me'" (II Chron. 28:23). The divine title Rimmon which we encounter as a compound of the theophoric name of King Tab-rimmon, son of Hezion, and which was common among the Arameans at least from the beginning of the 9th century B.C., became particularly important after Damascus became the metropolis of Aram.[26]

The formation of the Aramean empire raises the problem of the official language used in royal offices in Damascus, in the districts throughout the empire, in trade, and in contact with neighboring states. This problem is linked with the origin and dissemination of imperial Aramaic which, as is known, was current as the *lingua franca* in the Persian empire from India to Ethiopia, and to a lesser degree was the official language of diplomacy, administration, and business under the Assyrians and Babylonians in the 8th–6th centuries B.C. We shall merely point to the fact that already in the 8th century Aramaic had spread well beyond the boundaries of Aramaic-speaking countries. Assyrian documents from the 8th–7th centuries mention Aramean scribes in the service of the Assyrian government. Also the officers of Hezekiah, king of Judah, turn to Rabshakeh saying: "Pray speak to your servants in the Aramaic language, for we understand it; do not speak to us in the language of Judah within the hearing of the people who are on the wall" (II Kings 18:26).[27] Evidently

[26] On *Rāmān*, see H. Schlobies, *Mitteilungen der deutschen Orientgesellschaft*, I: 3 (1925), 9. In one list of gods (see O. Schröder, *Keilschrifttexte aus Assur verschiedenen Inhalts*, 64, V, 5), *Rāmān of the Mountain* is identified with *Amurru*, an identification which raises him to the status of the god of the west (Syria), apparently because of the unique position attained by the Aramean empire and its metropolis, Damascus. *Rāmān*, the epithet of Hadad, is clearly of Aramean origin, and Schlobies' view, that he is originally the ancient pre-Semitic god of Damascus, cannot be accepted.

[27] For official or imperial Aramaic, see the summaries of F. Rosenthal, *Die aramaistische Forschung* (1939), pp. 24 ff., A.

Aramaic emerged as the official language of the Aramean empire by the second half of the 8th century and spread beyond its borders, particularly in the Aramean countries, all the way to Ya'diya (Sam'al) in the north and to the Euphrates regions of the Khabur and Balikh (for example in Gozan and Hadatta) in the northeast. Of particular importance is the stele of Bir-hadad, king of Aram, dedicated to Melqart found near Aleppo. It testifies that Bir-hadad's empire reached to the northern districts of the Arameans; by the time of Ben-hadad II, imperial Aramaic was the official language of the unified Aramean state. Also worth mentioning is the ivory plaque from a bedboard found at Hadatta (Arslan-tash) on the Euphrates, with an Aramaic inscription dedicated "to our lord Hazael" (*lmr'n ḥz'l*),[28] in all probability none other than Hazael, king of Aram, who ruled in Damascus after the death of Bir-hadad II, founding a new dynasty, and appreciably extending Aramean dominion. Also, the stele of Zakir, king of Hamath and Lu'ash, inscribed in official Aramaic, is to be attributed to the end of the 9th century, or at the latest to the first quarter of the 8th.[29] In the 8th century, Aramaic was

---

Dupont-Sommer, *Les Araméens* (1949), pp. 82 ff. For the Aramean scribes in the Assyrian administration, see Lewy, *HUCA*, XXV (1954), 188 ff. H. Tadmor brought to my attention the fact that an Aramean epistle (*egirtu armītu*) is mentioned in a document from the second half of the 9th century, in a letter of an Assyrian clerk to Ashur-dan-apli, son of Shalmaneser, most likely Shalmaneser III. See A. T. Olmstead, *JAOS*, XLI (1921), 382.

[28] See F. Thureau-Dangin *et al.*, *Arslan-Tash* (1931), Pl. XLVII, p. 112a; R. D. Barnett, *A Catalogue of the Nimrud Ivories* (1957), pp. 126 f.

[29] Lewy, *Orientalia* XXI (1952), 418; M. Noth, *ZDPV*, LII (1929), 124 ff. The stele was found at Apis about forty miles southeast of Aleppo. In the Aramean inscription Zakir describes his victory over Bir-hadad, king of Aram, that is Ben-hadad III, son of Hazael, who had, with his allies, laid siege to Hadrach (Zech. 9:1), Zakir's fortress in the land of Lu'ash. Lu'ash, which was populated by Arameans, was properly part of the Aramean empire, but after Adad-nirari's defeat of Damascus it was attached to Hamath, which was at that time an Assyrian ally. As can be gathered from the inscription, Ben-hadad III did not succeed in retrieving Lu'ash for Aram, and it remained under the authority of Hamath, a fact attested by Zakir's title: King of Hamath and Lu'ash. It seems that due to the annexation of this important Aramean country, Aramaic became the official language of Hamath

already accepted throughout Syria and Aram Naharaim. What is more, these inscriptions, dating from the second half of the 9th century, are written in a distinct Aramean script, which differs from the Phoenician script of that period.

Theories concerning the origin and dissemination of official Aramaic, that it was first instituted in the offices of the small Aramean kingdoms in the Euphrates region, or in the offices of the Assyrian government, are not convincing. It is more reasonable to assume that it originated in the Aramean idiom of Damascus where it developed and crystallized into a written language. When Ben-hadad II founded the Aramean empire, Aramaic began to be used as the administrative language in all of its provinces. Then it became the official language of diplomacy and business, and thus spread beyond the borders of the Aramean empire. With the spread and consolidation of Assyrian rule over Transeuphrates, and in particular over the provinces of Aram, the Assyrian administration inherited official Aramaic as one of the languages of the empire. This assumption is supported by the fact that official Aramaic has none of the characteristics of east Aramaic dialects.

The preceding discussion does not exhaust all the implications of the establishment of a united Aramean empire in the middle of the 9th century. Particularly deserving of mention is the cultural influence of the Aramean empire upon the neighboring countries, including Israel and Judah. As is known, Palestine was for a long time under the political and cultural influence of the Phoenicians, from the time of David to the end of the Omri dynasty. Traces of this influence, viewed against the alliance between the courts of Israel and Tyre, are clearly discernible in Palestine's economic, religious, and cultic life, as well as in architecture, court practice, and upper class manners, and are strongly reflected in biblical literature and in material remains discovered all over the country. When the Israel-Tyre alliance ended with the bloody purge of Jehu, Phoenician influence on Israel and Judah waned. Political, economic, and military pressure from Damascus brought Israel under the influence of Aram, and mutual

---

alongside hieroglyphic Hittite; in the course of time it even banished Hittite. This is an illuminating example of the expansion of Aramaic as the official language of Syria. Some Aramaic inscriptions discovered at Hamath are from the 8th and 7th centuries.

relations affecting all areas of life developed between them. This explains the great changes in the culture of the country during the second half of the 9th century, particularly towards the end of that century, as evidenced by archaeological excavations on the one hand and biblical literature on the other. This would mean that along with the decline of Phoenician influence, the country came under the influence of the eclectic culture of the Aramean empire, which blended ancient Syrian with Phoenician and neo-Hittite elements, and also absorbed a constant stream of material and spiritual influence from Assyria.[30]

The biblical source discussed above (I Kings 20) implies that after the defeat of the Arameans at the gates of Samaria and the implementation of Ben-hadad's reforms, Aramean pressure on Israel did not cease, but was renewed with greater vigor. "In the spring Ben-hadad mustered the Arameans and went up to Aphek to fight against Israel" (I Kings 20:26). The war took place in the plain southwest of Aphek, the border fortress of the former kingdom of Geshur, which was subsequently annexed to the Aramean empire. The Aramean army was again defeated and negotiations between Ben-hadad, who was entrenched in Aphek, and Ahab, ended with an agreement and a peace treaty (I Kings 20:26–34). It appears that this treaty was made in anticipation of the great showdown at Qarqar (853 B.C.) where, according to the Assyrian source, a coalition of Syrian, Palestinian, and Phoenician kings, joined by Egyptian and Arabian auxiliary forces, lined up against the mighty army of Shalmaneser III;

[30] The clarification of this highly important problem in the cultural history of Syria and Palestine is awaiting a large scale and exhaustive study of Syrian architecture, sculpture, pottery, ivories (see Barnett, *The Nimrud Ivories* [1957], pp. 44 ff.), and seals in the 9th and 8th centuries and their influence on Palestine in that period. On the basis of indications from ceramic chronology, Y. Aharoni and R. Amiran (*IEJ*, VIII [1958], 171 ff.) proposed to divide the Iron Age in Palestine into three secondary periods; Iron I, 1200–1000, Iron II, 1000–840, Iron III, 840–587. However, G. E. Wright (*BASOR*, No. 154 [April 1959], pp. 13 ff.) argues convincingly that a date about 800 (or 815 more correctly) rather than 840 is the critical transition point from Iron II to Iron III. From the cultural-historical point of view, the transition between Iron II and III is expressive of the decline of Phoenician influence and the rise of its great neighbor, the Aramean empire, before Syria and Palestine became an integral part of the Assyrian empire.

in fact they succeeded in halting it. At the head of the coalition we find Hadadezer, who, as has been pointed out, is Benhadad II, and with him his two sworn adversaries, Ahab, king of Israel, and Arhilenu, king of Hamath, together with Gandabu the Arab and Baasha the Ammonite, and auxiliary forces from the coastal cities (north of Byblos) and from Egypt. Such a distribution testifies to large scale and thorough planning, the result of Ben-hadad's initiative.[31]

This coalition, however, was created only to meet a crisis. Aram's pressure on Israel was renewed and even intensified, and Ben-hadad succeeded in gaining control over Ramothgilead and its district, undoubtedly for the purpose of imposing his authority on Transjordan and perhaps also on the whole kingdom of Israel. When Shalmaneser III's expeditions against Damascus in the years 841 and 838 weakened the Aramean empire, the old alliance fell apart. Hazael was left to stand alone against the mighty Assyrian army, while Jehu, the founder of the new Israelite dynasty, chose a policy of submission to Assyria. But when Assyrian pressure on Syria subsequently ceased, the empire under Hazael revived its strength. It succeeded not only in regaining control over Aramean countries in northern Syria and the Euphrates region, but also in conquering Israelite territories in Transjordan (II Kings 10:32–33; Amos 1:3) and perhaps in dominating the "king's highway" throughout its length to the bay of Elath. In 815–814, Hazael launched his great expedition into western Palestine, proceeding along the coast to Gath on the border of Judah. Joash, king of Judah, was forced to capitulate to Aram and to pay Hazael a heavy tribute (II Kings 12:18–19); the Philistine kingdoms possibly became Aramean dependencies at this time also. That is the indirect implication of the inscriptions of Adad-nirari III, who obviously aimed at gaining control not only of Aram but also of its dependencies. Adad-nirari mentions the fact that Israel (Omri-land), Philistia, and Edom were among the states which paid him tribute after his expedition to Damascus.

Consolidated by an efficient imperial regime and dominating the major trade routes, the Aramean kingdom thus reached the summit of its greatness and extent as the strongest and most influential power in the western Fertile Crescent.

[31] See W. W. Hallo, *BA*, XXIII (1960), 39 f.; reprinted below, pp. 159–60.

The biblical historiographer is justified: "Hazael, king of Aram, oppressed Israel all the days of Jehoahaz" (II Kings 13:22; cf. II Kings 8:2), "and the anger of the Lord was kindled against Israel, and he gave them continually into the hands of Hazael. Then Jehoahaz besought the Lord . . . and the Lord gave Israel a savior, so that they escaped from the hand of the Arameans" (II Kings 13:3–5). This "savior" was none other than Adad-nirari III, king of Assyria, who by his military expeditions to Syria and Palestine succeeded in raising Assyria again to the level of a mighty military-political force and in weakening the power of the Aramean empire.[32]

In summary, we can say that, beginning with the middle of the 9th century, the kingdom of Israel was severely tried by the mighty Aramean empire which had attained the level of a decisive ethnic, political, and cultural force in Syria, this at a time when the Assyrian giant had already begun to overawe the Transeuphrates region and was destined ultimately to swallow up Aram and Israel. Aram-Israel relations from the end of Ahab's rule down to Jehoash's time become clear if we bear in mind that Ben-hadad II consolidated the Aramean kingdoms in Syria into one state, officially named Aram, with its capital at Damascus. This was a vast empire occupying a central position in the political and economic life of the Near East. Aram achieved this position by its successful consolidation of all the Aramean tribes, its excellent organization of civil and military administration, and the spread of Aramaic as the official language of business and diplomacy. Hazael, the founder of the new dynasty in Damascus, not only managed to preserve the stability of the empire, but also to broaden and strengthen it internally and externally. The turning point in the fate of the Aramean empire came during the reign of Ben-hadad III, his successor. The expeditions of Adad-nirari III, king of Assyria, brought about the dissolution of the empire; Damascus declined and was even conquered by Jeroboam II of Israel. Damascus continued its decline for a long time, but regained some of its strength under Rezin several years before it was finally conquered by Tiglath-pileser III and was converted into a district capital, a stronghold of Assyria in Transeuphrates.

[32] See B. Mazar (Maisler), *JPOS*, XXI (1948), 124 ff.

The Sefire Treaty and Aram in the Eighth Century

An impressive phenomenon in the history of the Arameans in Syria is their tradition of unity and distinctiveness, which remained unimpaired even in their period of decline, when they split up into small kingdoms and northern Syria replaced Damascus as the center of importance. This is strongly attested in a treaty between Mattiel, king of Arpad, and Birga'-yah, king of *Ktk*, dating from approximately the year 745. This treaty was written in Aramaic and preserved on three stelae which were discovered at Sefire about fifteen miles southeast of Aleppo.[33] This important document informs us that Mattiel, of the aggressive Bir-gush Aramean dynasty, succeeded in raising Arpad to a position of leadership in the Aramean empire in Syria; the ruler of *Ktk* most likely was a vassal of the mighty state of Ararat (Urartu) which from 749 ruled over southern Anatolia and began to compete with its enemy Assyria for dominion over northern Syria.[34] According to the treaty, Mattiel represented not only Arpad (stele AI, line 4), but also all of the Aramean states (i.e., "all Aram"). Furthermore, the term "all Aram" (*'rm klh*) includes two separate regions of Aram, i.e., "upper Aram" in northern Syria including Arpad, and "lower Aram" in southern Syria (*kl 'ly 'rm wthth*). However, the decisive passage in the treaty appears in stele BI, lines 9–10. It explicitly informs us that "all Aram"—with its division into upper and lower Aram—includes all Aramean territories in Syria, that is all of the provinces previously in the Aramean empire.

Regrettably, this important passage is defective, and its restoration is highly problematic. It undoubtedly contains a

---

[33] A. Dupont-Sommer, *Les inscriptions araméennes de Sfiré* (1958) for stelae I and II; *idem. Bulletin du Musée de Beyrouth*, XIII (1956), 23 ff. (stele III). Stele I was first published by P. Ronzevalle, *Mélanges de l'Université Saint-Joseph*, XV (1930–31) as the stele from Sujin in the vicinity of Sefire, and has hence been known as the contract from Sujin. See also Alt, *Kleine Schriften*, III (1959), 214 ff., and recently J. A. Fitzmyer, *JAOS*, LXXXI (1961), 178 ff.

[34] Dupont-Sommer at first proposed to identify *Ktk* with Kaška mentioned in Assyrian documents together with Tubal and Halah, later postulated that Birga'yah is but the title of Sardur II, king of Ararat.

detailed description of Aram's boundaries, patterned after parallel biblical descriptions which delineate the boundaries of Canaan and the land of Israel. Dupont-Sommer published the following transcription of the text with some restorations:

9. mn] rqw w'd y'd[y w]bz mn lbnn w'd yb-
10. [. . . . .]q w'r'rw wm..w.[wm]n bq't w'd ktk

The italicized letters are uncertain. On the basis of a careful analysis of the photograph published in Dupont-Sommer's book, and in the light of biblical, Akkadian, and Greek sources for the historical geography of Syria, I propose emendations in the reading and an attempt to restore the two lines as follows:

9. mn ']rqw w'd y'd[y] w.z mn lbnn w'd yb
10. [rdw wdms]q w'r'rw wm[nṣ]wt [m]n bq't w'd ktk

Again italics indicate uncertain letters. The translation that emerges, then, is "from Arqu to Yad[iya and .]z, from Lebanon to Iab[rud, and Damas]cus, and Aroer and Ma[ns]uate, from the valley (of Lebanon) to *Ktk*."

Should this restoration of the text prove correct, it would contain a delineation of the boundaries of upper and lower Aram, in sum, of "all Aram." "Upper Aram" is the region stretching from Arqu (which is Arqa in the vicinity of Zumur on the coast, known from Tiglath-pileser III's inscriptions and from the Arkite of Genesis 10:17, and now Tell 'Arqa not far from the basin of the Nahr el-Kabir[35]) up to Aramean Ya'diland, the capital of which was Sam'al (now Zenjirli), and thence to a place or province the name of which is not explicable in any satisfactory way.[36] As for "lower Aram," its boundaries are well defined in spite of the defects in the document. The north(western) border of "lower Aram" is marked

[35] This is the city 'Arqata mentioned in the Amarna letters and Egyptian documents. In the inscriptions of Tiglath-pileser III, the spelling is "Arqā" and in the Greek sources "Arke." The nominative suffix (cf. 'Ar'arw in l. 10) deserves special attention.

[36] While Dupont-Sommer's proposed restoration y'd[y] is acceptable, his supposition, proposed with some hesitation, that the second name is *bz* (that is, Buz, known from Jer. 25:23 ff.), is doubtful. More likely is *ḥzz*, mentioned in the Sefire inscription (face A, l. 35) as a "daughter-city" of Arpad and known as Hazāzu from Assyrian texts (Arabic 'Azāz, to the north of Arpad).

by Mt. Lebanon,[37] whereas the southern border is described by four names only one of which, Aroer, has been preserved intact. But the proximity between the name ending with "q" and Aroer brings to mind the passage in Isaiah 17:1–2: "An oracle concerning Damascus. Behold, Damascus will cease to be a city and will become a heap of ruins. The cities of Aroer are deserted; they will be for flocks, which will lie down, and none will make them afraid." Thus it is clear that Aroer is the fertile stretch of land in the vicinity of Damascus; hence, the word ending in "q" may be restored to read Dmśq (Damascus). This would suggest that the two other names refer to cities or districts east and west of Damascus. We may therefore restore the first name, the first two letters of which are "yb" to read ybrd, the city Iabrud, known from an Assyrian source and from the Hellenistic-Roman period.[38] Even now Iabrud is the name of a village located in an area rich in springs on the eastern slopes of Mt. Senir in the vicinity of Nebk on the main road from Damascus to Aleppo, which branches off east to Palmyra. As to the fourth name, of which only the letters m . . . wt are preserved, I propose to restore it to read m[nṣ]wt, referring to Mansuate of the Assyrian documents, located in the southern valley of Lebanon, west of the oasis of Damascus.[39] To outline the boundaries, the author uses names of countries and of political and administrative units.[40] It is noteworthy that Iabrud, Damascus,

---

[37] It is noteworthy that Lebanon serves, in many instances in the Bible, as the mark of the northern border of Canaan (Deut. 11:24, Josh. 1:4), analogous to the fixed border point Lebo Hamath which is north of the valley of Lebanon.

[38] Iabrudu is mentioned in Ashurbanipal's campaign to Arabia (together with Zobah, Ammon, Edom, etc.; see *Ancient Near Eastern Texts*, ed. J. Pritchard [2nd ed.; 1956], p. 298). Cf. also A. Rust, *Die Höhlenfunde von Jabrud* (1950), pp. 3 ff.

[39] Mansuate is mentioned in Assyrian sources beginning with Adad-nirari III who made military expeditions to Mansuate in order to gain control over this important district of the Aramean empire, which was blessed with rich iron deposits, down to the later Assyrian period, when it was a district in the Assyrian empire (see Noth, *PJB*, XXXIII [1937], 42 f.).

[40] This approach brings our document quite close to Ezek. 47–48. Ezekiel outlines the future borders of Israel on the basis of the ancient "land of Canaan in its full extent" (Num. 34), but inter-

Aroer, and Mansuate are, in all likelihood, counted among the sixteen districts of the Aramean state mentioned by Tiglath-pileser III in connection with the conquest of its metropolis. At the end of the passage, the author sums up the whole area of Aram by emphasizing its extreme borders; from the Biqa't to *Ktk*, that is from the valley of Lebanon[41] in the south to the border of Anatolia. We have thus exhausted the content of the passage in stele I which spells out, in detail, the boundaries of Aram, and which indicates that as late as the third quarter of the 8th century "all Aram" was an accepted ethnic-territorial concept in Syria, though two or three generations had already passed since the united Aramean empire had disintegrated.[42]

---

sperses his description with names of districts to bring the reader closer to the realities of his time. Cf. H. Tadmor, *IEJ*, XII (1962), 114 ff.

[41] In Josh. 11:17, 12:7, 13:5, in place of Mt. Hermon the sacred place Baal-gad in the valley of Lebanon marks the northern border of Canaan. Against that, our document refers not to a particular border point, but to the whole valley. The valley of Lebanon is now called *el-Biqa'*, "the valley."

[42] In the light of the Sefire inscriptions and a renewed investigation of the cuneiform sources (cf. H. Tadmor, *Scripta Hierosolymitana*, VIII [1961], 232 ff.), one gets the following impression of the unfolding events during the years 748–738.

748/7: the death of Jeroboam II; disorder in Israel; the end of Israel's rule over Damascus (the beginning of Rezin's reign?); the ascendancy of Arpad in upper Aram to the chief Aramean state in Syria.

746/5: Sardur II's expedition to Kumuhhi and its transformation into a satellite state; Carchemish a protectorate of Ararat; Tiglath-pileser III ascends the throne of Assyria; establishment of the Aramean states' league ("all Aram") headed by the king of Arpad.

745/4: Tiglath-pileser fights the Chaldeans in Babylon and Namri on the Medean border; the treaty between Mattiel, king of Arpad, and Birga'yah, king of *Ktk*.

743: Tiglath-pileser's war against Sardur II: defeat of the Ararat army and its Syrian allies in the vicinity of Arpad.

742/1: Tiglath-pileser's march on northern Syria; the siege of Arpad.

740: the fall of Arpad.

739: Tiglath-pileser's march on Ullaba on the border of Ararat; Azariah, king of Judah, at the head of the Syrian coalition.

738: Tiglath-pileser's march on Syria; disintegration of the al-

"All Aram" and "Upper and Lower Aram"

These territorial expressions, "all Aram" and "upper and lower Aram," coined in the days of the Aramean empire, were preserved, surprisingly enough, down to the Hellenistic period, despite political changes that occurred with the passage of time. It appears that already in the Persian period the Greeks were accustomed to use the name Syria in a double sense: a) for Transeuphrates as the general name for Syria, Phoenicia, and Palestine (including Philistia), a name established apparently in the time of Sargon and current in the Persian period as the name of the fifth satrapy; b) for Aram, that is, the territories of the Arameans in Syria, without Phoenicia and Palestine. This is the reason why Aram is generally translated in the Septuagint as Syria. The composite term *Koile Syria* appears already in the first half of the 4th century as the name of Syria proper in its restricted meaning, whereas the coastal area is called *Phoinike*, Phoenicia. This is the case in the *Periplus* of Pseudo-Scylax, which gives a description of "Syria and Phoenicia." This division reflects the ethnic-territorial difference between the population of interior and northern Syria and the Phoenicians on the seashore.[43]

The etymology of the word *Koile* is interesting; E. Schwarz had already postulated that it is a Grecized form of the Hebrew word *kol*.[44] A. Shalit[45] added further evidence and proved convincingly that *Koile Syria* is identical in meaning with the normal expression in Greek for "all Syria." However, the Greeks probably formed the name *Koile Syria* on the basis of the ancient term *arām kolā*, "all Aram," current among Aramaic speaking people, the antiquity of which is attested by the Sefire inscription discussed above. Furthermore, the division of Syria into "upper Syria" stretching from the Cilician border to the Orontes river and "lower Syria" south of

---

liance and the defeat of Judah; conquest of Calneh; organization of Assyrian prefectures in northern Syria and on the seacoast; tribute paid by Menahem, king of Samaria, and Rezin, king of Damascus, to Tiglath-pileser; Damascus' recovery and rise to the level of political center of lower Aram.

[43] Cf. K. Galling, *ZDPV*, LXI (1938), 69 ff.; E. Bickerman, *RB*, LIV (1947), 257.

[44] E. Schwarz, *Philologus*, LXXXVI (1931), 309.

[45] A. Shalit, *Scripta Hierosolymitana*, I (1954), 64 ff.

the Orontes, was still prevalent in the Hellenistic period. It is amply clear that this geographical division reflects a tradition prevalent in Aramaic Syria and based on the old division found in the Sefire inscription.

After the conquest of southern Syria by Ptolemy I (Lagos), *Koile Syria* began to be used to designate the area of the Ptolemaic conquest; such use of this name was consistent with Lagos' claim to the right of ruling all of Syria. The name was thereby given a new meaning, from the point of view of the Ptolemaic rulers, and it was used in this new sense by Diodorus, who actually uses *Koile Syria* for "lower Syria" in distinction from "upper Syria" which was within the area of Seleucid rule.

The entire discussion of these names demonstrates that the concepts "all Aram" and "upper and lower Aram" were used in Syria from the time of the Aramean empire through the Assyrian, Babylonian, and Persian periods, down to the time of the Diadochi, except that in Greek "Syria" was substituted for "Aram."

10

FROM QARQAR TO CARCHEMISH: ASSYRIA AND ISRAEL IN THE LIGHT OF NEW DISCOVERIES

WILLIAM W. HALLO

The history of the divided monarchy has been written many times, most recently in 1959.[1] The neo-Assyrian empire has had its chroniclers too.[2] But not till now has the time seemed so propitious for correlating the annals of both areas. The reasons for this optimism are to be found on both sides of the fence. The gaps in Assyrian historiography are being closed one by one through textual discoveries made both in the field and in the museums.[3] The last three decades have witnessed the systematic excavation, publication or even partial restoration of such sites as Dur-sharrukin (Khorsabad) and Shibaniba (Tell Billa) by American expeditions; Kalah/Kalhu (Nimrud), Sultan Tepe and Carchemish by the British; Ashur and Gozan/Guzana (Tell Halaf) by the Germans; Bit Adini (Til Barsip) and Hadattu (Arslan-tash) by the French; Kakzu by the Italians, Nineveh and the plains east and west of Nineveh by the Iraqis. All these discoveries have illuminated new periods or areas in the neo-Assyrian record.

The principal results of the Dur-sharrukin excavations were published by Gordon Loud and others, *Khorsabad* (2 vols.; = *Oriental Institute Publications* 38 and 40, 1936–38).[4] For

[1] John Bright, *A History of Israel* (1959), chaps. VI–VIII.

[2] The most recent treatment is by Hartmut Schmökel, *Geschichte des alten Vorderasien* (1957), chap. XIII. For a brief synthesis in English, cf. Svend A. Pallis, *The Antiquity of Iraq* (1956), chap. XI.

[3] For an important "museum find," see below, n. 102.

[4] The famous Assyrian king list from Khorsabad was published by I. J. Gelb, *JNES*, XIII (1954), 209–30 and Pls. XIV–XVII. For the most recent Iraqi soundings at Khorsabad, cf. F. Safar,

Shibaniba, see J. J. Finkelstein, "Cuneiform Texts from Tell Billa," *JCS*, VII (1953), 111–76. For Kalah, see M. E. L. Mallowan, "The Excavations at Nimrud (Kalhu)," *Iraq*, XII (1950), and succeeding volumes, and the convenient summary by Mallowan in his *Twenty-five Years of Mesopotamian Discovery* (1956), pp. 45–78. For Sultan Tepe, see O. R. Gurney, and W. G. Lambert, "The Sultantepe Tablets," *An. St.* II (1952) and succeeding volumes. For Carchemish, see C. L. Woolley and others, *Carchemish* (3 vols.; 1914–52). For Ashur, see especially C. Preusser and others, *Wissenschaftliche Veröffentlichungen der Deutschen Orientgesellschaft*, LXIV ff. (1954 ff.) and the texts published by E. Weidner and others *passim* in *AfO*. For Guzana, see M. von Oppenheim, *Tell Halaf*, trans. G. Wheeler, (1933); *idem et al.*, *Tell Halaf*, (4 vols.; 1943–62); J. Friedrich and others, *Die Inschriften vom Tell Halaf* (= *AfO Supplement* VI, 1940). For Bit Adini see F. Thureau-Dangin and M. Dunand, *Til-Barsib* (1936). For Kakzu, see G. Furlani, *Rivista degli Studi Orientali*, XV (1935), 119–42. For the area between Asshur and Erbil see M. El-Amin and M. E. L. Mallowan, "Soundings in the Makhmur Plain," *Sumer*, V (1949), 145–53 and VI (1950), 55–68 and Fuad Safar, "Sennacherib's project for supplying Erbil with water," *Sumer*, III (1947), 23–25 and *ibid.* II (1946), 50–52. For the Sinjar area see Seton Lloyd, "Iraq Government Soundings at Sinjar," *Iraq*, VII (1940), 13–21.

On the Palestinian side, the spade of the archaeologist has not been idle either. Its progress has been closely followed in the pages of this journal, and need not be gone into here. For the purpose of synchronizing Assyrian and Israelite history, the crucial advance here is rather the new solution of the chronology of the divided kingdom by Edwin R. Thiele. This solution, based ultimately on the comparison of biblical and Assyrian sources, manages to account for all the chronological data in Kings and Chronicles without emendation. It thus bids fair to escape the stigma of subjectivity which has attached to every previous reconstruction of Israelite chronology in modern scholarship. In what follows, it is made the basis of Israelite chronology for the period under discussion.

This procedure should require little defense. It is obvious

Sumer, XIII (1957), 219–21 and Pls. I–IV (facing p. 196 of the Arabic section).

that Israelite history, including especially that of the divided monarchy, cannot permanently be based on a "personalized" approach to chronology in which each historian constructs his own chronological hypothesis, or, what amounts to the same thing, takes over another's "with modifications."[5] Chronology is, after all, the backbone of history, and a chronological system like Thiele's, as carefully worked out as it is generally admitted to be, deserves to be tested, "without modifications," against an actual attempt to write a history on its basis, incorporating also, and in particular, data not available when it was first constructed. Whether the present essay supports the feasibility of this attempt and thus of Thiele's system must be left to the reader to decide.

Thiele's theories, first presented in 1944,[6] were developed in full in *The Mysterious Numbers of the Hebrew Kings* (1951) and defended, adjusted, and elaborated in various articles since then.[7] Some of the biblical figures are, of course, irreconcilable. But they are based on ancient errors or distortions, and Thiele is able to account plausibly for each of them without resort to the assumption of scribal errors in the transmission of the figures. For once such scribal errors are admitted, scholarly unanimity with respect to the proper emendation becomes almost impossible to achieve.

In attempting to present the present status of studies covering two-and-a-half crucial centuries of Assyrian and Israelite history within the pages of one issue of the *Biblical Archaeologist*, certain limitations that hardly require apologies impose themselves. Palestinian archaeology, as noted above, must be left to others. Babylonian, Anatolian, and Egyptian data, even where clarified by recent discoveries, cannot be adduced where they depend on, rather than provide for, the Assyro-Israelite synchronisms. Nor is it deemed possible to cite the earliest authority for each finding. The reader's familiarity with or access to such earlier works as those of A. T. Olmstead (notably his *History of Assyria*) and those cited by D. D. Luckenbill in his *Ancient Records of Assyria and Babylonia (ARAB)* has been taken for granted. Numerous bibliographical references may also be found in the notes and

---

[5] For the latest proposals along this line, cf. C. Schedl, *VT*, XII (1962), 88–119.

[6] *JNES*, III (1944), 137–86.

[7] E.g., *VT*, IV (1954), 185–95; *BASOR*, No. 143 (Oct. 1956), pp. 22–27; W. *Irwin Anniversary Volume* (1956), pp. 39–52.

comments to the inscriptions translated by A. L. Oppenheim, W. F. Albright, and F. Rosenthal in J. B. Pritchard's *Ancient Near Eastern Texts relating to the Old Testament* (1950; 2nd ed., 1955; *ANET* and *ANET*[2]). The present author has, therefore, attempted to supplement these sources from the most recent periodical literature, particularly in English. His task is facilitated by the constantly increasing proportion of original research being published in that language. Although earlier works[8] remain standard for the period, the new discoveries have contributed many improvements, both major and minor, that help to justify emphasis on the more recent literature.

What follows, then, is a synthesis of neo-Assyrian history as reflected in its impact on Israel. Often enough, ancient history must be read out of the records of one side alone, and few indeed are the periods documented, through the accidents of preservation or discovery, from two or more sides. Such are the reign of Hammurabi, the Amarna age, and the time of the Achaemenids. It is therefore gratifying to find the impact of the Assyrian expansion upon Israel, the changing fortunes in that unequal but protracted struggle, so richly documented on both sides.

Assyrian history, especially her "foreign policy," was dominated by the personalities of her monarchs or, in times of royal weakness, of her high officials, during the period under discussion. It is therefore convenient to divide it accordingly. An initial phase of Assyrian ascendancy, associated with Shalmaneser III, lasted for three decades, to be followed by forty years of consolidation under his son and grandson, and forty more of retreat when, with three weak brothers succeeding each other on the throne, effective power was vested in the military commander. The Assyrian resurgence under Tiglathpileser III, Shalmaneser V, and Sargon II occupied the next four decades; it set the stage for the phase of Assyrian hegemony which ended halfway through Ashurbanipal's reign. The last forty years of Assyrian history were marked by a persistent decline that occasional recoveries could not check. They conclude the present survey.

[8] Note especially E. Forrer, *Die Provinzeinteilung des assyrischen Reiches* (1921); J. Lewy, *Die Chronologie der Könige von Israel und Juda* (1927); A. Ungnad, article "Eponymen" in *Reallexikon der Assyriologie*, II (1938), 412–57. On the last, cf. the important review article by E. F. Weidner, *AfO*, XIII (1939–41), 308–18.

I. The Assyrian Resurgence (859–829)

The Assyrian year, like the Babylonian, began on the first day of Nisanu, a date which fell at varying points in March or April as restated in terms of the Julian calendar.[9] Thus the accession of Shalmaneser III actually took place sometime between March/April 859 and March/April 858, and the last year prior to the outbreak of the rebellion which resulted in his death ended in March/April 828. It would therefore be more accurate to render these dates as 859/8 and 829/8 respectively. For convenience, however, and in keeping with the literature, all Assyrian dates are rendered by single Julian figures.

When Shalmaneser III succeeded his father in 859 B.C., he inherited a kingdom on the ascendant. His ruthless if artistic predecessor had been, in the judgment of Olmstead, a master of military tactics. If he was not equally accomplished in military strategy or in diplomacy, the new king supplied these wants. Where Ashurnasirpal's object had been little more than plunder, Shalmaneser's expeditions bore the earmarks of a grand design. He measured his capacities, annexed those areas which he could, imposed regular annual tribute on those still strong enough to maintain, as loyal vassals, a measure of autonomy, and sought trade relations with yet others, too powerful or too distant to be reduced to vassalage. The repeated, hammer-like blows of Shalmaneser's armies were directed with an almost single-minded dedication and persistence against Assyria's western neighbors, and brought about the first direct contact between Assyria and Israel.

In Israel, the year 859 marked the 16th of King Ahab, son of Omri.[10] He too inherited an expanding kingdom, newly

[9] See R. A. Parker and W. H. Dubberstein, *Babylonian Chronology, 626 B.C.–A.D. 75* (= *Brown University Studies* XIX, [1956]; = 3rd ed. of The University of Chicago Oriental Institute's *Studies in Ancient Oriental Civilization* No. 24) chap. i: "The Babylonian Calendar"; and J. Lewy, *Archiv Orientální*, XI (1939), 35–46.

[10] The dates of the kings of Israel and Judah are based on Thiele's studies. Israelite years began in Nisan, as in Assyria, and Judahite years in Tishri. Thus they, too, represent parts of two Julian years each. But in many cases the biblical synchronisms between these two systems of dating enable us to date events to a six

entrenched at Samaria, which sought by trade, conquest and alliance to secure its place in the developing constellation of 9th century powers. Moab acknowledged Ahab's sovereignty over Gilead/Gad (Mesha Stone, ll. 10 ff.)[11] "and sent him tribute (II Kings 3:4); Sidon's alliance and trade were no doubt won together with the hand of Jezebel, the daughter of its king (I Kings 16:31); Jehoshaphat of Judah, Ahab's contemporary, made peace with him (I Kings 22:45) and this alliance too was cemented by marriage (II Chron. 18:1). These successes no doubt were registered in the time of Ashurnasirpal who, though he reached the Mediterranean and claimed receipt of tribute from as far south as Tyre,[12] apparently left Israel undisturbed in the enjoyment of successful diplomacy and domestic prosperity.

The prosperity of the time is exemplified above all by the luxuriant use of ivory, as attested both in the Bible and in Palestinian excavations.[13] The magnificent ivories found at Kalah include numerous pieces from the 9th century and throw an entirely new light on the history of this Phoenician medium.[14] Ahab's house of ivory (I Kings 22:39) in particular, now finds a parallel and explanation in the "great ivory screen which once overlay the mud brick of the north wall" in one of the rooms of the Assyrian building (the AB palace) at Kalah.[15]

The accession of Shalmaneser changed this situation. From now on, an annual campaign by the king or his commander-in-chief became a commonplace, so much so that it began to serve as an auxiliary system of dating in Assyria, producing

---

month period, i.e., to the spring and summer of a single Julian year or to the fall and winter of two successive Julian years. The table by Thiele, *Mysterious Numbers*, facing pp. 74 f. may be consulted for this more precise placement of the dates of Israel and Judah.

[11] W. F. Albright, *ANET*, p. 320.

[12] A. L. Oppenheim, *ANET*, p. 276.

[13] For Palestinian ivories of the 9th century, see esp. J. W. and G. M. Crowfoot, *Early Ivories from Samaria* (1938).

[14] Mallowan, *Iraq*, XIII (1951), 1–20; XIV (1952), 8; and *passim* in succeeding volumes. For additional illustrations of the Nimrud ivories, some in color, see *ILN*, CCXXI (1952), 256; CCXXIII (1953), 199 f.; CCXXVIII (1956), 130 f.; CCXXXI (1957), 869–73, 934–37, 968 f.

[15] Mallowan, *Iraq*, XX (1958), 104. For the date of the paneling, cf. R. D. Barnett, *Catalogue of the Nimrud Ivories* (1957), pp. 59, 124.

the so-called "Eponym Chronicle" which provides us with a record of the major military (or, occasionally, religious or civil) events of each year from the middle of the reign of Shalmaneser to the first years of Sennacherib.[16] The king's inscriptions supply the details.

The Assyrian royal inscriptions were collected in translation by D. D. Luckenbill, *Ancient Records of Assyria and Babylonia* I–II (1926–27) = "Historical Records of Assyria" (*ARAB* I–II). Most of the portions bearing on the Old Testament have been newly translated by A. L. Oppenheim, *ANET*, pp. 274–301. For a new compilation and German translation of some of Shalmaneser's inscriptions, see E. Michel, *Die Welt des Orients*, I (1947), and succeeding volumes. We now have at least five "editions" of Shalmaneser's annals, prepared respectively in 853, 850 (or 848), 842, 839 and 828,[17] in addition to some shorter inscriptions.[18]

The Assyrian inscriptions inform us of the Battle of Lutibu near Zinjirli (Sam'al) where, in 858, Shalmaneser met the combined forces of Sam'al, Hattina, Carchemish, and Adini.[19] This north Syrian confederacy succeeded in disputing Shalmaneser's march toward Cilicia and his control of the strategic routes to Asia Minor. Nothing daunted, Shalmaneser therefore concentrated his next effort against the nearest of the allies, Bit Adini. This area, lying between the river Balikh and the westernmost part of the Euphrates, was ruled by the Arameo-Hittite Ahuni from his fortress at Til Barsip, modern

[16] For bibliography, description and samples of the Eponym Chronicle, also called Eponym C(anon) b, see *ANET*, p. 274; but note that the king generally gave his name to his 2nd year, not his first, and correct Adad-nirari II to Adad-nirari III in l. 15. For an English translation of the entire text, see A. T. Olmstead, *JAOS*, XXXIV (1915), 344–68; reproduced *ARAB* II, § 1198, and, with some corrections, in Thiele, *Mysterious Numbers*, Appendix F. For additional corrections and restorations, see especially Tadmor, *JCS*, XII (1958), 85, 94–97.

[17] 853: *ARAB* I, §§ 594–611; 850: *ARAB* I, §§ 612–25; 842: G. C. Cameron, *Sumer*, VI (1950), 6–26, and *ARAB* I, §§ 626–63; 839: F. Safar, *Sumer*, VII (1951), 3–21; 828: *ARAB* I, §§ 553–93.

[18] *ARAB* I, §§ 664–712; D. J. Wiseman, *Iraq*, XIV (1952), 67, ND 1127 f.; J. Laessoe, *Iraq*, XXI (1959), 147–57; O. R. Gurney and J. J. Finkelstein, *The Sultantepe Tablets*, I (1957), No. 43, now edited by W. G. Lambert, *An. St.*, XI (1961), 143–58; J. V. Kinnier Wilson, *Iraq*, XXIV (1962), 90–115 and Pls. XXX–XXXV.

[19] *ANET*, p. 277.

Tell el-Ahmar, on the east bank of the Euphrates.[20] In three successive campaigns (857–855), Shalmaneser chased Ahuni from his capital, renamed it after himself, annexed Bit Adini to Assyria, and captured Ahuni. A hundred years later, Amos was to recall the downfall of perhaps this very "scepter wielder from Beth-eden,"[21] and its fate still served Assyria as an intimidating example another fifty years later.[22] In 854, the Assyrian success was consolidated with an expedition to Mt. Kashiari (= Tur Abdin) at the headwaters of the Khabur river.

The lesson of Shalmaneser's tenacity was not lost on the kingdoms of Syria and Palestine. Ben-hadad II of Aram-damascus[23] had for two years been attacking Ahab deep in his own kingdom (I Kings 20:1–30), but in the face of the common threat, Ahab made peace with him (I Kings 20:31–34). Together with Cilicians, Egyptians, Arabians, Ammonites and various Phoenician contingents, both joined the grand alliance under Jarhuleni of Hamath which met Shalmaneser at Qarqar on the Orontes river in 853.[24] Thus a new south Syrian con-

[20] For the hieroglyphic Hittite stele of the son or grandson of Ahunas (=Ahuni) from Bit Adini, see Barnett, *Carchemish*, III (1952), 263, and Albright, *An. St.*, VI (1956), 76 f. For other monuments from the same site, cf. Thureau-Dangin and Dunand, *Til-Barsib* (1936), pp. 135–40; *Syria*, X (1929), Pls. XXVIII–XXXIII.

[21] Amos 1:5; but cf. below, n. 71.

[22] II Kings 19:12 = Isa. 37:12.

[23] The Bible knows of at least three kings of Aram called Benhadad. The first was an ally of Asa about 896 (I Kings 15:18–20; cf. Thiele, *Mysterious Numbers*, p. 59). The second, his son (cf. I Kings 20:34 with 15:20) must be identical (in spite of the reservations of A. Jepsen, *AfO*, XVI [1952–53], 316) with the Adadidri (Hadadezer) of Damascus who, according to the Assyrian inscriptions, opposed Shalmaneser in 853, 849, 848 and 845. The third was a son of the Hazael who, having murdered Ben-hadad II (II Kings 8:15), opposed Shalmaneser in 841. One of these three has left us an inscription, the so-called Melqart stele, in which he calls himself Bar-hadad of Aram (F. Rosenthal, *ANET*², p. 501 and literature cited there); this stele is usually attributed to Ben-hadad I, but the patronymic is destroyed and the attribution is tentative. [But see W. F. Albright in *BASOR*, No. 87 (1942), pp. 27 f., and Bright, *A History of Israel*, pp. 215–21, esp. 221. Ed.]

[24] *ANET*, pp. 278 f. For the identification of Shian, one of the Phoenician allies, with biblical *Sin (Gen. 10:17 = I Chron. 1:15) cf. M. El-Amin, *Sumer*, IX (1953), 45.

federacy was called into being, comparable to the north Syrian confederacy that had engaged Shalmaneser in the first five years of his reign.

The battle of Qarqar, and all other Assyrian dates before Shalmaneser IV (782) are raised one year by some scholars. The basis for the uncertainty lies in the Eponym Canon, some recensions of which show four names, instead of three, in the interval between the 24th and the last (28th) year of Adad-nirari III. Even those lists which have, in keeping with the Assyrian king list, only three eponyms in this interval,[25] diverge as to the names and their order. It seems fairly certain that four names originally occupied the interval, but that, perhaps due to the death of one eponym while in office, they covered only three years, and that the different recensions found different solutions to overcome this discrepancy. We have therefore followed Thiele and others in accepting a 28-year reign for Adad-nirari III and 853 as the date of Qarqar.

Shalmaneser claimed an overwhelming victory at Qarqar, but there are several indications that the confederacy actually carried the day. First of these is the total silence in which the Bible passes over the great event. Had Ahab and his allies really suffered the massive defeat which the Assyrian annalists inflicted on them, an account of the battle would certainly have served the didactic purposes of the canonical book of Kings.[26] Equally telling is the fact that Shalmaneser's next three campaigns (852–850) were conducted considerably closer to home, while Damascus and Israel, two of the principal partners in the coalition, indulged in the luxury of renewing their old conflict. It was, apparently, immediately after the engagement at Qarqar that Ahab broke with his late ally by assaulting Ramoth-gilead (I Kings 22). Jehoshaphat of Judah accompanied Ahab and, if we may accept Thiele's hypothesis,[27] he appointed Jehoram his coregent just before his departure. The precaution, if such it was, was not

[25] Note especially the newly found eponym lists from Sultantepe: O. R. Gurney, *An. St.*, III (1953), 15–21 = Gurney and Finkelstein, *The Sultantepe Tablets*, I (1957), Nos. 46 f.

[26] Cf. C. F. Whitley, *VT*, II (1952), 137–52, esp. 150.

[27] *W. Irwin Anniversary Volume* (1956), pp. 41–3; cf. *Mysterious Numbers*, pp. 62 f., n. 6.

excessive, for though Jehoshaphat survived the expedition,[28] Ahab did not, and his successor Ahaziah was displaced, before a year had elapsed, by another son of Ahab, a namesake of the Judahite coregent. Much of Elisha's ministry must have fallen during the reign of this Israelite Joram, and it is thus in his reign that we may place the siege of Samaria by Benhadad II of Damascus (II Kings 6:24 ff.). Whether this was in reprisal for Ahab's breach of the alliance or not, it produced conditions of cannibalism in the besieged city that can now be paralleled from Mesopotamia in the closing years of the Assyrian empire.[29]

Perhaps the most important clue to the effectiveness of the south Syrian coalition at Qarqar in 853 is the fact that it opposed Shalmaneser again in 849, 848, 845 and 841.[30] It was only after the last of these encounters that Shalmaneser could truthfully claim the submission of the western states, for whom 841 was in many ways a critical year.[31] The biblical record is again silent regarding the Assyrian's role; but it reflects the unsettled conditions of the time in its account of the accession of Hazael in Damascus, Jehu in Israel and Athaliah in Judah (II Kings 8:7-15, 25-29; 9:1-28). The result of the Assyrian success and the upheavals in Palestine was the extinction of the house of Omri in Israel and its survival in Judah in the person of Athaliah. Athaliah was a daughter of Ahab and Jezebel,[32] the widow of Jehoram and

[28] He died five years later, in 848, and Jehoram became sole ruler of Judah in the 5th year of Joram of Israel (II Kings 8:16).
[29] A. L. Oppenheim, *Iraq*, XVII (1955), 79 and n. 34.
[30] It is essentially the same coalition throughout, though Israel, perhaps because of the death of Ahab, is not again specifically mentioned.
[31] The new "fourth edition" of Shalmaneser's annals, written in 839 (cf. above, n. 17), provides added details of this campaign, including a new synchronism between Assyria and Tyre, for which see J. Liver, *IEJ*, III (1953), 113-20; J. M. Penuela, *Sefarad*, XIII (1953), 217-37; and, for a different view, W. F. Albright, *BASOR*, No. 141 (Feb. 1956), p. 27. 841 is also critical for "a new scheme for the sub-division of the Iron Age in Palestine" proposed by Y. Aharoni and R. Amiran in a rare example of the (independent) convergence of artifactual and philological evidence, *IEJ*, VIII (1958), 171-84.
[32] Such at least is the general opinion, based on II Kings 8:18. For a different view, based on II Kings 8:26 (II Chron. 22:2),

the mother of the short-lived Ahaziah. Her triple claim to royal authority enabled her to sit first behind, then beside, and finally on the king's throne, and her career seems the more credible in the light of three Mesopotamian queens whose roles are emerging ever more clearly: Sammuramat (Semiramis), Naqia (Zakutu) and Adad-guppi.[33]

With the south Syrian coalition definitively reduced, and the successions in Damascus, Samaria and Jerusalem to some extent stabilized, Shalmaneser was once more enabled to turn his attention to north Syria and the lands beyond it. The campaigns of 839–828 were primarily directed against the northwest, although the Medean and Armenian frontiers received some attention in 834–831. Jehu, as a loyal Assyrian vassal,[34] and Joash, who came to the throne of Judah in Jehu's 7th year (835), found their weakened kingdoms bearing the brunt of Hazael's military designs, and a single punitive expedition by Shalmaneser (838) was not enough to deter the Syrian usurper.

II. Revolt and Restoration (828–783)

Shalmaneser III's reign ended in disaster. In the midst of a two-year campaign against the northeastern frontier a revolt erupted in Nineveh and other Assyrian centers which occupied the next six years of the Eponym Chronicle (827–822).[35]

---

see H. J. Katzenstein, *IEJ*, V (1955), 194–97, and previously, J. Begrich, *ZAW*, LIII (1935), 78 f.

[33] For Sammuramat and Naqia, see H. Lewy, *JNES*, XI (1952), 264–90. For Adad-guppi, see the articles by B. Landsberger, *Halil Edhem Anniversary Volume* (1947), pp. 115–51, and E. Dhorme, *Recueil Dhorme* (1951), pp. 325–50. The excavations at Haran by D. W. Rice have turned up an important new parallel to this inscription, now published by C. J. Gadd, *An. St.*, VIII (1958), 35–92 and Pls. I–XVI. For other Oriental queens, cf. N. Abbott, *AJSL*, LVIII (1941), 1–22.

[34] He paid tribute to Shalmaneser in the year of his accession (*ARAB* I, § 672 = *ANET*, p. 280), and this or a later submission of the same kind was immortalized on one of the panels of Shalmaneser's Black Obelisk (*The Ancient Near East in Pictures*, ed. J. B. Pritchard [hereafter, *ANEP*; 1954], fig. 355), which, as observed by A. Parrot, *Ninive et l'ancien testament* (1953), p. 25, preserves for us the only contemporary representation of an Israelite figure known from the Bible.

[35] *ARAB* I, § 715. Only Kalah seems to have remained loyal;

As a result of this upheaval, all of Shalmaneser's western conquests were nullified. Though Shamshi-adad V, his son and successor, was able to quell the revolt in his second year (822),[36] he had to acknowledge the overlordship of Babylon for this purpose.[37] His recorded campaigns were directed first against the north and then, when he felt powerful enough to throw off the Babylonian vassalage again, against his late sovereign there.[38] But the areas west of the Euphrates were lost, and Til Barsip on the Euphrates became the westernmost outpost of Assyrian influence (*ARAB* I, § 716). Excavations at Til Barsip show that this citadel remained under Assyrian control throughout the period of weakness that followed.[39] But a degree of independence was manifested even in such relatively nearby areas as the middle Khabur valley, where the "priestdom" of Mushezib-ninurta is attested by a votive seal of this period.[40]

Hazael of Damascus, meanwhile, continued his depredations against the divided kingdom, unchecked by Assyrian restraints.[41] The death of Jehu in 814/3 even enabled him to march through the length and breadth of Palestine in order to capture Gath (II Kings 12:18), for both events seem dated

---

the royal "building boom" which it enjoyed presently (see below) may have been its reward.

[36] So according to Weidner, *AfO*, IX (1934), 89.

[37] E. F. Weidner, *AfO*, VIII (1932), 27-29; cf. M. Noth, *ZDPV*, LXXVII (1961), 143, n. 73.

[38] Weidner, *AfO*, IX (1934), 89-104, who includes new additions to the texts of this king in *ARAB* I, §§ 713-28. (*ARAB* I, § 729, does not belong to Shamshi-adad V; *ibid.*, p. 89, n. 7). In 1961, an inscribed strip of ivory veneer from the throne of Shamshi-adad was found at Kalah; D. Oates, *Iraq*, XXIV (1962), 3 (ND. 10152).

[39] Thureau-Dangin, *Til-Barsib*, pp. 141 ff.

[40] E. Unger, *BASOR*, No. 130 (April 1953), pp. 15-21, and Albright, *H. Goldman Anniversary Volume* (1956), pp. 148 f. It is in this reign, too, that most scholars date the independence of Guzana on the upper Khabur; cf. Mallowan, *Iraq*, XIX (1957), 17, n. 1, and B. Hrouda, *Tell Halaf*, IV (1962), 113-17, against Albright, *An. St.*, VI (1956), 75-85, who would place it in the 10th century. Mallowan also considers the possibility of connecting the Kapara dynasty with the revolt of Guzana in 759-58 (see below, n. 58).

[41] There is no record of any Assyrian campaign to the west between 831 and 806.

to the 23rd year of the long reign of Joash of Judah.[42] Nor did the accession of a new Assyrian king in 811 immediately relieve Jehoahaz, the son and successor of Jehu, of the Aramean pressure. For Adad-nirari III was a mere child when his father died, and for four years his mother Sammuramat (the Semiramis of Greek legend) ruled in his name.[43] When, in 805, he was at last able to turn his attention against the Arameans, he was regarded as a veritable deliverer by Israel (II Kings 13:5).[44]

The reign of Semiramis and Adad-nirari III indeed marked a partial recovery in the general decline which followed the great revolt. The new excavations at Kalah show that this residence city was now thoroughly rebuilt. In the northwest corner of the outer city, Adad-nirari erected his own palace.[45] Within the citadel area proper, there arose two smaller palaces, the so-called Burnt Palace and the high-lying AB palace,[46] as well as a great temple of Nabu called, like its Babylonian prototypes, Ezida.[47] The cult of Nabu, thus introduced into Assyria, meant a cultural reconciliation with Babylonia, perhaps at the instigation of the Babylonian queen-mother. The completion of the new temple was marked by the dedication of two statues at its entrance, inscribed on behalf of Adad-nirari and Semiramis and ending in the well-known

[42] II Kings 12:7 and 13:1; for the proposed synchronism, cf. A. Jepsen, *AfO*, XIV (1942), 159. Note the different wording of II Chron. 24:23–25.

[43] Cf. H. Lewy, *JNES*, XI (1952), 264 f., n. 5. How young he was can be gauged from the fact that he was succeeded by three of his sons, the last of whom perished as the result of a revolution sixty-five years after Adad-nirari's accession.

[44] Schmökel, *Geschichte des alten Vorderasien*, p. 259, n. 4. If this identification is accepted, it would represent the earliest biblical reference, albeit oblique, to an Assyrian king (apart from the legendary Nimrud), antedating the first explicit reference in II Kings 15:19 by more than sixty years. Cf. already H. Winckler, *Geschichte Israels*, I (1895), 154; *OLZ*, IV (1901), col. 197. A. Jeremias, *The Old Testament in the Light of the Ancient East*, II (1911), 213, thinks that "the later Jewish edition . . . expunged the name of Adad-nirari" here.

[45] *Iraq*, XVI (1954), 153 ff.

[46] Oates, *Iraq*, XX (1958), 111–13, for these dates. Oates supposes that one of these palaces might have belonged to Semiramis or to the crown prince.

[47] Mallowan, *Iraq*, XVIII (1956), 9.

lines: "In Nabu trust: trust in no other God!" (*ARAB* I, § 745). They were dedicated by Bel-tarsi-ilumma, the new governor of Kalah, who is known, in addition, not only as eponym for the year 798, but also from administrative tablets found in the "governor's palace" which was newly erected for him in the citadel of Kalah at this time.[48]

Thus Kalah was transformed into a major—perhaps *the* major—capital of Assyria. Undoubtedly, too, it was turned into a staging area for the military operations which began, even during Adad-nirari's minority, to assume again some of their old effectiveness. The Medes and Manneans were attacked in the east, while the way to the west was opened with the recapture of Guzana (Tell Halaf) in 808. It is possible that this date marks the end of the independent Kapara dynasty there;[49] at any rate the archive of its governor, Mannu-ki-ashur, discovered on this site shows clearly the close supervision that Adad-nirari presently exercised over this important outpost.[50] His own coming of age was marked by the previously mentioned campaign against Damascus and Palashtu.[51] Israel too appears, under its Assyrian designation of House of Omri, among the willing tributaries recorded for this campaign. It was followed up by the strikes against more northerly Syria (Arpad, Hazazu, Ba'li, 805–803) until, in 802, the Mediterranean Sea itself was reached.

But Adad-nirari could not hold the west. Except for a single campaign against Mansuate in northcentral Syria in 796, his armies, for the rest of his reign, were engaged closer to home, north, east and south of Assyria. At the same time, the Urartean kings began to make their influence felt[52] and, until their pretensions were decisively challenged by Tiglath-pileser

[48] Mallowan, *Iraq*, XII (1950), 167–69.
[49] Cf. above, n. 40.
[50] E. F. Weidner, *Die Inschriften vom Tell Halaf* (= *AfO Suppl.* VI [1940]), pp. 1–46.
[51] *ARAB* I, § 734 = *ANET*, p. 282. This is the first time that the land of the Philistines appears by this name in the Assyrian records. For other references, cf. Tadmor, *JCS*, XII (1958), 83, n. 235.
[52] Beginning about 800, Menua of Urartu claimed tribute from Milid. For a convenient new summary of Urartean history, cf. A. Goetze, *Kleinasien* (2nd ed., 1957), pp. 187–200. The Urarteans also appear in scholarly literature as Haldians, but this alleged native designation remains doubtful; *ibid.*, p. 191, n. 6.

III at Kummuh in 743, they were apparently "recognized as overlords of the mountain country reaching to the Mediterranean, and even as far south as Aleppo."[53] Thus Adad-nirari's claim that "the country of the Hittites, Amurru-country in its full extent, Tyre, Sidon, Israel (*mat Ḫu-um-ri-i*), Edom, Palestine (*Pa-la-as-tú*), as far as the shore of the great sea of the setting sun"[54] all acknowledged his sovereignty and paid him tribute, was at best of temporary truthfulness.

III. Assyria in Retreat (783–745)

When Shalmaneser IV succeeded his father Adad-nirari III in 783, both Judah and Israel were firmly ruled by two long-lived princes who had taken over the throne in the lifetime of their fathers. Azariah of Judah had begun his coregency in 791, the 6th year of his father Amaziah, and Jeroboam II in 793, the 5th year of his father Jehoash, becoming sole ruler of Israel in Shalmaneser IV's first regnal year (782). Elsewhere, too, the new Assyrian king found powerfully entrenched rulers for, during his reign and that of his successor (Ashur-dan III), Urartu was ruled by Argishti I, who continued the Urartean domination of Syria. He attacked Assyria from both east and west, and the six campaigns of Shalmaneser IV against Urartu (781–778, 776, 774) were really defensive actions. Even the central provinces maintained only a tenuous loyalty to Assyria, for the various governors ruled in virtual independence of the king at Kalah. One of them, Shamshi-ilu, inscribed his own monuments at Kar-shalmaneser (Bit Adini) in quasi-royal style[55] and, even after this fortress had to be abandoned,[56] he virtually ruled the empire as *turtanu* (commander-in-chief).

Shalmaneser IV was succeeded by his brother Ashur-dan III in 773, but the situation did not change materially. Though the new king attacked Damascus once (773) and Hatarika (biblical Hadrach; cf. Zech. 9:1) on the Orontes three times (772, 765, 755), the main direction of Assyrian

[53] J. du Plat Taylor *et al.*, *Iraq*, XII (1950), p. 69.
[54] *ANET*, p. 281.
[55] F. Thureau-Dangin, *Til-Barsib*, pp. 141–51 and *RA*, XXVII (1930), 11–21.
[56] The last dated evidence for any official Assyrian occupation of this site prior to Esarhaddon's restoration is a Kalah tablet from 778; cf. D. Oates, *Iraq*, XXI (1959), 104, 126.

military efforts, such as they were, continued to be south and east. There are no more historical records for this reign than for the preceding one,[57] but the Eponym Chronicle reveals the Assyrian weakness clearly enough. For the first time—except 810—the king and his armies stayed at home, and this no fewer than four times (768, 764, 757, 756). The Assyrian weakness was aggravated by plagues (765, 759) and internal revolts (763–759). The last of these revolts was in Guzana (Tell Halaf) and, though it called forth Assyrian countermeasures (758), an independent dynasty may have taken over Guzana at this point.[58]

The third son of Adad-nirari III succeeded to the throne of Assyria in 755 under the name of Ashur-nirari V. Assyrian fortunes had now reached a nadir, and half of Ashur-nirari's decade of rule was spent "in the land." The campaign of his first regnal year (754) was directed against Arpad, and its temporary success may be read out of the famous treaty which he concluded with Mati'-ilu of Arpad.[59] But its ink—or rather clay—was hardly dry before Mati'-ilu broke it to enter into a similar vassal relation with Bar-gayah of *Ktk*.[60]

Summarizing the first half of the 8th century, it may thus be said that Assyrians, Arameans and Urarteans fought each other to a standstill in Mesopotamia and Syria. Given the internal stability that chanced to prevail in Judah and Israel at the same time, it is no wonder that the divided kingdom briefly regained the economic strength and territorial extent of the Solomonic empire. Judah exploited the southern desert (II

[57] However, the name of Ashur-dan III (*Asaradanas*) may occur in a hieroglyphic Hittite inscription from Carchemish; cf. Th. Bossert, *Belleten*, XVI (1952), 534–37; Güterbock, *JNES*, XIII (1954), 105.

[58] Cf. above, n. 40.

[59] *ARAB* I, §§ 749–60; E. F. Weidner, *AfO*, VIII (1932), 17–34. Arpad was not permanently conquered until 740; cf. M. V. Seton Williams, *Iraq*, XXIII (1961), 68–87 and Pls. XXXI–XLI.

[60] *ANET*², p. 504. The Sujin steles have now been (re-)edited by A. Dupont-Sommer, with J. Starcky, in *Les inscriptions araméennes de Sfiré* (*Stèles I & II*) (Paris, 1958) and Stele III in *Bulletin du Musée de Beyrouth*, XIII (1956), 23–41 and Pls. I–VI. Cf. also J. A. Fitzmyer, *Catholic Biblical Quarterly*, XX (1958), 444–76; Franz Rosenthal, *BASOR*, No. 158 (April 1960), pp. 28–31; Martin Noth, *ZDPV*, LXXVII (1961), 118–72; and Fitzmyer again, *JAOS*, LXXXI (1961), 178–222.

Chron. 26:1–15) and its land and sea trade routes,[61] while Israel won back all the Transjordanian lands lost to Hazael and much Aramean territory besides (II Kings 14:25, 28).

Yet the very prosperity enjoyed by the petty kingdoms of Syria and Palestine nourished the seeds of their destruction, and those astute enough to see this (Amos 1–2) knew that it could not outlast the fortuitous coincidence of stability in the west and weakness in Assyria. It required only a turn of the wheel of fortune to bring the Assyrian down upon Israel once more (Amos 6:14). And so it was. Jeroboam II died in 753 after a reign of forty-one years (twenty-nine of them as sole ruler) and his son Zechariah was unable to perpetuate the dynasty of Jehu. Within the year, his throne was usurped, first by Shallum and then (752) by Menahem. Even Menahem's rule did not go unchallenged for, as Thiele has shown, a later view assigned all of Menahem's ten years to *his* successor-by-usurpation, Pekah.[62] In Judah, meanwhile, the long reign of Azariah (Uzziah) ended in illness and, in 750, he turned over effective power to his son and successor, Jotham. Thus ended forty years of internal stability and external prowess for Israel and Judah.

In Assyria, however, the change of rulers had the opposite effect. Here too rebellion was the order of the day. This time it broke out in Kalah, and although the excavations have not turned up any physical evidence of its virulence, it served to sweep away the old ruling family and paved the way for a new resurgence. In the excavator's words, Ashur-nirari "perished in Kalhu . . . as the result of a revolution which reflected the culmination of discontent at the end of nearly forty years of disastrous Assyrian weakness."[63] Perhaps Israelite tradition reflected the memory of these forty lean years by attaching the legend of the near-collapse of Nineveh to Jonah, a prophetic contemporary of Jeroboam II or, con-

---

[61] Cf. especially N. Glueck, *Rivers In The Desert* (1959), pp. 168–79.

[62] Thiele, *Mysterious Numbers*, chap. vi. Even though Thiele (p. 114) rejects the theory that Pekah may actually have ruled a part of Israel during Menahem's reign, the claims of some other rival king could have given rise to the late conflation.

[63] Mallowan, *Iraq*, XII (1950), 172; cf. D. Oates, *Iraq*, XXI (1959), 126 f.

versely, by assigning the Jonah of legend to the reign of Jeroboam (II Kings 14:25).[64]

IV. Divide et Impera (745–705)

Tiglath-pileser III was a usurper, though perhaps of royal blood. The newly discovered duplicate of the Assyrian king list even calls him the son of his predecessor Ashur-nirari V.[65] He was certainly the beneficiary of the revolt which unseated Ashur-nirari, and even arrogated that ruler's last year to himself instead of counting his regnal years, as was the Assyrian practice, from the New Year following his predecessor's death. He and his first two successors changed the whole balance of power in the Near East, destroying Israel among many other states, and reducing the rest, including Judah, to vassalage. They found Assyria "in a difficult, even desperate, military and economic situation," but "the next forty years saw Assyria recover and consolidate control of all its old territories and re-establish itself firmly as the pre-eminent military and economic power in the Middle East."[66] Though this change of fortunes may have been due more to administrative reforms than to external victories,[67] it is the latter which primarily affected Israel, and they will therefore occupy us here.

The Assyrian campaigns of the next four decades not only assumed a new intensity but also covered greater distances and followed more numerous directions than ever before. Israel felt the effects of the new policy almost at once. In 743, the year of his own eponymate (traditionally the 2nd year, but the 3rd in his own system of counting), Tiglath-pileser was in Arpad,[68] apparently to receive homage from the loyal

[64] For the critical problem involved, cf. W. W. Hallo, *JAOS*, LXXXIII (1963), 175, n. 68. Note that Jonah's estimate of 120,000 inhabitants for Nineveh seems reasonable in the light of the 65,000 inhabitants who settled the newly rebuilt Kalah in 878, since the walls of Kalah enclose only one-half of Nineveh's area; cf. Mallowan, *Iraq*, XIV (1952), 20–22 and D. J. Wiseman, *ibid.*, p. 28.

[65] Cf. above, n. 4. That he was yet another son of Adad-nirari III (*ARAB* I, § 822:1) is less likely.

[66] H. W. F. Saggs, *Iraq*, XXI (1959), 176.

[67] *Ibid.*

[68] So according to the Eponym Chronicle. A new tablet from Kalah (ND 475; *Iraq*, XIII [1951], 114) has the notation "in Ashur" after the eponym, but this may be a simple dittography for *šar māt* <*aš*> *aš-šur*ᵏⁱ.

kings of the west, and to direct the launching of a massive campaign against those Anatolian, Syrian and Palestinian rulers who did not at once submit. Among the tributaries was Menahem of Israel (*Me-ni-hi-im-me* of the *Sa-me-ri-na-a-a*) while Azariah of Judah (*Az-ri-a-u* of the *Ia-ú-da-a-a*) was prominent among the rebels (*ANET*, pp. 282 f.). Unfortunately, the annals are not conclusive on the exact date of these two important synchronisms, but Thiele has reasoned cogently that both events fell near the beginning of a six-year campaign against the west, perhaps within 743.[69] This year marked the 9th, both of Jotham, coregent of Judah under Azariah, and of Menahem. Menahem's insecure position at this late stage of his reign may be indicated not only by the motive which II Kings 15:19 assigns to his submission to Assyria ("in order to secure the kingship in his hand") but also by the fact that his son Pekahiah, who succeeded him in the following year, was presently killed in the revolt of Pekah.[70]

The exact course of Tiglath-pileser's first great campaign against the west (743–738) is thus difficult to follow. But various details are emerging from obscurity. Evidently the Assyrians were organizing the nearer Syrian provinces under Assyrian administration, regulating the successions to their liking in the middle tier of states, and waging war against the more distant ones all at the same time. The semi-autonomous Assyrian proconsulships were broken up into smaller administrative units, and their governors thereby deprived of the virtually sovereign power that the interval of royal weakness had allowed them to assume.[71] The Urartean empire in north

[69] *Mysterious Numbers*, chap. v. H. W. F. Saggs, *Iraq*, XVII (1955), 144 f. criticizes Thiele's position, preferring to date the reference to Azariah 742 and to Menahem 741. A. L. Oppenheim, *ANET*, pp. 282 f., dates the reference to Azariah 743 and considers the date of the Menahem reference unknown. The widely accepted date 738 for the Menahem passage in the Annals may be considered definitely unproven. The resort to a "Northern Judah" with its own Azariah may also be dispensed with in the light of the proposed synchronisms.

[70] D. J. Wiseman notes that the biblical figure for Menahem's tribute, fifty shekels per head (II Kings 15:20), corresponds to the average Assyrian slave-price current at Kalah in the next century; it may thus have represented a kind of "ransom"; *Iraq*, XV (1953), 135.

[71] Cf. A. Malamat, *BASOR*, No. 129 (Feb. 1953), pp. 25 f. Malamat would identify Shamshi-ilu with the "scepter-holder of Beth-eden"; but cf. above nn. 21 and 56.

Syria was destroyed, Pisiris of Carchemish became a loyal vassal, and the main cities of northern Phoenicia were annexed and formed into the new province of Unqi after Tutannu of Unqi had been sent captive to Assyria. Presently, Phoenician cities as far south as Tyre and Sidon occupied the attention of the royal administration at Kalah.[72] In the more northerly Sam'al, Panamu II was installed by Tiglath-pileser in an attempt to end a troubled period that witnessed the assassination of his father, Bar-sur.[73]

Faced with these and similar examples, Menahem of Israel had probably sought support for an eventual succession by his payment of tribute. If so, that support was ineffectual, for Pekahiah had reigned only two years when, in 740/39, the revolt of Pekah unseated him in what certainly represented an anti-Assyrian reaction. In Judah, Azariah died in the same year, and Jotham, the coregent, began his sole reign. Apparently he was still enough of a free agent to undertake the subjugation of the Ammonites, for these do not appear in the early tribute lists of Tiglath-pileser; they had paid tribute to Azariah (II Chron. 26:8) and Jotham forced them to continue this practice for three years (II Chron. 27:5), after which we find them paying tribute to Tiglath-pileser alongside Ahaz (*Ia-ú-ha-zi*) of Judah (*ANET*, p. 282). Ahaz became coregent of Jotham in Judah in the three-year interval when Tiglath-pileser turned his attention to the northern and eastern frontiers,[74] in what may well have been a pro-Assyrian coup designed to appease Tiglath-pileser on his imminent return to the west.[75] His payment of tribute is, at any rate, in marked contrast with the anti-Assyrian and expansionist policies of Azariah and Jotham.

The second phase of Tiglath-pileser's western activities falls in the three years 734–732. According to the Eponym Chronicle, these were marked by one Assyrian campaign against Philistia and two against Damascus. They are illumined by

[72] Cf. the Nimrud letter ND 2715+2606; Saggs, *Iraq*, XVII (1955), 127–31.

[73] Cf. B. Landsberger, *Sam'al* (1948), pp. 60–72.

[74] The capture of Kullani in 738 marked the close of the first western campaign of Tiglath-pileser. It may be reflected in the Kalnoh of Isa. 10:9, an identification which goes back to Winckler, though the actual reference may rather be to the revolt of Kullani in 721; cf. Saggs, *Iraq*, XVII (1955), 147 f.

[75] Cf. Thiele, *Mysterious Numbers*, p. 117.

new texts from Kalah, among them a fragment of the annals,[76] supplementing the shorter version hitherto known; a parallel to *ARAB* I, §§ 815-19,[77] and a letter.[78] The focus of anti-Assyrian resistance was now Rezin of Damascus. Tiglath-pileser's strategy was therefore to attack the various lesser allies beyond Damascus first and then, having isolated Rezin, to turn on Damascus itself. This strategy was the more appropriate as he was already master of the Phoenician cities. Those that had not been included in the province of Unqi (see above, p. 171) were now united in a new province around Hamath bordering, presumably, on Unqi in the north, the House of Omri (i.e. Israel) in the south, and the House of Haza'ili[79] (i.e. Damascus) in the east. According to II Kings 16:7 (cf. II Chron. 28:16), however, the Assyrian strategy was inspired by Ahaz' call for help.

B. Landsberger has pointed out[80] that the Masoretic spelling *r^eṣîn* and the Greek spelling *rasōn, raasōn*, etc., give the Canaanite version, Akkadian *ra-hi-a-nu* (not **ra-zun-nu*, a value *zun/sun* for HI.A being otherwise unknown) gives the Aramaic version of an original Hebrew **raṣyôn*, Aramaic **ra'yān*.

Rezin had paid tribute as early as 743 (*ARAB* I, § 769) and again (in the same year?) in the company of Menahem of Israel.[81] Now, however, emboldened by Tiglath-pileser's preoccupation in the north, he conspired with Pekah of Israel and perhaps with the Philistines and Edomites in a new anti-Assyrian coalition. No doubt the coalition was intended to include Judah too but there, though Jotham was still alive,[82] effective power was now in the hands of the pro-Assyrian party and the coregent Ahaz. The Syro-Ephraimite coalition

[76] ND 400, published by D. J. Wiseman, *Iraq*, XIII (1951), 21-24.

[77] ND 4301+4305, published by Wiseman, *Iraq*, XVIII (1956), 117-29 and Pls. XXI-XXIII.

[78] ND 2773, published by H. W. F. Saggs, *Iraq*, XVII (1955), 131-33; re-edited by W. F. Albright, *BASOR*, No. 140 (1955), pp. 34 f.

[79] Not the "House of [Nafta]li as restored conjecturally in *ANET*, p. 283; the new text ND 4301+4305 (above, n. 77) is preserved at this point.

[80] *Sam'al* (1948), pp. 66 f. n. 169; cf. W. von Soden, *Das akkadische Syllabar* (1948), p. 108, No. 241.

[81] *ANET*, p. 283; cf. above, p. 170 f. and n. 69.

[82] Cf. the wording of II Kings 15:37.

sought, therefore, to substitute a more tractable king in Judah; the newly discovered Kalah letter which Saggs interpreted as reflecting the general unrest in the small states south of Palestine at this time has been shown by Albright to contain the geographical name Tab-el, so that the Ben-tab'al of Isaiah 7:6 may well have been a son of Azariah or Jotham by a princess from Tab-el.[83]

Ahaz, however, maintained his throne without yielding to the coalition, backed up, no doubt, by Isaiah's reassurances.[84] Under attack from all sides, he called on Tiglath-pileser for help and the campaign against Philistia ensued. Ashkelon and Gaza were defeated and Gezer too was captured.[85] Tiglath-pileser accepted tribute from Judah and her eastern neighbors, Ammon, Edom and Moab, but dealt more severely with Israel. Judging by II Kings 15:29, the Northern Kingdom was shorn of most of its territory, including all of Gilead and much of Galilee.[86] The inhabitants, perhaps because Pekah had drawn much of his strength from across the Jordan,[87] were exiled (cf. also I Chron. 5:26), the huge stronghold of Hazor was destroyed,[88] and the proud kingdom of Israel reduced to little more than a vassal state which Isaiah and Hosea now properly enough called simply Ephraim, where Amos had still called it Joseph. The ultimate step of incorporation into the Assyrian provincial system remained, under these circumstances, little more than a formality. It was postponed for a decade because, while Tiglath-pileser was successfully concluding his siege of Damascus in 732, a pro-Assyrian revolt in Samaria finally cost Pekah his life and elevated as loyal Assyrian vassal the last northern king, Hoshea. If Tiglath-pileser did not actually put

[83] Cf. above, n. 78.
[84] Cf. however, W. C. Graham, *AJSL*, L (1934), 210–16 and, for a different analysis of Isa. 7–8, S. Blank, *Prophetic Faith in Isaiah* (1958), chap. ii.
[85] This event, though not attested by the inscriptions, is confirmed by the caption on an Assyrian relief depicting the campaign, according to M. El-Amin, *Sumer*, IX (1953), 37.
[86] For the Galilean campaign, cf. Yohanan Aharoni, *The Settlement of the Israelite Tribes in Upper Galilee* (in Hebrew; 1957), pp. 129–32.
[87] I owe this suggestion to J. B. Curtis; cf. now *JBL*, LXXX (1961), 362 f.
[88] Cf Y. Yadin, *BA*, XX (1957), 34–37; see below, p. 195.

Hoshea on the throne himself, as he claims,[89] he was certainly not dissatisfied with this regulation of the succession.

Throughout the west, the royal successions were similarly regulated to Assyria's satisfaction.[90] About 733, the Assyrian vassal Panamu II had died fighting loyally at his master's side before Damascus,[91] and his son Bar-rekub received the throne of Sam'al from Tiglath-pileser, as he admitted freely in his own inscription (*ANET²*, p. 501). Ambaris of Tabal was recognized at the same time as vassal king of Hilakku (Cilicia). Damascus fell in 732 and, with Rezin dead, was at last incorporated into the Assyrian empire (II Kings 16:9). In Judah, at the same time, Tiglath-pileser had the satisfaction of seeing the loyal Ahaz become sole ruler upon the death of Jotham.

Tiglath-pileser's second western campaign was thus even more decisive in its effect than the first, and from the Taurus mountains in the north to the river of Egypt in the south, the entire Mediterranean littoral now paid him homage, whether as province or as vassal kingdom. If the vassals, such as Israel and Judah, Tabal and Cilicia, and even Carchemish, were not at once reduced to provinces it was because, now as in 738, Tiglath-pileser's attention was once more diverted elsewhere. In 731, the eponymate of Nergal-uballit of Ahizuhina,[92] a rebellion broke out in Babylonia, and a certain Ukin-zer replaced the loyal Nabu-nadin-zer. Tiglath-pileser moved energetically against this threat in his rear, "taking the hands of Bel" himself in 729, and disputing Ukin-zer's claims by setting himself up as Pulu, king of Babylon.[93] The Ukin-zer rebellion is thrown into new relief by several letters found at Kalah in 1952;[94] its importance for Israel lay in the fact that it occupied Tiglath-pileser till the end of his reign. When he did finally turn his attention to Damascus again in 727, it was his last recorded act; judging by the Eponym Chronicle, Shal-

[89] *ARAB* I, § 816 = *ANET*, p. 284.

[90] For a new parallel to Hoshea's installation see now ND 4301+4305 (above, n. 77) and especially Wiseman's remarks, *Iraq*, XVIII (1956), 121.

[91] Landsberger, *Sam'al*, p. 70.

[92] For an instructive letter from this governor, see now Saggs, *Iraq*, XX (1958), 187–90.

[93] This is the form of the name in II Kings 15:19, and in I Chron. 5:26 where it is "glossed" by the Assyrian form.

[94] Saggs, *Iraq*, XVII (1955), 44–50.

maneser V took the throne before the campaign had really started.

The new king's brief reign of five years (726–722) is so far not illuminated by a single inscription[95] and, were it not for records from Babylonia (where he reigned as Ululai) and Israel, he would scarcely even be credited with the capture of Samaria, his greatest achievement. During his first regnal year he stayed "in the land," apparently content not to interfere with the Phoenician-Palestinian rebellion that had, almost inevitably, greeted his accession (cf. II Kings 17:4). But in 725 he began his countermeasures. Shechem was captured,[96] Samaria invested, and a siege of Tyre begun at the same time.[97] The five-year siege of Tyre was destined to be completed by Sargon, but Samaria fell in August or September 722, Hoshea having been deported sometime before.[98] Shalmaneser V died in December of the same year, i.e., *after* the fall of Samaria, and those scholars who, like Olmstead,[99] argued that II Kings 17:6 and 18:10 implied as much seem now definitely to be proven right. Although Sargon may have shared as second-in-command in the siege of Samaria, he misappropriated his predecessor's triumph late in his own reign in order to fill the gap in military activities that, in the earlier records of his reign, loomed in his first year.[100]

Besides the Bible, the "Babylonian Chronicle" notes the destruction of *Sa-ma-ra-'i-in* as the outstanding event of Shalmaneser's reign, and the hesitation in the past to equate this name with biblical *Shomron/Sham'rayin* (Ezra 4:10) had little philological foundation.[101]

The Babylonian Chronicle is a most important and, in some senses, even impartial record of Near Eastern history which,

[95] The text *CT* 37:23 which Luckenbill, *AJSL*, XLI (1925), 162–64 and *ARAB* I, §§ 829 f. took for an inscription of Shalmaneser V was shown by Meissner, *AfO*, III (1926), 13 f. to belong to Esarhaddon. Cf. now R. Borger, *AfO Suppl.* IX (1956), § 20.

[96] Cf. L. E. Toombs, *BA*, XX (1957), 99.

[97] A. Malamat, *IEJ*, I (1950–51), 152.

[98] It is for this reason that Sargon's new Kalah prisms refer to the "Samarians" rather than to their king at the start of the siege, according to H. Tadmor, *JCS*, XII (1958), 37.

[99] So already in 1905; cf. *AJSL*, XXI (1905), 179–82.

[100] Tadmor, *JCS*, XII (1958), 33–40.

[101] *Ibid.*

when complete, covered the entire "Nabonassar Era" (747–539), the greater part of it year by year. So far there is no single edition or translation of all its extant portions, but Oppenheim has translated those dealing with the years 702–667, 616–609, and 555–539 in *ANET*, pp. 301–7, while Wiseman has edited the newly discovered Chronicles for 626–556 in *Chronicles of Chaldaean Kings* (1956).[102]

The exile which Shalmaneser V imposed on Samaria was no more severe than Tiglath-pileser's exile of the Transjordanian Israelites ten years earlier. Nor was he the king who repopulated Samaria with the motley victims of other campaigns.[103] If the events of 722 nevertheless had such an impact on Jewish religious thought, it was because the literary prophets saw in them the first decisive fulfillment of their collective interpretation of history, as the Babylonian exile of Judah was to be the second. The exiles themselves were probably quickly acclimatized in such strongholds of Assyro-Aramean symbiosis as Guzana (Gozan) and Haran (II Kings 17:6; I Chron. 5:26). They may soon have penetrated even the capital cities of Assyria, for presently we find such good Israelite royal names as Menahem at Kalah[104] and Hoshea at Nineveh.[105]

The reign of Sargon, though it may mark the beginning of a new "Sargonid" branch of the royal family, is more appropriately considered, in the present context, as the closing chapter in the period of Assyrian conquest and expansion. The seventeen years of Sargon's reign were marked by almost continuous warfare, and his later scribes would have it appear that every single year witnessed a major campaign. It is this *Tendenz* which was responsible for a number of chronological contradictions within the records of Sargon's reign similar to that indicated for 722 (above). In the light of new historical sources, however, it is now possible to resolve these contra-

[102] On this most important "museum-find," see D. N. Freedman, *BA*, XIX (1956), 50–60.

[103] Cf. below, pp. 180 and 186–87.

[104] J. B. Segal, *Iraq*, XIX (1957), 139–45. W. F. Albright, *BASOR*, No. 149 (1958), pp. 33–36 dates it between about 725 and 675.

[105] *Corpus Inscriptionum Semiticarum*, part 2, vol. I, text 17, dated 680. The cuneiform text has *Ú-ši-'a*, the Aramaic endorsement *hwšʿ*.

dictions, and to adduce some important new synchronisms with biblical history and literature.[106]

Whether Sargon was a son of Tiglath-pileser, as a text published by E. Unger[107] claims, remains open to doubt. His accession seems to be based on the tumultuous circumstances alluded to in the Harper Letter No. 473.[108] The documents from Nineveh published by R. F. Harper, *Assyrian and Babylonian Letters* (14 vols., 1892–1914) and translated by L. Waterman, *Royal Correspondence of the Assyrian Empire* (4 vols., 1930–36) and, in part, by R. H. Pfeiffer, *State Letters of Assyria* (= *American Oriental Series* VI [1935]) are an important source for the history of the new dynasty, and were heavily drawn on by Olmstead and by F. M. Th. de Liagre Böhl, "Das Zeitalter der Sargoniden," *Opera Minora* (1953), pp. 384–422, 519–25.[109] They do not, however, make much mention of western affairs, perhaps, if a guess may be hazarded, because these may have been administered from Kalah.[110]

The change of Assyrian rulers was, as usual, greeted by a rebellion. In the west it was led by a certain Yaubidi,[111] a commoner (*hupšu*) who, having succeeded in seizing power in Hamath, and winning followers among the newly conquered cities of Damascus, Simirra, Arpad, Hatarika and Samaria, found allies in the still independent Hanuni ("Hanno") of Gaza and the commander-in-chief (*turtanu*) of lower Egypt,

[106] H. Tadmor's study, *JCS*, XII (1958), 22–40, 77–100 is of fundamental importance in this connection. Note also his clarification of the Eponym Chronicle (p. 85), and his summary of historical sources (pp. 94–97).

[107] *Forschungen und Fortschritte*, IX (1933), 254 f., republished *AfO*, IX (1933–34), 79; more fully in *Sargon II. von Assyrien der Sohn Tiglatpilesers III.* (*Publik. der Antiken-Museen zu Istanbul*, IX [1933]).

[108] Cf. R. C. Thompson, *Iraq*, IV (1937), 35–43 and the literature cited there.

[109] For a more recent treatment, cf. W. von Soden, *Analecta Biblica*, XII (1959), 356–67.

[110] Cf. Saggs, *Iraq*, XVII (1955), 126–60 for twelve Kalah letters bearing on "relations with the west." Cf. however D. Oates, *ibid.*, XXIV (1962), 23, for "the decline of Calah itself after Sargon established his new capital at Khorsabad" at the end of his reign.

[111] M. El-Amin, *Sumer*, X (1954), 27 proposes the reading Iluyaubidi instead.

whose name has hitherto been generally read as Sib'e.[112] However, Sargon did not at once move to quell the rebellion. Like Shalmaneser V before him (above, p. 175), he seems to have spent his first regnal year "in the land."[113] When he did open hostilities in 720, it was against the south that he first turned his attention. At the great battle of Der, before the Iranian foothills, the Assyrians met the combined force of Humbanigash of Elam and Marduk-apal-iddina II (Merodach-baladan), the new king of Babylonia, who was destined to be a focus of anti-Assyrian resistance for a generation. Since he was left in control of Babylon for a decade following the battle, it is apparent that the encounter at Der was, at best, undecisive for Sargon who now, as the Eponym Chronicle shows, turned his attention "against [Hatt]i," i.e., the west.

The battle of Der is interesting not only as a prelude to Sargon's first western campaign but also because it is unusually well documented. In C. J. Gadd's words,[114] "There are now three different accounts of the battle of Der . . . , victory being claimed in almost the same terms for Humbanigash [by the Babylonian Chronicle], for Sargon [*ARAB* II, §§ 4, 118, 137, etc.], and now for Merodach-baladan, whom the [Babylonian] Chronicle itself had contemptuously dismissed as arriving too late for the action." Merodach-baladan's version has been recovered on a barrel-cylinder from Uruk which Sargon had brought to Kalah and then replaced with his own.[115]

Against the western rebellion Sargon was considerably more successful. Yaubidi was defeated near Qarqar and executed; Hamath, his base of operations, was destroyed together with Hatarika (Hadrach),[116] and the other rebellious cities, in-

[112] E.g., *ANET*, p. 285. But R. Borger, *JNES*, XIX (1960), 49–53, has argued instead for a reading *Re'e* which, if accepted, renders the usual identification with "So', king of Egypt" (II Kings 17:4) untenable; see now H. Goedicke, *BASOR*, No. 171 (Oct. 1963), 64–66.

[113] Tadmor, *JCS*, XII (1958), 25, contrary to previous opinion that placed the suppression of the revolt in this year.

[114] *Iraq*, XV (1953), 128.

[115] *Ibid.*, pp. 123–34; cf. also R. Follet, *Biblica*, XXXV (1954), 413–28.

[116] Thus according to the "Acharne Stele" which Sargon erected along his line of march to commemorate his victory; cf. A. Malamat,

cluding Samaria, were recaptured. The "subjugation" of Judah, i.e., its payment of tribute,[117] was a natural consequence. The campaign climaxed in a victorious sweep of the Philistine coast. Eqron and Gabbatunu (biblical Gibbeton) were razed,[118] as well as Gaza, the center of Philistine opposition, and the Assyrians advanced to the very gates of Egypt which for the first time was defeated and forced to pay tribute. Finally, the siege of Tyre begun by Shalmaneser V was brought to a successful conclusion in this campaign.

Thus Sargon showed in no uncertain manner that he was prepared to carry on in the aggressive footsteps of his two predecessors. And he saw to it that the lessons of his energetic campaigning would not be lost on his subjects and vassals. At Dur-sharrukin ("Sargonsburg," today Khorsabad), he spent most of his reign erecting an entirely new capital city for himself, with a magnificent palace whose walls he decorated with reliefs illustrating this and subsequent campaigns.[119] The execution of Yaubidi and other rebels was depicted in realistic detail in Hall VIII as a warning to visiting princes, while Hall V was given over to the rest of the campaign of 720.[120] It would be no wonder if Sargon's first western campaign left a deep impression on Judah and, indeed, it has been argued that it was referred to with awe in a prophecy as late as Zechariah 9:1–5, whose topographical allusions can now all be linked to this campaign.[121]

A respite followed for the west, but it lasted only two years (719–718), during which Sargon was engaged in the far

---

IEJ, I (1950–51), 153; A. L. Oppenheim, *ANET*, p. 281, n. 1. For the incorporation of the defeated Hamathite troops into the Assyrian army, cf. now Barbara Parker, *Iraq*, XXIII (1961), 15 and 40 f. (ND 2646).

[117] Tadmor, *JCS*, XII (1958), 38 f., n. 146.

[118] As shown by the captions to the reliefs of Hall V in Khorsabad; cf. below, n. 119. For the proposed identification of Gibbeton, cf. now B. Mazar, *IEJ*, X (1960), 71 f.

[119] M. El-Amin, *Sumer*, IX (1953), 35–59, 214–28, and X (1954), 23–42.

[120] The capture of Hamath, a center of the Phoenician ivory craft, may have supplied the models, materials, craftsmen, and even some of the finished pieces for the vast program of ivory decoration that now ensued at Khorsabad and Kalah; Mallowan, *Iraq*, XV (1953), 17.

[121] A. Malamat, *IEJ*, I (1950–51), 150–52.

north. In 717, according to a newly-published text,[122] Carchemish conspired against Assyria and Sargon unleashed a two-year show of strength (717–716) throughout the entire west which effectively quelled whatever opposition was left after 720. Carchemish was defeated and incorporated into the empire, another Assyrian province was organized in Palestine, and captive Arabian tribes were settled in Samaria.[123] Finally, Sargon marched to the Egyptian border once more and, according to a newly published fragment from Asshur, defeated Shilkanni, king of Egypt, at the city of the river of Egypt, probably identical with Raphia/Rapihu.[124]

In the midst of these events, there occurred the death of Ahaz of Judah, the "broken rod" of Isaiah 14:28–32.[125] The historical Isaiah had perhaps never been such a partisan of Ahaz as "the Isaiah of legend";[126] he either sensed or himself contributed to the decisive change in Judean policy implied by Hezekiah's accession. Sargon did not recognize it, or more likely was already on his way back to Assyria. Otherwise he would surely have invaded Judah now, instead of waiting till 712. Certainly Hezekiah showed his hand at once, for in his first or 2nd year (715 or 714) falls the proclamation of his Passover, together with an invitation that embraced not only Judah but the new Assyrian province in Israel as well.[127] Thus he inaugurated not only a great religious reform but also an anti-Assyrian policy both of which, resumed by Josiah, ultimately enabled Judah to survive Assyria.

In the meantime, Sargon was again occupied on the northern frontier, carving out new provinces and waging mountain warfare of the type made famous by the account of his eighth campaign.[128] But the diversion was short-lived for, in 712,[129]

[122] H. Tadmor, *JCS*, XII (1958), 22 f.

[123] For dating this event to 716, not 715, see *ibid.*, p. 78.

[124] E. F. Weidner, *AfO*, XIV (1941), 40–53; cf. the restorations by Tadmor, *JCS*, XII (1958), 77 f. The identification of Shilkanni (i.e., Shirkanni) with the 3rd or 4th pharaoh preserved in Greek transcription as Osorkon (i.e. Sorkon) has the support of Albright, *BASOR*, No. 141 (Feb. 1956), pp. 23–26.

[125] So at least W. A. Irwin, *AJSL*, XLIV (1928), 73–87.

[126] S. H. Blank, *Prophetic Faith in Isaiah* (1958), chap. ii.

[127] II Chron. 30:1–31:1. Cf. Thiele, *Mysterious Numbers*, pp. 129–32.

[128] Cf. most recently E. M. Wright, *JNES*, II (1943), 173–86;

[1] Statue of Lamgi-mari, one of the kings of Mari in the early 3rd millennium.

[2] A Nuzu "lion," from the Hurrian level.

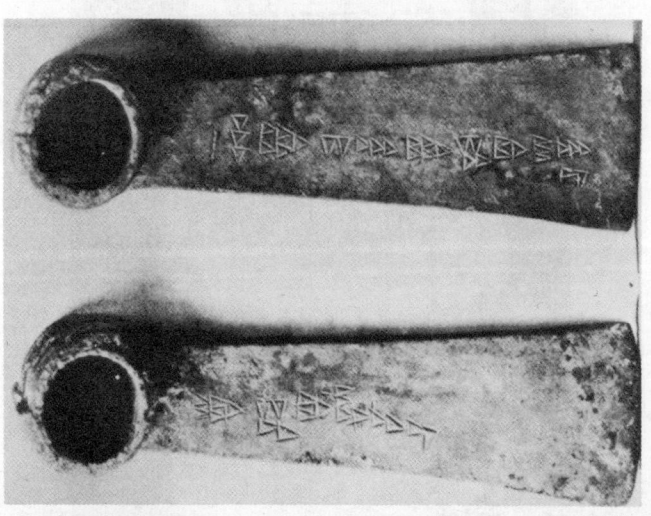

[3] Adzes from Ugarit, now in the Louvre Museum in Paris. The upper one reads "Kharusenni, chief of priests" (ḫrsn rb khnm). The lower one is one of four reading simply "chief of priests" (rb khnm).

[4] A bas-relief from Ugarit showing the Canaanite weathergod Hadad (familiarly Baal 'Lord') brandishing his thunderbolt and lightning. The small figure at his knees is probably the king, hands lifted in prayer. He stands on a chest or tub with a lid, reminiscent of the "bronze platform" upon which Solomon stood to pray at the dedication of the temple (II Chron. 6:13).

[5] Figurines near Buseirah (Bozrah) in Edom.

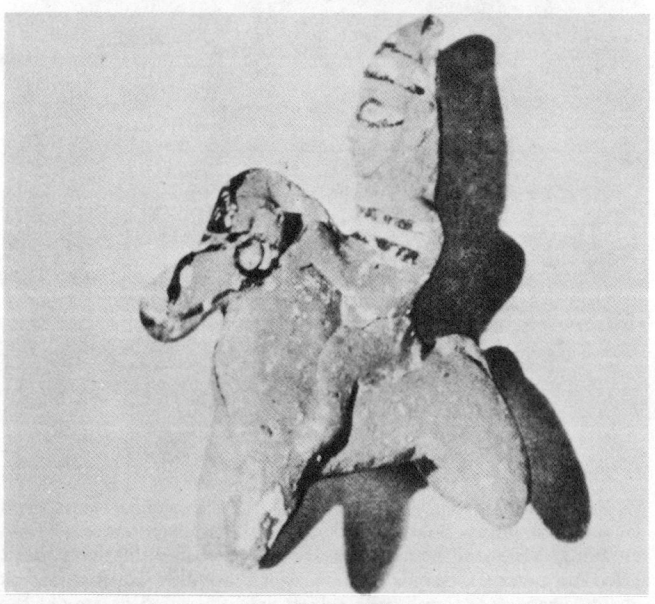

[6] A horse-and-rider pottery figurine from an Ammonite tomb at Meqabelein, near Amman, Jordan.

[7] Statue of Yarah ʿazar, found outside the city wall of Amman. On the base of the statue is a short inscription identifying the official depicted.

[8] A frankincense tree, *Boswellia Carterii,* on the plain of Dhofar along the Indian Ocean in southern Arabia.

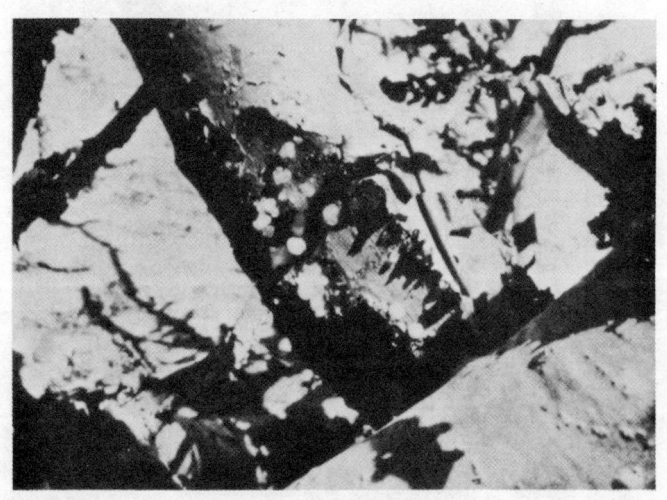

[9] Tears of gum resin exuding from the tapped branch of a frankincense tree in Dhofar.

[10] A stele dedicated to Melqart by Bir-hadad, king of Aram, found in the vicinity of Aleppo.

[11] The stele IB from Sefire, containing in lines 9 and 10 a description of the boundaries of Aram in the mid-8th century B.C.

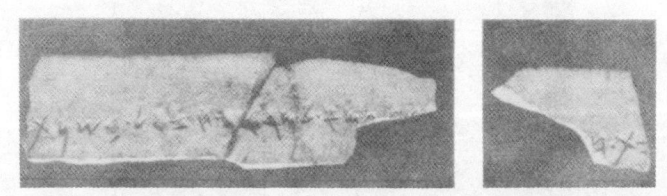

[12] An ivory plaque from the sideboard of a bed, found at Arslan-Tash (ancient Hadatta) on the Euphrates River. The inscription in Aramaic is dedicated to "our lord Hazael."

[13] A statue of the Assyrian king Shalmaneser III, found at Nimrud.

[14] A cuneiform tablet containing a vassal treaty of Esarhaddon, found at Kalah on the Tigris River.

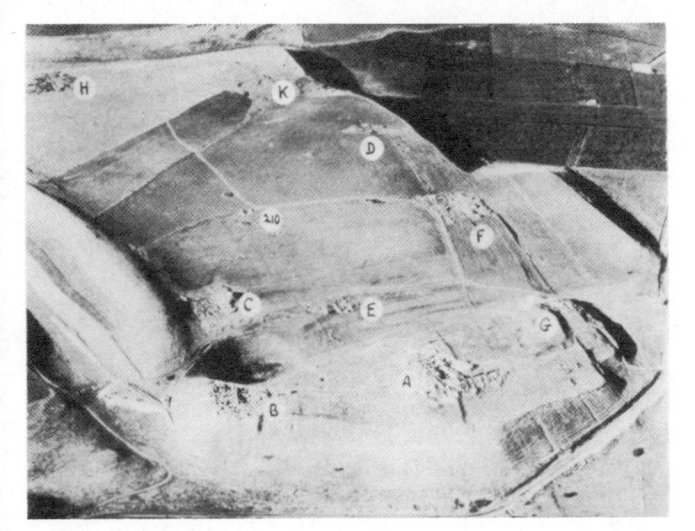

[15] An aerial view of the site of Hazor, looking to the north. The various excavated areas can be located by the letter key. The heavily fortified tell proper is at the bottom of the photograph, while the lower city fills the plateau north of it.

[16] The Holy of Holies in the Canaanite orthostat temple at Hazor, showing the two phases of Temple I. The standing pillar and the square base belong to the later floor (Ia, 13th century B.C.); the two column bases belong to the older and original floor (Ib, 14th century B.C.).

[17] A view of the furnishings in the Holy of Holies of Temple Ia, as they were found on its floor.

[18] A close aerial view of Area A at Hazor after the conclusion of the dig. At the right is Solomon's gate, with the casemate wall running down into the center of the picture. The pillared building of Ahab's time (stratum VIII) is at the center left, and left of it is a fine private house, similar to one found at Shechem, of stratum VI–V (8th century B.C.). Below Solomon's gate is the Late Bronze Age palatial building with orthostat entrance found in 1958, while below the casemate wall is the monumental staircase. A huge MB II building lies in the center of the picture, to the right of the pillared building. Below it are Early Bronze houses.

Palestine once more felt the full impact of the Assyrian arms. Sargon stayed "in the land" according to the Eponym Chronicle, which confirms Isaiah's statement that his commander-in-chief, the *turtanu*, led the operations,[130] against the claims of Sargon's annalists (*ANET*, p. 286), that he personally led the operation. The provocation for Sargon's third and last western campaign came from Ashdod, where a certain Iamani or Iadna[131] had been elevated to kingship by the anti-Assyrian party in a rebellion that implicated all the southern states including Judah and Lower Egypt. Ashdod was captured in the same year and organized into a new Assyrian province;[132] Lower Egypt was given to the Nubian ruler of Upper Egypt as a reward for extraditing Iamani; Judah was defeated, and foreign captives were settled in the Philistine cities. A Kalah letter mentioning the tribute of Egypt, Gaza, Judah, Moab, Ammon (*ba-an am-ma-na-a-a*), Edom, and Eqron may date from this campaign;[133] then a period of relative stability settled over the area.

For the rest of his reign (710–705), Sargon was largely occupied with the restless Arameans penetrating Babylonia from the Sealand at its extreme south. Indeed, it is possible to see in the sequel to Isaiah's Ashdod prophecy a reference to the Sealand campaign of 710.[134] The ever-dangerous Merodach-baladan was removed from the throne of Babylon and Sargon himself "took the hands of Bel" and assumed the kingship of Babylon (709). Merodach-baladan was allowed to remain as prince of Bit-jakin, but presently his capital of

---

A. L. Oppenheim, "The City of Assur in 714 B.C.," *ibid.*, XIX (1960), 133–47.

[129] For this date and re-edition of texts bearing on the campaign, cf. Tadmor, *JCS*, XII (1958), 79–84.

[130] Hebrew *tartan;* Isa. 20:1. He may have been the Zer-ibni of the Harper Letter No. 1073, according to R. C. Thompson, *Iraq*, IV (1937), 35–42. Cf. also M. El-Amin, *Sumer*, IX (1953), 216–19.

[131] Usually understood as the "Ionian (Greek)"; but cf. now Tadmor, *JCS*, XII (1958), 80, n. 217.

[132] [Fragments of a stele of Sargon II were discovered at the site of ancient Ashdod by an archaeological expedition in the summer of 1963.—Ed.]

[133] ND 2765, published by Saggs, *Iraq*, XVII (1955), 134 f.

[134] E. Dhorme, *Recueil Edouard Dhorme* (1951), pp. 301–4.

Dur-jakin was destroyed,[135] and the mission which he later sent to Hezekiah (II Kings 20:12 ff. = Isa. 39) must be dated during his subsequent exile. An important new Kalah letter, probably written by Sargon to the crown prince Sennacherib about this time, refers to Merodach-baladan as Apla-iddina, thus throwing light on his curious patronymic in the biblical account.[136] The letter is primarily concerned with war and diplomacy on the northern frontier, and it was there that Sargon met his death in battle in 705.

V. Pax Assyriaca (705–648)

The accession of Sennacherib, usually dated 12 Abu 705,[137] symbolized in many ways the start of a new phase in the Assyrian impact on western Asia. No longer did the Assyrian army march annually towards new conquests. The Eponym Chronicle, which had, in effect, dated the years by campaigns since Shalmaneser III (above, p. 158), typically enough ends with the first years of Sennacherib. Only eight campaigns marked the twenty-four years of his reign besides two conducted by his generals, and the royal annalists made no attempt to edit the record (as they had with Sargon) in order to make it appear otherwise.[138] Assyrian power was, in fact, approaching the natural limits of which it was capable, and the thrusts which were now made into more distant regions such as Persia, central Anatolia, or Egypt were either repulsed or only temporarily successful. Although the warlike ideals of their forebears continued to color the records of the later Sargonids, the impression of sustained militarism that they create is an exaggerated one. The real spirit of the time is revealed, on the one hand, by such marvels of civil engineer-

[135] For the proposed identification of Dur-jakin cf. H. W. F. Saggs, *Sumer*, XIII (1957), 190–95 and Pls. I–II.

[136] "Son of Baladan"; cf. Saggs, *Iraq*, XX (1958), 182–87, 202–8 (ND 2759). On this letter, cf. J. Friedrich, *AfO*, XIX (1959–60), 151.

[137] But see the arguments of J. Lewy, A. Deimel Anniversary Volume (= *Analecta Orientalia* XII [1935]), pp. 225–31.

[138] In abandoning the cumbersome fiction of the annual campaign (*palu*) they restored the system of counting by actual campaign (*girru*) used previously in the period of Assyrian weakness by Shamshi-adad V; cf. Tadmor, *JCS*, XII (1958), 29–32.

ing as Sennacherib's aqueduct at Jerwan[139] and, on the other, by the greatly increased attention to administrative matters reflected in the growing amount of royal correspondence (above, p. 177). Literature and learning too came into their own, and the vast library assembled by Ashurbanipal is only the most dramatic expression of the new leisure. In spite of their protestations to the contrary, the Assyrian kings were inclined to sit back and enjoy the fruits of empire.

The new "Pax Assyriaca" stabilized the relations of Assyria and her western vassals to some extent. Where we have outlined no less than six major Assyrian campaigns to the west in the preceding forty years, there were only three of comparable magnitude in the nearly sixty years here under review, namely, Sennacherib's invasion of Judah in 701, Esarhaddon's capture of Sidon in 677, and the more or less continuous decade of warfare against Egypt by Esarhaddon and Ashurbanipal (673–663). The Assyrian records of these campaigns are presented in considerable detail in *ANET* (pp. 287–301) and, apart from the vassal treaties of Esarhaddon (see below, p. 185), new additions to the inscriptions of Sennacherib,[140] Esarhaddon[141] and Ashurbanipal[142] since then have not thrown much further light on Judeo-Assyrian relations.

Sennacherib's campaign against Hezekiah in 701 is well known.[143] It presents us with an unusually complete account of a single event told from both sides—if indeed it was a single event. In part because of the very different interpretations put on it by the biblical and the Assyrian sources, Albright[144] has argued that there were actually two contests between

[139] Thorkild Jacobsen, *Oriental Institute Publications*, XXIV (1935).

[140] Cf. especially A. Heidel, *Sumer*, IX (1953), 117–88. This prism is a duplicate of *ARAB* II, §§ 285–92.

[141] Now collected by R. Borger, *Die Inschriften Asarhaddons* (= *AfO Suppl.* IX [1956]), to which add A. Heidel (and A. L. Oppenheim), *Sumer*, XII (1956), 9–37; R. Borger, *AfO*, XVIII (1957), 113 ff.; J. Nougayrol, *ibid.*, pp. 314–18; Borger, *ibid.*, XIX (1959–60), 148; A. R. Millard, *Iraq*, XXIII (1961), 176–78; P. Hulin, *ibid.*, XXIV (1962), 116–18 and Pl. XXXV, and below, n. 151. For the stamp and cylinder seals of Esarhaddon, cf. Barbara Parker, *ibid.*, p. 38 (ND 7080).

[142] Cf. below, pp. 185 f.

[143] Cf. the bibliography given in *ANET*, p. 287, n. 1 (bottom).

[144] Most recently *BASOR*, No. 141 (Feb. 1956), pp. 25 f. Cf. also John Bright, *A History of Israel* (1959), pp. 282–87.

Sennacherib and Hezekiah and that the Assyrians won the first but lost the second. This theory is plausible, for it would not be out of character for the Deuteronomist to dismiss the defeat of a good king in three verses,[145] nor for Sennacherib to pass over his defeat in total silence. By the same reasoning, however, we would have to suppose that there had been two or even three battles of Der (above, p. 178)! As a matter of fact, it is difficult to see where, in Sennacherib's reign, a second campaign against Judah should be placed. His exploits are well known through 691, and do not include any further attacks on Palestine; even the campaigns against Cilicia and Tilgarimmu (696–695) were conducted by his generals. And by this time, as Thiele has shown, Hezekiah was "sick unto death" and Manasseh was coregent of Judah;[146] the account of II Kings 18:17–19:35 would make little sense in this context.

An interesting sidelight to the siege of Lachish that accompanied Sennacherib's attempt on Jerusalem is provided by Barnett.[147] His comparison of the Nineveh reliefs depicting the captives at Lachish with those illustrating the bodyguard of the king in Assyria show some of them wearing the same peculiar headdress and tunics. He takes these Lachishites to be the earliest historical example of a "Jewish regiment." The famous speech of the Rab-shaqeh has also been put in a new light. The Assyrian policy of resettlement was not without its positive sides; to some extent it represented an attempt to cope with the vestiges of Aramean nomadism, and the attractions of resettlement that are put in the Rab-shaqeh's mouth in II Kings 18:32 find a parallel in Tiglath-pileser's diplomatic approach to the Babylonian rebels thirty years earlier.[148]

Manasseh reigned for fifty-five years (696–642), forty-five of them as sole ruler. It was probably his loyalty to Assyria, both politically (*ANET*, pp. 291, 294) and culturally (II Kings 21), which enabled him to hold the throne for this

[145] II Kings 18:14–16; these verses are entirely absent from the account in Isa. 36 and in II Chron. 32.

[146] *Mysterious Numbers*, pp. 155 f. Hezekiah became ill about the time of the siege, fifteen years before his death in 687 (cf. II Kings 20:6), and made Manasseh coregent in 696 at the age of twelve (II Kings 21:1), i.e., as soon as he was old enough for the purpose.

[147] R. D. Barnett, *IEJ*, VIII (1958), 161–64.

[148] Saggs, *Iraq*, XVII (1955), 47; XVIII (1956), 55.

unprecedented length of time. Even the assassination of Sennacherib in 681[149] did not entice him to revolt as it did Babylonia.[150] Moreover, the new Assyrian king made sure that the next succession would proceed more smoothly. Fragments of eight "grand tablets" (*tupkallu*) found at Kalah in 1955 show how Esarhaddon in 672 forced his Iranian vassals to swear to support the accession of his sons in Assyria and Babylonia after his death.[151] Similar treaties may well have been imposed on the western vassals.[152] Esarhaddon's planning bore fruit, and for seventeen years his designated successors ruled the empire side by side, Ashurbanipal from Nineveh and Shamash-shum-ukin from Babylon. But in 651, civil war broke out between the two brothers. After four years of bloody warfare, Ashurbanipal won the victory, but at a heavy price. The Pax Assyriaca had been irreparably broken, and the period of Assyrian greatness was over.[153]

[149] On the death of Sennacherib (II Kings 19:37) see E. Kraeling, *JAOS*, LIII (1933), 335–46. For the extensive literature in German on the same subject, see *ANET*, p. 288, n. 1. For new documents bearing on it cf. J. Nougayrol, *Syria*, XXXIII (1956), 158 f. n. 6, and R. C. Thompson, *The Prisms of Esarhaddon* (1931), pp. 7 f.

[150] Cf. E. F. Weidner, *AfO*, XVII (1954–56), 5–9, for a letter showing an unsuccessful attempt to enlist Elamite support for rebellion against Esarhaddon in this or the following year. R. Labat, *Archiv Orientální*, XVII:2 (1949), 1–6 has thrown further light on this period.

[151] D. J. Wiseman, *The Vassal-treaties of Esarhaddon* (= *Iraq*, XX:1 [1958]). Together with the ivories, these treaties constitute the most important of the many rich fruits of the new British excavations at Kalah. They contain much illustrative material for biblical covenants, some of which has already been brought out by Wiseman, *ibid.*, pp. 22–28 and M. Tsevat, *JBL*, LXXVIII (1959), 199–204.

[152] For a somewhat earlier treaty with Ba'al of Tyre which, however, has more of the character of a parity treaty, cf. Langdon, *RA*, XXVI (1929), 189–94; E. F. Weidner, *AfO*, VIII (1932–33), 29–34.

[153] For the possible involvement of Judah on the side of Babylon, cf. II Chron. 33:11 and W. F. Albright, *The Biblical Period* (1963), p. 79.

VI. Decline and Fall (648–609)

The last forty years of Assyrian history were marked by constant warfare in which Assyria, in spite of occasional successes, was for the first time in a century on the defensive. The principal historical source for these years is the Babylonian Chronicle, recently augmented by important new finds (above, p. 175). Assyrian royal records are sparse, and even the order of the eponyms is uncertain after 648.

The inscriptions of the last Assyrian kings were collected by M. Streck, *Assurbanipal und die letzten assyrischen Könige* (= *Vorderasiatische Bibliothek* VII [1916]), supplemented by Th. Bauer, *Das Inschriftenwerk Assurbanipals* (= *Assyriologische Bibliothek* I [1933]). For additions to the corpus, see particularly B. Meissner, *AfO*, VIII (1932–33), 51; E. F. Weidner, *ibid.*, pp. 175–203; *idem*, *AfO*, XIII (1939–41), 204–18; D. J. Wiseman, *Iraq*, XIII (1951), 24–26, and R. Borger, *AfO*, XVII (1954–56), 346 (Ashurbanipal). E. Ebeling, *A. Deimel Anniversary Volume* (= *Analecta Orientalia* XII [1935]), pp. 71–73 and D. J. Wiseman, *Iraq*, XII (1950), 197 (ND 284) (Ashur-etil-ilani). F. X. Steinmetzer, *A. Deimel AV* (= *Analecta Orientalia* XII [1935]), pp. 302–6; F. M. Th. de Liagre Böhl, *Akkadian Chrestomathy* (1947), No. 25; M. Falkner, *AfO*, XVI (1952–53), 305–10; cf. *eadem*, *AfO*, XVII (1954–56), 321 (Sin-shar-ishkun).[154] For an attempt to restore the order of the "post-canonical" eponyms cf. *eadem*, *ibid.*, pp. 100–20.

The new state of affairs was not without its repercussions in Judah. Though Amon succeeded his long-lived father in orderly enough fashion in 642, and continued his pro-Assyrian policies (II Kings 21:20 f.; II Chron. 33:22), the unrest that gripped the empire (Elam revolted in 641) spread to Judah. Amon was murdered after just two years of rule in what was certainly an anti-Assyrian move. It was probably a part of the uprising of all the western territories which Ashurbanipal moved quickly to quell in 640.[155] Even Samaria may have joined the revolt, for the foreign populations which "Asnap-

---

[154] Note now also J.-M. Aynard, *Le prisme du Louvre AO 19.939* (1957) with the review by Borger, *Bibliotheca Orientalis*, XVI (1959), 137–39; *idem*, *AfO*, XIX (1959–60), 153 (Ashurbanipal); *ibid.*, p. 143 (Ashur-etil-ilani).

[155] Cf. A. Malamat, *IEJ*, III (1953), 26–29.

par" settled there (Ezra 4:9 f.) could well have been prisoners of the Elamite revolt.[156] At the approach of the Assyrian king, the "people of the land" grew fainthearted, slew the rebels, and made Josiah king (II Kings 21:24; II Chron. 33:25), thus apparently avoiding further Assyrian retribution.

But Josiah was no Amon. By 632, "though he was still a young man,"[157] he began to revive the anti-Assyrian political and religious policies of Hezekiah, and the death of Ashurbanipal in 627[158] assured the success of these policies. In this same year, his 12th, Josiah annexed the Assyrian provinces of Samaria, Gilead and Galilee,[159] enabling him to extend his reforms, including presently the Deuteronomic reform (622), to all Israel. The last kings of Assyria[160] were powerless to oppose him, nor were they a match for the great coalition of Media, Babylon, and Palestine that now began to close in on Assyria. The complete annihilation of all the Assyrian capitals—Nineveh, Kalah, Asshur, Dur-sharrukin—in 612 is attested in part by the Babylonian Chronicle and even more graphically in the archaeological evidence from these sites. Its impact on the contemporary world can still be measured in the ode of Nahum, and possibly in Zephaniah. Only Egypt remained loyal to Assyria, and Pharaoh Necho's effort to aid the last remnants of Assyrian power at Haran under Ashur-

[156] *Ibid.*, p. 28.

[157] II Chron. 34:3; he was sixteen years old at the time.

[158] So according to the important new duplicate of the Adad-guppi inscription from Haran; cf. above, n. 33. This inscription shows that Ashurbanipal reigned forty-two years, and makes his identification with Kandalanu of Babylon, who also died in 627, once more highly probable.

[159] II Chron. 34:3b–7. Cf. F. M. Cross, Jr. and D. N. Freedman, *JNES*, XII (1953), 56–58. They took "the annexation of the Assyrian provinces by Josiah in 628" (i.e. 628/7) as an example of "the tendency of vassal states to revolt after the death of a strong king," (p. 57 and n. 10). That this "strong king" was Ashurbanipal rather than Ashur-etil-ilani is now all the more likely.

[160] Ashur-etil-ilani ruled at least four years, and Sin-shar-ishkun, another son of Ashurbanipal, at least seven, but it is impossible to reconcile all the known data for these kings with the new figures from Haran (note 158 above) except perhaps on the attractive but unproved hypothesis of the identity of the two; cf. R. Borger, *Wiener Zeitschrift für die Kunde des Morgenlandes*, LV (1959), 62–76. Ashur-uballit II, the last Assyrian king, ruled approximately 611–609.

uballit II were seriously impaired by Josiah at Megiddo (609). Four years later, the battle of Carchemish finished what Josiah had begun: Egypt bowed to Nebuchadnezzar and a new era opened for the entire Near East. Lacking an army to fill its coffers with the tribute of her neighbors, or a monarch to divert the waters of a dozen rivers to its fields and cities, the land of Assyria became deurbanized, returning to a primitive stage of civilization such as it had not known for two thousand years; when, finally, it re-emerged as the vassal kingdom of Adiabene under the Parthians of the first century of our era, a supreme irony of history decreed that its royal house convert to Judaism.[161]

[161] Cf. G. Goossens, *Compte rendu de la 3me rencontre assyriologique internationale* (1954), pp. 84–100.

Part II

MAJOR EXCAVATED CITIES OF PALESTINE

11

EXCAVATIONS AT HAZOR* (1955–1958)

YIGAEL YADIN

[*The following article represents a digest of the reports presented in the* Biblical Archaeologist *written at the conclusion of each of the campaigns at Hazor. Since the running presentation of the progress of a dig has its own fascination, something of that flavor has been retained, but a considerable amount of repetition and back-reference has been removed, and the reports on each of the areas of excavation have been pulled together so as to depict the excavators moving toward their conclusions as their work progressed. The reader will find that reference to the chart appended to the article by Professor Yadin for this volume will be helpful in following stratigraphic and chronological matters.*—THE EDITORS.]

Hazor is one of the few ancient cities in Palestine about which many historical facts were known, even prior to excavations, owing to the numerous data related to it and found in many literary documents from Egypt, Palestine, Mesopotamia and, of course, the Bible itself. The city is mentioned for the first time in the famous 19th century B.C. Egyptian Execration texts, listing potential enemies in the external provinces of the Egyptian empire. Two letters, published not long ago from the well-known archives of Mari (modern *Tell Hariri* on the middle Euphrates) dating *ca.* 1700 B.C., inform the king of Mari that certain messengers from various cities in Mesopotamia are on their way to Hazor. In another letter the king is informed that a caravan has arrived from Hazor and Qatna, accompanied by Babylonian envoys. Thus Hazor was at that time one of the most important cities in Palestine, in fact the only city from that area to be mentioned in those documents.

* The James A. de Rothschild Expedition at Hazor, operated on

Later on, Hazor is mentioned among the conquered cities by Thutmosis III, Amenophis II and Seti I. An interesting allusion to Hazor is found in the famous Papyrus Anastasi I (13th century B.C.) in which Hori, a royal official, challenges Amen-em-opet, the scribe, to answer him on various military and topographical problems. The passage relating to Hazor is "Where does the *mahir* [a swift military courier] make the journey to Hazor? What is its stream like?"

The most important data concerning Hazor from external documents have come from the famous letters found in the archives of el-Amarna, in Egypt, from the 14th century B.C. Those letters were written mainly from the petty kingdoms in the Near East and are addressed to the Egyptian kings. In four letters, Hazor is the subject of the correspondence. In two letters the kings of Tyre and Ashtaroth, respectively, complain that Abdi-tarshi, the king of Hazor had rebelled against the pharaoh, and taken several cities from the plaintiffs. In the other two letters the king of Hazor denies all these complaints and, while pledging his loyalty to the pharaoh, takes the opportunity to complain about his neighbors.

Hazor became "famous" in our era, however, owing to its prominence in the biblical narratives concerning Joshua and Deborah. Indeed, those narratives had led Prof. J. Garstang to suggest the location of Hazor within the ruins of the big *Tell el-Qedah* or *Waqqas* in the Huleh plain. The victory of Joshua by the "waters of Merom," according to the biblical narrative, marks a decisive phase in the conquest of northern Canaan:

> And Joshua at that time turned back [after the battle of the Waters of Merom], and took Hazor and smote the king thereof [i.e. Jabin] with the sword: for Hazor beforetime [i.e. at the time of Joshua, but no longer at the time of the narrator] was the head of all these kingdoms . . . and he burnt Hazor with fire. . . . But the cities that stood on their mounds [lit. on their tells] Israel

---

behalf of the Hebrew University, Jerusalem with funds contributed by the P.J.O.A., the Anglo-Israel Exploration Committee (headed by Sir Maurice Block, Mr. Israel Sieff and Dr. A. Lerner) and the Government of Israel. The director was ably assisted by Mr. M. Dunayevsky (the architect of the Expedition), in addition to the members of the staff whose names are mentioned in the course of this article.

burned none of them, save Hazor only did Joshua burn (Josh. 11:10–13).

Later on, during the time of the Judges (according to Judg. 4:2), "The Lord sold them into the hand of Jabin king of Canaan, that reigned in Hazor; the captain of whose host was Sisera, which dwelt in Harosheth of the Gentiles."

Two more biblical passages inform us about Hazor in later periods. Solomon rebuilt Megiddo, Gezer, and Hazor (I Kings 9:15), the three strategic cities dominating the plains of Aijalon, Jezreel and the Huleh, and turned them into garrison cities. The last we hear of Hazor in the Bible is that, "In the days of Pekah king of Israel came Tiglath-pileser [III], king of Assyria, and took Ijon and Abel-beth-maachah, and Janoah and Kedesh and Hazor and Gilead and Galilee, and the land of Naphtali, and carried them captive to Assyria" (II Kings 15:29) in the year 732 B.C.

The latest historical reference to Hazor is in I Maccabees 11:6 in which we are told that Jonathan fought against Demetrius (147 B.C.) in the "plain of Hazor."

The Ruins of Hazor

The ruins of Hazor lie in the Huleh plain at the foot of the eastern ridge of the mountains of upper Galilee, about fourteen kilometers, due north of the sea of Galilee, and about eight kilometers southwest of Lake Huleh. It is located in one of the most strategic areas of ancient Palestine—dominating the several branches of the famous Via Maris leading from Egypt to Mesopotamia, Syria and Anatolia. The present highway leading to Damascus runs about two kilometers south of it while the road leading north, literally traverses it.

The site comprises two distinct areas:

1. The tell (mound), bottle-shaped, stretches for about 600 meters—its "neck" in the west and its "base" in the east—and has an average width of about 200 meters, thus comprising more than twenty-five acres in area (compare the area of Megiddo, which is fifteen acres). Its very steep slopes rise up from the surrounding ravines to about forty meters.

2. A huge rectangular plateau—1000 meters in length and 700 in average width—lies immediately to the north of the mound. This plateau, which is also raised above the three surrounding ravines, is protected on its western side by a big

beaten-earth wall, still rising to a height of about fifteen meters, and its width at its foot is about 100 meters. This side of the rectangle, being originally at the same height as the area near it, was further protected by a gigantic moat to the west of the wall. The other three sides of the rectangle were steep enough to provide natural protection; and a glacis built on them turned the whole area into a well-fortified enclosure. This type of site—which is quite rare, and only Carchemish and Qatna in Syria could be compared with it in type and size—led Garstang to suggest that the "camp enclosure was large enough to accommodate in emergency 30,000 men with a corresponding number of horses and chariots." Garstang made soundings at Hazor in 1928 chiefly in order to fix the date of the Exodus and occupation of the country by Joshua. Unfortunately, except for a brief description in his famous book *Joshua-Judges*, his results were never published in detail. His main conclusion was that during the 15th century B.C. (the period in which according to him the story of Joshua began) the camp-enclosure "was apparently occupied only by temporary structures, for troops or travellers passing through, whether tents of goat-hair or maybe huts built of papyrus reeds" (p. 185). Moreover, he reached the firm conclusion that during the 14th–13th centuries B.C. the days of the big city were over, a conclusion that has baffled most scholars who believe that the main phase of the Exodus and conquest of Canaan fell precisely at that period. Garstang based his conclusion on "the complete absence of Mykenaean specimens" (p. 383); Mycenean pottery appears in this area from Greece and Cyprus only after about 1400 B.C. and disappears before the end of the 13th century B.C.

The Rothschild Expedition

The James A. de Rothschild Expedition had the following objectives as it approached the first of four campaigns:

1. To examine the character and nature of the big enclosure. Was it just a "camp" or a real city? If a city, when was it first built, what was its history, and when was its last destruction?

2. To explore the stratification of the mound proper and to establish the date of its final destruction.

3. To gather data for the determination of the material culture of northern Palestine, since before Hazor no serious

excavation had been carried out north of the sea of Galilee.

The four campaigns at Hazor took place in August–October 1955; mid-July to the end of October 1956; August–October 1957; and August–October 1958. Ten different areas were investigated, although work in only a few of them continued through all four seasons. Areas A, B and G were on the mound proper, while areas C, D, E, F, H, K and probe 210 were all in the enclosure.

AREA A
(Excavated under the supervision of Dr. Y. Aharoni in all four seasons.)

Area A was chosen near a row of columns discovered by Garstang in the center of the mound, attributed by him to the Solomonic period, and considered to be part of a stable for horses. Four strata, each representing a different city were uncovered in the first season; the first (from top to bottom) contained the remains of a town dating back to the end of the 8th and the beginning of the 7th century B.C. It represents a small settlement after the capture of the city by Tiglath-pileser III in 732 B.C. The second stratum revealed a city very effectively destroyed by fire. Its fallen roofs and the many beautiful vessels of basalt and pottery found still intact in their original place, proved that the population was driven away in haste, not to return. The date of the destruction, ascertained with the aid of the pottery, was the second half of the 8th century B.C. It was therefore assumed by us that this is the city which was destroyed by Tiglath-pileser III in 732 B.C. The third city contained typical 9th and 8th century pottery; the fourth stratum contained among other things many vessels of the Samaria type and we fixed the date of its construction, tentatively, to the period of Ahab in the third quarter of the 9th century. The most important building of this stratum is a big public structure with two rows of monolithic columns of nine pillars each. The first row was partially uncovered by Garstang in a very narrow trench and the second was discovered by us.

The later strata all made use of the pillars within their walls, or broke them up in those areas in which they interfered with the plans of the builders. The tops of the pillars were embedded in and formed part of the floors of the latest stratum. Although the exact function of the building (during both phases of its occupation) could not be ascertained in the first campaign, it proved definitely not to be a stable, but rather a big public building with two rows of pillars (about two meters in height) supporting a second story. A narrow trench proved that even below the floor of this building there were at least three more strata of Iron Age cities, which were left to be excavated in subsequent seasons. The most important single object from Area A is a bone handle of a scepter or mirror bearing beautiful and unique carvings of a four-winged figure holding in its outstretched hands a stylized "tree of life" in the so-called Phoenician style (9th century B.C.).

In the 1956 (second) season, work was concentrated mainly around four points:

1. The big public building with its two rows of pillars was completely cleared. It became obvious that the building had two periods of occupation, the first (Stratum VIII; note that the numbers of strata used are the final numbers for strata for the whole mound and are explained in the chart at the end of this article) during the time of Ahab and the second (Stratum VII) during the time of his successors. This building with its adjoining paved courts must have stood out majestically in the neighborhood. We believe it may have served as a storehouse of the type which must have existed in the neighborhood (as is attested by II Chron. 16:4): "And Ben-hadad . . . sent the captains of his armies against . . . all the store cities of Naphtali."

2. South of this building, where we had discovered in the first season the buried remains of City V (destroyed by Tiglath-pileser), there awaited us the first Hebrew inscriptions from the times of the kings of Israel ever discovered in Galilee. After removing the buildings of Stratum V we came upon buildings of Stratum VI, which belonged to wealthy merchants from the time of Jeroboam II (786-746 B.C.). In one of these houses we found two inscriptions in the old Hebrew script. One, which was incised on a jar, read LMKBRM, i.e., *belonging to Makhbiram,* a Hebrew name unknown either from the Bible or from inscriptions. We called the house where this inscription was found the house of Makhbiram. In the same house we found a second inscription, this one painted on a jar, which is unfortunately incomplete; what remains of it might be read YRB' (= Jeroboam?) and in the second line BN 'ELM (= the son of ELMATAN or ELIMELEKH). In the same house we also discovered a

beautiful cosmetic palette made of ivory, with a carving of a stylized tree-of-life on one side, and a head of a woman on the other, with two birds flanking the head carved on the narrow sides of the palette. It probably belonged to Mrs. Makhbiram.

Before leaving Stratum VI in this area, it is perhaps worthwhile to mention that the walls of this house were heavily damaged by an earthquake. Could this be the earthquake referred to in Amos: "The words of Amos . . . which he saw concerning Israel . . . in the days of Jeroboam the son of Joash, king of Israel, two years before the earthquake"?

3. East of the building with the pillars, and belonging to Stratum X, we discovered a well-built casemate city wall, which was most probably constructed by Solomon. The fact that the wall traversed the mound in its center suggests that Solomon built on only part of the mound and turned it into a garrison city (I Kings 9:15). This city wall was abandoned in later periods when the city expanded eastwards, and the casemates were turned into workshops, living quarters, etc. In one casemate we found about twenty jars of wine or oil, covered by the fallen roof of the room, while in another we struck a unique find: a big Red Sea shell used as a trumpet (9th century B.C.) in a manner still common among many primitive tribes in various parts of the world.

4. In order to establish the relation between Stratum X (Solomon) and that belonging to the latest Canaanite city in the Late Bronze Age (13th century) we cut a deep trench east of the casemate wall and perpendicular to it. This trench yielded most important historical data: between the Solomonic and the Late Bronze cities at least one other stratum was discovered belonging to the first centuries of the Iron Age, i.e., between 1200 and 950. Fixing the exact age of this intermediate stratum would make it possible to decide finally concerning the relation between the capture of Hazor attributed to Joshua and what took place according to Judges 4 at the time of Deborah (on this see below).

During the 1957 season, work in Area A was concentrated in three spots. First, it was determined that an elaborate residence south of the pillared building of Ahab's period was built in Stratum VI and continued to exist, after being ruined by an earthquake and rebuilt, in Stratum V. Signs of the earthquake here were clearly evident: large pieces of the plastered ceiling were scattered all over the rooms and remains of the pillars were found tilted. There was no evidence of man-made destruction or fire. The building's plan is most interesting and one of the finest examples of a well-to-do residence of the Israelite period ever discovered in the northern part of the country. The general plan is a square fifteen by fifteen meters, consisting of a large court at the southeast corner while its west and north sides are flanked by rows of rooms. Part of the court was covered, as is evident from the well-dressed stone pillars found in place. Here we also found household pottery, as well as other items, among them a cosmetic jar with engraved decorations.[1]

Most of the work in Area A was centered around the two northern halls of the pillared storehouse of Stratum VIII (Ahab's time). We had noticed during the previous season rectangular depressions in the floors of those halls, and had assumed, therefore, that the paving, built on ruins of earlier strata, had sunk in those places which corresponded to the space between the walls of the previous stratum. And, indeed, when the floors were now removed, structures of Stratum IX appeared beneath them of a layout similar to the sunken rectangles. In this stratum, two building phases were uncovered, the upper one most probably being the result of the restoration of the structures after their destruction (by Ben-hadad of Damascus?). Between the structures of Stratum IX and the casemate wall, we uncovered the pavement of a street, also belonging to that stratum. This confirmed our assumption that the wall continued to exist through Stratum IX. The interesting finds of this stratum include a terra-cotta statuette of a stylized head of a horse with a sun-disk-and-cross-impression on its forehead. Below Stratum IX, structures of Stratum X were found (two phases again) belonging to Solomon's time. Between the structures and the casemate wall the pavement of a street was once more discovered. The interest in deepening the dig here lay in the fact that the next city seems to belong to Late Bronze II (13th century), as is evident from the pottery. At this point in our work it seemed that there was a clear gap between the Canaanite era with its Late Bronze II pottery, and the restoration of the town by Solomon. Iron I pottery was scarcely found, and the little of it discovered indicated a temporary settlement only. This

[1] R. de Vaux has found similar fine Israelite homes, though earlier, at Tirzah: *RB*, LXII (1955), 575 ff.

fact proved later of great importance in solving the problems connected with Joshua and Deborah.

The outstanding find in Area A, and in fact in the whole Israelite city, was the gate of Stratum X, belonging to the Solomonic casemate city wall. We went about discovering it with Bible in one hand and spade in the other. The report that Solomon rebuilt Hazor and Megiddo (I Kings 9:15) enabled us to outline in advance, on the surface, the plan of Solomon's city gate by simply copying that of the gate discovered at Megiddo some years back by an expedition of Chicago's Oriental Institute. When finally the gate at Hazor was revealed, and actually turned out as expected, our laborers thought we were wizards indeed. The gate consists of six chambers, three on either side, with square towers on the external walls. Its plans and measurements (some twenty meters long) are identical with those of the Solomonic gate found at Megiddo, Stratum IVB. This fact not only confirms quite clearly the biblical narrative but even indicates that both gates were built by the same royal architect.

In the final season, we concentrated on three fields in Area A: the area immediately below the Solomonic building, the gate area, and the big trench which we began in the 1956 season east of the Solomonic casemate wall. All three fields yielded important results.

Below the Solomonic building (Stratum X) we came across the ovens and silos of the first Israelite settlement (Stratum XII) above the ruins of the last Canaanite city. This corroborated the evidence from Area B to be described below. These silos and ovens had been built on accumulated dirt which had been leveled. This proves that a gap of several decades must have elapsed, during which the dirt had accumulated, between the destruction of the Canaanite city and the first Israelite attempt to resettle it. No remains of Stratum XI (see Area B) were found in Area A, which further proves the limited size of this settlement.

Below the remains of Stratum XII we came upon the Canaanite strata, with richer Canaanite finds than in Area B. Here, as in the lower city, we found two levels belonging to the Late Bronze Age II (1400–1200). The later one (Stratum XIII) was relatively poorer than the earlier (Stratum XIV) belonging to the 14th century, i.e., the Amarna period. Stratum XIII consisted of several buildings and constructions which partially used remains from the previous building and showed a certain decline after the grandeur of Hazor in the Amarna period. Enough was discovered to indicate that here as in the lower city, occupation continued until the middle or the second half of the 13th century B.C. Two of the most interesting finds of Area A were discovered at this level, although both belonged originally to the earlier stratum.

The first is a tall stele or a sacred stone pillar set up in the earlier city but used also by the later occupants. When found, its top was broken off as though it had been deliberately chopped away. This was probably part of the idol destruction carried out by the conquering Israelites. The other object, although found incomplete, is one of the finest pieces of art found at Hazor. It is part of a basalt orthostat of exactly the same dimensions and features as the lion orthostat from the Area H temple described below. It bears the sculptured head of what seems to be a lioness. It is a door orthostat which belonged originally to a palatial building in Stratum XIV. This enables us to correlate the 14th century structure with the temple of 1B, and the 13th century Stratum XIII with the reconstructed temple in 1A.

This palatial building of Stratum XIV, the remains of which covered the whole area of excavation, was only partially uncovered since the rest of it extended outside the excavated area. Nevertheless enough was found to give us the following pattern: A large entrance in the east, consisting of a fine stone-built staircase and gate, led to a fenced court on the south. In the northern section was another court which gave access to the rooms of the main building which were west of it. Below the Solomonic gate, we found an entrance built of well-dressed basalt orthostats and sill-slabs put together by a master-mason. The orthostats, with the drilled holes at their top to take the joints of the brick and wood construction of the walls, are identical with those of the orthostat temple, a further indication of the link in this Canaanite period between the upper and lower cities.

The southern part of the building complex consisted of a large finely-paved cobbled court. Its purpose became apparent only when we found a huge underground water reservoir between this and the fenced court. It was fed by waters during the rainy season which accumulated in the paved court and flowed into the reservoir. The fine basalt inlet was still well preserved within the inner walls of the reservoir. The reservoir itself is about thirty meters long and its walls are finely plastered. It is of two parts: a large tunnel hewn out of the rock, ending in three chambers forming a trefoil; and a vaulted corridor leading into the tunnel with steps, some of which were built and others cut in the rock.

The basalt water inlet is an integral part of one of the corridor walls. The reservoir has a capacity of about 150 cubic meters. To fill it with an average annual rainfall of 500 millimeters (20 inches), the cobbled floor area would have to have covered at least 300 square meters. This is about the size of the area which we discovered. This reservoir must have served the occupants of the palatial building in time of siege. Similar techniques of collecting rain water were used in the lower city, even in the private houses.

Incidentally, it is probable that the reservoir tunnel may originally have been a tomb cave, and was converted into a reservoir by plastering its walls and building the additional corridor in the 14th century.

We had our biggest surprise in this area by being curious as to why the natural rock was much higher than we had anticipated. This prompted us to change our original plans and try and reach the earliest settlement on the mound. We were well rewarded, for the effort has given us the complete history of Hazor from its beginning to its end. From this "operation rock bottom" the following results emerged:

1. Stratum XV proved to be of the 15th century, and corresponded to level 2 in the lower city. We found a palatial building here, too, its thick walls built mainly of bricks which were partially reused in the similar building of Stratum XIV.

2. Strata XVII and XVI consisted of two floors representing two periods of occupation of a huge Middle Bronze II building (18th–16th centuries B.C.). This was either a fort or a palace, similar in dimensions and technique of construction to the one of the same period found in 1957 in Area F. The thick walls of this building, situated south of the building of Stratum XV were of considerable height. They were used by the Late Bronze population sometimes for other than structural purposes. Two stone steps, built in Stratum XIII leading to the top of these walls suggest their use as a platform of some kind, possibly a *bamah*, or high place. This building serves as further proof of the great size of Hazor as early as the Hyksos period, when the Lower City too was established, and suggests how Hazor developed into the largest of all the cities in Palestine.

3. Immediately below these strata we found in Stratum XVIII a large quantity of pottery of Middle Bronze I (2100–1900) but, alas, no buildings to go with it. Nevertheless the discovery is of historical importance, for it is at this period that the first mention of Hazor appears in ancient documents, i.e. in the earlier group of Egyptian Execration texts.

4. Immediately below this stratum we found three strata of buildings, the lowest (Stratum XXI) built on bedrock. Its houses were the first to be built at Hazor, some time in the second quarter of the 3rd millennium B.C. The other two (XX–XIX) contributed "Khirbet Kerak ware" typical of the Early Bronze Age III (26th–24th century B.C.). There would thus appear to be a gap in the history of the city between the end of the 3rd millennium and the occupation in Stratum XVIII at the beginning of the 2nd millennium.

With the excavation of this area, the number of strata at Hazor reached twenty-one (or twenty-two, if we add a possible additional phase in MB II), covering a span in time of nearly 2500 years. This conclusion was further confirmed in our dig in the big trench, east of the casemate wall. Here, too, we managed to reach bedrock and find upon it the first settlement of Hazor.

But the prize find of this dig was a tremendous city wall, twenty-five feet wide, built of bricks on a stone foundation and covered with very fine plaster. It was built in three sections, the outer and inner ones very well and neatly laid out while the center one was rather crude. This city wall with a fine drainage system made of clay pipes, found nearby, was constructed sometime in the Middle Bronze II period and must have served as the innermost wall guarding the heart of the Acropolis. Its construction was so sturdy that it must also have been used in the Late Bronze Age, and it is even possible that in Solomon's time it served as a revetment to hold the terrace on which his walls were built.

AREA B
(Excavated under the supervision of Mrs. Ruth Amiran in all four seasons.)

Area B lies at the western tip of the mound in its most protected part (see Plate 15). Here were discovered a number of citadels, one above the other. The latest proved to be of the Hellenistic period, while below it lay a citadel built sometime in the late 8th century or early 7th century but reconstructed and reused during the Persian period in the 5th century B.C. The plan of this building is square, with a central open court flanked on the north and south by oblong halls. The whole building was surrounded by small living rooms. During the reconstruction of the building and among other changes, a dividing wall was built in the northern hall, which contained many niches and it is most probable that during that period the building served as a base for a small cavalry garrison, as could be inferred from the many mangers added to the building.

We decided in 1956 to remove the well-preserved Persian citadel in the hope of uncovering below it the yet older citadel belonging to the Israelite period. We were amply rewarded for our decision; below the late building we discovered a most imposing citadel, inferior in construction only to the royal palaces discovered at Samaria, the capital of the northern kingdom of Israel. The citadel contained two parts: in the center the fort proper and to its north and south an annex containing the living quarters of its occupants. The plan of the fort is a simple one: a square with a row of square rooms as its northern and southern flanks, with two long and narrow halls in the center. The characteristic feature of the fort, however, is its method of construction: very thick walls (up to two meters in thickness) occupying about forty per cent of the total area of the fort, and very deep foundations, at places going down to about three meters below the floor. The corners of the building were built with imposing ashlar stones, some of them about a meter and a half long. But the most interesting, although tragic aspect of the dig at this area, was the evidence of the terrific destruction which befell the citadel. All the rooms were covered with a layer of ashes about one meter thick; the stones were all black and numerous charred planks and fragments of plaster from the ceiling were scattered all over the area. The eastern side of the citadel—the direction from which the fort was attacked—was destroyed to such an extent that at some places only the foundations below the floor level were visible. What a striking example of the method of destruction described so vividly by the Psalmist: "Raze it, raze it, even to the foundation thereof" (137:7).

The most important single find from the Israelite citadel is a partly broken ivory box (Samaria style) bearing carvings of a winged sphinx and a kneeling figure, praying before a "tree of life."

The type of pottery scattered on the floors—and other considerations—indicated quite plainly that we were looking at the remains of the destruction wrought by Tiglath-pileser III in 732 B.C.—a tragic illustration of the laconic biblical description of this event: "In the days of Pekah king of Israel came Tiglath-pileser, king of Assyria, and took . . . Hazor . . . and carried them captive to Assyria" (II Kings 15:29). A brief inscription on one of the wine jars discovered in the citadel added a somewhat intimate touch to the already highly dramatic site: LPQH, i.e., "for Pekah." The kind of the wine was indicated too: SMDR, i.e. *semadar*. This word occurs three times in the Bible, all in the Song of Songs. The word is translated as "tender grape:" "The fig tree putteth forth her green figs, and the vines with the *tender grapes* give a (good) smell" (Song of Songs 2:13). The occurrence of the word *semadar* on the jar will serve as a starting point for a fresh study of its exact meaning.

From the many interesting pieces of pottery and other objects found in this area, we should like to mention the discovery of a "cultic incense ladle" made of local marble and bearing a beautifully-carved palm on its back, its fingers grasping the "cup" of the ladle. One should bear in mind that the Hebrew word for a spoon or ladle is "palm."

All these discoveries were made in the debris of the last phase of occupation of the citadel, belonging to the days of Pekah, king of Israel. We found ample evidence, however, that the citadel was built about a century earlier, probably in the time of King Ahab, at the same time as the big building with the pillars in Area A was built. In the citadel we also found evidence of a major earthquake; at a certain period (probably that of Menahem) a big wall was added further to protect the city, a wall which was built through the northern part of the living-quarters annex.

The Israelite citadel had such thick walls and sturdy construction that it continued to exist a long time without the accumulation of occupation layers (resulting from the resurfacing of floors). The only way to solve the problem of its history was to excavate a wide area on three sides (north, east and south) of it with a view to uncovering the adjoining buildings which were destroyed and rebuilt more frequently. This we undertook in 1957.

The results of these excavations were most important, although less spectacular than those of the other areas. It is possible for us to relate the history of the citadel from its period of construction (Ahab; Stratum VIII; 9th century), up to its destruction in 732 B.C. (Stratum V) by the Assyrian king, Tiglath-pileser III.

In the areas adjoining the citadel, several public buildings were found, such as service rooms, storehouses, and towers, used mainly in connection with the citadel, as well as living quarters for the officers and their families. Among the finds from this area one should mention a large number of cosmetic palettes, an "incense-ladle" made of black stone, a terra-cotta woman's head, as well as two short inscriptions. One of the last mentioned (Stratum V) was incised on the exterior of a deep bowl and its only clearly readable word is *q-d-sh*, which can be interpreted in various ways: *qodesh* 'holy;' or *Qadesh*, the name of the neighboring city.

To understand the complicated problems of walls in this area, we had at first to overcome many difficulties, and only at the end of the season did we reach a solution. We found out that the builders of the citadel in Stratum VIII (Ahab) had used the casemate wall of Strata IX–X (Solomon), remains of which were discovered both north and south of the citadel, and did not build a new wall of their own. On the western part of the tell, they built their citadel on top of the casemate wall without any further addition, because the slope was sufficiently steep at this point to assure protection. The western wall of the citadel, therefore, served simultaneously as the city wall in this place. But owing to the serious Assyrian menace during the second half of the 8th century, the inhabitants of Stratum V did not find these precautions sufficient, but built their own wall on top of the structure, surrounding the whole citadel.

Thus the clearing of the casemate wall in Area B completes our information on the Solomonic fortifications.

In 1958, we concentrated on a section east of this citadel. We decided to remove the public buildings of Strata VI–V (8th century B.C.) which were found in 1957, to enable us to dig down to the Canaanite strata. And we were well rewarded.

Above the plastered floor of the open area of Stratum VII in front of the main entrance to the citadel, we had our first surprise. Two beautiful proto-Aeolic (or Ionic) capitals were lying on the floor, one upside down, the other with its carved face upwards. They formed a right-angle in which stood a well-preserved clay oven. This type of capital is the most characteristic architectural element of the public buildings in the time of the kings of Israel and Judah, and some had already been discovered in Megiddo, Samaria and Ramathrachel (near Jerusalem). It was clear that the capitals were not in their original positions, but had been used by later occupants as shelters for the oven when the original building was in ruins. It was equally obvious to us that the only building of which such large objects could have formed a part was the nearby 9th century citadel. We cleared the gap between the citadel and the adjacent service house and there we found on the sill of a well-paved corridor traces of a pilaster. This was near the original building which housed our finds. Thus for the first time in Palestinian archaeology we can reconstruct with certainty a location for this type of capital. Having been in secondary use above the Stratum VII floor, they can be attributed without doubt to the 9th century B.C., either to the period of Ahab (Stratum VIII) or a little later (Stratum VII).

Three feet below the very spot where the two capitals lay we came upon the most important historical, artistic, and theological find in this area. Digging through the thin layers of Strata VIII, IX and X we discovered a well-paved area, with flat stones, which ran below the foundations of Solomon's casemate wall (Stratum X). Yet at the same time it contained pottery of the early Israelite period (Iron Age I). This revealed that before Solomon turned Hazor into a garrison town but after the Canaanite destruction, there existed in Hazor a small Israelite settlement, apparently without a city wall. This in itself was important. But of greater interest was the significance of the paved area which soon became clear. It turned out to be what may be described as an idolatrous Israelite cult place, the first ever discovered. This was indicated by the two incense stands which were found, similar in shape to those from Megiddo (Stratum VI—11th century, B.C.); a unique jar, full of votive bronzes including a seated figurine of a war god, and an abundance of weapons, including a lugged axe, a sword, two javelin heads and butts, as well as some fibulae and other objects. This is indeed vivid evidence of a local Israelite cult place such as existed according to biblical record in many parts of Israel during the pre-monarchical period (cf. Judg. 18).

We have already mentioned the discovery of pre-Solomonic

Israelite remains, a fact of historical interest. When we dug further we discovered below it yet an earlier Israelite settlement (Stratum XII), the very first on the site of the destroyed Canaanite city. This bore all the marks of a very poor settlement, poorer even than its successor, and can best be described as the temporary dwelling of a seminomadic people. Its only remains consisted of rubble foundations of tents and huts, numerous silos dug into the earth for the storage of pottery and grain, and crude ovens sometimes made of disused store jars. This establishes the significant point that after the Israelite destruction of Canaanite Hazor, the city was not reconstructed as a solid fortified town until the time of Solomon, as recounted in the Bible (I Kings 9:15). Moreover, the fact that some nomadic Israelites did settle there temporarily, as far back as the middle of the 12th century, helps to confirm another theory. It seems to me to indicate that the contemporary Israelite settlements found in Galilee belong to the "post-conquest" period and were not the result of a peaceful infiltration prior to the conquest as Aharoni holds. However, the most important deduction to be made from the gap between the last Canaanite *city* (Stratum XIII) in LB II and Solomon's city (Stratum X) is that during Deborah's time there was *no city at Hazor at all!* This means that Judges 5 (The Song of Deborah) is the true historical record of her battle, which took place at Megiddo, and not Judges 4, in which the later editor tried to connect her battle with Jabin, king of Hazor.

AREA G
(Excavated under the supervision of Mrs. T. Dothan)

Area G, excavated only in 1957 during the third season of excavation, is on the eastern slope of the mound proper. The main discovery in this area was the Israelite fortifications. It emerged that the whole terrace was surrounded by a double wall (sometimes reminiscent of a casemate wall) with two large towers flanking the eastern and western side of the northern wall respectively. In one phase a brick tower was built on top of the western tower base, and its northwest and northeast corners were rounded off. Eastward, and close to the tower, there was a small gate within the wall, built of large ashlar stones. It is noteworthy that during the last phase of the fortification's existence (Stratum V) the inhabitants of Hazor blocked this gate hurriedly. The blocking itself is made of bricks, but its exterior to the north, facing the enemy, was covered with a thin layer of rubble stones, clearly to camouflage the previous existence of the gate. On the eastern part of the northern wall we found a well-preserved basalt sewage outlet.

In the center of the terrace a huge rectangular silo was discovered, built to the depth of about five meters with walls lined with rubble stones. This silo was not wholly cleared but the part excavated was covered with a thick layer of fine ashes, indicating the heavy fire which must have burned the grain therein. The silo might also explain the location of the small gate found near it and facing the vast fields north of the tell. This gate was perhaps meant to facilitate the bringing in of the wheat from the field. Just before the siege it could no longer serve that purpose and instead became a point of weakness for the defense, and was therefore hastily blocked.

The excavations here spread out west of the terrace along the slope between it and the upper area of the tell. Here, once the mass of stone debris had been cleared as well as some late structures of the Persian period, a large city wall was revealed running from north to south across the slope, part of which was also discovered on the west side of the tell. The wall here was preserved to a height of six meters. In order to establish its date and its connection with the terrace wall, we deepened the excavation on the tell west of the wall. This not only supplied us with the exact date of the wall, i.e. Stratum VIII (Ahab), but also revealed a residence close by, which continued to exist in various ways from Stratum VII until the city's fall in Stratum V. The residence consisted of two stories and the ashlar staircase leading to the second story was well preserved *in situ*.

To conclude the description of excavations in this area, one of the most interesting finds concerning the Canaanite fortifications should be mentioned. On clearing the north and east slopes of the eastern terrace, we discovered under the Israelite wall, an enormous glacis (sloping revetment) made of stone, which surrounded the terrace. At its bottom was a deep, narrow moat, of which the western wall was the wall of the glacis, while the eastern wall, too, was made of stone. Pottery found in the moat and trial trenches near the glacis within the terrace, proved that this glacis was built during Middle Bronze II. After the moat was filled with earth, the upper part was still used during the Israelite period, when the Israelite walls mentioned above were built on top of it. It is interesting to note the surprising resemblance between this wall-glacis and the famous wall of the same period in Jericho, discovered exactly fifty years before.[2]

The Lower City

Altogether seven areas were investigated in the "enclosure." Areas C, D, and E were first opened in 1955, Area F in 1956, Area H and probe 210 in 1957, and Area K in the final season in 1958.

AREA C
(Excavated under the supervision of Mr. J. Perrot in 1955, of Mrs. T. Dothan in 1956.)

Area C is located in the southwestern corner of the big rectangular enclosure, in the immediate vicinity of the beaten-earth wall. The excavations here had the threefold objective of verifying the nature of the "camp area," or "enclosure," ascertaining the date of its last occupation, and determining the technical details concerning the construction of the earthen wall.

All three aims resulted in startling and important discoveries and conclusions. Firstly, it appeared that the whole area, just one meter below the surface, was occupied by a well-built city with houses and drainage systems. Secondly—and greatly to our surprise—we found the floors of these houses littered with Mycenean pottery as well as many other vessels and objects of local make, all dating back to the last phase of the Late Bronze Age, i.e. the 13th century B.C.! In other words here was definite proof that the last city in the big enclosure met its end about the same time as the actual conquest of the country by Joshua, according to the date given by most scholars.

Now, one of the stumbling blocks concerning the whole theory of the Conquest has been Garstang's conclusion that the city was destroyed about 1400 B.C. This has been removed. Another important conclusion from this area is the fact that below the stratum of the 13th century B.C., we discovered several layers containing earlier cities ranging from the Middle

[2] Note also Wall A of the 17th–16th century fortification of Shechem, described in *BA*, XX (1957).

Bronze Age II (the so-called Hyksos period of the 18th to 16th centuries) down to Late Bronze IIA in the 14th century.

But the biggest discovery of the season came, as usual, in the last fortnight of excavations! Two small Canaanite temples one on top of the other, dating from the Late Bronze II period, were discovered at the foot of the beaten-earth wall. Only the central part of the temples was cleared in 1955, but even so it yielded a very rich harvest. In the central niche of the rooms, high above the floor, the "holy of holies" was found. In it was a basalt sculpture of a male (deity?), seated on a throne, holding a cup. A row of several stelae, with rounded tops, was placed just to the left of the sculpture. All of these were devoid of reliefs, except for the central one which bears a very effective and simple design: two upstretched hands in the attitude of prayer below the emblem of the deity—a crescent and a disk within. The whole row was flanked by a basalt orthostat, bearing the head and forelegs of a lion on its narrow side, and a relief of a crouching lion— its tail coming up from between its hind legs, on its wide side. This group is unique in Palestinian archaeology (and in fact in many respects in the Near East as a whole), and although it clearly shows northern influence, it is local Canaanite in execution and detail. The many vessels found in place together with the sculptures and the clear stratification of the temple, all point to its final destruction in the 13th century. Here we have bold representations of Canaanite art on the eve of Joshua's invasion, art of which very little has been known up till now.

In 1956, we continued the dig in the area to clarify further some vital points. The season's work was no less rewarding. The clearing of the vicinity of the sanctuary disclosed another room, filled with stelae, thrown in disorder and lying in heaps. Was this a storeroom of the sanctuary or were the stelae thrown into it by conquerors? This we could not establish. While clearing this area, and to our great surprise, we discovered an intricate system of stone walls and buttresses supporting the lower slopes of the earthen wall—some of them dating to the Middle Bronze period (18th–17th centuries B.C.) when the great earthen wall was erected, and some to the Late Bronze period, in the final phases of the occupation of this site. These walls, together with others found in trial digs in other parts of the rampart show that that type of earthen rampart was much more intricately built than could have been assumed before. In order to investigate further the remains of the Canaanite city which met its end in the 13th century we greatly enlarged the area of excavations to the north. This area yielded numerous interesting and striking finds. It appeared that the whole vicinity of the sanctuary was occupied by storerooms full of big jars, as well as potters' workshops, all probably connected with the sanctuary.

In one of the potters' workshops we discovered a complete potter's wheel (made of two pieces of basalt) *in situ*, with one of the potter's last products, before he had to abandon the place: a beautiful clay cultic mask, with holes pierced at its sides for fastening to the face. In what appears as the storeroom of the potter we discovered about forty complete vessels: chalices, bowls, lamps and juglets. But the greatest prize was still to come. Hidden below a heap of bowls, and stored in a specially prepared jar, we found one of the most interesting of our finds in this area: a cultic standard. The standard is a bronze plaque, with a tang for fastening it to a pole. The face of the standard, silver-plated, bears the image of the snake-goddess holding a snake in each hand; above her is her emblem: a crescent and a conventional sign of a snake, which also appears in the lower part of the standard. This standard must have belonged, too, to the treasures of the sanctuary, and was used probably in the cultic procession, in which the priests carried the standards of various gods.

In order to establish the date of the earliest occupation of the enclosure, we removed Stratum 1A (the latest city) in the area excavated in 1955. Below it appeared the remains of Stratum 1B, dating to an earlier phase of the Late Bronze Age (14th century, the Amarna period). Removing Stratum 1B, we reached still another city (Stratum 2) of the Late Bronze I period, below which two more strata were found (3 and 4). The lowest (4), appears to be built on virgin soil (end of the 18th century) and is thus the oldest in this area City 3, belonging to the last phase of the Middle Bronze Age (17th–16th centuries), was effectively destroyed by fire, most probably by one of the Egyptian pharaohs of the New Kingdom (Ahmosis). A most pathetic sight was to be discovered below the floors of the houses of the oldest city: scores of infant burials in jars. Each contained a skeleton of an infant accompanied by one or two juglets which might have contained water or milk; in some cases the jars were found to contain the skeletons of two infants. This practice is known also from other sites of the same period, but the great number of burials in each room may indicate a plague as the cause of death.

The excavations in Areas D (under the joint supervision of Miss C. Epstein and Mr. M. Megiddon) and E (under the supervision of Mr. J. Perrot) were also within the great enclosure. These were excavated only during the first campaign and were intended to show whether the conclusions reached at Area C were characteristic of the whole 180 acre enclosure. Indeed they were! In both areas we found the same features: the latest buildings belong to the 13th century B.C. and are built upon previous cities, the oldest of which dates back to the Hyksos period. In these two areas many water cisterns were discovered, some of them as much as nine meters deep. They yielded a rich harvest of pottery and scarabs coming from burials and silos which belong to the secondary usage of the cisterns in different periods of their occupation.

The most important single object from Area D was a small fragment of a jar bearing two letters in the Proto-Canaanite alphabet (the alphabet from which evolved the old Hebrew script and later the Latin alphabet): . . . *LT* . . . This is the first time that that script has been found in Galilee and its date (the 13th century) is close to that of a very similar jar bearing an inscription of the same kind, found some years ago by the late J. L. Starkey in Lachish.

A small trench, Area 210, dug in the center of the lower Canaanite city, confirmed our conclusion that the whole enclosure was inhabited from the middle of the 18th century to the end of the 13th. The one important conclusion that can be drawn from the fact that the whole area of the enclosure was a real city, is that during the Middle and Late Bronze periods, Hazor was indeed one of the greatest cities in Canaan, and with its estimated 40,000 population justly deserved the description given it in the book of Joshua: "For Hazor beforetime was the head of all those kingdoms."

AREA F
(Excavated under the supervision of Mr. J. Perrot.)

This was a new area in 1956 and was dug again in 1957. It lies a few hundred yards south of Area D in the enclosure. The direct reason for our dig in this area, was a big stone protruding from the ground. This stone turned out to be a huge altar, weighing five tons and hewn from one block of stone. It was obvious that some attempts were made at the latest phase of occupation of the site to pull the altar down. After clearing the neighborhood of the altar, the following picture emerged of the last phase of occupation (Stratum 1A; 13th century B.C.): the altar, already built in the earlier period, stood at the center of an open court, an open canal leading to it, flanked on two sides by a series of large rooms containing many big stone jars, extremely fine Mycenean pottery, a stand for incense vessels and an offering table (?) made of basalt; at the northern side of the court, a big platform made of small rough stones was discovered, which served most probably as a cultic high place or *bamah*. A stand for incense was found on it and a beautiful two-piece alabaster vessel was lying just to the south of it, in a niche.

The whole area was obviously a holy place. A further proof of this conclusion was the basalt sculpture of a seated figure, found in one of the rooms. The building proper was situated perhaps south of the altar, while its storerooms and the living quarters of its staff were to the north and south of it. A very interesting feature of this area is the intricate complex of underground canals, sometimes a meter in height, all built of stones, and covered with huge slabs. These canals running west-east and south-north, belong to an earlier period (Strata 3-4) of Middle Bronze II. The builders of the altar in Stratum 1B (14th century) reused them by joining a much smaller canalization system (which came from below the altar) to them. This earlier system of underground canals belonged to a large complex structure with walls about two meters in thickness, which was largely destroyed. Not enough of it remains to allow reconstructing its plan or ascertaining its exact function, although it was thought to be a part of a fortified *temenos* (a holy enclosure).

As is usual in excavations we had to face the greatest surprise in the last fortnight of excavation, when we struck an opening in the rock, about five meters below the foundation of Stratum 3. The opening, which was closed with huge boulders, turned out to be the entrance to a large tunnel hewn out of the rock, about twelve meters long and two meters high. When we moved into it we had the feeling it had just been hewn because it was so well preserved. But alas, when we reached its end we could not proceed because the debris of the fallen ceiling of the chamber, to which the tunnel led, blocked the outlet completely. It was very dangerous to proceed, but the temptation was too great. We decided to enter the room by digging a vertical shaft, from the outside, and at a depth of eight meters we reached the room. Unfortunately when the season came to its end, we had only succeeded in clearing about six meters through the length of the room and there was still no end to it. In the meantime another tunnel with many offshoots, about thirty (!) meters long was discovered in the vicinity, but again it was too dangerous to clear in a hurry. What was the purpose of these tunnels? Were they part of an intricate and hidden necropolis of "V.I.P.s?"

The excavation in Area F in 1957 began with searching for the remains of the large Middle Bronze complex with thick walls, which belonged to Stratum 3 of the lower city. During this search we came across a cave hewn in the rock outside the northeast corner of the building, accessible through a small vertical shaft, the opening of which was blocked by two stone slabs, a meter and a half in length. This cave, used as a burial place during Late Bronze II, was littered with an abundance of pottery (some 500 vessels) which complemented the repertoire of pottery of that period found elsewhere in Hazor. Among these, the following are worthy of special mention: a large group of beautiful imported Mycenean pots (type IIIA from the 14th century), more than ten "bilbils" from Cyprus, two ribbed pots (of the Cypriote Bucchero-ware type), of which only very few specimens have hitherto been found outside Cyprus, and a number of local pots (mainly bowls, lamps and jars). It should be said that the bones of skeletons found in the cave were not in place, but were piled up and thrown towards the back of the cave. This fact, as well as the large amount of pottery, testifies that the grave must have been in use for a long period and seems to have been cleared from time to time as the need arose.

However, our main efforts in Area F were devoted to the rock-hewn tunnel (Stratum 4) of the Middle Bronze II period. The season's excavations made it clear that the tunnel and its chamber were actually part of a ramified network of underground tunnels. These tunnels must have been already known to the inhabitants of the "large structure," who used them as reservoirs and outlets for the canals, and also by the residents of the Late Bronze period who looted whatever was still available in them. In many places we found the entrances to the tunnels blocked off by rubble stone walls and we could not always determine the exact date of such blocks. Except for the chamber discovered in 1956, we did not succeed, for technical reasons, in getting to the end of the tunnels. But it can be assumed that they too, during their early stage, led to chambers which must have served as burial places for the aristocracy. This assumption was unexpectedly confirmed when at the end of the season, we cleared the debris covering the large vertical shaft (approximately eight meters square) hewn near the first tunnel. At its bottom, on the west, we discovered three enormous caves, rock-hewn, of which the largest was seventeen meters long and three meters wide and high. These caves accessible through the deep shaft were certainly meant for burial, but it is doubtful whether their hewers managed to use them for that purpose or for any other. They were found completely empty (except for a few pots and jugs most probably left there by the laborers); and the southernmost cave in that group was abandoned still unfinished. This set of tunnels, shafts and caves, however, has no parallel so far in this country, and it testifies to the high technical skill and engineering ability of the Middle Bronze people at Hazor.

AREA H
(Excavated under the supervision of Miss C. Epstein and Mrs. T. Dothan.)

Our prize find in the Lower Canaanite city was the temple, discovered by chance at the northern tip of the enclosure in Area H, first opened in the third season, 1957. This temple is most interesting for the following reasons: its plan, its building system and the finds therein. The plan is rather simple, consisting of three chambers built in succession from south to north: a porch, a main hall and a holy of holies. The building's length is twenty-five meters and its width seventeen meters. A large opening leads from the porch—which is somewhat narrower than the rest of the building—to the main hall; and a similar opening on the same axis in the center of the building leads from there to the holy of holies. In the porch, on either side of the opening leading to the main hall, we found two round pillar bases made of basalt. The technique of building in this temple is unique in the country. The walls of the porch and holy of holies are lined at the lower part with beautifully dressed basalt slabs (orthostats) up to 1.70 meters long and an average of sixty centimeters high with a varying width of twenty to forty centimeters. The narrow top edge of each orthostat had well-drilled round holes four centimeters in diameter (usually there were two holes at both ends of the slab). The row of orthostats was lying on a ledge of rubble stones (two meters wide), forming the lowest part of the building's wall. In this building system, typical of Hittite Anatolia and northern Syria, the round drilled holes served as a socket for pegs securing the horizontal wooden beams meant to strengthen the brick or mud built above the stone foundation.

The Holy of Holies and Cult Furniture of the Temple

In 1957 we proceeded to clear, in addition to the porch and the hall, the holy of holies, which had a wealth of ritual vessels, especially near the square niche at the narrow northern wall of the building. Since the building was destroyed by fire, as is testified by the charred beams found on the floor, it must have collapsed quickly and thus buried most of the implements. Among these, the most complete set of ritual implements and furniture so far found in this country, the following are noteworthy:

1. An incense altar made of basalt, about fifty centimeters square and 1.40 meters high. On one side and on top there is a relief of a disk in a square frame with a four-pointed star in the center, i.e. the emblem of the sun-god in the Canaanite pantheon. Below this are chiseled two elongated depressions giving the front of the altar the impression of a column's relief. At the back the surface is similarly dressed except that the dented square frame has no relief. The other two sides of the altar have a long upright depression in each, completing the general pattern.

2. Near the altar we found a large basalt basin, some eighty centimeters in diameter.

3. South of the altar and the basin, in the center of the holy of holies we found *in situ* and at some distance from each other, two large earthenware pots, and near them a large number of dipper juglets. These pots served as containers for oil, wine, or other liquid, and were used in connection with the temple's rituals.

4. Between the containers and the altar we found two basalt slabs, both of which had rectangular depressions at the

corners. These slabs must have served as offering tables for the liquids mentioned above.

5. Near the southern container a carinated basalt bowl was found, fifty centimeters in diameter and forty centimeters high, its upper part decorated with a relief of a fine running spiral design.

6. In the southeast corner we found an offering table with several rectangular depressions and one small round indention at each of the four corners.

7. Left of the entrance to the holy of holies and inside it, there was a small basalt statue of a man sitting on a chair and holding a goblet in his right hand. The head, broken off, was found close by. The shape of the chair and its workmanship are identical with the similar statue found (headless) in Area F during the second season.

8. Four bronze figurines. The first is that of a deity with outstretched arms and a conical helmet. This figurine must have been stuck in a wooden or other base, as may be inferred from its pointed bottom. The second is that of a bull, made of wrought bronze; here again the four legs must have been stuck in a base of some sort. The third and fourth are two figurines of female deities, the facial features of which were barely indicated by shallow incisions in the thin metal foil from which they were made.

9. A sizable group of cylinder seals and faience beads scattered on the western part of the floor of the holy of holies. One of the seals, made of hematite, bears a complicated engraving superbly executed, in its center a deity sitting on a chair under a winged sun-god disk, and in front a king offering presents with a line of present-bearers behind him. This cylinder seal is one of the finest examples known of the Syro-Mitannian type.

10. A large amount of pottery, including ritual vessels, scattered on the floor and on the stone bench which ran along the walls of the holy of holies.

11. A large scarab seal, bearing the name of Pharaoh Amenophis III, identical in measurements and workmanship with the scarabs found in the third phase of a temple at Lachish (13th century) and with a scarab of the same period found in a temple in Beisan.

The finds of this temple belong mostly, as is indicated by the pottery, to the last Canaanite settlement at the end of the Late Bronze period (Stratum 1A), although the temple was founded in the 14th century, according to the date of the scarab (Stratum 1B).

This temple sheds important light on a number of problems and it is interesting to note that in the character of its ritual vessels and particularly the use of the orthostats, it is almost identical with a temple (less well preserved) discovered by Sir Leonard Woolley at Tell Atchana (Alalakh) in Syria, which also belongs to the 14th–13th centuries. We have here proof of a direct or indirect affinity between the Canaanite culture of Hazor and that of northern Syria and Anatolia. Even the temple's plan is interesting, since we have here a prototype of Solomon's temple, with the two pillars on the porch emphasizing the resemblance. Until now, the only example known of a temple in Asia resembling that of Solomon was the temple of Tell Tainat in Syria (8th century).

When the 1957 season came to its end, we had nearly completed the excavation of the holy of holies. The tasks we set ourselves in the final season were: to finish excavating the main hall and the porch, and to dig below the floor of the temple. For here we had found the base of a column projecting from the floor of the holy of holies, a sure indication of an earlier phase of the building below.

To save the reader the suspense which we ourselves experienced, it can be said that by the end of the season we had not only uncovered the two phases of the orthostat temple, the earlier belonging to the 14th century B.C.; but we had found two more temples, the first built on virgin soil, belonging to the Middle Bronze Age, 18th–17th century B.C., and the second to the Late Bronze Age I, the 15th century B.C.

I follow with a description of these four temples from latest to earliest (i.e., top to bottom).

Temple 1A.

This temple was the last in Canaanite Hazor, which was destroyed by the Israelites at the end of the Late Bronze Age II, in the second half of the 13th century B.C. It was, in fact, a reconstruction of the earlier temple with most parts of the latter's walls still in use. We have good reason to believe that most of the furniture saved from the previous ruins was reused. The general plan of this temple turned out to be what we had expected. It comprised three wings, a porch, a main hall and a holy of holies, each with its own entrance built on a single axis. On clearing the main hall, however, we found that its western section held a two-roomed tower, probably with a staircase leading to the roof. In the center and right of the hall was some ritual furniture, including a fine offering-table made of basalt. On the porch, before the entrance to the main hall, stood two pillars, their fine basalt bases still *in situ*. Most of the furniture of the temple was in the holy of holies, but two items found in the other rooms were of considerable importance. One enabled us to date the temple's destruction, the other gave us the identification of the temple's deity. On the floor of the main hall a small clay figurine of an animal was found intact. This figurine is of Mycenean style of the 13th century B.C. and is the only Mycenean piece to come from the temple proper, though many others were found elsewhere in the dig. The other object is a broken basalt statue of the temple's god. This was discovered in the debris just in front of the entrance near a cult obelisk, bearing on its breast the crossed sun-disk identical with that of the altar found in 1957 in the holy of holies. Another broken piece of basalt found in the vicinity and depicting a bull, proved to be the base of the god's statue. Thus again we have the sun-god associated with a bull which was the emblem of Hadad, the storm-god Baal of Canaanite religion.

The Lion's Den—Temple 1B

One of the most exciting experiences of the whole dig occurred during the excavation of the southwest corner of the porch. Here the main wall of the temple was missing. In trying to trace its foundations we struck a heap of stones under which appeared a beautiful nearly life-size head of a lion made of basalt. When the stones were removed a basalt orthostat was revealed 1.75 meters long, one side bearing the relief of a crouching lion with its fully sculptured head fashioned from the front of the stone. The top had two drilled holes, exactly like those on the orthostats of the porch and holy of holies, thus indicating that the lion orthostat was part of the entrance jamb. But its location was a mystery which remained unsolved until we had cleared the whole area. We noticed then that the lion had been thrown into a pit, deliberately cut through the two cobbled floors of the earlier temples (2 and 3) and then covered with a heap of stones. It is difficult to determine whether this had been done by the people of temple 1A, when they reconstructed the temple and found no further use for the lion, as in the case of Idrimi's statue from Alalakh in Syria, or by the conquerors who may have been motivated by ritual considerations. But whatever the reason, their act preserved for us one of the finest and most ancient orthostats in the whole of the Fertile Crescent.

Under the holy of holies little was found of temple 1B, except for two column bases, just below the two of temple 1A, and several valuable small objects, among them a well-made cylinder seal of hematite and a strange figurine of a woman, 3300 years old, very suggestive of the contemporary work of Picasso.

The plan of the reconstructed temple 1A was clearly identical with that of 1B, except for the main hall where the eastern tower was entirely abandoned. These two temples, 1B and 1A, 14th and 13th centuries B.C., respectively, with their interesting plan and unusually rich hoard of objects and statues, are among the most interesting temples found in Palestine, and the material, when thoroughly studied, will enrich our knowledge of Canaanite cult and art.

Temple 2 lay immediately below the foundation of 1B. The latter's foundations had in fact been built upon the ruins of temple 2 wherever it suited the architects. Temple 2 consisted of only one room, identical in plan and dimensions with the holy of holies of temple 1. At its southern end there was an open entrance flanked by two rectangular towers, resembling somewhat the temples of Shechem and Megiddo, though of different proportions. In front of the entrance there was a large cobbled open court, with a big rectangular *bamah* (high place) and several small altars. To its south—and this is a remarkable feature of this temple—there was a large propyleum, a monumental gateway, its sill made of basalt slabs and benches in the main room. A drainage system was found just east of the propyleum and the temple. Its sections consisted in part of disused *incense stands*—only a temple can afford that!—while the rest was built of field stones.

In the court we also found a potter's kiln, no doubt used for producing votive bowls to judge by the scores of small bowls found intact inside it. Among the few objects discovered in the temple the most important was found in a heap of pottery near the altar. During four years of excavations we had hoped, fervently but in vain, to find a cuneiform inscription. And then, in the last week of the season, we finally came across one. The object was a clay model of an animal's liver with inscribed omens for the use of the temple's diviners. This model is the only one with an inscription found in Pales-

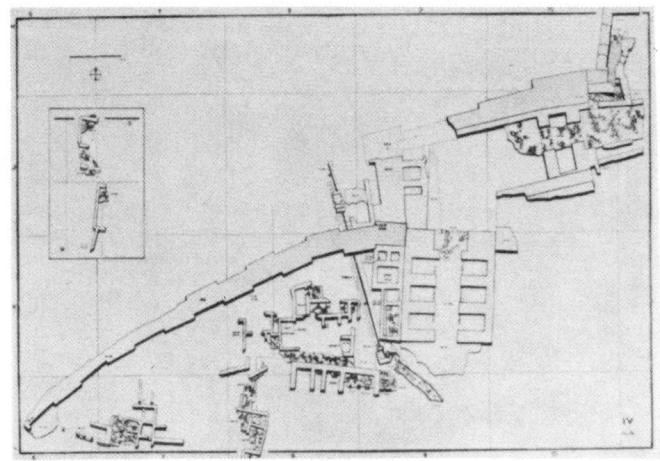

[19] Plan of the Megiddo city gate of the time of Solomon. The unique four entryway plan is exactly like the east gate of Solomon's temple enclosure in Jerusalem as described in Ezekiel 50:5–16, and is duplicated at Gezer and Hazor. The "offsets and insets" wall shown here now is to be dated to the 9th century, and Yadin has found beneath it remnants of a casemate wall which belongs with the gate.

[20] A proposed reconstruction of the Solomonic gateway at Megiddo. It is to be doubted that the doors had round arches; more probably the space between them was roofed with the use of horizontal beams. Also, the main city wall was doubtless of casemate construction.

[21] One of the Hellenistic round towers at Samaria, with the older Israelite wall appearing at the right. The new architectural plan of these towers suggests the change to the pagan city of Samaria, from which the Samaritans fled to Shechem.

[22] Remains of the Fortress Temple at Shechem, viewed from the east and looking toward the front entrance. The standing stones and columns marking various periods of its history have been reconstructed in their respective places. The retaining wall around the temple "fill" is modern.

[23] A fine Assyrian adorant seal from the ruins of stratum VII at Shechem (*ca.* 724 B.C.). Note the hole in the bottom margin; the seal hung around its owner's neck.

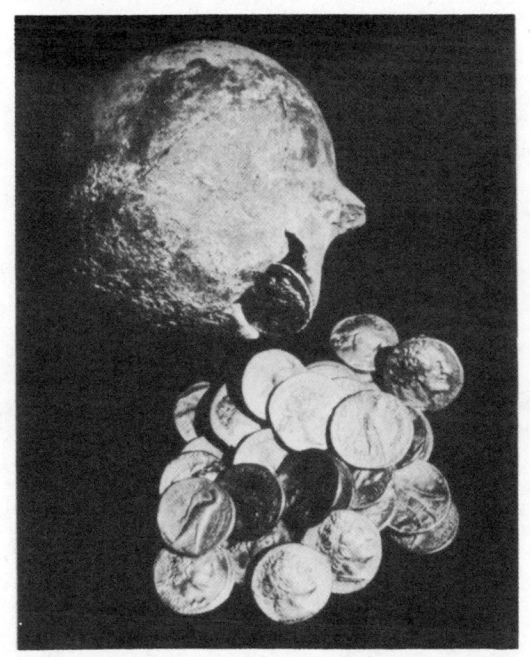

[24] A cache of silver Ptolemaic tetradrachms, the latest of which dates to 193 B.C., from stratum III of Shechem.

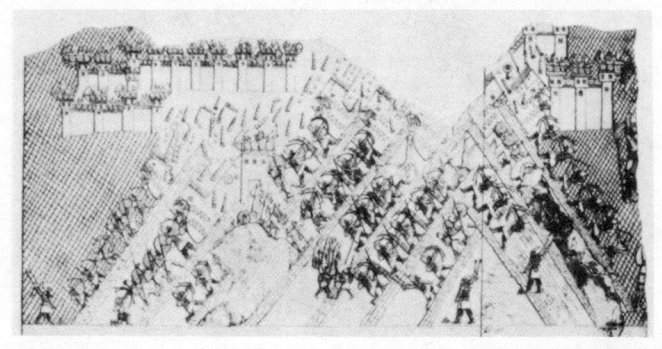

[25] The siege of Lachish as depicted in the reliefs of Sennacherib at Nineveh.

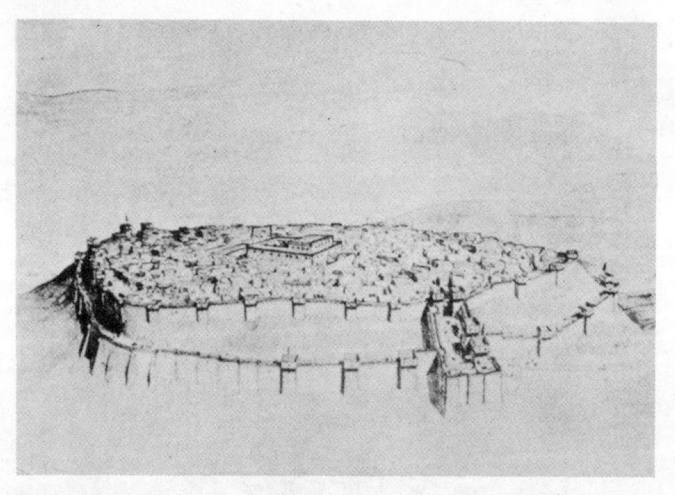

[26] A reconstruction of the city of Lachish as it looked shortly before its destruction by Nebuchadnezzar in 598.

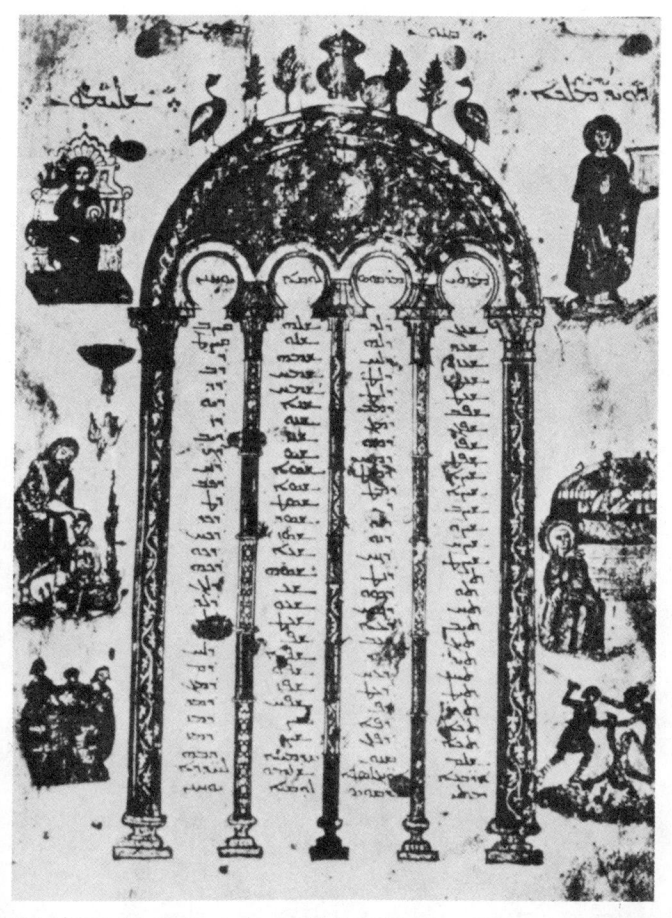

[27] Folio 4, verso, of the Rabbula Gospels, a Syriac manuscript dating from A.D. 586. The illustrations in the margin are excellent examples of the type of art developed in the church at Antioch.

[28] The Chalice of Antioch, found in a well at Antioch in 1910. The central figure represents Christ.

[29] A reconstruction of the west portico of the temple of Artemis (Diana) at Ephesus, as designed and erected with the aid of Croesus, king of Lydia, in the 6th century B.C. Accounted one of the seven wonders of the ancient world, it was burned in 356 B.C., but reconstructed on the same plan.

[30] A reconstruction of the center Harbor Gate at Ephesus. It was at one end of the Arkadiane, the marble-paved street which ran from the Great Theater (Acts 19:29).

[31] The basilica on the east side of the main street of Hierapolis, possibly a church dedicated to Philip. Note the *chi-rho* monogram in the keystone over the door.

[32] The Acropolis at Athens, with the Areopagus in the foreground; hence, this is the view that one standing on the Areopagus would see.

[33] The Areopagus in Athens from the south. On this rocky eminence Paul delivered his speech to the men of Athens (Acts 17:22).

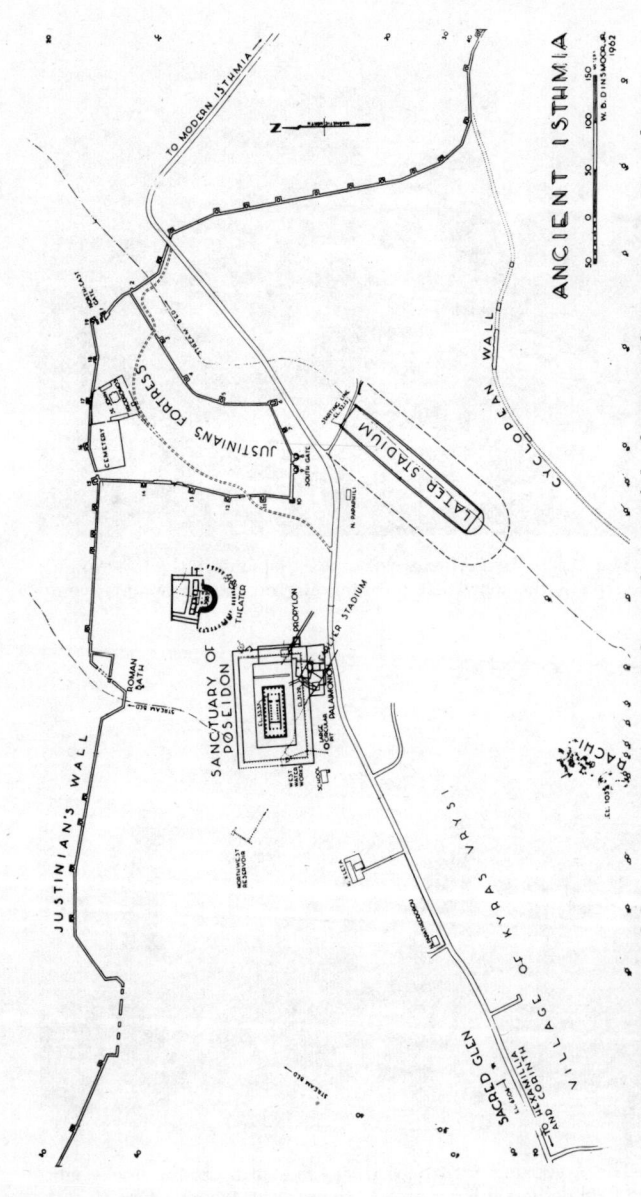

[34] A plan of the structures at ancient Isthmia, the site of the famous Isthmian games. Note the earlier and later stadia.

[35] The temple of Poseidon at Isthmia, seen from the west. The depredations made by the engineers of Justinian were thoroughgoing, but the trenches cut into the rock for the foundations permit restoration of the plan.

[36] The starting line at the Early Stadium in Isthmia. The starting device, called *balbides,* has been reconstructed; Professor Broneer is in the pit where the ancient starter stood.

[37] A marble head of a victorious athlete (left). [38] A marble torch flame (right). The young boy wears the crown of pine branches awarded victors in the Isthmian games. The torch, from the later stadium at Isthmia, represents the one carried by athletes in the torch race. Only the flame was found; the handle, probably of wood, was attached by a metal dowel.

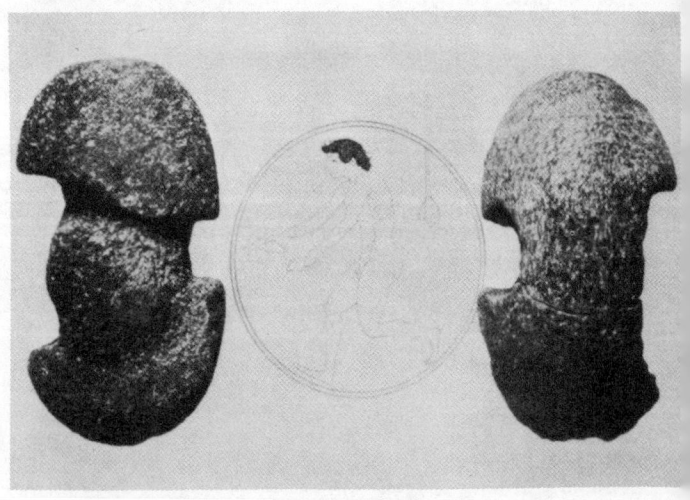

[39] Jumping weights (*halteres*) found at Isthmia. A drawing from an ancient vase shows how the weights were used.

tine and one of the very few from this period, 16th–15th centuries B.C., found in the entire Middle East. The sun-god, being the god of the liver diviners, must also have been the deity of temple 2.

Temple 3. Of temple 3, the earliest and the first to be built on the site, relatively little was found, but enough to show that it had been a very elaborate building and that it was constructed about 1700 B.C. Like temple 2 it consisted mainly of one room, similar in plan and dimensions to the temple built on its ruins. But in front of it there must have been a large platform reached by a flight of three steps, as is indicated by the beautifully dressed basalt ashlar steps found below the cobbled floor of the court of temple 2. Temple 3 also had a large open court in front of it, but its cobblestones were of much finer work than the later structure and even today it looks like a mosaic floor. The two small basalt bases of capitals and the many basalt ashlar stones reused in temple 2, all indicate that temple 3 was a fine edifice matched only by temple 1, built about 300 years later.

Area H, with its four strata of temples reveals that the tradition of a holy place lasted for centuries. Our excavations here gave us proof, confirmed by excavations in the other areas, that the lower city was established in the Middle Bronze II period and came to its end in the 13th century B.C. with the conquest of the Israelites.

AREA K
(Excavated under the supervision of M. Dothan)

Finally, let me offer a few words about the dig in Area K to complete our picture of the lower city's defenses. From aerial photographs and from our excavations nearby, we were convinced that one of the city gates must have been located in the northeastern part of the lower city. We decided to dig here in the final season, calling the site Area K. We started from what we suspected was the jamb of a gate, with huge ashlar stones which we found protruding from the ground. With the turn of almost the first spade, our theory was confirmed. The city gate of the Late Bronze Age lay bare. It turned out to be one of the most formidable gate structures ever found in this country. Below it were gates of the Middle Bronze Age II. Together they offered us the complete history of the defenses of the lower city, from the first beaten earth rampart and slopes, later strengthened by additional revetments, until its final destruction in the Late Bronze II period.

Space limits us here to a brief description of only one of the gates, that of LB II and the large revetment wall. This Late Bronze Age gate with its ashlar stones, some of them two meters long was erected on the foundations of the earlier Middle Bronze Age II gate, and is identical in plan. The gate passage with its floor of fine cobbles was flanked on each side by three pairs of pilasters, the two extreme ones forming the jambs of the outer and inner entrances respectively. The middle ones served to support the ceiling. On either side of the entire gate structure was a two-roomed tower. This gate must have been destroyed in a violent conflagration, though the exterior walls still stand to a height of three meters. Traces of the burnt bricks of its inner walls and the ashes of the burnt beams still cover the floors in thick heaps.

Access to the gate which was on the very edge of the slope was gained by a road built on a specially constructed rampart. This was reinforced by a platform in front of the gate. To carry both rampart and platform the Middle Bronze Age engineers built a great revetment wall, strengthened by huge basalt boulders, to a height of four meters. We found this wall intact; it is a magnificent feat of engineering. These formidable defense works illustrate the biblical report that this 180 acre city was indeed the largest and most heavily defended city of the country.

Conclusion

This brings us to the end of our current dig. We have had four seasons and there is work for another 400! Nevertheless we have been able as a result of this expedition to reach a number of important conclusions concerning the history of Hazor both in biblical and earlier times. And great quantities of objects were discovered, which, when finally assessed, will throw new light on many aspects of the material and spiritual culture of the Holy Land.

The first two volumes of Hazor, covering the 1955 and 1956 seasons, have already been published, as has the plates part of Vol. III–IV, covering the final two seasons. The general results may be summarized as follows:

1. During the 3rd millennium B.C., the city of Hazor was located only within the area of the mound proper.

2. The 2nd millennium was Hazor's most flourishing era. During the Hyksos period, the second half of the 18th cen-

Date and/or Period	Strata of Upper City	Strata of Lower City	General Remarks
Hellenistic	I	—	A fort
Persian	II	—	A fort
Assyrian	III	—	A fort
Israelite 8th–7th cent.	IV	—	A small undefended settlement built after destruction of 732 B.C.
8th cent.	V	—	Destroyed by Tiglath-pileser III, 732 B.C.
8th cent.	VI	—	Destroyed by earthquake; see Amos 1
9th cent.	VII	—	Post-Ahab
9th cent.	VIII	—	Ahab rebuilds Hazor
10th–9th cent.	IX	—	Post-Solomonic
10th cent.	X	—	Solomon's city
12th–11th cent.	XII–XI	—	First Israelite settlements—meager remains of seminomadic character Period of Deborah
13th cent. LB IIB	XIII	1A	Destroyed by Joshua, ca. 1230 B.C.
14th cent. LB IIA	XIV	1B	Amarna Period
16th–15th cent. LB I	XV	2	Large, well-fortified city
17th–16th cent. MB II C	XVI	3	Large, well-fortified city
18th–17th cent. MB II B	XVII	4	Foundation of lower city, ca. 1750, with its defenses
21st–19th cent. MB I	XVIII	—	Meager remains
27th–24th cent. EB III–II	XXI–XIX	—	Well-fortified cities

tury B.C., the Lower City was built, covering an area of approximately 180 acres.

3. The downfall of Hazor, "the head of all those kingdoms," occurred in the second half of the 13th century B.C. when the Israelites destroyed it completely, as recorded so vividly in Joshua 11 and confirmed emphatically by our work.

4. Between the destruction of Joshua and the rebuilding of Solomon, there existed no *city* at Hazor; thus, Deborah's battle had nothing to do with Jabin, king of Hazor; this conforms to Judges 5.

5. It was only from Solomon's times onwards that Hazor experienced a revival, albeit within the acropolis area, until it came to its end as a major city towards the end of the 8th century B.C., as also is related in the Bible. What followed Solomon's period were Israelite settlements and cities, built and destroyed over a span of not more than 200 years. Later only small citadels or pillboxes of the Assyrians, Persians, Greeks and, in the 20th century A.D., of the British, were to crown its peak. Indeed the site is one of the most strategic locations of the Holy Land, guarding as it does the high roads from inner Syria to the south and west in that piece of land called the cradle of our modern civilization.

The chart on page 223 will help to clarify the stratigraphic and chronological problems discussed above.

12

THE DISCOVERIES AT MEGIDDO
1935–1939

G. ERNEST WRIGHT

In 1948, there were published two large volumes, entitled *Megiddo II: Seasons of 1935–39*, written by Gordon Loud, the excavator, and published by the University of Chicago Press (cost $30). Megiddo is so rich in wonderful material and the technical job of publication so beautifully done that a review of the discoveries there described ought to be given.

Megiddo, one of the most important cities of ancient Palestine, has been more thoroughly excavated than any other city of the country of comparable size, unless Macalister's work at Gezer between 1902 and 1909 be excepted. The site was purchased by the Oriental Institute of the University of Chicago, and the late Dr. James Henry Breasted planned that it should be excavated completely as a model of modern scientific technique. Work began in 1925 under the direction of Dr. Clarence S. Fisher; he was succeeded by Mr. P. L. O. Guy in 1927 who continued as director until 1935. During this decade the first four strata of the mound were completely cleared, a beginning was made on Stratum V, a section of the eastern slope was dug to bedrock to make ready a place to dump the debris, and a great water tunnel was investigated whence the city secured its water about 1200 B.C. The first stratum contained the scattered ruins of the Babylonian and Persian periods, the site being virtually abandoned not long after 400 B.C. Strata II and III belong to the Assyrian period of the 8th and 7th centuries, the most notable feature being the large palaces which were probably used by Israelite and then by Assyrian governors, the latter ruling the province of Galilee with Megiddo as capital after 733 B.C. Stratum IV began in the 10th century and is well known for the presence within it of the large stables for horses. The results were published by Lamon and Shipton in *Megiddo I: Seasons of 1925–34* (1939), and supplemented by Guy and Engberg, *Megiddo Tombs* (1938); Engberg and Shipton, *Notes on the Chalcolithic and Early Bronze Age Pottery of Megiddo* (1934); May, *Material Remains of the Megiddo Cult* (1935); and Lamon, *The Megiddo Water System* (1935).

By 1935 it was seen that the site could not be completely dug with the resources available. Between 1935 and 1939 an expedition directed by Gordon Loud selected certain areas for deeper probing. In the north by the city gate an area labeled AA was excavated through Stratum XIII (*ca.* 18th century B.C.); at the east in area BB where the first stables were discovered the digging went down to bedrock on which the earliest remains in Stratum XX were discovered; an exploratory trench was dug at the south in area CC but abandoned when more interesting material appeared in the other two areas; and finally an attempt was made to connect areas AA and BB (in an area labeled DD) but lack of time prevented its completion. The results are published in *Megiddo II*, though they must be supplemented by Loud, *The Megiddo Ivories* (1939) and by Shipton, *Notes on the Megiddo Pottery of Strata VI–XX* (1939).

The Early History of the City

The mound of Megiddo is situated in a very important location; it is on what was once the main route between Africa and Asia at the point where the pass through the Carmel range opens into the plain of Jezreel (Esdraelon). The first villagers settled there about 4000 B.C. or slightly before. It was not the first town to be settled in Palestine; the first occupation at Jericho was still earlier, dating from a time before the invention of pottery. Indeed, the latter was probably the oldest known village in the world until the spring of 1948 when Robert J. Braidwood of the Oriental Institute discovered a similar cultural horizon at Qalat Jarmo in northern Iraq.

The first coherent architecture is not found at Megiddo until Stratum XIX which belongs to the age designated Early Bronze I, about 3000 B.C. or just before. Here was found in area BB a small temple built against a heavy mud-brick enclosure wall nearly ten feet thick. This area continued as the city's sacred quarter until the destruction of the Late Bronze Age city, Stratum VII, between about 1140 and 1100 B.C. A small temple of the same date as the one in Megiddo XIX has been found at Jericho, though its plan is slightly different.

With Megiddo XVIII we enter the second Early Bronze Age, roughly contemporary with the First Dynasty in Egypt and Early Dynastic I in Mesopotamia. The surprising feature of this stratum is the appearance of a city wall, made of stone, which is the most massive fortification ever erected on the site; its original thickness was between thirteen and sixteen feet, which was later extended to nearly twenty-six feet. When found it was still standing more than thirteen feet high.[1]

The massive size of the Megiddo XVIII wall is to be compared with a mud-brick wall of great strength, dating from the preceding Early Bronze I period, discovered in 1945-46 by an Israeli excavation at Beth-yerah (Khirbet Kerak), a site along the southern coast of the sea of Galilee. This wall was also some twenty-six feet thick; it was built with an upright wall in the center with sloping additions on both sides. Fortifications of the same general period, also very massive, have been found at Taanach, Dothan and Tirzah, and further south at Jericho and Ai.

We may thus say that the age between about 3200 and 2800 B.C. was the first "boom" age of Palestine. The great increase in the number and amount of archaeological deposits indicates a rapid increase in population. World trade was underway, for Egyptian, Mesopotamian, and Syrian objects have been found, while material from Palestine, Syria, and Mesopotamia has been found in Egypt. The first fortified cities and monumental architecture were erected, though earlier examples of fine architecture may turn up in the future. Sudden acceleration in other arts of civilization is also evident; pottery appears in a greater variety of shapes than ever before and great care is occasionally used in decorating it. Palestine thus reflects the situation in the whole of the Near East at this time. In Mesopotamia also, for example, population increased greatly. Certain towns became fortified cities, from which it is inferred that the city-state system began, that the local ruler obtained greater power, that he was able to command an army for offense and defense, and that with population growth social organization became more elaborate. The same may presumably be inferred for Palestine. By this time, urbanism has begun, and anthropologists believe that the necessary

[1] See K. M. Kenyon, *Eretz Israel*, V (1958), 51-60.

specializations were present to permit the use of the term "civilization."[2]

The Dark Age

In Strata XVII and XVI the chief feature was a large building, evidently a palace, the stone walls of which were given a thick mud coating and finished with a white lime plaster. Also erected at this time, the excavators believe, was a large altar for burnt offerings in a separate enclosure. It was built of stone rubble (cf. Exod. 20:25), and is exceptionally interesting because it is the only one of its type and size yet found. Its diameter at the top is twenty-six feet and its height four and one-half feet. In a careful check of plans and levels it is clear that there were two phases of the altar; that is, it was rebuilt at least once. However, the levels and accompanying architecture strongly suggest to this writer that this altar should not be dated to this period, but must go with the temples of Stratum XV (see below).

Strata XVII and XVI are dated by the excavators between 2500 and 1950 B.C. For reasons which cannot be presented here, however, it is quite certain that they are to be dated within the period from about the 28th to the 26th centuries B.C. Then the city was evidently destroyed and not reoccupied, at least in the area excavated, for some five centuries.

The situation in Palestine at the end of the 3rd millennium is very curious. Every Early Bronze Age city thus far excavated was apparently destroyed between the 26th and 23rd centuries, so that we do not have a clear picture of what was going on in the years before 2000 B.C. The age is the equivalent of the First Intermediate period in Egypt, where an invasion of Asiatics seems to have brought an end to the Old Kingdom, best known as the age of the pyramids. Settled population decreased in Palestine, as did the level of cultural achievement, witnessing to the breakdown of the social organization in the city-states. Yet it is also the age when villages first appear in southern Transjordan and the Negev, as

[2] In recent years the literature in this area has been increasing rapidly. See, e.g., Henri Frankfort, *The Birth of Civilization in the Near East* (Doubleday Anchor Books, 1956); Robert J. Braidwood, *The Near East and the Foundations of Civilization* (1952); Braidwood and Gordon R. Willey, *Courses toward Urban Life* (1962); Emmanuel Anati, *Palestine Before the Hebrews* (1963).

we know from the explorations of Nelson Glueck. In other words, in that region nomads began to settle for the first time in urban communities. We can only infer that great invasions were taking place, perhaps to be connected in some way with the "Amorite" movement which between 2000 and 1700 B.C. seems to have dominated the whole Fertile Crescent area.

A brief revival of Early Bronze Age traditions in pottery occurred in Middle Bronze I, in the period from about 2000 to 1850 B.C. Towns began to be re-established all over the country, though the occupation was thin. The pottery, while made for the most part after the older models, is much finer, the clay being beautifully cleaned and baked and easily distinguished. Megiddo was resettled at this time, as we know from pottery found on the mound and from a large number of tombs, some of which contained vases imported from Syria. The excavators include this material in Stratum XV which is dominated by the entirely new ceramic culture of Middle Bronze II, though in none of the find-spots as published were the two types of pottery mixed together. Evidently the builders of Stratum XV destroyed most of the distinguishable architecture of Middle Bronze I, whatever it may have been, so that the new buildings rested directly on top of the remains of Stratum XVI.

Megiddo's Golden Age

The Middle and Late Bronze Ages at Megiddo present the most prosperous picture of the city's history, with the possible exception of the 10th century. Strata XV–XIII belong to Middle Bronze IIA, now to be dated *ca.* 1850–1750 B.C., and provide the best collection of material from that age which we now have. The country was probably controlled by Egypt; a portion of an Egyptian statue of one Thuthotep has been found at Megiddo. His tomb at el-Bersheh in Egypt has been excavated; he was high priest of Thoth at Hermopolis and nomarch of the Hare Nome (county) in Middle Egypt during the 19th century. It is highly probable that at some time in his life he was Egyptian ambassador or high commissioner at Megiddo.[3]

The most interesting discovery of this period was that of

[3] J. A. Wilson, *AJSL*, LVIII (1941), 225 ff.

three well-designed temples of Stratum XV.[4] These together with the large temple of Early Bronze III (possibly built in II) at Ai are among the finest examples of temple architecture yet found in Palestine. The great altar continued in use at their rear and probably received the offerings presented to the three different deities whose palaces the temples were. One of the buildings was re-used in Stratum XIV, but the foundations of the great fortress-temple above were set so deep as to make it unclear what kind of temple existed there in Strata XIII–XII, which span the 18th century. A fortification wall and a unique city gate, erected in this period, were of mud brick on a stone foundation; though excellently constructed they were by no means as massive as the fortifications of XVIII, the wall being but five feet wide. Yet in type the fortification is comparable to the wall of Stratum G at Tell Beit Mirsim, to Wall D at Shechem, and perhaps to a brick wall at Jericho, all evidently dating from the first half to the middle of the 18th century.

Strata XII–X belong for the most part to Middle Bronze II B and C, and date within the period *ca.* 1750–1550 B.C. Stratum XII presents a new town plan, but re-uses and doubles the brick wall of the preceding age. In Stratum X, it is thought, a new fortification system was erected, of which the gate was found. It was built of hewn stone, carefully fitted together on the face, with the interior filled with rubble and dirt. Within it were two chambers formed by three pairs of piers projecting from the two sides of the entrance passage, this type of gate being the customary one of the period and well known from a number of sites.

The city gate of Stratum X continued in use through Strata IX–VII, which cover the Late Bronze Age, beginning about 1500 B.C. or slightly before and ending about 1150 B.C. in the first part of the Iron Age. Stratum IX dates for the most part in the early 15th century and is thought to contain the city which was conquered by the great Egyptian conqueror Thutmosis III in his first campaign against a rebellious Palestine-Syria about 1468 B.C. A coalition of forces against Egypt had collected at Megiddo, headed by the king of Kadesh in Syria. The annals of the pharaoh tell us that the Canaanite army quickly abandoned their horses and chariots

[4] For a very different interpretation of these temples, see Kenyon, *Eretz Israel*, V (1958), 51–60.

and fled into the walled city, the people pulling many of the soldiers over the wall by their clothing. The annals continue: "Now, if only the army of his majesty had not given their heart to plundering the things of the enemy, they would have captured Megiddo at this moment, when the wretched foe of Kadesh and the wretched foe of this city were hauled up in haste to bring them into this city. The fear of his majesty had entered their hearts, their arms were powerless." As it was, the trees of the district were cut down and a walled enclosure was erected around the city so that no one could escape; thereupon the city soon surrendered. The booty taken was very great. It included 924 chariots, among which were those of the kings of Kadesh and Megiddo, each wrought with gold, 200 suits of armor, including those of bronze belonging to the two kings (said to have been very beautiful), 502 bows, 1929 cattle, 2000 small cattle (probably goats), and 20,500 small white cattle (sheep).

The palace of the kings of the city was just inside the gate in the northern quarter (area AA). It was built and rebuilt in the successive strata from X through VII A when it was finally destroyed. It extended some 180 feet along the perimeter of the mound, and in size must have rivaled the one which Solomon built in Jerusalem. Its general plan seems to have been an enlargement of the typical home of a wealthy person of the time, an open court or series of courts surrounded by a large number of rooms of varying sizes. In one of the rooms belonging to the Stratum VIII palace (*ca.* 1400–1250 B.C.) a hoard of gold and ivory treasure was found buried beneath the floor, evidently in the hope that it would escape the detection of a threatening enemy—which it obviously did. Among other things it contained numerous gold and lapis lazuli beads, an ivory wand, lapis lazuli cylinder seals, a glass scarab set in a gold or electrum finger ring, a gold bowl, gold headbands and rosettes, a pair of heads in gold foil, stone and gold cosmetic jars, etc. In Stratum VII A of the early 12th century there was found a series of three basement rooms in the debris of which was a large collection of carved ivories. They have been published in a special volume, *Megiddo Ivories* (1939). These form a valuable addition to our knowledge of Canaanite ivory work, previously known from Cyprus (14th–12th centuries), Arslan-tash (9th century), Samaria (9th–8th centuries), Nimrud (9th–8th centuries), Khorsabad (8th century), and elsewhere. A wall in the last phase of the palace's history preserved a hint of its original interior decoration. The mud-plastered surface had been painted; and while the design could no longer be made out, the colors recognized were blue, green, red, yellow, black, and white.

An imposing feature of the Late Bronze Age was a massive temple in the city's sacred area (BB). The excavators believed it was originally built in Stratum VIII, though its foundations were dug so deeply that they actually rested on ruins of Stratum XIV. Two phases of repair and reconstruction are credited to Strata VII B and A (*ca.* 1250–1140/1100 B.C.). It ceased to exist after the destruction of the last Bronze Age city (VIIA).

A similar fortress-temple exists at Shechem, and while place names appear to indicate that several of the type once existed (for example, Migdal-el, Migdal-gad, etc.), the Megiddo and Shechem buildings are the only archaeological examples so far found. The Megiddo one was rectangular, about seventy feet long and fifty-four feet wide, with projecting wings or towers at the front and perhaps with two columns between them at the entrance, forming the portico. The unusual feature of the temple is the width of its walls, which on the two sides were about eleven and one-half feet wide. In the earliest phase there was a niche in the rear wall opposite the door for the statue of the god; in the later phases a platform is known to have existed there for the same purpose. The building at Shechem was even larger and more massive: eighty-six and a quarter feet long by sixty-nine and two-thirds feet wide with walls seventeen feet, five inches, thick.[5] At Ugarit in Syria walls of a similar massive character have been found in a temple, though the plan is different. Professor Albright suggests that the heavy walls may indicate that the buildings were two or more stories high, the superstructure being built of mud brick. If so, their type may be reflected in the many-storied house-shrines found both at Megiddo and at Bethshan.[6] There has been some debate over the function of the Shechem building, but in the light of the Megiddo discovery there can no longer be much doubt that it is indeed the temple of El-berith, mentioned in Judges 9:4, 46. Its size and

[5] See *BASOR*, No. 161 (Feb. 1961), pp. 28 ff.; No. 169 (Feb. 1963), pp. 18 ff.; *BA*, XXIII (1960), 110–19.

[6] W. F. Albright, *The Archaeology of Palestine*, (hereafter *AP*; 4th ed., 1960), p. 104.

strength would certainly have made it an ideal refuge for the men of Shechem, though Abimelech is said to have burned it over their heads.

Israel at Megiddo

The latest datable object in the city of Stratum VII was a statue-base of Pharaoh Rameses VI, to be dated shortly after the middle of the 12th century. To the east at Beth-shan in the Jordan valley a 12th century temple was found in Level VI, one which was rebuilt from a 13th century temple in Level VII. Associated with it in debris was a door lintel bearing an inscription of an Egyptian official of Pharaoh Rameses III (early 12th century). It is thus evident that throughout the first part of the 12th century the Egyptian pharaohs of the 20th dynasty were able to exercise some measure of control over this area of Palestine; the city-states of Megiddo, Beth-shan, and probably others along the coastal plain were subservient. Yet in the hill country of central Palestine are a number of sites which have been excavated and which we know to have been occupied by Israel at this time. The contrast between the two is instructive, revealing the extraordinary simplicity and comparative poverty in the material arts of life which are characteristic of Israel's earliest settlements.[7] Both Megiddo and Beth-shan were among those city-states which withstood the first assaults of Israel (cf. Josh. 17:11-12; Judg. 1:27).

City VII at Megiddo must have been completely and violently destroyed, because the new city of Stratum VI bears no resemblance to it in plan. The Late Bronze Age fortifications were no longer in use. Remains of a small city gate seem to have been found, but it is trivial indeed compared to the earlier one. In the northern part of the mound two very different building phases were found in VI, in the later of which the remains of a small but substantial palace appeared. In the east and south the two phases were not so clearly distinguished. The pottery vessels found are typical of the period elsewhere in Palestine, so that we must date the stratum plus or minus 1125–1050 B.C. This city was violently destroyed by a fierce conflagration, and charcoal-filled debris varying from two to six and one-half feet covered the ruins.

[7] See further W. F. Albright, *AP*, pp. 119 f.; and the writer, *JBL*, LX (1941), 30 ff.

Albright believes that the Song of Deborah in Judges 5, celebrating the victory of Israel over the Canaanite forces headed by Sisera, must be dated between the destruction of City VII and the building of City VI.[8] His argument is based upon the topography of the area and the poetic statement in Judges 5:19 that the battle took place "at Taanach, by the waters of Megiddo." In vs. 21 these waters seem further to be identified with the river Kishon, which flows by the mound of Megiddo; the perennial stream of the Kishon arises in the springs near the mound. It is highly probable, therefore, that the battle actually took place near Megiddo. Yet why is Taanach mentioned, when it is five miles away to the southeast? It is very strange that the writer, an eyewitness of the events, did not simply say that the battle took place at Megiddo, particularly since this was the strongest city of the whole Esdraelon area. Albright believes that the victory must have occurred at a time when Megiddo was in ruins, unoccupied as a city. Taanach would then have been the nearest town by which to fix the location, though the "waters of Megiddo" could also be used. The verse (Judg. 5:19) would mean, therefore, "In [the district of] Taanach, on [the stream called] Waters-of-Megiddo." If so, then Deborah's song must be dated between about 1150 and 1125 B.C., during the interval between Strata VII and VI.[9]

Megiddo as an Israelite Government Center

The great problem at Megiddo, however, is the question as to what ruins belong to the time of David and Solomon in the 10th century. In *Megiddo I: Seasons of 1925-34* (1939), the excavators published a remarkable series of constructions in Stratum IV which they attributed to the time of Solomon. A new stone city wall was erected around the perimeter of the mound, slightly over one-half mile in circumference. Its average thickness was about twelve feet. In certain areas it was made of roughly coursed rubble, but in others, perhaps where extra strength was needed, blocks of hewn stone were carefully fitted together along the faces of the wall. At the east were the remains of what was once an excellent palace, presumably for the local governor, set in a walled courtyard of its own.

[8] *AP*, pp. 117 f.
[9] See *BASOR*, No. 62 (April 1936), pp. 26 ff.

Most interesting of all, however, were the remains of four large buildings which once were stables for horses. Careful measurements indicate that the capacity of these stables was 480 horses. In addition, there was a small stable unit adjoining the palace which could have housed about a dozen more. The typical unit was about eighty feet long; it contained a central passage about ten feet wide, paved with crushed, unslaked lime. This passage was flanked by two rows of stone pillars which served as tie-posts (the tie-holes were preserved) and as supports for the roof. Between the posts were mangers, each hollowed out of a solid block of limestone. Behind them on each side was an aisle, parallel to the central passage and of equal width, in which the horses stood. These aisles were paved with cobblestones to keep the animals from slipping. Five of these units were put together to make each of the three larger stables; the fourth stable employed but two units. Each unit held about thirty horses, except in one of the large buildings where the aisles were slightly smaller and would have held only about twenty-four horses.

The masonry of these structures in Stratum IV is entirely different from anything found in the preceding strata, though it is well known from the discoveries in the Omri-Ahab period of the 9th century at Samaria. Characteristic of it is the use of well-cut stones laid in the header-stretcher method: that is, two or three stones were laid across the thickness of the wall (headers), whereas above, below, and beside them stones were laid lengthwise (stretchers). Such an alternation of stones laid made for great strength; it was a building device probably borrowed from the Phoenicians.

Immediately to the east and adjoining the large stable in the southern quarter of the mound (the other three stables were in the eastern section, the foundations of one of them resting on the ruins of the Stratum VIII temple) was a special building which had its own paved courtyard and fortified gate. Since the city wall was erected over a portion of its southern part, it must have been built before the main phase of the Stratum IV construction, though it was reconstructed and used at the same time as the stable. The masonry of the original building, however, is the same as that in the other IV buildings. Consequently, the excavators attributed the structure to Stratum IV B; but they found nothing comparable elsewhere on the mound and concluded that the city was unoccupied at the time except for this isolated fortress which may have served as the headquarters of the local governmental official and tax collector.

Digging below Stratum IV in areas not disturbed by the deep foundations of the stables and palaces, the excavators found the remains of Stratum V. The architecture was of a domestic nature and no large constructions were discovered. The date given to Stratum V was *ca.* 1060–1000; IV B was considered Davidic, dating from the early 10th century; and Stratum IV proper was credited to Solomon though it continued in use through most of the 9th century.

In reviewing this material Albright pointed to the evidence of two stratigraphic levels on the plans of Stratum V in the eastern area of the mound. At least certain buildings attributed to V were erected over earlier V remains. He thus suggested that these buildings should be attributed to IV B, since it is surprising that IV B remains were not found in the eastern quarter as well as in the southern. Furthermore he believed that the pottery of V was mostly from the early 10th century. His revised dating for the strata was as follows: V. *ca.* 1050–975 B.C.; IV B, *ca.* 950–918; IV A, *ca.* 918–815. This would make IV B Solomonic in date, ending with the Shishak invasion from Egypt (a portion of a stele of Shishak was found on the mound), an event which Albright dates *ca.* 918 B.C. City V, on the other hand, would have been destroyed by David about the same time as he destroyed Bethshan.[10] After a careful study of the pottery, this revision in the dating of the Megiddo material seems to the writer to be highly probable.[11]

Now with the publication of *Megiddo II* new information has come to light. In the northern area of the mound (AA) two phases of V were found. The older of these, labeled V B, contains pottery which in my opinion is identical with the bulk of the V material published in *Megiddo I*. Furthermore the later of the northern phases, called V A, contains precisely the same type of pottery as that which Albright and I had previously distinguished as IV B in the east and south. Consequently, there seems no escape from the conclusion that V A and IV B are one and the same stratum and to be dated from some time in the reign of David until the invasion of Shishak, five years after Solomon's death (I Kings 14:25). The ques-

[10] *AASOR*, XXI–XXII (1943), 2–3, n. 1.
[11] *Ibid.*, pp. 29–30, n. 10.

tion now is: Just what did David and Solomon erect in this stratum?

In the northern quarter after the destruction of the fine Late Bronze Age gateway at the end of Stratum VII, there was constructed in Stratum VI a small, unimposing gate, the weakness of which is in striking contrast to the strength of the former. This gate was rebuilt in Stratum V; in addition, there was found in V a paved road leading up the side of the mound and into the gate. Now for some unexplained reason the excavators attribute this gate to V A, the later of the two V phases. Yet it rested directly upon the ruins of VI A. Consequently, it is highly probable that this gate actually belongs to V B, that is to City V proper which was destroyed by David.

Above the V gate and the road leading up to it there was discovered the finest fortified gateway yet found in early Palestine. The excavators attribute it to Stratum IV and believe it to be Solomonic, which it certainly is. It is the gate of the fine Solomonic city wall previously discovered in the southern and eastern quarters. Yet if it belongs to Stratum IV proper, then we have one gate too many in the strata of Israelite Megiddo. The reasoning is as follows: in Stratum III (ca. 780–733 B.C.) the gate was composed of two parallel sets of piers, forming a double entryway. Immediately below it was the foundation of another gate with three pairs of piers, forming a triple entryway. This also is attributed to Stratum III; but to do so the excavators must assume that it never actually came into use, being replaced by the double gate immediately after it was erected. This now appears as an unnecessarily awkward point of view. It would be much simpler to assume that the triple gate actually belongs to the preceding Stratum IV, now dated from the end of the 10th century to the end of the 9th. This means that the newly discovered gateway with *four* sets of piers and four entryways could be placed in Stratum V A-IV B of the 10th century. In fact, a study of the plans makes it highly probable that this is its correct attribution. If so, then the whole fortification system, including the city wall, previously attributed to Stratum IV, is actually from Stratum V A-IV B.

The gate with the four doorways is unique, though double and triple doorways have been found a number of times at other sites. The masonry was massive and the workmanship excellent. The stones were cut and fitted together in a regular bonding pattern on the wall faces, while the interiors were filled with mud and rubble. The masonry was laid dry without mortar, but the joint between any two stones is said to have been so perfect that not even a thin knife blade could be inserted between them. The width of the main doorway between the tower piers was about fourteen feet; this may have been the only one provided with wooden doors. There were probably two of them, one on each side; when open they could be swung back into the side chambers. A stone socket on which one of the doors turned was found in place. Outside the gate was a strongly fortified courtyard with a small outer gate; from the side of the latter a series of steps led down the steep slope of the mound for the use of pedestrians. As Albright was the first to observe, the main gate with the four doorways is remarkably similar in plan to the east gate in the enclosure to the Solomonic temple in Jerusalem, as described in Ezekiel 40:5-16—a further witness to the importance of Ezekiel 40-42 for the reconstruction of the Jerusalem temple.[12]

After these things had been noted, the writer in 1950 attempted to reconstruct the events in 10th century Megiddo as stated in this and the next paragraph. As the Israelite king, David, in the early part of the 10th century sought to extend his control over all of Palestine, he was forced to attack certain strong cities in the north in order to secure his dominion over the Esdraelon and the northern Jordan valley. In so doing, he destroyed Beth-shan, which guarded the eastern opening of the Esdraelon into the Jordan valley. At the same time, he probably destroyed Megiddo V. Various bits of evidence for reoccupation in Stratum V A-IV B have been found; but the largest construction thus far discovered is that of the palace. It was provided with its own walled enclosure and covered gateway, thus suggesting that the mound's fortifications at the time were by no means strong. Whether the V city gate was still in use or completely in ruins we have no means of knowing. It is likely that David was responsible for the building of the palace as the residence of the official in charge of the Esdraelon district.

In the reign of Solomon, Megiddo was made the capital of

[12] C. G. Howie, *BASOR*, No. 117 (Feb. 1950), pp. 13 ff.

his fifth administrative district,[13] which included the Esdraelon and extended to the Jordan valley. Its governor was Baana, son of Ahilud (I Kings 4:12). An elaborate plan for the rebuilding of the city was evolved and carried out by extremely able architects. The new fortification wall and gate were built. It is also highly probable that the various stables for horses were erected (cf. I Kings 9:15–19), since the city gives evidence of having been planned and built as a whole.

Between 1955 and 1958, an expedition directed by Yigael Yadin worked at the great Galilean site of Hazor (see chap. 11 of this volume), where among other things a four entryway city gate was found which was very close in size to the one at Megiddo. Instead of being attached to a heavy "offsets and insets" wall, as had been believed to be the case at Megiddo, it was found to have been erected as a part of a casemate fortification—that is, a fortification consisting of two parallel walls with small rooms or "casemates" in between. Previously, this type of wall had been found in the Judean provincial centers, Beth-shemesh and Debir, where it was known to have been introduced by the royal court in the 10th century. I Kings 9:15 says that King Solomon fortified Jerusalem, Hazor, Megiddo and Gezer. A careful study of the plans of Macalister's excavation at Gezer identified a casemate wall and four entryway gate which had been incorrectly dated.[14] Hence, if Beth-shemesh, Debir, Hazor and Gezer had casemate walls erected by the 10th century royal court, it was strange that Megiddo did not have one to go with its Solomonic gate.

In the spring of 1960, Yadin conducted a small test excavation at Megiddo along the northwestern edge of the tell. Below the heavy "offsets and insets" fortification he discovered a casemate wall connected with a beautifully built fort which ran beneath one of the stable compounds. This discovery means, then, that Solomonic Stratum V A-IV B had a four entryway gate and a casemate wall, whereas Stratum IV A of the 9th century possessed a three entry gate, an "offsets and insets" wall eleven and one-half feet wide, stables and governor's palace. A governor's palace of IV B is known, but it is by no means certain what else in the city may be Solomonic.

[13] See Wright and Filson, *Westminster Historical Atlas to the Bible* (rev. ed., 1956), p. 50 and Pl. VIIA.
[14] Yadin, *IEJ*, VIII (1958), 80–86.

ns city.[15]

NEW LIGHT ON SOLOMON'S MEGIDDO

YIGAEL YADIN

"And this is the reason of the levy which king Solomon raised; to build the house of the Lord and his own house, and Millo, and the wall of Jerusalem, and Hazor and Megiddo and Gezer" (I Kings 9:15).

It all started with the brief biblical account of Solomon's building activities. In fact hardly ever in the history of archaeological digging has such a short verse in the Bible helped so much in identifying and dating actual remains found by the spade.

When the magnificent six-chambered and two-towered gate was found at Megiddo by the expedition of the Chicago Oriental Institute, it was correctly attributed by the excavators to the Solomonic city.[1] Furthermore, Albright was able to show the striking resemblance between the plan of that gate and the east gate of the enclosure in the Solomonic temple in Jerusalem as described in Ezekiel 40:5-16.[2] When a similar gate was found during our excavations at Hazor in a level attributable to Solomon on the grounds of stratigraphy as well as pottery,[3] the attribution of the Megiddo gate to Solomon became certain.

These discoveries led me sometime ago to re-examine Macalister's report on his excavations at Gezer, and to my great

[15] See Yadin, *BA*, XXIII (1960), 62-68, reprinted herewith in this volume. For further details, see the excavation volumes themselves, and the critical reviews written before the Yadin sounding by W. F. Albright and the writer in *AJA*, LIII (1949), 213-15, and *JAOS*, LXX (1950), 56-60; see also the discussion with comparative charts by the writer in *The Bible and the Ancient Near East*, ed. G. E. Wright (1961), pp. 73-112.

[1] Robert S. Lamon, *apud* G. Loud, *Megiddo* II (1948), pp. 46-57.

[2] *AJA*, LIII (1949), 213-15; Carl G. Howie, *BASOR*, No. 117 (Feb. 1950), pp. 13-19.

[3] *IEJ*, VIII (1958), 80-86.

surprise and delight a similar gate emerged from one of his plans, which he had entitled a "Maccabean Castle."[4] That this gate was indeed Solomonic was clear not only from its plan and method of construction, but also from the fact that it was part of a casemate city wall, similar to the one found at Hazor which was also connected with the Solomonic gate. It occurred to me, therefore, that the nature of the city wall of Megiddo attributed to Solomon (Stratum IV) would have to be reconsidered; while the gates at Hazor and Gezer belonged to a casemate city wall, the one at Megiddo—as shown on the plans of the excavations[5]—belonged to a solid wall built with "offsets" and "insets." This anomaly could not be explained away by the different character of the three cities.[6] It is axiomatic that the strength and character of a wall are determined by the tactics, strength, and siegecraft of the enemy against whom it is erected. Gezer in the south and Hazor in the north could theoretically have been fortified against two different potential enemies, yet both had the same type of fortifications. There was no reason why Megiddo in the center of the land should be protected by a different type of fortification, one which was obviously stronger.

I suspected, therefore, that a casemate wall was hidden beneath the solid wall and when the solid wall was built, the former was filled up, and for some reason was not recognized by the excavators. A similar situation was found at Hazor, where at some places the older casemate wall was filled up by the builders of the solid wall at the beginning of the 9th century.[7]

Another fact connected with the problem of the solid wall at Megiddo created great difficulties for the excavators and for all who studied the Megiddo report. At the southern part of the mound, east of the southern complex of stables, the excavators discovered a huge palatial building constructed of fine ashlar blocks. This building, which was obviously Israelite, nevertheless lay in part immediately beneath the solid "Solomonic" wall. Furthermore, another building (1482) of the same level, west of the palatial building, was shown to

[4] *Ibid.*

[5] *Megiddo* II, Figs. 105, 389.

[6] As suggested by Y. Aharoni, *BASOR*, No. 154 (April 1959), pp. 35–39. Cf. Yadin, *The Kingdoms of Israel and Judah* (in Hebrew; 1961), pp. 66–109.

[7] See *Hazor* Vols. III–IV (forthcoming).

be covered partly by the stables. The excavators attributed the stables and solid wall to Stratum IV, while the palace and building 1482 were attributed to a newly-named stratum IV B—the designation "V" having already been taken up by another stratum.[8]

Since the solid wall and stables had been attributed to Solomon, the lonely palace or fort had to be attributed either to David or to an early Solomonic phase; both alternatives allowed for the belief that Solomon himself tore down this fine building in order to build the city wall, the stables, etc.[9] In spite of the brilliant and tireless efforts of Albright and Wright,[10] who have introduced considerable clarity into the complex problems of the Megiddo stratigraphy (particularly by showing that the remains of V A are in fact part of the IV B city), the difficulty remained. Either the lonely fort was built by David (for which there is no biblical support) or by Solomon himself, who in either case would be charged with demolishing one of the finest buildings of Israelite Megiddo for no apparent reason.

In view of these difficulties and in search for a hoped-for casemate wall, I carried out a short dig during January 1960 at Megiddo. The results, which were really startling, will soon be published in detail with plans in a forthcoming issue of the *Israel Exploration Journal*.[11] There too the full implications concerning Strata V-IV and III will be discussed. At the request of Prof. Wright, I submit herewith a concise report of the dig and the general conclusion which may be drawn from it.

The most promising area for the soundings seemed to be the northeastern sector of the site, due east of the city gate,

[8] Robert S. Lamon and Geoffrey M. Shipton, *Megiddo* I (1939), p. 9.
[9] *Ibid.*, p. 59.
[10] See G. Ernest Wright in *Biblical Archaeology* (1957), pp. 120 ff., which lists further bibliography; and "The Discoveries at Megiddo," pp. 225–240 of the present volume (from *BA*, XIII [1950], 28–46).
[11] This dig, carried out on behalf of the Hebrew University and through the generous support of Mr. John Wilks of Corona Del Mar, California, lasted from January 13th to 15th and again for several days in the second half of the same month. I was assisted by Mr. I. Dunayevsky, chief architect of the Hazor Expedition, with whose collaboration the full report will be published.

near the eastern group of stables. On the one hand, the remains of the solid wall in that spot were still intact and had not been removed by the excavators, and, on the other, air photographs showed some structures which obviously extended beneath the city wall.[12] Even before we began the actual digging, we were surprised to notice that what seemed to be the lower courses of the outer face of the solid wall, in square K13,—as exposed by the excavators—were built of big ashlar blocks, some smoothly dressed, some with marginal-drafting, like those of the Solomonic city gate. This was unlike the rest of the wall, which was built of smaller stones. Furthermore, these courses extended for a considerable length without any "offsets and insets." No conceivable reasons were apparent why that sector should be built differently; our suspicion grew when we noticed that these courses at the north end came to an abrupt end in a straight vertical line. The only *a priori* explanation was that these courses did not originally belong to the city wall, but to an earlier huge building, on whose ruins the solid wall was built. To examine this theory the lower courses of the solid wall above the end of the ashlar blocks were carefully removed, and immediately we struck a surprise, the first in a series. A solid wall one and one-half meters wide, built of large ashlar stones, appeared just below the city wall, extending in a right angle toward the city. This wall formed a corner with the ashlar courses. We followed the wall of this building for more than ten meters well inside the city, until we were satisfied that the building was lying not only below the solid city wall, but also below the foundations of the adjacent partially excavated stables.[13]

As though these facts were not in themselves enough, we were fortunate in finding in the corner room of the newly discovered building, just below the lower courses of the "offsets and insets" wall, a fine group of whole vessels, all typical of the V A-IV B period, i.e. the Solomonic times: typical cooking-pots, deep bowls with hand burnishing, a number of store jars and a fine imported Cypriote juglet.

The next problem was to locate the other corner of the building, i.e. the eastern corner. This was a more difficult task since that part was almost completely destroyed even prior to the building of the "offsets and insets" city wall. Due

[12] *Megiddo* I, Fig. 119, Squares K12–13; L15.
[13] *Ibid.*, plan on Fig. 49.

south of the hypothetical corner at a distance of about fifteen meters, lies the "finger" of the deep "BB" cut made by the Megiddo excavators.[14] In this section were visible huge ashlar stones (unmarked in the plans of the Megiddo excavators) forming a wall of exactly the same width (i.e. one and one-half meters), lying clearly *beneath* the floors of Stable 407. Several trial soundings along the hypothetical line revealed, immediately below the walls and floors of the stable, the eastern outer wall of the newly discovered building. Thus this building turned out to be a huge structure, its northern face measuring twenty-nine meters, a few meters more than the "palace" of IV B, previously discovered in the south, and it was lying in similar stratigraphic conditions, i.e. beneath the solid city wall and stables.

Our second effort was concentrated west of the western wall of this palatial or fort-like structure (to be called the "Northern Fort"). The fact that the northern wall of the fort was built on the very edge of the mound indicated either that there was no city wall to be connected with it, or that the outer wall of the fort also served as part of a city wall which abutted on the building west and east of it. West of the building two facts demanded clarification:

1. West of the outer wall of the fort, and in straight line with its outer face, a wall built of slightly masoned boulders was visible. This wall was also lying below the foundations of the "offsets and insets" city wall.

2. About five meters south of this latter wall and parallel to it, right inside the city in the narrow strip between the inner face of the "offsets and insets" wall and the northern wall of the stable complex, the top of a fine wall built of carefully laid headers and stretchers was visible. Although its top is visible on the air-photograph published in Megiddo I[15] it is not marked on any of the published plans. The excavation of the two walls mentioned above, by carefully removing the foundations of the "offsets and insets" city wall when that was necessary, revealed a series of casemates, measuring four by five meters. Each casemate had a carefully built entrance in its southwest corner, and the dividing wall (or diaphragm) served also as the western jamb of the door. It was interesting to note that the dividing walls also built of ashlar blocks, were

[14] *Megiddo* II, Fig. 377 (Square L13).
[15] *Megiddo* I, Fig. 119, Square K12.

well bonded into the outer wall, which, as already mentioned, was built of slightly masoned boulders. The westward extension of the series of casemates cannot be traced, since here lies the Schumacher trench (dug in 1903–5). But that these casemates did extend westward is clear since the western part of the third casemate and the beginning of a fourth are clearly marked in the sketch plans in Megiddo II, where the buildings found by Loud in the strip between the eastern edge of the Schumacher trench and the present edge of the trench are marked.[16] Some of the casemates yielded a considerable number of domestic vessels, all identical with those found in the corner room of the Northern Fort.

A second sounding was made east of the newly discovered Fort. Here again, the straight line of a wall became visible, parallel to and beneath the outer broken edge the "offsets and insets" city wall.[17] The removal of the foundations of the "offsets and insets" city wall in several places revealed below a fill of loose earth and stones, a series of long casemates measuring on the average seven and one-half meters in length and two meters in width (between the walls). While one casemate was found intact (on all sides), of the others only the inner and dividing walls were found (of casemate No. 2, parts of the outer wall were also discovered). The outer walls, built on the very edge of the mound, have disappeared, together with the outer edge of the "offsets and insets" wall. It is interesting to note that part of the second casemate lay bare before we began excavating and in fact is visible on the air photograph.[18] As mentioned above, the area around the eastern corner of the Fort was utterly and deliberately destroyed even before the erection of the "offsets and insets" city wall. Because of this fact, no remains of the casemate wall were found in the immediate area of the Fort's corner; nevertheless it was interesting to note that the remains of the nearest casemate, lying at a distance of some six meters east of the Fort, show that it was built in a sharp curve intended to meet the Fort's bastioned corner. Furthermore, this casemate had a series of at least two dividing walls built close to each other, thus strengthening the curve.

This casemate wall is built on a much flimsier foundation

[16] *Ibid.*, Fig. 114, Square K12, northern part.
[17] *Ibid.*, air photograph, Fig. 119, Square L14.
[18] *Ibid.*

than that west of the Fort and in fact than that of Hazor. This may be explained by the fact that it was located on the highest part of the site, where the slope to the north is extremely steep, thus making any conceivable attack with engines of war practically impossible from that direction. The area west of the Fort is much lower and is adjacent to the city gate.

The stratigraphic position of the Fort and the series of casemates in relation to the stables, and the "offsets and insets" wall of Stratum IV A, was clear and decisive: the former lay immediately below the latter. There remained the problem of fixing the relation of the newly discobered IV B constructions to the earlier strata. This was done with the aid of several soundings below the Fort and casemates on the one hand, and checking the exposed section of the Schumacher trench on the other. The Fort was found to be built above the remains of walls which in turn were built above the clearly discernible burnt brick walls of Stratum VI A. Thus again the newly discovered stratum had to be attributed to IV B-V A, even when counting the strata from below upwards, i.e. from the burnt brick walls of Stratum VI A; the remains above them and below the foundations of the Fort were V B and the Fort itself was V A-IV B. This conclusion was further corroborated when a sounding near and beneath the eastern corner of the Fort revealed the corner of a room, badly burnt and filled with a large unmber of whole vessels of the VI A types.

Before trying to apply the conclusions of these finds to the other discoveries at Megiddo, let us sum up the facts:

1. A huge Fort, built of ashlar blocks, dressed similarly to those in the other IV B structures, was found immediately beneath the solid IV A city wall and the northern complex of stables. The pottery associated with this Fort is typical V A-IV B.

2. This Fort is part of a casemate complex of fortifications, built east and west of it; the outer wall of the Fort served at the same time as part of the casemate system.

Conclusions

1. The first and most important conclusion to be drawn from the above facts is that the southern palace, or Fort, discovered by the excavators of Megiddo, should no longer be considered as an isolated fort built in an undefended city; on the contrary, it was part of a big city (Stratum V A-IV B), well defended by casemate walls, the formidable six-cham-

bered city gate and the newly discovered Northern Fort which dominated from above the approaches to the city gate. To these two forts should be attributed quite a number of public and private buildings, some of which were considered by the excavators as belonging generally to Stratum V or more specifically to V A. Such a city, of the 10th century, was probably not built by David, if we base our judgment both on general historical considerations and especially on I Kings 9:15. This city, with its system of fortifications similar to those of Hazor and Gezer, must have been the Solomonic city referred to in the biblical verse, quoted above.

2. The second automatic and unavoidable conclusion is that City IV proper (IV A) with its solid city wall of the "offsets and insets" type (built in part on a filling of the older casemate wall), the two complexes of stables and the four-chambered city gate (the unfinished III B gate in the terminology of the excavators),[19] is *not* Solomonic but was built after the destruction of the Solomonic city by Pharaoh Shishak in the 5th year of the reign of Rehoboam. The work was that of a later sovereign, most probably King Ahab, whose great force of 2000 chariots is mentioned in the annals of Shalmaneser III. This does not exclude the possibility that Solomon's city had stables too, but these were not the excavated ones, nor would they have been in the area in which these were found.

3. It is to Stratum III, then, that the last of the city gates of Megiddo, the one with the two chambers,[20] should be attributed.

Many problems which require fresh consideration will be dealt with in the forthcoming article in the *Israel Exploration Journal;* these will include the problem of building 338, the exact relation of the various gates (including the one attributed by the excavators to Stratum V), the duration of Stratum IV, etc.

Let me conclude by saying that the few days of soundings in Megiddo were most exhilarating for all of us. The finds made in a short time only show how much more can be done in this magnificent mound. The tremendous pioneering work done by the Oriental Institute of the Chicago University enables us now to probe further into the mysteries of this city with relatively small effort.

[19] *Megiddo* I, Gate 1 on Fig. 86.
[20] *Ibid.*, Gate 2.

13

SAMARIA

G. ERNEST WRIGHT

After a long delay, the publication of the Samaria excavations has been completed. This great site was first dug in 1908–1910 by a Harvard University expedition, directed by George A. Reisner and Clarence S. Fisher. The publication of the results was delayed by the First World War until 1924.[1] Between 1931 and 1935 a second expedition worked at the site under the direction of J. W. Crowfoot, ably assisted by E. L. Sukenik, Kathleen M. Kenyon, and Mrs. Crowfoot, if we list only those who bore major responsibility for publication. In the first three of the four campaigns it was called the "Joint Expedition," because five institutions joined in sponsoring the project: Harvard University, Hebrew University, the Palestine Exploration Fund, the British Academy, and the British School of Archaeology in Jerusalem.

The complete publication of the results was delayed, this time by the Second World War. The first volume (*Samaria-Sebaste I: The Buildings*) was published in London by the Palestine Exploration Fund in 1942. The second volume (*Samaria-Sebaste II: Early Ivories*) had actually appeared earlier (1938), while the final volume, long awaited, did not leave the press until 1957 (*Samaria-Sebaste III: The Objects*). It is perhaps worthwhile to celebrate the completion of this important project by reviewing briefly some of the main results of the Expedition's work. It may be observed that the distinguished French archaeologist, André Parrot, has written a fine summary of the city's history and archaeology in his small volume, *Samarie, capitale du royaume d'Israel* (Paris, 1955). This book has been translated and published in England by the Student Christian Movement Press as No. 7 in their Biblical Archaeology series, and is warmly recommended.

[1] Reisner, Fisher and Lyon, *Harvard Excavations at Samaria* (1924).

The importance of the work at Samaria is obvious. Not only is the site significant because of a history rich in architectural, inscriptional, and artistic remains, but it is also important because of the excellence of the archaeological work done there by both expeditions. The Samaria volumes are a monument to archaeologists who have done their work exceedingly well under the most difficult circumstances.

The primary reason for the difficulties is the fact that Samaria was one of Palestine's chief pagan cities during the Hellenistic and Roman periods, when architects built their buildings to last a long time. Foundations for important structures were likely to be laid in trenches on bedrock, and there was no hesitation about large scale earth removal, leveling and excavating. As a result, in a city which once flourished as a thriving metropolis between the 3rd centuries B.C. and A.D. one must expect earlier ruins to be badly disturbed, if not destroyed. And so it is at Samaria. Early fortifications were replaced by later ones, so that the earlier ones became a convenient quarry for fine masonry. The Israelite city gate on the summit of the mound seems to have been in the area leveled for the Roman forum, a large flat place still used as the threshing floor of the village of *Sebastyeh*. Herod the Great built his remarkable temple in honor of Caesar Augustus at the highest point on the western summit, a spot which the Israelite dynasty of Omri also considered a choice one, because that was where the palace of the Israelite kings was erected.

History of the City

Samaria's day as the capital of Israel and rival of Jerusalem lasted about as long as Washington, D. C. has been the capital of the United States (*ca.* 870–721 B.C.). The site was purchased by a former army general, Omri, for the royal residence and the private possession of the Israelite king.[2] It is a high hill, easily defended, with a marvelous view westward to the Mediterranean, though higher hills to the north, south

[2] An important monograph by the great German scholar, the late Albrecht Alt, deals with this subject (*Die Stadtstaat Samaria* [1954]). He argues from the Naboth vineyard story in II Kings 22 that Israel was peculiar in having two capitals, one at Samaria and one at Jezreel to the north in the plains of Jezreel (Esdraelon). Furthermore, King Omri was able to purchase the hill of Samaria, but his son, Ahab, could not buy property in Jezreel. Alt interprets

and east hem in the view in those directions. The Assyrians called it the "house of Omri," and continued to do so long after Omri's death and the annihilation of his dynasty and family in the revolution of Jehu (*ca.* 842 B.C.). After a long siege, the city was destroyed by Sargon II early in 721 B.C. and the kingdom of Israel brought to an end (II Kings 17). It was rebuilt, however, as the administrative capital of the Assyrian province of Samaria, and it continued to be used as a provincial capital by the Persian government. There in the time of Nehemiah during the third quarter of the 5th century B.C. a strong man, named Sanballat, was evidently governor and the most prominent individual west of the Jordan (Neh. 2:19; 4:6).

In the Hellenistic Age its history is an interesting contrast to that of Shechem. The latter city, some five miles to the south at the opening of the pass between Mts. Ebal and Gerizim, was the old religious, as well as political, center of the whole area. Its political hegemony was taken over by Samaria, but during the latter part of the 4th century it was rebuilt on a large scale as the metropolis of the Samaritan sect of Judaism.[3] Samaria, on the other hand, was taken by Alexander

---

this to mean that Samaria was possessed by a large Canaanite remnant in Israel and that the hill was actually at the center of a typical Canaanite city-state, governed by Canaanite commercial law. Jezreel, on the other hand, was Israelite and governed by Israelite property law. The dynasty of Omri, he argues, adopted a compromise government, a thoroughgoing dualism, with two capitals symbolizing the rule over two peoples, and with complete religious toleration. This marvelously balanced system was upset by the Elijah-Elisha revolution against such toleration. The monograph is a fine example of logical construction, though its logic rests on too narrow a basis. The Jezreel palace of the kings of Israel is usually interpreted very simply as a "winter house" (Amos 3:15), while Omri's ability to buy at Samaria but not at Jezreel need be nothing more than a powerful person's gaining his ends by legal ingenuity (Omri need only to have had himself "adopted" as a son by the selling family or clan to have made the purchase "legal": cf. the Nuzi documents where this type of action was common, and also the protests of Amos and Isaiah). Jezebel's method of securing Naboth's vineyard for Ahab was much more heavy-handed, but it was successful and attempted to preserve the fiction of legality (Naboth was executed for blasphemy, false though the charge indeed was).

[3] This we know from the Drew-McCormick excavations at Shechem in 1956, 1957, 1960 and 1962; see *BA*, XX (1957), Nos.

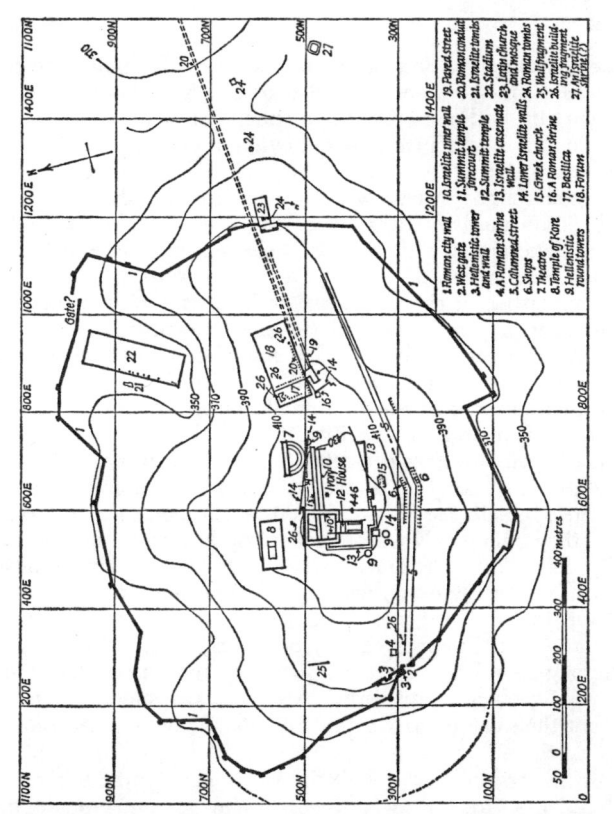

FIGURE 4. Plan of Samaria. Wall 1 surrounds the city of Herod the Great. The summit is enclosed by the Israelite inner wall (wall 10) and the casemate wall (wall 13), while a suspected Israelite city gate would lie south of the Roman forum and Roman basilica (area 17). The old approach road came up the northern slopes along the line of the wall by the theater, marked 14. The late Roman-columned street with shops is on the south (5 and 6). Building 23 at the east limit is the mosque of the modern village, built from the remains of a Latin church.

the Great, who is said to have destroyed the city, and to have given it to Macedonians. Many of its inhabitants evidently moved to Shechem which they rebuilt as their rival to Jeru-

---

1 and 4; XXIII (1960), No. 3; *BASOR*, Nos. 144 (Dec. 1956), pp. 9–20; 148 (Dec. 1957), pp. 11–28; 161 (Feb. 1961), pp. 11–54; and 169 (Feb. 1963), pp. 1–60.

salem. Both cities now flourished, the one a Samaritan center and the other, whence the Samaritans took their name, a pagan city with a foreign population. The old Israelite fortifications of Samaria were reused by the proteges of Alexander, but were strengthened at critical points by beautifully constructed round towers. Mr. Crowfoot says of the tower his expedition unearthed that it is "the finest monument of the Hellenistic age in Palestine. It is also one of the least Palestinian buildings in the country. A work as foreign to the land as the castles of the Crusaders, it is an enduring witness to the strong grip of the early Macedonian adventurers."[4]

On a terrace north of and below the summit where the ruins of the Israelite palace and the Augustus temple are, Sukenik unearthed beneath a small Roman shrine the remains of a small temple for the Egyptian goddess, Isis, in its own sacred enclosure. It was erected in the 3rd century B.C. In the mid-2nd century the people of the city evidently became alarmed about the threat from the Hasmoneans in Judah, and they built a new wall ("Hellenistic fort wall") around the city, following approximately the line of the Israelite fortifications. Yet the Judean ruler priests were persistent. Between about 111 and 107 B.C. John Hyrcanus took Samaria and, according to Josephus, destroyed it with such violence and thoroughness as to leave no sign that the city had existed. Since Shechem's prosperous existence was suddenly ended about the same time, it is probable that John wreaked similar havoc there.

In the first century, rebuilding began at Samaria, but it was Herod the Great who between 30 and 20 B.C. brought the city back to the glory it had in the Israelite period. It was both a fortress city to protect his hold on the country and an advertisement to the world of his gratitude to Caesar Augustus, whose client he was. Six thousand of his mercenary soldiers from various parts of the Roman world were settled there and given land. The city's name was changed to Sebaste

[4] *Samaria* I, p. 27. The Harvard Expedition found two of the towers in 1908–1910, and dated them in the Israelite period, but Dr. Ben Dor, who directed the excavation of the northeastern one for the Joint Expedition, found early Hellenistic pottery in debris contemporary with the tower's erection. Eusebius (*Chron.* ed. Schoene, II, 118—so Mr. Crowfoot) says that one Perdiccas who died in 321 B.C. rebuilt the city. The towers may have been his work, or they may have been erected during the subsequent quarter-century in the midst of many alarms and excursions.

(= Augusta) in honor of Augustus, and the great temple was built at the highest point on the summit. The latter was raised on a podium so as to be the most prominent feature of the whole area. In order to provide a court of sufficient size for the building, a great area about 225 feet long and almost square was leveled over the remains of Israelite and Hellenistic fortifications and on retaining walls over the edge of the hill itself. A new city fortification was built around the mound's lower slopes and out into the valley at the north, to enclose a large, irregular oval, about a kilometer wide at its greatest extent. Towers for defensive purpose were spaced at intervals along the wall; their erection would have demanded a tremendous amount of labor because of the size of the area being enclosed, even though the work was by no means equal in craftsmanship or defensive strength to that of the earlier Israelite structures.

The wall may have been extended into the valley to protect a stadium which Herod built in Doric style: an oval some 638 feet long for a regulation-size track was surrounded by a wall and a covered passageway, supported by Doric columns, for the comfort of spectators. Herod had a great interest in athletics; he built another stadium at Caesarea where the 192nd Olympiad was held at his expense. As already mentioned, a forum or civic center and market place was created at the eastern end of the summit by a great leveling operation, an area which today serves admirably as a threshing floor for the modern village.

Space prevents a detailed description of later developments. The next and final period of extensive building at Samaria was between about A.D. 180 and 230 when the stadium was rebuilt in Corinthian style, colonnades were added to the forum, a fine basilica was erected at the northeastern corner of the forum, a theater on the northern slope, a temple of Kore over the ruins of the earlier temple of Isis, an aqueduct to supply the city with needed water, and a new gate and columned street along the mound's southern slope. Before this time the road to the summit had led along both natural and artificial terraces over the northern side of the hill. Now a new street, bordered by columns and shops, followed a fairly level ledge immediately below the summit on the south. Samaria, like Caesarea along the coast, must have been a city so westernized as to make any Roman or Greek feel almost at home.

The Israelite Period

Most of the architectural remains found at Samaria are Roman or Israelite, and the latter were only discovered at points where later leveling had happened to cover them. The most astonishing feature of the Israelite period is the city walls around the summit. Their masonry is of such excellence that, while it has been equaled, it has never been surpassed in the later history of the country. Before that time only some masonry of the Solomonic period at Megiddo and Gezer can be said to resemble it. To see it is to gain a new respect for 9th century Israelites, particularly King Ahab, who was ultimately responsible for at least one phase of the work, though as in Solomon's day imported architects from Phoenicia may have supervised the actual workmanship. While most of the stones have been taken away by later builders, the lower courses often remain. Even where they have been completely removed the line of the walls can be traced because not only were the foundations laid on bedrock but trenches were dug in the rock to make sure of a perfect footing for the wall. Courses left below ground usually had a raised boss remaining, but above ground the stones were finely cut, fitted and laid, with ends and sides showing alternately: the "header-stretcher" method.

One of the most important parts of the Joint Expedition's work was a vertical slice or section cut through the debris from north to south across the summit east of the Israelite palace. This work was directed by Kathleen M. Kenyon, who through her careful study of the various types of debris in relation to walls was able to establish a succession of building periods. Period I was the time when the site was first fortified. An enclosure wall was built around the summit; it was 1.60 meters wide (*ca.* five feet) and enclosed an area *ca.* 178 meters by 89 meters. This is called the "Inner Wall" or "Wall 161" in the publications. The royal palace was erected at the western side; another building in the north center called the "ivory house" was built, and a large courtyard existed along the southern side, evidently related to the palace. The hill once had a ridge. Hence the enclosure wall served both as a fortification and as a retaining wall for the dirt needed to make a level place inside the enclosure on the slopes of the ridge. Parts of at least two other walls are known to exist lower down the slope. The approach road came up a terrace on the north side along Wall 573, and the gate or gates were evidently in the area later leveled for the Roman forum. Remains of one of them are thought to have existed just south of the basilica though if this is the case another approach road may have existed at the south. It is of interest to observe that the summit rectangle was only about five acres in extent. Consequently this area can only be considered as a governmental center. Most of the families of servants, retainers, and soldiers must have lived around the slopes of the hill both inside and outside the lower fortifications.

Period II is the time when the summit fortifications were greatly strengthened by a casemate wall on the north, west and southwest. At the southeast the older Inner Wall was re-used and its thickness tripled. The casemate wall consists of two parallel walls connected by crosswalls which make small chambers ("casemates"). The outer wall is 1.80 meters (about six feet) thick, the inner one meter, and the space between seven meters on the north side but narrower on the west and southwest. The whole fortification was nearly thirty-one feet thick on the north and there added over fifty feet to the width of the summit platform.

In Period III a wholesale rebuilding of the "ivory house" and of the royal palace suggests that a catastrophe had brought Period II to a close. Period IV represents only alterations to the "ivory house" and perhaps a repair in the casemate wall, though it seems to me that the latter could just as well have been done in Period III. Period V was the time when the "ivory house" was reconstructed. Over its floors was "a thick layer of debris, with much burnt matter, including a considerable quantity of burnt ivory" (*Samaria III*, p. 97). This is surely the evidence for Sargon II's destruction of Samaria during the winter of 722–721 B.C. "Period VI" is a designation given some debris piled against Wall 573 down the slope, but the writer does not believe it can be separated from V; it must belong to the same period.

It is the dating of the periods and the interpretation of the debris-layers in relation to the walls that occasion the greatest difficulty in the volumes. Period I is attributed to Omri, who purchased the site for his capital. Period II is assigned to Ahab, Omri's son, after whose day there was a destruction and the major buildings were rebuilt (Period III), presumably by Jehu, the army official who led the revolution against the Omri dynasty. Thus the major construction of Period I, the casemate fortification of Period II, a major destruction and reconstruction (Period III) are all dated in a thirty-five year period (*ca.* 875–840 B.C.). Yet Omri reigned so short a time that it is difficult to see how he could have completed everything in Period I within his short reign.[5] It would be better to assume that Period I was begun by Omri and completed by Ahab, while Period II represents Jehu's strengthening of the summit fortifications. The destruction of Period II can safely be attributed to the Arameans from Damascus who in the reign of King Jehoahaz of Israel (*ca.* 815–801 B.C.) brought Israel to her knees (II Kings 13:3–7; cf. vss. 22–25 and 12:17–19). To the same people at the same time must be credited also the destruction of Megiddo (the city of Stratum IV A) and Hazor (Stratum VII).

To such a redating Miss Kenyon would reply that the pottery of Periods I and II is so similar that a lengthy time interval cannot be assumed between them. The pottery of III, on the other hand, differs much more and can be separated in time from that of I–II, as it also can be separated from IV which is very close to V–VI. The answer to Miss Kenyon's views involves a very complex analysis of the stratigraphy, for the details of which I must refer to another article.[6] To oversimplify the situation, I would describe the ceramic picture as follows: the pottery assigned to Period I comes from the first occupation level on the rock surface, except for some pieces dating from about 3000 B.C. from rock pockets (Early Bronze I). Otherwise the date of this Period I pottery is 10th or early 9th century, with at least one piece going back to the 11th century. *When Omri purchased Samaria, he was not buying an empty hill, but a hill with a small village on it.* The pottery assigned to Period II does not differ from that of Period I because it was in fill used to level up inside the casemates. That is, the builders of the casemate wall threw in dirt fill from elsewhere on the mound; and most of it was dirt

[5] I Kings 6:21 ff. says that Omri reigned twelve years, six of them being a time of civil war with part of the nation following Tibni. That this figure has something wrong with it seems indicated by the following: Vs. 23 says Omri began to reign in the 31st year of King Asa of Judah and reigned six years in Tirzah. Vs. 29 says that Ahab began to reign in King Asa's 38th year. This would leave only *two years* for Omri's residence in Samaria (so Albright, *BASOR*, No. 100 (Dec. 1945), pp. 20–21, n. 15), scarcely time enough to complete the vast building operation which the excavators would attribute to him.

[6] See the writer, *BASOR*, No. 155 (Oct. 1959), pp. 13–29.

from the pre-Omri village. Except for occasional broken pieces in the fill of II, one would need to look under III floors to find 9th century pottery to date the walls of I–II. Yet all pottery *below* III is what Miss Kenyon assigns to III; all that *under* IV to IV, etc. This may be true in part, but the pottery *below* floors is usually very mixed and scarcely homogeneous. Much of it belongs to the preceding period or periods, unless there is some special circumstance to indicate otherwise. In any event, this is certainly the case for much of the pottery from the Samaria section. Consequently, my redating of the Israelite stratigraphy at Samaria is approximately as follows (at the risk of oversimplification):

	Samaria		*Hazor*
ca. 3000 B.C.	Village	Pottery in rock pockets	
10th–early 9th cent.	Village	Pottery I–II	X–IX
ca. 870–842	Bldg. Per. I }	Most of Pottery III	{ VIII
ca. 842–810	Bldg. Per. II }		VII (?)
ca. 810–750	Bldg. Per. III	Pottery IV	VI
ca. 750–735	Bldg. Per. IV	Pottery V (below floors)	V
ca. 735–721	Bldg. Per. V–VI	Pottery VI	

Space does not permit the discussion of the marvelous pieces of ivory inlay discussed in *Samaria II*, nor the ostraca found by the two expeditions. Most of those discovered by the Harvard Expedition were found in an administrative building west of the palace between the inner and casemate walls. They belong in Building Period IV from about 738 B.C.[7] But these and many other interesting discoveries at Samaria are another story for which we cannot now pause. While it is almost inevitable for opinions to differ on details, the world of biblical archaeology is forever indebted to the excavators of Samaria for a great achievement.

[7] See Y. Yadin, "Ancient Judaean Weights and the Date of the Samaria Ostraca," *Scripta Hierosolymitana*, III (1960), 1–17. For a brief review of the main group of ostraca, see the writer, *Biblical Archaeology* (Rev. ed.; 1962–63), pp. 163–64. The ivories belong in type to a sizable collection of Phoenician and Syrian ivory work of the 9th–8th cents. After that time, the elephants along the upper Euphrates seem to have become extinct, and Syro-Phoenician artists turned increasingly to metal. For a comparative study of the ivories of this age, see especially R. D. Barnett, *The Nimrud Ivories in the British Museum* (1957).

14

SHECHEM IN EXTRA-BIBLICAL REFERENCES

WALTER HARRELSON

Egyptian References

The two earliest occurrences of place names which may refer to the biblical city of Shechem are found in texts from the 12th Egyptian dynasty. The first to be examined appears in one of the texts of execration published by Posener.[1] These texts, which are written on the bodies of clay figurines representing bound captives of the pharaoh, contain over seventy names of Asiatic cities, among them a considerable number from Palestine. The texts have the following form: "The ruler of ———— [name of city], ———— [name of ruler]," thus providing a large number of place names as well as personal names. Albright dates the texts to the middle of the 19th century;[2] Alt proposes a date around 1800 B.C.[3] Posener places them at the end of the 12th dynasty (1991–1778 B.C.).[4]

The text which may contain a reference to the city of Shechem reads as follows: "The prince (or ruler) of *Skmimi*, 'Ibshddw."[5]

Albright has proposed that the word be vocalized Sakmami or Sakmemi, meaning "the two shoulders."[6] Such a meaning would fit the region of biblical Shechem excellently: the city dominated by the two mountains Ebal and Gerizim. He con-

[1] G. Posener, *Princes et pays d'Asie et de Nubie* (1940), p. 68.
[2] *BASOR*, No. 81 (Feb. 1941), pp. 16–21.
[3] *ZDPV*, LXIV (1941), 21–39.
[4] Posener, pp. 31–35.
[5] Posener, p. 68. There are various ways to vocalize the word but this is Posener's preference.
[6] *BASOR*, No. 81 (Feb. 1941), pp. 18–19, n. 11.

siders the term to refer to the biblical Shechem.[7] Posener says no more than that it is generally thought to refer to Shechem.[8]

This text gives no clear indication of the size or importance of the city, since it occurs in a list of city names some of which are strategically located and of considerable size (at least in certain periods), others of which are apparently of little military or political significance. We have no way of knowing to which category Shechem may have belonged at this period, until more adequate archaeological evidence is at hand.

The second 12th dynasty text appears in the Khu-sebek inscription which is dated to the reign of Sesostris III (*ca.* 1880–1840 B.C.).[9] The inscription contains a number of difficulties, particularly in its depiction of the sequence of events related.[10] The relevant portion of the text for our purposes is translated by Wilson as follows (the italics indicate uncertainty of the reading): "His majesty proceeded northward to overthrow the Asiatics. His majesty reached a foreign country of which the name was Sekmem. His majesty *took the right direction* in proceeding to the Residence of life, prosperity, and health. Then Sekmem fell, together with the wretched Retenu."[11]

As indicated above, the term *Skmm*, here vocalized Sekmem, is generally taken to refer to the biblical city.[12] Here we have to do with a larger geographical entity, it would appear. Kurt Sethe maintained that the land of Retenu referred to Palestine and that Sekmem (= biblical Shechem) was the capital city.[13] Alt once argued that there were two monarchical entities in Palestine at the time: one with its capital at Lydda (= Retenu) and the other at Shechem (= Sekmem).[14] Such a view could no longer be maintained after the publi-

[7] *Ibid.*
[8] Posener, p. 68. See also Wilson in *Ancient Near Eastern Texts*, ed. J. B. Pritchard (hereafter *ANET;* 2nd ed., 1955), p. 329, n. 9.
[9] Wilson, *ANET*, p. 230.
[10] *ANET*, p. 230, n. 8.
[11] *ANET*, p. 230.
[12] *ANET*, p. 230, n. 7.
[13] *Erläuterungen zu den ägyptischen Lesestücken* (1927), p. 135, referred to by Alt in *Die Landnahme der Israeliten in Palästina* (1925), pp. 35–36, n. 5.
[14] Alt, *ibid.*

cation of the Execration texts.[15] It would appear that Sekmem was a term used in the Khu-sebek inscription to refer to the central Palestine area where, perhaps, opposition to the pharaoh had its center at Shechem. Even this much is by no means certain. It could be that the country of Sekmem meant no more than the region dominated by the influence of the city of Shechem; or, at the most, that a regional confederation of city-states, with its center at Shechem, provided the major opposition to the forces of the pharaoh.

No further references to Shechem are found in the large number of historical documents from the 18th dynasty. It may be worthwhile to point out, however, that in the many references to Palestinian cities in the general region of Shechem from the reigns of Thutmosis III, Amenophis II, Thutmosis IV, Amenophis III, Haremhab, Seti I, Rameses II, Rameses III, and Shishak I, there are three occurrences of the place name Jacob-el and two of Joseph-el.[16] If Shechem were in existence at this time it is remarkable that it should not have appeared in the lists of captured cities. This is all the more striking since we do have a reference to Shechem in a literary text (to be examined below). It could be that the places Jacob-el and Joseph-el (either or both) refer to Shechem, since we know from the Old Testament that both Jacob and Joseph were closely associated with the city.

The last Egyptian occurrence of Shechem appears in Papyrus Anastasi I,[17] a popular letter in a satirical and rhetorical vein used in the training and instruction of apprentice scribes. The Shechem reference appears as follows:

> "Pray, teach me about the mountain of User. What is its head like?
> Where does the mountain of Shechem come? . . ."[18]

---

[15] See *PJB,* XXXVII (1941), 19–49 for Alt's modification of his earlier position.

[16] *ANET,* pp. 242–43.

[17] See Alan H. Gardiner, *Egyptian Hieratic Texts;* Series I: *Literary Texts of the New Kingdom* (1911), p. 23 and n. 10. The text is dated by Gardiner (p. 4*) to the reign of Rameses II (*ca.* 1290–1224 B.C.). Wilson in *ANET,* pp. 475–79 gives a new translation and dates the text to "the late Nineteenth Dynasty (end of the thirteenth century B.C.)."

[18] *ANET,* p. 477. The word appears in the form *Sa-ka-ma.* See also A. T. Olmstead, *History of Palestine and Syria* (1931), pp. 229–31, and Gardiner, p. 23*.

The reference to Shechem here is of questionable historical worth. It may not even support the conclusion that Shechem is in existence at the time of the document, since the author may have relied on traditional materials for his geographical and topographical observations.

The Egyptian sources thus contain three texts which may with reasonable confidence be taken to refer to Shechem. They indicate that the city is known by its biblical name as early as the 19th century B.C. One of them (the Khu-sebek inscription) *may* suggest that the region of Shechem is a center of significant opposition to the pharaoh. The fact that the city is not mentioned in any recognizable form in the historical texts from the 18th and 19th dynasties could be taken to support the conclusion that the Late Bronze Age Shechem was less important than its predecessors (until the Amarna period, at any rate).[19]

Shechem in the Amarna Period

While the Tell el-Amarna letters[20] contain only a single reference to Shechem, their importance for the history of the city extends much beyond this reference. The city is referred to in letter 289. 'Abdi-kheba, prince of Jerusalem, writes to the pharaoh (probably Akhenaten) for aid to withstand the enemies who are attacking the land of the pharaoh. If such aid does not come quickly, 'Abdi-kheba is doomed. In this context, 'Abdi-kheba raises the question: "Or should we do like Lab'ayu who gave the land of Shechem to the 'Apiru?"[21] Thus we have the name of Shechem and also the name of the prince of the city. "The land of Shechem" must be taken to refer to the city and the adjacent territory under its control.

Lab'ayu's name appears in several other letters. It is difficult to assess his precise place in the history of the Amarna period, of course, but the following general sketch appears to be fairly reliable.[22] Lab'ayu's own letters (252–54) are ad-

[19] Study of the scarabs found at Shechem leads to similar conclusions. See Siegfried H. Horn, *JNES*, XXI (1962), 1–14.

[20] See Edward F. Campbell, Jr., *BA*, XXIII (1960), 2–22, for a recent analysis. Campbell also deals with the letters discussed below.

[21] Albright's translation in *ANET*, p. 485.

[22] The relevant letters are the following: 32; 237 (name damaged); 244–45; 249 (name damaged); 252–54 (from Lab'ayu

dressed to the pharaoh Amenophis III (*ca.* 1406–1370 B.C.). In the first of these (252) he replies in defiant terms to the charge of disloyalty and maintains that his enemies will be resisted.[23] The dispute between him and his enemies concerns two towns, one of which is the ancestral town of Lab'ayu. This town cannot be Shechem, his capital city (on the basis of letter 289), since the loss of Shechem would have meant, we must suppose, the loss of significant influence in Palestine. The other two letters from Lab'ayu depict him as a loyal vassal of the pharaoh, although they contain his acknowledgment that in Gazri (Gezer) he had complained publicly about the pharaoh's unfair preference of Milkilu of Gezer over him. Milkilu elsewhere is found as an ally of Lab'ayu but he apparently suffered a change of heart and renewed his loyalty, a fact which the pharaoh has acknowledged with suitable concessions.

In letters 242–46 we learn that the 'Apiru[24] have attacked Megiddo (243); that Lab'ayu has laid siege to the city (244); that upon orders of the pharaoh he had been captured but had managed to bribe his way to escape and had subsequently been killed before the pharaoh's order could be carried out (245). We also learn that a son of Lab'ayu has gone over to the 'Apiru (246).

Letters 237 and 263, in which Lab'ayu's name occurs, do not yield any definite information for our purposes. In letter 290a Albright supposes that the attacks upon Shuwardata, the sender of the letter, by the "chief of the 'Apiru" and his forces may have included Milkilu and/or Lab'ayu.[25] In a later letter from Shuwardata to Akhenaten (280) we learn that Lab'ayu's name has become a byword for treachery and rebellion: "Now behold, 'Abdi-kheba is another Lab'ayu, and he takes our cities!"[26]

Four facts, among others, are clear from these letters. 1)

---

himself); 263; 289; and 290a (Mercer's numbering of a letter published by Thureau-Dangin in *RA*, XIX [1934], 91–108).

[23] In this letter he utters what may be a Canaanite proverb to the effect that if ants are smitten, they bite the hand of their smiter (cf. the ant proverbs in Prov. 6:6; 30:25); see W. F. Albright, *BASOR*, No. 89 (Feb. 1943), pp. 29–32.

[24] We use the term 'Apiru to refer both to the SA.GAZ and to the *Kha-bi-ri* of the Amarna letters.

[25] *ANET*, p. 487, n. 16.

[26] Albright's translation in *ANET*, p. 487.

Lab'ayu is the prince of Shechem; 2) Shechem includes sufficient territory adjacent to it to be referred to as the *land* of Shechem; 3) Lab'ayu is very closely related to the 'Apiru and has apparently made a contract or covenant with them; and 4) he has given Shechem into the control of the 'Apiru. This last point may indicate nothing more than the third: that Lab'ayu and his people are in covenant relationship with the 'Apiru and are supporting their attempts to gain control of other lands and cities belonging to the pharaoh's province in Palestine.

There are also important references to the sons of Lab'ayu. If these sons continued to control the Shechem region as had their father, then their deeds may provide further information on the history of Shechem in the Amarna age.[27]

In letter 246 these sons of Lab'ayu are accused by Biridiya of Megiddo of having given silver to the 'Apiru, among others, to wage war on him. Letter 250 tells a similar story: Ba'lu-UR.SAG reports that the sons of Lab'ayu and Milkilu of Gezer have been applying pressure on him to rebel against the pharaoh. Letter 255 appears to be from one of these sons, Mutba'lu, who protests his utter loyalty to the pharaoh. And in 289 'Abdi-kheba tells the pharaoh that Milkilu is in league with the sons of Lab'ayu and with the sons of Arzayu to take the land for themselves. He then goes on to refer to Shechem, as we have noted above.

It is clear, therefore, that the sons of Lab'ayu carry on the tradition of their father. They too are in league with the 'Apiru. They too join forces with other Palestinian princes to extend their territory.

Shechem in the Amarna period (end of the 15th and first two-thirds of the 14th centuries) is therefore a city of considerable importance. The city is a major center of opposition to the pharaoh's authority on the part both of its princes and of the 'Apiru. These 'Apiru are not necessarily a group of invaders. They may represent the population elements which have not gained, or have lost, legal and social standing among the Palestinian peoples who are organized into a city-state system under the waning authority of the pharaohs. It appears more probable, however, that at least a portion of the people referred to as 'Apiru *are* invaders who are attempting

[27] The relevant letters are 246, 250, 255, and 289.

to take over the land as the opportunities permit. It should be stated, though, that this point is today debated.[28]

Lab'ayu and his sons, from their headquarters at Shechem, are collaborators with the 'Apiru. The story of Lab'ayu and his sons has many parallels to the Genesis traditions connected with Shechem (33:18–20; 34; 48:21–22; 49:5–7). Yet it would be rash to *identify* the sons of Hamor with Lab'ayu and his sons or Jacob and his family with the 'Apiru. The events are *comparable* but certainly not identical. More significant is the fact that Shechem was not captured in the conquest of Canaan under Joshua. Rather, according to traditions which are in their present form rather late (Deut. 11:26–32; Josh. 8:30–35), the city appears not only to have been under the control of a people sympathetic with the invading Israelites, but was already an acknowledged setting for Israelite worship.

Shechem in Later Extra-Biblical Sources

One other reference to Shechem requires comment here. In the ostraca found by the excavators of the city of Samaria there is one occurrence of the word "Shechem" in an interesting context.[29] On ostracon 44, only a portion of the text of which has been preserved, the text reads: ["In the] ninth [year], from Shechem, . . . to . . . wine." Shechem is thus sending produce to the king at Samaria, perhaps Menahem,[30] along with other cities of the tribe of Manasseh. Other cities mentioned include Helek, Hoglah, Noah, Shemida, and Abiezer, all of which (together with Shechem) appear in the lists

[28] George E. Mendenhall argues against an invasion by 'Apiru in *BA*, XXV (1962), 66–87. I find it difficult to accept his argument in its entirety. "Outsiders" need not once have been "insiders." The difficulties with the 'Apiru may reflect both an internal struggle in Canaan and conflicts with groups seeking entrance into Canaan from the "outside."

[29] G. A. Reisner *et al.*, *Harvard Excavations at Samaria 1908–1910* (1924), I, 227–46. Ostracon 43 appears to be a part of the same text found on ostracon 44.

[30] Y. Yadin, *Scripta Hierosolymitana*, VIII (1961), 9–25, who corrects the older reading from "fifteenth" to "ninth" and clears the way for placing the ostraca later in the 8th century than has previously been possible. Cf. Albright, *Archaeology of Palestine* (4th ed.; 1960), p. 220.

of cities belonging to the district of Manasseh (Num. 26:28–34 and Josh. 17:1–3).[31] The importance of this fact has been indicated by Albright.[32] Many Canaanite towns have simply been incorporated into the tribal lists and have been given "names" in the lists of descendants of the various Israelite tribes. Thus, one of the ways in which the Israelites have taken possession of Canaan was that of treaty-making with the local inhabitants.

In order to complete the references to Shechem in extra-biblical materials it would be necessary to include references in the Apocrypha, Pseudepigrapha, and other later Jewish writings (including Josephus, the *Biblical Antiquities* of Pseudo-Philo, etc.). This is not possible in a brief sketch of the materials, although the writer is convinced that a good deal of highly relevant evidence may be adduced from their inclusion and evaluation. Samaritan sources, Jewish coins, and other items also help to fill in the picture. It is important that such sources not be overlooked in any definitive writing of the history of Shechem.

THE PLACE OF SHECHEM IN THE BIBLE

BERNHARD W. ANDERSON

In its present form the Old Testament comes to us from Jerusalem (Judean) circles. Thanks to the brilliant achievements of David and the political fortune which favored his successors, Jerusalem outranked all other Palestinian cities—even Samaria, the great city built by Omri of northern Israel. After the fall of Samaria, northern traditions were inherited and edited in Judean circles, as can be seen from northern literature like Hosea.

Jerusalem, however, did not always have this pre-eminence, certainly not in the period before David when other cities were vying for supremacy. As a result of critical study of the biblical traditions, aided by archaeological discoveries, we are now able to see behind the present Jerusalem bias of the Old Testament into the time of struggle when many of Israel's

[31] Reisner, p. 229.
[32] *The Biblical Period from Abraham to Ezra* (1963), pp. 30–34.

traditions were formed. One city, Shechem, looms up through the mists of the past, a city which Albrecht Alt has called the "uncrowned queen" of Palestine. This article will draw attention to the biblical traditions concerning Shechem and some recent studies bearing on its history.[1]

The Navel of the Land

An apocalyptic passage in Ezekiel describes the gathering of the hosts of Gog for the final battle of history at Mount Zion, "the navel of the land" (Ezek. 38:12). The notion that Jerusalem is the "center of the nations" (Ezek. 5:5) appeared later in pseudepigraphical (Jubilees 8:19) and rabbinic literature, as well as in medieval maps which pinpointed the Holy City at the center of the world. Long before Jerusalem achieved this centrality, however, the expression "navel of the land" was applied to a mountain overlooking Shechem, undoubtedly Gerizim (Judg. 9:37). In the ancient period it was claimed that Shechem was the center of Canaan.

Shechem figures prominently in the patriarchal stories. Although Abraham was associated primarily with the southern shrine of Mamre, near Hebron, the Yahwist—seeking to unify the tribal traditions around the theme of God's promise—could not avoid connecting him with two important northern shrines, Shechem and Bethel, which were joined by a main highway (cf. Judg. 21:19). According to Genesis 12, Abra(ha)m's first stop in Canaan was at "the place (*maqom*) of Shechem," where he received the promise and built an altar to Yahweh (Gen. 12:1–7). Thence he moved on to the vicinity of Bethel where he built another altar and the promise was reaffirmed.

Near Shechem was the oak of Moreh, a sacred tree associated with oracle-giving (cf. Judg. 4:4–5). As if to apologize for Abraham's visit to a Canaanite sacred spot, the narrator comments that "at that time the Canaanites were in the land" (Gen. 12:6). This story, although overlaid with later theological interpretation, may preserve the memory that it was at Shechem, a strong Canaanite shrine (*maqom*) in the 2nd

---

[1] The most thorough and up-to-date studies are Eduard Nielsen, *Shechem: a Traditio-Historical Investigation* (1955) which has a full bibliography; and Walter J. Harrelson, *The City of Shechem, Its History and Interpretation* (unpublished dissertation, 1953).

millennium B.C., that the ancestors of Israel first came into contact with the natives of the land.[2]

Shechem is associated primarily, however, with the northern tribal heroes, Jacob and Joseph. On his return from Paddan-aram, Jacob came in a peaceful spirit (*shalem;* cf. 34:21) to Shechem, which lay at the commercial crossroads of Canaan (33:18–20). Desiring to settle among the people, he bought a parcel of land from "the sons of Hamor" and there he erected an altar (or probably a sacred stone, *maṣṣebah*) which he named "El, the God of Israel." This tradition is resumed in Genesis 35:1–4 which tells how Jacob's clan engaged in ritual acts (purification, change of garments, burial of idols and earrings beneath the oak of Moreh) and made a pilgrimage from Shechem to Bethel.[3] Joseph is also connected with Shechem, for his brothers pastured their flocks in its fields (Gen. 37:12–14), and his burial place was there (Josh. 24:32)–a traditional site which is supposedly marked by the present-day *qubr yusef,* "tomb of Joseph," a Moslem shrine.

These traditions show that at an early time Hebrews entered into friendly relations with the citizens of Shechem, profiting by the commercial advantages of this strategic city and being influenced by Canaanite religion and culture. The tradition of Jacob's peaceful covenant with the Canaanites of Shechem is difficult to square with the statement in Genesis 48:22, according to which Jacob took "one mountain slope" (*shekhem*) by military action. Undoubtedly the Hebrews played their part in the struggle for Shechem, both by alliance and by the sword, as a story found in Genesis 34 seems to show.

The Attack against Shechem

The story of the rape of Dinah, although now organically related to the Jacob traditions on both sides of Genesis 34 (Gen. 33:18–20 and 35:1–7), seems to have had an independent origin. Here the relations between the Shechemites and

---

[2] Nielsen, *Shechem,* p. 216.

[3] Albrecht Alt finds here the memory of an ancient cultic rite once celebrated at Shechem and elaborated in the time of Jeroboam I when the sanctuary of Bethel became prominent. See *Kleine Schriften zur Geschichte des Volkes Israel* (hereafter *KS*), I (1953), 79–88.

the Hebrews are portrayed in the guise of individuals. Shechem, "the son of Hamor the Hivite," having fallen in love with Jacob's daughter, asked his father to negotiate with Jacob for her hand in marriage. Hamor's appeal to Jacob was based on the economic advantages which would come from intermarriage between the two peoples, and Jacob seemed perfectly agreeable to the covenant. But his sons, hearing of the rape of their sister, came from the fields and denounced the incident in language later used of crimes within the Covenant Confederacy (34:7; cf. Judg. 20:6, 10). They consented to the *connubium* only on the condition that the males of Shechem be circumcised. This "marriage price" was acceptable to Hamor and Shechem. They persuaded their fellowmen that the land was big enough to include the newcomers and, besides, they could easily get the best of them economically. Scarcely had the circumcision been performed, however, when Simeon and Levi made a surprise attack on the city, killed Hamor and Shechem, plundered the city, and made off with Dinah. The story ends with Jacob's protest against a deed which was apt to put him in bad with the Canaanites of the region.

This legend reflects the historical situation of the patriarchal period when Hivites,[4] related to the Hurrians, constituted the ruling class of Shechem, as evidenced by the portrayal of Hamor as the father of Shechem (cf. 33:19; Josh. 24:32). These Hurrians are "the men of Hamor" (cf. Judg. 9:28). The name Hamor ("ass") recalls the Hurrian custom of slaughtering an ass to make a covenant (cf. Jer. 34:18–19). Thus, according to Harrelson's interpretation, we are given a veiled picture of the citizens of Shechem, under Hurrian (Hamorite) leadership, making a covenant with the invading Hebrews.[5]

All of these patriarchal traditions show that in the early period Shechem claimed a position of pre-eminence in Ca-

[4] Probably the text should read "Horites," following the Septuagint of Gen. 34:2.

[5] See also the remarks of W. F. Albright on the same point, *From The Stone Age to Christianity* (hereafter *FSAC*; 3rd ed., Doubleday Anchor Books, 1957), p. 279. Albright's view that *bene hamor* refers to "members of a Confederacy" is supported by Folker Willesen, who draws attention to a South Arabic inscription in which "ass" (*ḥmrm*) designates a covenant alliance, *VT*, IV (1954), 216–17.

naan. Shechem was, indeed, the "prince" (*nasi'*) of the land of Canaan and the most honored of all his kinsmen (34:2, 19). At Shechem the Hebrews first came into contact with Canaanites and settled down in their midst on amicable terms.

The Shechem Assembly

In Joshua 24, after initial successes in Canaan, Joshua is pictured convening the Hebrew tribes at Shechem "before God," near the oak of Moreh. He started by reciting a *kerygma*—the story of Yahweh's mighty acts made known especially in the Exodus and the victories against the Amorites (Canaanites). Then he summoned the people to put away all "foreign gods," whether brought from Mesopotamia or adopted from the Canaanites among whom they had settled. Despite his warning that Yahweh is a "jealous" God who brooks no rivals or any form of idolatry, the people responded affirmatively to the challenge, and a covenant was made that day. The covenant-making included the giving of the law and the erection of a "great stone" or stele beneath the oak of Moreh.

In its present form the chapter has suffered expansion, but there can be little doubt that it rests upon an authentic tradition. The ceremony represents the inauguration of a twelve-tribe confederacy, modeled after the type of organization known as an amphictyony in ancient Greece.[6] One of the striking aspects of the conquest tradition is that Joshua waged no battles in the area of Shechem. From this silence scholars have inferred that Joshua found himself on friendly ground at Shechem, owing to the fact that Hebrew tribes previously had made a covenant with the ruling class of the city. Joshua's accomplishment, then, was to extend the covenant to include twelve tribes and to ground the covenant on the Exodus faith.

The name of this confederacy was "Israel." What the name means is uncertain; but the group was a theocratic community of tribes bound together loosely by common cultic, legal, and military responsibilities. Many of the traditions now embedded in various literary strata of the Old Testament had

[6] Martin Noth, in *Das System der zwölf Stämme Israels* (1930), has shown that the twelvefold pattern of Israel's tribal structure reaches back to the earliest stage of Israel's life in Canaan, and that this type of organization was similar to the six or twelve-tribe alliances known in Greece and elsewhere.

their origin at Shechem. Albrecht Alt argues that the Canaanite-style case law (the *mishpatim* of the Covenant Code in Exod. 21–23) were first given to Israel by Joshua at Shechem and later on were administered by the minor judges of the Confederacy (Judg. 10 and 12). On the other hand, he maintains, the apodictic laws (like the Ten Commandments) were native to the Mosaic period.[7] Moreover, it has been persuasively shown that many of Israel's liturgical traditions, now found in Deuteronomic literature, go back to the earliest times of the Confederacy. This holds true not only for the basic elements of Israel's *kerygma* or Credo, but for various rituals belonging to the covenant renewal ceremony, as we shall see below.

Abimelech's Kingdom

During most of the period of the Confederacy, the central sanctuary was located at Shiloh (Judg. 21:19; I Sam. 1:3). Shechem, however, seems to have enjoyed a certain autonomy in the tribe of Manasseh, as the story of Abimelech suggests (Judg. 9). The story hangs loosely in its context as indicated, for instance, by its apparent assumption that Gideon of Manasseh actually accepted the kingship at Ophrah (see 9:2), contrary to 8:22–23.[8] Abimelech's mother was a Shechemite who had been brought into Gideon's harem (8:31). So, having blood ties with the Canaanites in Shechem, Abimelech persuaded the citizens there to support him in his bid for the kingship and even to give him money from the temple of Baal-berith. After murdering his seventy brothers (all except Jotham) who would be rivals to his throne, Abimelech was crowned king by the citizens of Shechem (the lower city) and Beth-millo (the acropolis in the upper city) by the oak of Moreh. The incident evoked a stinging rebuke from Jotham who, standing on a promontory of Gerizim, told his famous parable of the trees as a curse on Abimelech's violation of the Israelite theocratic ideal.

Abimelech's royal residence was at Arumah (9:31, 41). Shechem was the most important city in a kingdom which must have covered considerable territory, for Abimelech was harassed by raids on caravan routes leading to Shechem and

[7] *KS*, I (1953), 278–332.
[8] See Nielsen, *Shechem*, p. 143.

finally met his death in an attempt to storm the city of Thebez, on the road to Beth-shan. At the time of the annual harvest festival, a conspiracy developed against him under the leadership of a certain Gaal. Tipped off by his officer Zebul, who was in charge of the royal troops garrisoned in the city, Abimelech successfully intervened. The story (vss. 22–41) discloses unrest under a political regime formed by alliance between Abimelech and the "men of Hamor," the ruling class of the population. According to another story (vss. 42 ff.), Abimelech conquered the city and razed its foundations. When some held out in the tower of Shechem (the acropolis), taking refuge in the temple-fortress of El-berith, the stronghold was burned over their heads.

Abimelech's attempt to forge a kingdom out of Shechem and the surrounding area failed, for it went against the tribal and theocratic ideal of the Israelite confederacy. His destruction of Shechem, perhaps about 1100 B.C., eclipsed the importance of the city for some time. It was incorporated into the territory of Manasseh, according to the tribal list in Numbers 26:28–34 (cf. Josh. 17:1–2), which may come from the next century.[9]

The Revolt of Northern Israel

The fall of Shiloh (*ca.* 1050), the central sanctuary of the Confederacy, was followed soon by David's establishment of Jerusalem as the political and spiritual center of his kingdom. Desiring to strengthen his hold over the twelve tribes, he chose a city which was not included in any tribal territory and was thus elevated above sectional claims and jealousies. He sought to support his throne with the religious sanctions of the old Confederacy, and brought to Jerusalem the long neglected confederate symbol, the ark. He may have reinstituted the cities of refuge (one of which was Shechem), which had been under the charge of the Levites, the ancient covenant priesthood (Josh. 20; 21:20–22).[10] In other respects, how-

[9] Noth dates the list in the period between Deborah and David (*ca.* 1125–1000), and Albright regards it as a corrupted version of David's census.

[10] Scholars have argued that the list of cities and priestly towns in Josh. 21 (cf. I Chron. 6:54 ff.) comes from the time of David or Solomon. See W. F. Albright, *Archaeology and the Religion of Israel* (3rd ed., 1953), p. 121.

ever, David took steps to centralize power in the crown. For instance, plans were devised to create a system of twelve administrative districts, each supervised by a royal officer, which in several cases did not coincide with the old tribal boundaries. This plan was carried out by Solomon (I Kings 4:7–19) who may have stationed one of his administrative officers in Shechem, for in I Kings 4:8 the words "in the hill country of Ephraim" perhaps should be governed by the determinative "Shechem," as in other instances (cf. Josh. 20:7; 21:21; I Kings 12:25; I Chron. 6:67).[11]

These policies stirred up great unrest, especially in northern Israel, as witnessed by the revolt of Sheba during David's time (II Sam. 20). In an attempt to conciliate the northern tribes, Rehoboam, Solomon's son, went to Shechem to be crowned (I Kings 12). It is hardly accidental that he negotiated with the northern tribes, who had formerly been under Saul's rule, at this ancient meeting place of the tribal Confederacy. When Rehoboam spurned the request for a lightening of the burdens of tyranny, the northern tribes, remembering the days of tribal freedom under the Confederacy, raised a cry of revolt: "To your tents, O Israel!"

The first northern king was Jeroboam, the man whom Solomon had put in charge of forced labor in "the house of Joseph." His immediate problem was to consolidate his kingdom and offset the political and religious prestige of Jerusalem. He fortified ("built") Shechem as his capital, then moved to Penuel (I Kings 12:25), and finally to Tirzah (I Kings 14:17). Why he moved from Shechem we are not told. Certainly he must have been influenced by questions of military strategy, for Shechem, on the floor of the valley, was a poor defense site in comparison with Tirzah (*Tell el-Far'ah*).

Jeroboam's royal cult, however, was not centered in Shechem but in Bethel.[12] The whole account of his religious reform is so colored and distorted by Judean bias against the villain who "made Israel to sin" that it is difficult to get a clear picture of what actually took place. Probably he was attempting to found his kingdom upon the religious practices and beliefs of the old Confederacy which had been eclipsed

---

[11] F-M. Abel, *Géographie de la Palestine* (1933–1938), article on "Sichem."

[12] Nielsen, *Shechem*, pp. 190 ff., conjectures that one reason for Jeroboam's move from Shechem to Tirzah was Shechemite objection to making the Ephraimite city, Bethel, his royal shrine.

under David and Solomon. Harrelson, who advocates this view, plausibly suggests that the national-religious revival of the time stimulated the gathering together of the nucleus of the Elohistic traditions around Jacob, a northern figure associated with the very places that Jeroboam fortified: Shechem, Penuel, and Bethel. While Davidic theology was based on the idea of a covenant with the "anointed" Davidic king, which guaranteed the continuance of the Davidic dynasty, northern circles stressed the Mosaic covenant made at the time of the Exodus.[13] Thus Jeroboam, like Joshua at the ancient Shechem assembly, stressed the Exodus kerygma: "Behold your God, O Israel, who brought you up out of the land of Egypt."[14]

Shechem in the Deuteronomic Tradition

In the northern kingdom Shechem was soon overshadowed by Bethel and especially Samaria. But the influence of Shechem lived on in "Deuteronomic" circles. In its present *literary* form, of course, Deuteronomic literature comes from the last days of the kingdom of Judah. But a number of scholars maintain that Deuteronomy is a Judean adaptation of a northern Israelite tradition. Centralization of worship in "the place (*maqom*) which Yahweh shall choose" was not a Deuteronomic innovation, but harked back to the ancient Covenant Confederacy organized around the central sanctuary. Moreover, the special place given to rituals in the neighborhood of Gerizim suggests that the ultimate origin of Deuteronomic tradition was the sanctuary of Shechem.[15]

Several Deuteronomic passages refer to the Shechem liturgy.

1. Deuteronomy 11:26–32: When the Israelites enter Canaan they are to participate in the ceremony of putting the blessing on Mount Gerizim and the curse on Mount Ebal.

2. Deuteronomy 27:1–26 gives the same liturgy in more

[13] See George Mendenhall, *Law and Covenant in Israel and the Ancient Near East* (1955), especially Part II, pp. 44 ff., which is the same as *BA*, XVII (1954), 70 ff.

[14] The Judean historian changed God to "gods" in I Kings 12:28 and argued that the Bethel priesthood was non-Levitical. For a sympathetic evaluation of Jeroboam's reform, see W. F. Albright, *FSAC*, pp. 298–301.

[15] See G. Ernest Wright, *Interpreter's Bible*, II (1953), 323–26.

detail. Several ancient elements stand out from the late literary strata in which they are embedded: the altar of unhewn stones, the charge given by a leader of the community to be Yahweh's people *this day*, and the role of the Levites in the ceremony of blessing and cursing. The list of apodictic curses found in 27:14–26 is undoubtedly an ancient fragment of ritual, and the whole section (chaps. 27–30) is based upon ancient liturgical patterns.

3. Joshua 8:30–36: The Levites, carrying the ark, lead a procession from the oak of Moreh to a spot in the valley between Gerizim and Ebal. There the tribes divide, half standing in front of Gerizim and half in front of Ebal, for the hearing of the law, receiving the blessing and the curse, and the solemn renewal of the covenant.

Owing to the fragmentary character of the remains, it is difficult to reconstruct the ceremony of covenant-renewal in which through the years Deuteronomic materials were given shape. According to Harrelson's reconstruction, it contained the following elements:

1. an assembly of the tribes at Shechem for a pilgrimage to the Yahweh sanctuary by the oak of Moreh;

2. a recitation of the benevolent deeds of Yahweh by the leader of the community, accompanied by the demand for decision, the removal of foreign gods, and cultic purification;

3. and the march to the valley between the two mountains for the ceremony of the blessing and the curse. He concludes that the covenant-renewal ceremony was carried out annually at the central confederate shrine during the New Year's festival at harvest time (cf. Judg. 9:27).

The Later History of Shechem

After the time of Jeroboam I, Shechem fell into obscurity. Psalm 60:6–8 (= 108:7–9) refers to the dividing of Shechem, but the historical circumstances are vague. Hosea 6:9 refers to priests murdering on the way to Shechem, but it is not clear whether the prophet was referring to contemporary events or sacred traditions.[16] The last reference to Shechem in the Old Testament is found in Jeremiah 41:4–5 which tells of pilgrims from Shechem, Shiloh, and Samaria who stopped at Mizpah

[16] Artur Weiser (*Das Alte Testament Deutsch*, XXIV [1949]) thinks that the background of Hosea 6:7–11 is a cultic pilgrimage from east Jordan to Shechem and Bethel.

on their way to worship in the ruins of the Jerusalem temple.

In the post-exilic period Shechem rose to new importance, owing to the growing tension between Samaritans and Jews. It may have been a flourishing city in the time of Sanballat of Samaria who opposed Jewish efforts to rebuild the walls of Jerusalem (Neh. 4). It regained much of its ancient religious prestige when, in the middle of the 4th century B.C., the Samaritans built their temple on Gerizim. According to Josephus, the Samaritans escaped Seleucid persecution by calling themselves the Sidonians of Shechem,[17] but John Hyrcanus, one of the Maccabees, took and presumably destroyed the city in 107 B.C.[18] Despite this catastrophe the sacred memories of Shechem lived on. According to the well-known story, a woman of Samaria, speaking to Jesus at Jacob's well in the very shadow of Gerizim, reminded him that her people worshiped God "on this mountain" (John 4:20). Even today a small Samaritan community lives in Nablus, not far from the ancient site of Shechem.

THE EXCAVATION OF SHECHEM AND THE BIBLICAL TRADITION

EDWARD F. CAMPBELL, JR., AND JAMES F. ROSS

The role of biblical archaeology in the reconstruction of Israel's history has become a topic of heated debate in recent years. Several contributions to the *Biblical Archaeologist* have dealt with this subject,[1] and similar discussions are to be found in a wide variety of journals and books.[2] None of the scholars cited in these notes would subscribe to the view that archaeology "proves the Bible true." But there is a certain

[17] *Antiquities* XII. v. 5.
[18] *Antiquities* XIII. ix. 1; *Wars* I. ii. 6.
[1] See especially G. E. Wright's appreciation of Nelson Glueck's work in *BA*, XXII (1959), 98–108, and J. A. Soggin, *BA*, XXIII (1960), 95–100.
[2] J. Bright, *Early Israel in Recent History Writing* (Studies in Biblical Theology No. 19; 1956), pp. 25, 29, 87 ff., and 125, criticizing, among others, M. Noth, *The History of Israel* (Eng. tr., 1958). See also Chap. 1 of Wright's *Biblical Archaeology* (1957) and *JBL*, LXXVII (1958), 39–51.

amount of disagreement as to the relevance of archaeological data in the attempt to write the history of Israel. The reader can easily grasp the nature of the debate by comparing the two most recent histories of Israel, that of Noth, mentioned above, and of Bright.[3] In the former, archaeological data, both architectural and epigraphic, is cited only in passing, and primary emphasis is placed on the history of the biblical traditions. In Bright's work, however, a much greater significance is ascribed to the contribution of archaeology; excavation reports, editions of ancient Near Eastern texts, and topographical surveys are used as primary sources along with literary evidence from the Old Testament itself.

In this brief article it is not our intention to settle this vexed question. However, it may be of some help if, at this juncture in the debate, evidence from the excavation of one particular site is placed in conjunction with the biblical tradition. And that site, biblical Shechem,[4] is well suited as a test case. Its geographic location at the "center of the land" (Judg. 9:37 RSV) between the two great mountains Ebal and Gerizim (cf. Deut. 11:26-30; 27:11-26; Josh. 8:30-35) enabled its inhabitants to control both the east-west and north-south trade routes. Consequently Shechem was occupied by either Canaanites or Israelites, or both together, throughout the biblical period. Furthermore many of Israel's sacral-political traditions are associated with this ancient city. On the basis of information in Joshua 24 it has been widely assumed that Shechem was the first center of the twelve-tribe Israelite league or amphictyony, and that there Israel took upon herself obedience to the "statutes and ordinances" (vs. 25) of ancient Near Eastern common law. And it was natural that Rehoboam, Solomon's son, go to Shechem for his coronation, although he encountered the opposition of the northern Israelites who chose Jeroboam. The latter in turn "built Shechem" as his first capital (I Kings 12:1-25). Thus Shechem, "the uncrowned queen of Palestine," deserves our closest attention.

[3] Bright, *A History of Israel* (1959).
[4] See the preliminary reports in *BA*, XX (1957), 2-32 and 82-105; *BA*, XXIII (1960), 102-19; and also *BASOR*, No. 144 (Dec. 1956), No. 148 (Dec. 1957), No. 161 (Feb. 1961), and No. 169 (Feb. 1963).

Shechem in Patriarchal Traditions

Shechem appears as the site of more distinct patriarchal narratives than any other Palestinian city.[5] The Yahwist has Abra(ha)m visit the sacred place, with its "oak of Moreh,"[6] as his first stop in the land of Canaan. But it is Jacob and his sons who seem to be at home in or near Shechem.[7] After his encounter with Esau, Jacob "came safely to the city of Shechem" and "camped before the city"; he bought a piece of land from the sons of Hamor, Shechem's father, and erected an altar (possibly a pillar), calling it "El, the God of Israel" (Gen. 33:18–20). Furthermore, he led his clan in a purification rite whereby the foreign gods (amulets?) and earrings were buried under "the oak which was near Shechem" (Gen. 35:2–4). Inserted between these two Jacob traditions is the originally independent account of the "rape of Dinah" (Gen. 34) on which see further below. Joseph, moreover, was buried in the land which his father had purchased.

Shechem is thus associated with all of the patriarchs except Isaac, although the tradition connected with Abraham is probably secondary. Yet the picture of Shechem in the patriarchal age is not homogeneous. The most notable difference is between those passages in which the Hebrews enjoy peaceful trade relations with Shechem (Gen. 33:18–20; 37:12–14; Josh. 24:32) and those in which there is reference to armed conflict (Gen. 34; cf. 49:5–7).[8] Furthermore it is strange that Simeon and Levi, whom the Old Testament elsewhere

---

[5] For an excellent review of the biblical traditions see B. W. Anderson, *BA*, XX (1957), 10–19, which appears in this volume, pp. 265–275.

[6] *Moreh* means "teacher" or "instructor, oracle giver." The term "oak(s) of Moreh" also appears in Deut. 11:30. Whether *moreh* means "teacher" in the phrase "oak of Moreh" is an open question.

[7] According to W. J. Harrelson, *BA*, XX (1957), 4, the place names Jacob-el and Joseph-el in Egyptian conquest lists are "in the general region of Shechem." Harrelson's article is reprinted in this volume; see p. 260.

[8] See also Gen. 48:22, where the text can be read "I [Jacob] have given to you [Ephraim] rather than to your brothers one Shechem which I took from the hand of the Amorites with my sword and my bow."

localizes in the south, are found marauding in the north. We shall return to these questions after a review of the archaeological and epigraphical evidence.

Data from the excavation of Tell Balâṭah and extra-biblical texts are in close agreement as to the founding of Shechem as a city. Although there is scattered evidence of encampments from the early Chalcolithic period (*ca.* 4000 B.C.), the first real building activity so far found at Shechem is to be dated in Middle Bronze IIA (around 1800 B.C.). The 1962 Drew-McCormick expedition discovered a large earthen platform supported by a battered retaining wall approximately parallel to the later (MB IIB) wall enclosing the inner city. This platform, the purpose of which cannot yet be ascertained, is associated with a stone-lined pit under the lowest MB IIB street[9] and also with several fragmentary walls further to the west; possibly the earliest defense wall encircling the city on the north comes from the same period. Very interesting in this connection is a well-preserved cylinder-seal impression on a jar handle, which was discovered in the make-up for the first MB IIB building ("939 phase"). Dr. Edith Porada[10] points out that it carries Old Babylonian artistic motifs together with some "secondary motifs of Syrian origin," the combination being particularly characteristic of Mari. Apparently it has northern associations rather than southern. The implications, culturally and historically, have yet to be fully worked out.

The first extra-biblical references to Shechem[11] are from the same general period as this earliest level. One is in an "execration text" written on a clay figurine, and the other is a battle report by an officer of Sesostris III (1878–1843 B.C.); both suggest that Shechem, even at this early date, was a center of opposition to Egypt, anticipating the Late Bronze kingdom of the rebel Lab'ayu (see below).

The Shechem of Middle Bronze IIA—12th dynasty was, however, merely a faint anticipation of its successor, the city of the Hyksos (MB IIB–C, *ca.* 1750–1550 B.C.). The Hyksos, who are responsible for the Second Intermediate Period in Egypt (*ca.* 1720–1550 B.C.), passed through Palestine from

[9] *BASOR*, No. 161 (Feb. 1961), p. 18, Fig. 4, level 22.

[10] In a letter to the authors after the original appearance of this article. See H. Frankfort, *Cylinder Seals* (1939), Pl. XXIXa.

[11] Harrelson, pp. 258 f. of this volume.

their original home in the north and built or fortified several cities, of which Jericho, Hazor, and Shechem are best known archaeologically.[12] Shechem of the early Hyksos period (MB IIB, *ca.* 1750–1650 B.C.) had a double defense wall running under the level of the later temple. Parallel to this was another large wall (usually called the "temenos wall," wall 900 of *BASOR*, No. 161, Figs. 3, 7, and 8) separating the acropolis from the lower city. In the area thus enclosed the Drew-McCormick expedition discovered four building phases.

The earliest of these ("939 phase") was uncovered only in a few exploratory trenches, and no consistent structural pattern was ascertained. But the next two ("902 phase" and "901 phase") were laid bare in most of their extent in 1960 and 1962.[13] Of most significance is a large building, measuring, in the 902 phase, about fifty by one hundred feet. It had a large courtyard with a row of small rectangular rooms along its east and perhaps along its south side. In the northwest corner of the courtyard was a rectangular chamber which lay directly beneath the area occupied by the standing stone and altar of the Late Bronze temple. This plan bears a strong resemblance to a "courtyard temple" found at Hittite Boghazköy. This kind of sacred building is not well attested in Palestine; one in Stratum IX of Beth-shan is the only comparable example so far. But the possibility must be considered that Shechem's sacred precinct, represented by the large fortress-temple to be described below, stands on ground already considered holy.

At the northeast corner of this structure was a paved entrance hall into which the streets opened. Of special interest here is a well-preserved store jar burial.[14] The 902 people dug a trench through the accumulated debris down to the flagstone paving of the 939 phase and then inserted a large store jar containing the skeleton of a four to six year old child. A string of paste beads with a central scaraboid was found around the child's neck. The trench was finally filled in and

[12] It is interesting that Shechem and Hazor are mentioned together in a "satirical letter" of the late 19th dynasty (end of the 13th century B.C.); see J. A. Wilson, *Ancient Near Eastern Texts*, ed. J. B. Pritchard (hereafter *ANET*; 2nd ed., 1955), p. 477.

[13] *BASOR*, No. 161 (Feb. 1961), pp. 24–25, Figs. 7 and 8, and No. 169 (Feb. 1963), pp. 12–14, Figs. 6 and 7.

[14] For the burials found in 1960, see *BA*, XXIII (1960), p. 109, Fig. 4.

the flagstone paving of the 902 entrance hall laid over the top.

In the 901 phase, the courtyard and rectangular rooms were abandoned (at a date somewhere around 1710 B.C., when the Hyksos were now in control of Egypt and new groups, such as the Hurrians, may have pushed into Palestine behind them). The center of the structure now became a large chamber with a row of pillars along the north end. A lone column base, suggesting a freestanding pillar, was set south of this row. The whole room lay a little north and a little east of the large court of 902, but still present in this phase was the rectangular chamber beneath the altar of the later temple, and in it was another base which may conceivably have held a freestanding pillar. While the layout was different, then, the 901 and 902 buildings did have features in common. In addition to the rectangular chamber, both had the cobblestone street along the east and several walls of 902 were re-used by 901 builders.

The final MB IIB phase (909-910) is less well known because much of the evidence had been removed by previous excavations, both ancient and modern. However, we again find re-used walls which in some cases were built up to a higher level; this would seem to indicate that there was no sharp break in architectural tradition.

When we turn to a consideration of the later Hyksos period (MB IIC, *ca.* 1650-1550 B.C.) we do find such a break. Now the remains of the buildings mentioned above are covered by an artificial mound of fill, and the city defenses are moved further north. In the new city wall a gate (the northwest gate, excavated by the German expeditions) was built; it had three entryways made of pairs of parallel limestone blocks. The city wall was continued around to the east and very probably inscribed a complete circle or ellipse around the tell.

It is during this period that the great temple of Shechem was first constructed.[15] Covering an area approximately sixty-nine by eighty-five feet, it had walls about seventeen feet thick. The worshipers approached its entrance, which was in the narrow end to the southeast, along a sloping ramp beginning at wall 900, still standing after nearly 250 years of use. Somewhat later, but still in the Hyksos age, an earthen altar was constructed in the area once occupied by the ramp, and

[15] R. J. Bull, *BA*, XXIII (1960), 110-19.

the doorway of the temple was narrowed. The approach was then made from one of the sides, turning a right angle into the entrance, now flanked by a pair of *maṣṣebot* (pillars) in stone sockets.

Still another Hyksos construction of the later MB IIC period is the east gate. It was built along with a new defense wall approximately thirty-three feet inside the earlier wall mentioned above. Like the northwest gate, this gate also had entryways made of pairs of limestone blocks, but here there were only two of these, enclosing guardrooms on either side. In its brief existence of merely fifty years the east gate was destroyed not fewer than three times, eloquent evidence of the end of Hyksos and Middle Bronze Shechem.

How can the biblical traditions and the archaeological evidence be brought into fruitful relationship with each other? We may begin by noting that there is some evidence of Amorite settlement at Shechem, corresponding to Jacob's boast in Genesis 48:22 ("one Shechem which I took from the hand of the Amorites"). The earliest consistent archaeological level (the previously mentioned earthen platform) is from the end of the period generally assigned to the great Amorite migrations. Of even more importance, however, is the name "Hamor" in Genesis 34. This is a common Semitic word for "ass." And in the letters written by the Amorite inhabitants of Mari toward the end of the 18th century B.C.,[16] we frequently find references to "killing an ass" as the ritual for making a treaty or covenant of peace.[17] To be sure, the Amorite word is *ḥa(y)arum* (equivalent to Hebrew *'ayir*), but the difference is probably not significant. We may conclude that "sons of Hamor" really means "sons of the Ass-Covenant." It is no coincidence that the Shechemite sanctuary of Abimelech's time was called the "house of El (or Baal) of the covenant" (Judg. 9:4, 46). Amorite traditions were apparently preserved for centuries at the site.

Of greater significance, however, are the relationships between the patriarchs and the Hyksos. Modern scholars usu-

---

[16] G. E. Mendenhall, "Mari," *BA*, XI (1948), 1–19, reprinted in this volume, pp. 3–20; see also J. C. L. Gibson, "Mari," *JSS*, VII (1962), 44–62.

[17] Bright, *A History of Israel*, p. 73, n. 26, and works cited there; Albright in *ANET*, p. 482, and *From the Stone Age to Christianity*, (3rd ed., Doubleday Anchor Books, 1957), p. 279.

ally date the "sojourn in Egypt" to the Hyksos period. Indeed, the name Ya'qub (Jacob)-har appears as that of a Semitic leader of the early Hyksos. Nevertheless, it is apparent that many ethnic groups which later became Israelite tribes remained in Palestine. Perhaps among these were the ancestors of the Simeonites and the Levites.[18] The narrative of Genesis 34 will then reflect a period in which the Hyksos were defending their bastion in central Palestine against seminomads who were anxious to obtain a firm foothold in the Fertile Crescent.[19] In support of this thesis it may be noted that in Genesis 34:2 Hamor is called "the Hivite." However, the Septuagint reads here (and in Josh. 9:7) "the Horite." The Horites are now known to be the Hurrians, a people whose original home was in Armenia, but who spread throughout the upper part of the Fertile Crescent in the 2nd millennium B.C. It is quite probable that the Hurrians were connected with the Hyksos movement, either as a constituent part thereof or as a power which forced the Hyksos to move south.[20] Thus we should not be surprised to find Hurrian-Hyksos groups at Shechem. And as late as 1400 B.C. we have, from Tell Balatah itself, a cuneiform letter addressed to a certain Birashshena, whose name is most probably Hurrian.[21] However this may be, the Hurrians are likely to have been the ruling aristocracy in Hyksos Shechem. This may be reflected in the tradition that a particular Hurrian family was able to persuade the whole population to submit to circumcision so that a young man might have the wife he desired!

Of course it would be going far beyond our evidence to conclude that any one of the building phases at Shechem is

[18] Before the latter became a priestly tribe. Of course some of the Levites must have been in Egypt, since Moses and Aaron are associated with this group. The history of the Levites is full of confusions and contradictions. Note the difference between Gen. 49:5–7 and Deut. 33:8–11.

[19] For an alternate view, that Gen. 34 may reflect the disruptions of the Amarna period, see Bright, *A History of Israel*, pp. 122–24.

[20] For Hyksos leaders with Hurrian names and a discussion of the general problem, see W. F. Albright, *From the Pyramids to Paul*, ed. L. G. Leary (1935), pp. 9–26.

[21] W. F. Albright, *BASOR*, No. 86 (April 1942), pp. 28–31. For a general discussion of Hurrian names in Palestine see H. L. Ginsberg and B. Maisler, *JPOS*, XIV (1934), 243–67.

to be associated with any particular event recorded in the patriarchal traditions. Indeed these traditions give the general impression of a peaceful symbiosis between the Jacobites and the Shechemites, not the destruction and rebuilding of cities. But this tranquil scene is occasionally broken by warlike incursions such as those reported in Genesis 34 (cf. 49: 5–7) and 48:22. Perhaps the tremendous defense walls and the temple-fortress of the MB IIC city reflect such events. We have no "footprint of Jacob" at Shechem, but we do have evidence of the confusing times in which he and his sons lived.

Shechem and the Israelite Conquest

After the Egyptians of the 18th dynasty took Shechem in their reconquest of Palestine, the city entered a period of decline. The Late Bronze inhabitants of the site were content merely to re-use and rebuild the structures of their predecessors. At the east gate, for example, the innermost wall of the Hyksos complex was used as the foundation for a much weaker defense perimeter, and in the process a new pair of guardrooms was created. Similarly a new temple was built on the walls of the older sanctuary. But the new building had much less massive walls and was laid out on a different angle; it is possible that this reorientation was due to customs connected with solar worship. The most significant new feature was the erection of a huge *maṣṣebah* in a stone socket directly in front of the entrance to the temple; it will be remembered that the last Hyksos temple was provided with a pair of (smaller) *maṣṣebot* on either side of the door. Along with this new pillar an altar of stone was erected, resting on the earthen altar of the preceding period.

The most extensive information about Late Bronze Shechem comes, however, not from these fragmentary stones, but from the famous Tell el-Amarna letters.[22] Here we find Shechem as the capital of an extensive kingdom in the hill country of central Palestine. This territory was ruled by a certain Lab'ayu who, according to the complaint of 'Abdi-kheba of Jerusalem, rebelled against the pharaoh to the point of giving Shechem

[22] E. F. Campbell, Jr., *BA*, XXIII (1960), 2–22, and Harrelson, above, pp. 261–264. These letters were written to pharaohs Amenophis III and IV (Akhenaten) by their Palestinian vassals, and are to be dated approximately in the second quarter of the 14th century B.C.

to the 'Apiru.[23] Lab'ayu's own letters protest his innocence, but his tone is rather truculent and he obviously felt secure in his central stronghold.

When we turn to the biblical evidence for this period we find a significant gap. Shechem appears neither in the lists of cities destroyed by the invading Israelites nor among those too strong for them to conquer. Nevertheless we may assume from Joshua 24 that, by the end of the period of the conquest, Shechem was considered to be Israelite territory. Joshua 24 tells of the great assembly at Shechem. Here Joshua reminded the Israelites of Yahweh's mighty deeds, and challenged them to worship Yahweh and to "put away the gods which your fathers served."[24] After the Israelites affirmed their faith, Joshua made a covenant with them, "and he took a great stone, and set it up there under the oak in the sanctuary of Yahweh."

The question remains, how did Shechem become an Israelite city? We can only assume that the peaceful symbiosis reflected in the Jacob narratives eventually led to an Israelite infiltration of the city in the Late Bronze Age, and that the "conquest" of Shechem was achieved without resort to force of arms. Shechem may very well have been the first real Israelite city.

The archaeological evidence from Tell Balatah is parallel to the situation reflected in the biblical narratives. The Late Bronze city once ruled by Lab'ayu and his sons never suffered a destruction as did Lachish, Bethel, and Hazor. Rather there is a smooth and apparently peaceful transition from the Late Bronze Age to the pre-Philistine Iron Age (Iron IA). This is especially apparent in one of the guardrooms of the Late Bronze east gate. Here were found five levels of Late Bronze floors superseded, without an intervening destruction layer, by no less than fourteen superimposed Iron I floors. The same peaceful transition is found in the only other areas on the tell where these strata have so far come to light (Fields VIII and VI. 2). To be sure charcoal flecks were found in pits dug

[23] For an interpretation of this charge, see *BA*, XXIII (1960), 19.

[24] Note the same motif in Gen. 35:2-4. On the basis of these references, Albrecht Alt concluded that during the period of the divided monarchy the Israelites carried out a purification rite at Shechem before the great annual festival at Bethel. See his *Kleine Schriften* (hereafter *KS*), I (1953), 79-88.

through the floors of both the Late Bronze and Middle Bronze temples, but these are probably from the Abimelech destruction (see below). We may conclude that the Israelites represented by the tribe of Manasseh simply took over most of the territory once ruled by Lab'ayu without a significant struggle.

A few details of Joshua 24 deserve special attention. There is reference in verse 26 to a "great stone," an oak, and a "sanctuary of Yahweh." The reader is led to identify the oak with the "oak of the pillar" under which Abimelech was later crowned (Judg. 9:6).[25] But the stone and the sanctuary may very well have been the large *maṣṣebah* and temple of the Late Bronze Age. Certainly these were standing in the early Israelite period and for some time to come. And since the sanctuary is associated with Yahweh, it is probable that Israel used the Late Bronze temple for her own cultic purposes. But of this we have no archaeological evidence. Nor can the stones and sherds demonstrate that Shechem was the first center of the Israelite tribal league; here we are completely dependent upon an interpretation of the biblical material.

Shechem in the Period of the Judges

Shechem is the site of a particularly interesting episode recorded in the book of Judges (chap. 9). Gideon (sometimes called Jerubbaal) had died, leaving behind his concubine in Shechem and her son Abimelech, as well as seventy sons in Ophrah. Although Gideon had rejected the Israelites' attempt to make him king (8:22 f.), Abimelech had no such scruples. He persuaded his mother's relatives to start a whispering campaign against his half-brothers. They were to point out that Abimelech was of Shechemite stock, and that it would be better to have one ruler than seventy. The campaign was successful; Abimelech was even given money from the temple, the "house of Baal-berith (Lord of the covenant)," with which he hired assassins to kill his half-brothers in Ophrah (9:1-6). Only one, a certain Jotham, escaped. He climbed Mount Gerizim and proceeded to proclaim a fable about the trees in

[25] The trees of Gen. 12:6 and Gen. 35:4 seem to be different from this "oak of the pillar." They seem to have been located outside the city walls; Jacob "camped at the face of the city" (Gen. 33:18), and the oak of 35:4 is said to be "with (or near) Shechem." See below.

which Abimelech's treachery was roundly denounced (9:7–21). But it was too late. The usurper had already been crowned by the citizens of Shechem and the people of Beth-millo;[26] the event took place "by the oak of the pillar at Shechem."

Obviously Abimelech was trying to establish the sort of kingdom over which Lab'ayu had ruled, although he may never have heard the latter's name. It is said that Abimelech ruled over *Israel* (9:22). Shechem was not even his capital; this was located at Arumah.[27] The Shechemites, having supported Abimelech in his bid for power, were now treated as mere vassals. And so after only three years they regretted their action and began to set ambushes for their "brother"; at the same time they held up passing caravans, thus jeopardizing Abimelech's shaky hold on the territory (9:23–25).

The situation was ripe for a rabble-rouser, and he appeared in the person of a certain Gaal, who had recently moved to the city.[28] Just as the Shechemites had once been misled by Abimelech, so now they were persuaded by the oratory of Gaal (and by the aftereffects of the annual grape harvest festival). He pointed out that Abimelech was only *half*-Shechemite; the city should remember its former glories and revert to the rule of the native nobility (the sons of Hamor). Unfortunately for Gaal, Abimelech's deputy, Zebul, heard of the plot and sent or brought word to his master. He suggested that Abimelech and his followers rush upon the city early in the morning. When the day of battle came, Gaal went forth and stood in the entrance of the gate. He saw Abimelech's troops advancing from the tops of the mountains, but Zebul persuaded him that they were only shadows. Then Gaal saw men coming "from the center of the land" and one company "from the direction of the Diviners' oak." Zebul finally admitted his true loyalty, and goaded Gaal into advancing. But Abimelech, given this extra time, was able to chase the rebels

[26] The former term means literally "lords of Shechem." This may reflect the existence of a ruling nobility as in patriarchal times. For Beth-millo see below.

[27] Judg. 9:31, 41; the RSV corrects the former to agree with the latter. Arumah may be located at Khirbet al 'Urmah, about five miles SSE of Balatah.

[28] Judg. 9:26. The Hebrew verb translated in the RSV as "moved into" really means "crossed over." Does this mean that Gaal was from the other side of the Jordan?

back to the entrance of the gate; Gaal and his kinsmen were subsequently disowned by the Shechemites (9:27–41).

Another episode (9:42–45), perhaps from a separate source, tells how Abimelech was able to get between the Shechemites and the city. This time we hear that he captured the city, killing the people and razing the walls; finally the area was sowed with salt.[29]

The sequel (9:46–49) reports that the "lords of Migdal-shechem" heard of Abimelech's success and took refuge in the crypt of the "house of El-berith" (El of the covenant; compare vs. 4). But Abimelech and his followers gathered brush from Mount Zalmon, and burned the crypt; the inhabitants, "about a thousand men and women," perished in the flames.

Abimelech met his death at another town, Thebez.[30] A woman threw a millstone from the tower and crushed Abimelech's skull; rather than let it be said that he was killed by a woman, he had his armor-bearer slay him with a sword (9:50–54).

The biblical narratives here summarized are characterized by a note of reality and immediacy. Only infrequently does the Deuteronomic historian break in with a moralizing judgment (e.g., 9:24, 56f.). Possibly, as we have noted, some of the episodes are from originally independent tradition complexes. But we can be sure that the later Israelite inhabitants of Shechem preserved these stories and took great pleasure in passing them on from generation to generation.[31]

However this may be, the narratives of Judges 9 seem to preserve ancient traditions about the situation of Shechem in the time of the Judges. But there are notorious difficulties in the interpretation of the text. Perhaps the most confusing details are those having to do with ancient places:

1. The "Diviners' oak" of verse 37 was probably thought

[29] For an interpretation of the latter phrase see Stanley Gevirtz, VT, XIII (1963), 52–62, in which there is criticism of A. M. Honeyman, VT, III (1953), 192–95. See also F. C. Fensham in BA, XXV (1962), 48 ff.

[30] Modern Tubas, about nine miles NNE of Balatah on the way to Beth-shan.

[31] This is probably the case with the Genesis stories as well. The common motif is the gullibility of the Shechemites. They agree to an audacious bride price and are then deceived by the sons of Jacob. And later they fall prey to the pretensions of a half-Shechemite (Abimelech) and even a complete stranger (Gaal). The Shechemites were not noted for shrewd political sense.

to be identical with the "oak of the teacher" mentioned in Genesis 12:6, as well as with the (unspecified) oak of Genesis 35:4. It was obviously outside the city, and this would correspond to the implications of the other references. The "oak in the sanctuary of Yahweh" in Joshua 24:26 would then be a separate tree, but it may very well have been the same as the "oak of the pillar" in Judges 9:6. As for this pillar, it is most probably the *maṣṣebah* of the Late Bronze temple, and, if so, identical with Joshua's "great stone."

The official preliminary report of the 1962 campaign suggests another interpretation, and it deserves and will receive serious consideration. It is based on two sets of "constants." One set has been suggested above in the description of the acropolis, where the possibility exists that the spot below the altar and stone of the Late Bronze temple was considered "holy ground" back to at least 1750 B.C. We have yet to learn whether the MB IIA platform described on p. 278 itself indicates that the area was very important; it is noteworthy that, so far as we can now tell, that platform lies *outside* the fortification walls and would be outside the city. This is a very tentative matter, but we can suggest that a particular place along the western edge of the city held sacral significance for at least 650 years, from *ca.* 1750 to *ca.* 1100.

The second set of constants characterize the patriarchal and later narratives. The repeated theme involves a holy place (several Hebrew terms describe it), a tree (either an oak or a terebinth), and the long-standing covenant motif. One also cannot help noticing a continuing reference to a stone of some sort (again under several Hebrew terms).

The impact of these constants is such as to suggest the possibility that *all* of the stories about a sacred precinct at Shechem refer to the *same place*, namely the acropolis area, as their locus. Even the ones implying that the sanctuary is outside the city might fit the pattern, because it is possible that the MB IIA platform lies outside the city.

Notice that such an interpretation requires that the Diviners' oak of 9:37 and the oak of Moreh not be identical in location, even if later tradition equated them. There are two trees in Judges 9 anyway; the other one, in 9:6, may be the one to associate with the patriarchal traditions. It should be remembered also that the subject under discussion is not the *tree* but rather a remembered *location*. The old stories could easily be attached to whatever tree was visible and handy, long after the tree of the ancient occurrence was dead and gone. But that there was a sacred location marked by the structures on the west side of ancient Shechem pertinent to all of the narratives here discussed is a strong possibility.

2. "Beth-millo" is apparently distinguished from the city proper in verses 6 and 20. It has been thought that it was a village dependent on Shechem. The same name occurs in II Kings 12:20 (Hebrew, 12:21) as the place where King Joash was killed in a palace intrigue. Apparently this was inside the walls of Jerusalem, although the further reference, "on the way that goes down to Silla," is obscure. We also find references to a "Millo" in the accounts of building activity during the reigns of David (II Sam. 5:9), Solomon (I Kings 9:15, 24; 11:27), and Hezekiah (II Chron. 32:5). It is natural to derive the word from the Hebrew verb meaning "to fill" (a breach, hole, etc.), thus rendering "filling." And this is borne out by the excavations at Shechem. Here the Hyksos temple (MB IIC) was constructed on a massive fill of earth and decomposed limestone fragments. This fill covered the remains of the earlier (MB IIB) Hyksos structures and also served to extend the city to the north; at the same time the outer circumvallation wall was built along with its northwest gate. Furthermore a heavy wall was constructed inside the city, running from this gate to form a right angle with the earlier wall 900. In effect the acropolis of the city was both raised and extended, just as Jebusite Jerusalem was enlarged by David and Solomon. This quarter of Shechem came to be known as the "house," or "structure of the filling." The fact that the "citizens of Shechem" and "all Beth-millo" are distinguished in Judges 9 probably indicates merely that there was social stratification in the city; perhaps we have here still another reference to Horite ruling classes and their subjects.

3. Even more difficult is the identification of Migdal-shechem (RSV "Tower of Shechem") in verses 46–49. On the basis of the verb used ("all the people of the Tower of Shechem *heard* of it [Abimelech's destruction of the city]") many scholars have naturally concluded that Migdal-shechem is to be located at some distance from the city itself. It is more likely, however, that the verb is merely a feature of the

author's style.[32] If this is the case, we are to understand that the people (non-combatants?) of the acropolis "heard of" the destruction of the lower city and took refuge in the tower. As for the latter, it is most natural to identify it with the temple itself. The thick walls of the Middle Bronze temple were surely there for reasons of security. The Late Bronze temple, while a smaller and slighter building, would still serve as a place of refuge. At any rate the identification of Migdal-shechem as a part of the city finds support in Judges 8:9, 17, where we find reference to a tower *in* Penuel and then Gideon's destruction of "Migdal-penuel"; surely the same structure is meant.

4. Unfortunately we cannot now identify the "crypt" or "stronghold" (RSV) of the house of El-berith (vss. 46, 49). The only other occurrence of the Hebrew word in the Old Testament is in I Samuel 13:6, where it apparently means "cave of refuge." In post-biblical times the term was applied to rock-cut tombs,[33] but this is hardly relevant in the present connection.

One other topographical detail of the story deserves comment. Throughout we have references to only one gate (vss. 35, 40), and in verse 44 we are led to believe that it was the only gate of the city. This is in accord with the findings of the archaeologists. At the east gate the Late Bronze conquerors of the Hyksos city re-used the innermost wall of their predecessors and built new guardrooms, leaving the old entryways relatively intact. However, there is no sign of Late Bronze re-use of the northwest gate, judging from the preliminary reports of the German expeditions. Indeed these reports refer to an Iron Age house built northeast of this gate, and this would probably block it. At any rate, the east gate is certainly intended by the author of Judges 9. For Gaal, standing in the gate early in the morning, can be tricked into thinking that Abimelech's troops are merely the "shadow of the mountains as if they were men" (vs. 36).

What became of Abimelech's Shechem? If the identifica-

[32] E. Nielsen, *Shechem: A Traditio-Historical Investigation* (1955), p. 165. This work contains extensive discussions of many of the problems raised in this article.

[33] J. T. Milik, *RB*, LXVI (1959), 556 f., 560–62. Milik discusses the references in Judges 9 and comes to the conclusion that the sanctuary was located in a cave on the slopes of Mount Ebal.

tions suggested above are correct, we have an account of two separate stages in the destruction of the city. First the lower city was destroyed, beginning at the east (and only) gate. Then those who had fled to the acropolis (Beth-millo) were burned to death in the temple (Migdal-shechem). It must be admitted, however, that there are difficulties with this hypothesis. There is no clear destruction level from the Iron I period inside the cella of the temple. Rather we have MB IIC floors, then a layer of fill topped by the LB floor, which in turn is overlaid by red earth. On top of the latter was found the heavy plaster layer in which the stones of the Iron II (8th century B.C.) granary were set.[34] But the previously mentioned red earth cannot be destruction debris; it is simply the ordinary dirt from the slopes of Mount Ebal, probably brought in by the granary builders to level up the site. We are left, then, with the pits in the temple cella, all of which were sealed by the granary plaster floor.[35] Whatever the purpose of these pits may have been, they were all filled with dark earth, a great deal of charcoal, and Iron IA (early 12th century) pottery. This debris may very well represent Abimelech's destruction of Migdal-shechem.

Shechem under the Monarchy

The stratigraphic sequence of ancient Shechem has emerged from a procedure that has its analogy in the building of a transcontinental railroad; conditions at the site have permitted the study of earlier strata (stretching from about 4000 B.C. to about 1100 B.C.) in one place, while remains from the first millennium were emerging elsewhere. The teams of men studying the latter are progressing toward a junction with those studying the former. The two sections of the work should drive the "golden spike" that links them sometime in the fifth campaign, in the summer of 1964.

The gap not yet bridged extends through the latter part of the period of the Judges and then through the time of the United Monarchy, ending sometime early in the 9th century. During at least a part of that period Shechem played a highly important role; it was doubtless its reputation as center of

[34] See *BA*, XXIII (1960), p. 119, Fig. 7, and *BASOR*, No. 148 (Dec. 1957), p. 25, Fig. 4.
[35] Bull, *BA*, XXIII (1960), 116–19.

the covenant community early in Israel's history (reflected in Josh. 24) that led Jeroboam, at the head of the northern secession, to make it his capital late in the 10th century. As we have noted, the fact that Rehoboam went to Shechem to receive the crown suggests the city's prominence and probably suggests that there was at least something there in the way of a settlement.

We are not without archaeological evidence pertaining to this period. The excavation of the east gate in 1956 and 1957 showed a patching of walls within the two flanking gate towers, the ones dating from the Hyksos era 700 years earlier. Pottery associated with a poorly preserved surface in the gate tower belonged to the 10th or early 9th century and at least suggests that one activity of Jeroboam's "building" of Shechem (I Kings 12:25) was the rebuilding of the gate. Further, a probe under stones atop the late Hyksos fortification just south of the northwest gate proves a rebuilding there in early Iron II (apparently contemporary with our Stratum IXB). That is what is currently available to suggest the fortifications of the Iron II period, which begins about the time of the division of the monarchy in Palestine (*ca.* 922 B.C.).

What information have we about the Iron II period then? Pivotal to our knowledge is the evidence from Stratum VII (beginning from the latest, we can so far assign numbers to nine strata stretching back to the break in our sequence; after the 1964 campaign, we should be able to assign consecutive numbers to the strata already described above). Stratum VII is the Stratum V of earlier reports; evidence of two important intervening strata has forced us to renumber. Stratum VII is represented in one major field (Field VII) by the remains of a fine house, the 1727 house. Especially interesting is the huge hearth in the central courtyard; bins and a basin made out of a sheared-off jar bottom set in a stone foundation surround the hearth. Other houses of the same plan, especially from a slightly earlier period at Tell el-Far'ah nearby,[36] have no such hearth, although storage bins are quite prevalent. The hearth, and the abundance of lime coating its lip and coating stones of underground drainage channels under the rooms to the

---

[36] *RB*, LXII (1955), Pl. VI opposite p. 552; for a similar house at Hazor, see *BA*, XXI (1958), 29, Fig. 1, and *BA*, XXII (1959), 15, Fig. 11.

south, suggest that the owner of the house supplied lime for the community.

In any event, the house-owner lived well; his home represents the better class of housing in 8th century Shechem, with its roofed courtyards and two-storied plan. We can think of it as better class because of the contrast to be found in Shechem's "slums." The slums came to light in Field IX, located so as to probe dwellings nearer the spring of modern Balatah; here stratification quite similar to that in Field VII was found. Architecture was less impressive and the evidence as a whole suggests relative poverty. Stratum VII meant a fine house in the better part of town, only haphazard repair of existing structures in the slums. Perhaps more striking, the poor part of town appears not to have suffered destruction such as that which devastated the 1727 house; that havoc was described in *BA*, XXIII (1960), p. 106, and emerged even more vividly in 1962. As was stated in 1960, the end of this stratum must be associated with the Assyrian conquest about 724 B.C.

Stratum VII is pivotal in that it alone of five Iron II strata can be related with anything approaching certainty to an historical event known from biblical and/or extra-biblical sources. Stratum VIII, of which VII was a rebuilding in the slums, and into which the 1727 house cut deeply in Field VII, is of uncertain duration. Preliminary study in Field IX has led to the tentative conclusion that Stratum VIII had three phases there, and that especially the middle of these three phases (VIIIB) had a rather long history; the hard-packed earth floors were resurfaced several times during that phase.

This middle phase of Stratum VIII shows evidence of destruction by fire. This raises a question for the interpreter: does every burnt layer represent a military conquest? The question is important, because where written records are available, archaeology and annals most naturally intersect at the point of battles, sieges, and conquests. Nor is the question easy to answer. Presumably ancient peoples had accidental fires at least as often as modern people do. Modern archaeological technique works in confined areas, and it is at least a theoretical possibility that an accidental fire at one place in a city be misinterpreted as the effects of military attack. On the other hand, it cannot be a requirement of interpretation that one find weapons, such as arrowheads and slingstones, in the destruction debris of a house before he assumes that military attack brought the stratum to an end. There were times when destruction by fire at the hands of an enemy came about *after* the city had been seized and plundered; weapons would not be found everywhere in the debris under such circumstances, nor, probably, would fine possessions of the inhabitants be present.

Something must have brought the stratum to an end. The archaeologist, in assigning his stratum numbers, must do so on the basis of evidence of a real break in the life of the city, be that break a gap during which the city was unoccupied, or a new ground plan for the architecture, or clear and unmistakable evidence of destruction. Then he may with some justification sift his other resources for reconstructing history and try to explain the reasons for the end of a stratum.

What, then, is the historical context of Stratum VIII? We are inclined to see it covering the first half of the 8th century. The major part of this period falls during the reign of Jeroboam II in Israel; if we can trust the impression given by Amos and the historical accounts, there was prosperity in Samaria, represented there by the buildings of Miss Kenyon's Period III and pottery of her Period IV.[37] The first king after Jeroboam to reign for any length of time was Menahem, who overthrew Shallum, himself a man who came to the throne by force (II Kings 15:13-22). If we could be sure that Stratum VIII at Shechem really suffered violence, we would have to look to the events brought on by Menahem's behavior when he came to the throne; as a result he was paid a "visit" by Tiglath-pileser III (Pul) of Assyria. This is the suggestion of Professor Mazar, made when he looked over the Shechem evidence in the winter of 1962-1963. However, as has been noted, Stratum VIII simply merges into Stratum VII in one field of our work, while in the better housing district it gave way to the fine 1727 house, whose builder cut his foundations so deeply into Stratum VIII remains that nothing certain can be said about what brought VIII to an end. For the present, our best hypothesis seems to be that Stratum VIII belongs to the 8th century and that Stratum VII is sufficiently later than VIII so that a difference in pottery types is discernible. Stratum VIII probably ends around 750 to 745, while Stratum VII lasts about twenty years from roughly 745 to 724. The

[37] G. E. Wright, *BA*, XXII (1959), 67-68, reprinted in the present volume, pp. 254-256; see also his more technical discussion in *BASOR*, No. 155 (Oct. 1959), pp. 13-29.

builder of 1727 must have been an optimist! Assyria soon had enough of Israel's rebelliousness and wrote *finis* to her national existence before his house was more than twenty years old.

One further structure suggests the prominence of Shechem in the 8th century. The few sherds from the granary atop the temple ruins on the west side of the mound appear to be earlier than the pottery of the 1727 house and contemporary with our Stratum VIII or even with IXA to be described below. This counters the statement made in *BA*, XXIII (1960), p. 114. The pottery comes from the foundation of the granary and reflects the earliest possible date for the building of the structure. If it came into existence around 800 B.C., this would suggest that throughout Stratum VIII and indeed through Stratum VII, Shechem had a building in which to store taxes paid in kind; this conforms to the information coming from the Samaria ostracon which mentions Shechem, one of a group of receipts for delivery of goods to the court at Samaria from the districts of Manasseh.[38] According to the new interpretation and dating offered by Yadin, at least around the year 738 Shechem was the center of a small district in southeast Manasseh.[39]

Below Stratum VIII remains in the better part of town (Field VII), there is a complex of architecture which breaks up into at least three house units. Stratum IX has two phases, throughout both of which the major walls remained the same. The lower phase has fine flooring in some places, and the preserved house walls stand as high as four feet. Especially characteristic are pillars of large stones along one side of a room; apparently the builders used these to hold up roof beams along that side while still leaving the room as open to the outside as possible, an ancient "picture-window" effect.

Sometime during the existence of Stratum IX, a destruction took place which resulted in very little burning but in heavy accumulation of debris on the floors of the lower phase. Apparently the inhabitants returned and restored their houses immediately, with floor levels now riding about twenty inches above the original floors. Some of these new floors were sub-

[38] Y. Yadin, *IEJ*, IX (1959), 184–87.
[39] Y. Yadin, *Scripta Hierosolymitana*, VIII (1960), 1–17. See the map prepared by Frank M. Cross, Jr., in *BASOR*, No. 163 (Oct. 1961), p. 13.

stantially built of flagstones, while where there were beaten-earth floors several resurfacings can be discerned.

In terms of pottery evidence, the whole stratum belongs to the 9th century. Again we cannot be certain that military action brought either phase to its end; indeed, the way the preserved walls stand, askew and tilted, has suggested to more than one of the supervisors a natural calamity such as an earthquake. If military action is more likely, then one looks during this period to the Arameans and their activities.[40] The fortunes of Shechem from about 870 on are bound up with those of Samaria; Omri had made Samaria his capital about that time. It is likely that Aramean raids aimed at the capital would involve forays in the vicinity. While nothing approaching certainty can be said, we might tie the end of the lower phase of IX (IXB) to Ben-hadad's attack in *ca.* 856, described in I Kings 20, and the end of the upper phase (IXA) to some such Aramean threat as that of Hazael of Syria (II Kings 13:3), around 810 B.C. The years in between saw the re-use of the earlier buildings, and, as we have said, the resurfacing of floors, as many as four times.

When did Stratum IX begin? It may go back to Jeroboam I. In the one place where we have cut below it, in a trial trench, we have found striated debris going well back into Iron I, but we must withhold judgment until more information is available.

An Interlude of Lions

After 722/1, our information about the northern nation is slight. The Assyrian overlords "carried the Israelites away to Assyria," and imported populations of other captured cities to replace them (II Kings 17:24), as was their customary practice. An intriguing note included in the narrative at this point claims that Yahweh sent lions among the new inhabitants because they did not fear Yahweh; it became necessary for the Assyrian king to provide a priest for the religious instruction of the people who did not "know the law of the god of the land." The narrative suggests that this measure stopped the threat of the lions. It does not appear to have secured the peace of the land during the 7th century, however.

[40] B. Mazar, *BA*, XXV (1962), 106 ff., 115; Mazar's article is reprinted in this volume, pp. 127–151.

Along the south edge of the 1727 house, evidence appeared which suggests resettlement. The northern rooms were buried under tons of brick debris, but the southern row of rooms proved to have upper cobblestone surfaces. Spilling south down a slope from these ill-preserved signs of rebuilding was a scree of debris a major feature of which was a layer of lime which had been exposed to high heat. Under the lime, and coated with it, was a large quantity of broken pottery, and, beneath that, bricky debris of a different color from that covering the floors of the 1727 house. The pottery included fine Assyrian bowls and other forms unlike Stratum VII forms. Further investigation of the debris layers showed two phases; skimpy traces of wall may be present for each, although they are little more than rock jumbles now.

Here again the lower city slums may help explain the evidence. Two clear phases of this stratum, Stratum VI, are found there also; both show evidence of destruction and weapons are present in both bands of destruction. The walls appear to have been of mud brick on stone foundation; in some cases the same wall served both phases. It appears that the floors of the upper phase (VIA) were laid very soon after the destruction of the lower phase (VIB), since the ash layer on the lower phase was preserved without erosion. And the pottery is consistent throughout the two phases.

The picture is consistent then: two phases of occupation both of which suffered violent destruction. In Field VII particularly, the structures seemed little more than re-use of an old ruin for rude hovels. The site seems not to have been a walled city at all, although of that we cannot be absolutely certain.

About the Israel of this period we know very little. That Hezekiah and Josiah, the two great "reform" kings of Judah, made some attempt to assert control in old Israel is clear enough. There is no good reason to dismiss the tradition contained in II Chronicles 30:1–12 about Hezekiah, while a whole range of evidence suggests that Josiah extended his control both westward and northward. He could travel with his army to the battle at which he lost his life in 609 (II Kings 23:29), which took place at Megiddo well to the north of Samaria and Shechem. He is reported to have used force in destroying the altar at Bethel and the high places of the cities of Samaria (II Kings 23:15–20).

Josiah's activities date just about a century after Samaria's fall and may be a bit late for our evidence. Hezekiah's activity is not reported to have included military exploits. One other suggestion may apply to the interpretation of Stratum VI, made by Abraham Malamat and growing out of an article he wrote in 1953.[41] In the midst of the confused reports contained in Ezra 4:1-5 and 4:8 ff., the almost incidental note is sounded that in the days of Esarhaddon (681-670), and again under "Osnappar" (almost certainly Ashurbanipal, 669-*ca.* 627 B.C.), new peoples were settled "in the cities of Samaria" and the Assyrian province "Beyond-the-River." If the settlement of new populations followed the suppression of revolt (as it had in 722/1), it is quite possible that punitive expeditions were carried into the vicinity of Shechem on two occasions between *ca.* 673 and *ca.* 640, the first as an aspect of the successful campaign to Egypt of these two monarchs, and the second perhaps in connection with a revolt taking place at about the time of the assassination of Amon. Of this we cannot be sure, of course, but two destructions of a rather confined settlement on the site of Shechem did take place during the 7th century.

The settlement that followed was no more substantial (Stratum V). In Field VII, all that remains are a half-circle of fine cobbling which may have served as a permanent tent floor, and an oval structure which may have served as a pen for animals. The latter was hardly six feet long and little more than three wide, however. In the lower city, traces of mudbrick walls, sometimes on stone foundation, are found; the dominant impression is one of marked poverty. Nevertheless, to Stratum V belongs some fine black glazed Greek pottery, several impressions on jar handles of a seal, and one seal impression showing a lion which is quite similar to the one found at Ramath-rachel and depicted in Figure 9 of *BA*, XXIV (1961) on page 106. This last is interesting indeed, for it suggests that motifs characteristic in Judah were common to the region of Samaria also. Also to this stratum probably belongs the beautiful *lmbn* seal in blue chalcedony found in 1960.[42]

From the time of Samaria's fall until the 4th century, then, Shechem was not a great city. Jeremiah's mention of men

[41] A. Malamat, *IEJ*, III (1953), 26-29.
[42] Published by Frank M. Cross, Jr., in *BASOR*, No. 167 (Oct. 1962), pp. 14 f.

from Shechem, Shiloh, and Samaria who fell victim to Ishmael's brutality (Jer. 41:5) doubtless refers to pilgrims coming from a nostalgic visit to once-proud cities now hardly worthy of their great names. Erosion of the few scattered 6th–5th century remains at Shechem bear mute testimony to the total abandonment of the site until the beginning of the Hellenistic occupation.

Hellenistic Shechem

Shechem was reborn in the 4th century as an extensive and powerfully-defended city. This is the most salient point emerging from the archaeological evidence. As previous reports have indicated, a strong fortification system was established along the lines of the Hyksos city walls, and that fortification was re-established during the early 3rd century. It appears that another major earth-moving operation had the opposite motivation: apparently as an epilogue to the death of the city in 107 B.C., an enormous amount of earth was spread over the defenses along the west and the mound was leveled off. The explanation may be that John Hyrcanus, to whom the final destruction of the city is to be ascribed, wanted the city never to be re-established, and undertook a gigantic task to insure the neutralization of the western defenses.

Between the earliest Hellenistic stratum (involving IVB and IVA) and the final destruction of the city (ending Stratum I) there are two strata. Concerning Stratum III, it is possible to say that its end coincides with the shift of hegemony in Palestine from the Ptolemies to the Seleucids, near the year 190 B.C.

What is to account for the sudden re-establishment of the defunct city in the late 4th century? This question has called forth a most interesting article by the excavation's director, Professor G. E. Wright,[43] whose conclusions are summarized here. There are several written sources pertinent to the matter, the most significant of which is the composite report of Josephus in his *Antiquities*, Book XI (from § 302 until the end of the book). Also important are bits of information from Quintius Curtius, Eusebius, Jerome, and Syncellus. It is possible to assemble the material from these sources into the following synthesis. The Samaritans sought and received permis-

[43] G. E. Wright, *Harvard Theological Review*, LV (1962), 357–66.

sion from Alexander the Great to build a temple on Mt. Gerizim; the Samaritans rebelled against Alexander while he was in Egypt shortly thereafter; he retaliated by destroying Samaria and settling some of his Macedonian troops there, giving the city to them and thereby making it pagan;[44] the necessity then arose for the Samaritans to find a place where they could live unhampered by pagan influences and safe from the rival Jews of Jerusalem. This line of reasoning points toward Shechem, founded in the late 4th century directly beneath Mt. Gerizim where the temple stood, massively fortified, on the ruins of a city whose heritage was as anti-Jerusalem as that of any city in the land. The Hellenistic remains from Shechem probably represent the Samaritan capital from the time of Alexander until a Jewish high priest, John Hyrcanus, brought its checkered history to an end.

Finally, what can be said about Sychar of the New Testament? The excavation still has brought to light no Roman period remains and so little Roman period pottery as to mean nothing in the way of a Roman settlement. Field IX carried us as close to the modern water supply of Balatah and to the traditional location of Jacob's well as we are likely to be able to go, since modern houses cover the flanks of the mound in that quarter. It stands to reason that such a water supply attracted settlements of some sort at almost every period of history, but we cannot say now whether Sychar was on the slopes of the ancient mound, or at Askar on the slopes of Ebal nearby, or at some other place in the vicinity.

[44] Wright cites the Hellenistic round towers at Samaria which are unique in Palestine and may be due to new settlers from Greece, and the fact that Herod the Great could build a completely pagan city at Samaria (implying a history of pagan associations), as evidence from the archaeological sphere pertinent to this matter.

15

JUDEAN LACHISH

G. ERNEST WRIGHT

One of the important excavations in Palestine between the two World Wars was that at Tell ed-Duweir, biblical Lachish, frontier fortress guarding approaches to Jerusalem and Hebron. It was the work of a British expedition between 1932 and 1938, which came to a sudden halt when the director, J. L. Starkey, was murdered by Arab enemies. Since that time members of the staff, headed by Miss Olga Tufnell, have been publishing the detailed reports of the discoveries at the site. *Lachish I: The Lachish Letters*, dealing mainly with letters written to the military commander of the city just before its siege and destruction by Nebuchadnezzar in 589–588 B.C., was published in 1938. *Lachish II: The Fosse Temple* concerned itself with a small Canaanite temple of the 15th–13th centuries B.C. which the Israelites presumably destroyed shortly before 1200 B.C. when they conquered the city; this volume was published in 1940. In 1953 a two-volume work, entitled *Lachish III: The Iron Age*, appeared. Miss Tufnell was the main author. The material surveyed is from Levels I through V, dating between the 10th and 4th centuries B.C. A final volume, *Lachish IV: The Bronze Age*, by the same author and publisher, appeared in 1958. It is mainly given over to Bronze Age tombs and objects, dating between 3100 and 1200 B.C. and not otherwise fully published. Miss Tufnell labored for twenty years from incomplete records to publish this important material. She has now retired with the best wishes and gratitude of other Palestinian archaeologists for a difficult task well done.

Lachish was one of the largest cities of ancient Judah. Its summit, comprising some eighteen acres, is about the same size as that at Gezer, but much larger than Tell Beit Mirsim (Debir; seven and one-half acres), eight miles southeast on the road to Beer-sheba; it is even larger than Megiddo (thirteen acres) which guarded the pass through Mt. Carmel. Its ruins together with its position in the Lowlands (Shephelah) indicate that between the 10th and 6th centuries it was a key site in the Judean defense system, dominating the smaller cities of Moresheth-gath (Micah's home) and Mareshah by the main pass leading to Hebron.

The preparation of the results of the excavation for publication has been difficult, owing to the fact that most of the work before 1938 had been preparatory for the stratigraphical excavation of the mound. The northeast, northwest, and south slopes had been cleared for the disposal of debris, a work which brought to light a large number of tombs and the Canaanite temple mentioned above. In addition, the lines of fortification had been followed, the main city gate along the west side and the approaches to it inside and outside the walls had been cleared to Stratum III; the palace-citadel was only partially investigated, and a large shaft had been cleared on the mound. This shaft still seems to be considered by Miss Tufnell as a water tunnel, comparable to those at Megiddo, Gezer, Gibeon and Jerusalem, though in the opinion of this reviewer it is best considered as a quarry from which building stone was hastily secured in preparation for the Babylonian sieges of the city.

After the violent destruction of Level VI, presumably by the Israelites at the end of the 13th century, the mound seems to have been virtually deserted during the period of the Judges (12th–11th centuries). King David was probably responsible for bringing the city again to life in the early 10th century. During his time, at any event, the palace of a provincial official of the government was erected on the ruins of an old Canaanite building. Practically nothing of the superstructure remains, but the platform on which it was built is still to be seen. It was an earth-filled podium about 105 feet square, still standing on its western side to a height of twenty-three feet. This structure with its platform reminds us of the citadel, called the Millo (meaning "filling"), which David built in Jerusalem (II Sam. 5:9).

Adjacent to the palace of Level V was a thick-walled brick building with long parallel rooms which was probably a government storehouse, or royal granary. Some fifteen miles north of Lachish are the ruins of Beth-shemesh, a small city which once guarded the valley of Sorek leading up to Jerusalem.

There, too, was found a palace, which though never completely excavated was probably erected on a podium; near it were the thick stone foundations of a long-roomed storehouse. Both were erected in the early 10th century. When considered together with the Lachish installations, they appear to furnish evidence for some sort of Judean provincial administration in the time of David, before the Solomonic organization of the northern part of the country which is described in I Kings 4:7 ff.

The main fortifications of Lachish were presumably built by Solomon's son, Rehoboam, after 922 B.C. (II Chron. 11:5–12). The summit of the mound was surrounded by a brick wall, about nineteen and one-half feet thick, with alternating salients and recessed panels. Over fifty feet below it on the slope of the mound was a stone and brick revetment about thirteen feet wide, with alternate projecting and recessed panels except where the wall turned around the mound's corners. At these places an irregular series of recesses and salients replaced the paneling. In other words, the main wall at the summit was provided with a regular series of defense towers, while the lower wall had such towers only at the places where maximum protection was necessary. An idea of the nature of these fortifications has been provided by an Assyrian artist who reconstructed Sennacherib's siege of the city in 701 B.C. for the adornment of the palace at Nineveh. The masses of charcoal found around the bases of the walls by the excavators may have come from the projecting battlements, probably built of wood, which are shown on this Assyrian relief.

Along the west side of the mound the roadway ascending to the city gate from the valley was discovered, and the gate was found to be protected by a large freestanding bastion, which by Nebuchadnezzar's time had been incorporated into the line of the outer revetment. In the Assyrian relief there is a lower gate out of which Judeans are filing, and this may well have been intended to represent the bastion found by the excavators. Great ramps of soil, evidently brought up from the valley and piled against the bastion may have been part of the Assyrian siege-ramps, for in the relief the attack seems to be centered around the gateway area. An interesting object found buried in the mass of debris at the base of the outer fortification was a bronze crest mount which had traces of cloth and leather fastening still adhering to it, and which was once riveted to the top of a helmet. In the Sennacherib relief such crests are shown only on the helmets of Assyrian spearmen.

Strata V, IV and III cannot be distinguished as yet because stratigraphical excavation on the mound has not reached that deep in any systematic manner. Sometime during the late 10th or 9th centuries the 10th century podium of the palace (Palace A) was enlarged by an addition which lengthened the whole from 105 to 256 feet (Palace B). Subsequent to that a ten-foot strip along the east side was added (Palace C). None of these building phases can be closely dated. A series of ten steps leading up to a porch on the east side of the last phase was discovered in excellent condition, buried under a mass of brick fallen from the superstructure. Though these steps were made of the very soft *huwar* (a yellow chalky marl) of the neighborhood, there was no evidence that they had ever been scratched or worn. The presumption, therefore, is that the steps were completed only a short time before the final destruction of the building, and this is supported by the presence of a pile of *huwar* chips. Below this last flight of stairs were the remains of two earlier stairways. On the lowest, near the outer corner of one of the two preserved steps, the first five letters of the Hebrew alphabet were found to have been scratched. Until a recent discovery at Ras Shamrah in Syria, these letters were the earliest archaeological evidence for the conventional order of the alphabet. Both Diringer and Albright agree that, palaeographically, the letters should be dated to the late 9th or early 8th century. All three stairways were built against Phase C of the palace, which would mean that both Phases B and C were erected between *ca.* 900 and 750 B.C.

From the 8th and 7th centuries come large numbers of inscribed jar handles. The most common type consisted of those bearing the inscription "belonging to the king" and then the name of one of four towns, Hebron, Soco, Ziph and Mamshat. These probably belonged to jars made for the shipment of wine from royal vineyards. It is now generally agreed that they date from the last half century of the kingdom of Judah, before its destruction in 587 B.C.

A most intriguing problem of this period was a large pit which had once been a tomb (No. 120), found on the northwest slope. Associated with it were five other smaller pits. The astonishing thing about them was their contents: they were filled with a scattered and completely mixed conglomeration of bones. The main tomb held the remains of at least 1500 bodies, but the bones were in such a jumbled mass that no order could be discerned and the skulls, separated from the vertebrae, had rolled to the sides of the chamber from the top of the pile when thrown in. Some of the bones and skulls showed signs of having been burned, and it is clear that the remains had been gathered up from some other area and thrown into this repository after the flesh had decomposed or been burned. Over the solid mass of human bones and spilling over into adjoining pits was a layer of animal bones, most of which were from pigs!

Along with the bones were many pieces of pottery, a large proportion of which were broken fragments. Some of the dishes and bowls, among them fragments of cooking pots, were of the type of vessel which is rarely found in tombs though very common in the ruins of houses. In other words, this deposit was no ordinary cemetery but a place where bones were thrown after having been swept up along with pieces of pottery in some other quarter. First the human bodies were taken care of and then the animal remains. Mr. Starkey, the excavator, originally suggested that the deposit represented the clearance of the city after the siege of Sennacherib, and this explanation has much to commend it. It would explain the conglomerate nature of the deposit, the evidence of burning on some of the bones, and also the fact that few of the people here buried were old. The skeletons were of a group who, in one expert's opinion, were "considerably younger than such as is normally found in ancient or recent cemeteries." Furthermore, "the hypothesis that the bones were cleared from an existing cemetery is . . . unacceptable, both because of the lack of aged people and the high proportion of immature skeletons which are normally too easily damaged to survive more than one removal."[1]

[1] These are the remarks of D. L. Risdon as quoted by Olga Tufnell, *Lachish III: The Iron Age* (1953), p. 63. It may be added further that the pottery associated with the remains belongs, in this writer's opinion, to the 8th or early 7th century rather than to the period around 600 B.C.—a further support for Mr. Starkey's views. Miss Tufnell, p. 194 suggests as an alternate view that the tomb "might have been caused by a wholesale clearance of idolatrous burials during the religious reformation of Josiah" (*ca.* 621 B.C.). Yet to me this would necessitate too late a date for the pottery as well as negate the opinion of D. L. Risdon that the bones were scarcely from an existing cemetery.

One further interesting fact is that at least three of the skulls show evidence of the operation known as trepanning. They are the first specimens found in western Asia which show this operation. On two of the skulls the crude saw marks are still so clear where the piece of bone was removed to relieve the pressure on the brain that we must presume that the patients died almost immediately. Curiously enough, however, the bone of the third skull had begun to grow sufficiently to obliterate the evidence of the saw. This person, then, must have lived for some time after his operation. The evidence of these skulls is a surprising testimony to the advanced state of Judean medicine during the time of the prophet Isaiah.

The presence of so many pig bones in the pits is also surprising and somewhat puzzling in view of the Israelite dietary laws which for good reason forbade the eating of pork. As is well known, pork quickly becomes a dangerous food where good refrigeration is lacking. We know that this prohibition did not extend to Israel's neighbors, however, and it is not impossible that the pigs at Lachish were brought there as a part of the commissary of the Assyrian army.

The destruction of the city of Level II must be attributed to Nebuchadnezzar's second invasion in 589–587 B.C. The evidence for the city's complete demolition is as vivid as that at Tell Beit Mirsim (Debir), eight miles away. Miss Tufnell writes (p. 57): "Masonry, consolidated into a chalky white mass streaked with red, had flowed in a liquid stream over the burnt road surface and lower wall, below which were piled charred heaps of burnt timber. In the angle below the north wall of the Bastion and the west revetment, breaches which had been hurriedly repaired with any material available were forced again; indeed, evidence of the destruction by fire was not difficult to find anywhere within the circuit walls." It was in a guardroom of the gate which was destroyed at this time that eighteen of the well-known Lachish letters were found.

The city of Level III had suffered an equally violent destruction. The palace was demolished and, according to the excavators' opinion, not rebuilt in Level II. Judging from the distribution of the charred debris, it was burned from the inside and the brick walls overthrown by extraction of stones supporting them from beneath. Burnt brick from the superstructure was spread over the surrounding area, and in this debris huts of City II were built. The main brick wall around the summit was so damaged, at least near the gate, that its ruins were pulled down and in Level II a thinner stone wall was built upon its stumps. In other words, the destruction of Level III was so severe that the fortifications had to be reconstructed, at least in part, while the palace was left in ruins. Stone for the reconstruction of the wall was evidently quarried from the deep shaft at the southeast corner of the summit. Whether the reconstruction of events at the end of Level III is correct in all details, we cannot now be sure. Yet the evidence does suggest that the city was so weakened and the population so diminished that by 589 B.C., when Nebuchadnezzar attacked a second time, resistance could not have been as strong as in previous centuries.

When was City III destroyed? Mr. Starkey originally thought that it was at the time of Nebuchadnezzar's first invasion in 598 B.C. In *Lachish III* Miss Tufnell suggests that the differences in ceramics which she observes between III and II mean that a longer interval must separate them. Accordingly, she attributes the destruction of III to Sennacherib in 701 B.C. In the opinion of this and other reviewers, however, the evidence as published does not sustain her opinion but rather supports the view of Starkey.[2]

After a long period during which the mound was virtually abandoned, the Israelite fortifications were rebuilt and a new residency was erected on the podium of the Judean palace-citadel. This reoccupation was in the post-exilic period during the 5th and 4th centuries. The palace was a large structure— in plan a series of rooms erected around an open court—and it is comparable to a contemporary building found by Petrie at Tell Jemmeh and to slightly earlier structures at Megiddo. The mound seems to have been virtually abandoned, like Megiddo, after the 4th century. A small temple, probably erected about the same time as the palace, remained in use until the second half of the 2nd century, but the district center had shifted from Lachish to Marisa (Mareshah), three and one-half miles to the northeast.

During the Persian period Lachish was not a part of the province of Judah, but of the province of Arabia (or Idumea).

[2] For details see W. F. Albright, *BASOR*, No. 132 (Dec. 1953), p. 146; Briggs W. Buchanan, *AJA*, LVIII (1954), 335–39; and the writer's reviews in *VT*, V (1955), 97–105; and *JNES*, XIV (1955), 188–89.

The governor of this province in Nehemiah's time was "Geshem the Arab" (Neh. 6:1) and the Lachish palace was probably one of his residencies. Not long ago this man's name was found on a Lihyanite inscription from Dedan in Arabia south of Edom. Isaac Rabinowitz has reported on a small collection of silver vessels recently acquired by the Brooklyn Museum.[3] The objects are reported to have been found at Tell el-Maskhutah (biblical Succoth) near the Suez Canal in Egypt. Three of the vessels bear Aramaic inscriptions which say that they are offerings to the north Arabian goddess Han-'allat. The proper names mentioned, with one exception, are all north Arabic. One is of special interest: "Qainu son of Geshem [Gusham], King of Qedar." Here, then, is a second reference to Geshem outside the Bible. The evidence is accumulating that the territory ruled by his family was quite extensive, including southern Judah in which Lachish was a chief center, the ancient area of Edom, northern Arabia and extending as far as Succoth in the Nile Delta. Small south Arabian incense altars, found at Lachish, Gezer and Tell Jemmeh, are evidence of the flourishing nature of the Arabian trade which was carried on during his time.

This brief survey of the later history of Lachish does not begin to exhaust the interesting materials to be found in *Lachish III*. It is one of the major sources now available for the archaeological history of ancient Palestine.

In *Lachish IV: The Bronze Age* one is astonished at the size and richness of some of the family burial vaults. As an example, of the 400 Egyptian scarabs published, 150 of them were found in Tomb 4004 with a 14th century deposit of pottery. Tomb 216, on the other hand, contained a rich collection of imported Cypriote pottery in a context which I would date *ca.* 1350–1250 B.C. (against the author's date, 1450–1300 B.C.).

Of special interest to biblical students is the inscriptional material and the evidence for the destruction of Bronze Age Lachish. The earliest known examples of alphabetic writing are a small ostracon from Gezer, a plaque with representation of a goddess found at Shechem, and a dagger found in Tomb 1502 at Lachish. All appear to date in the late 17th or early 16th century B.C. Of particular importance is a small square seal (poorly published on Pls. XXXVII–XXXVIII:295) from

[3] *JNES*, XV (1956), 1–9.

Tomb 555. On one side it bears the name of the Egyptian pharaoh, Amenophis II (*ca.* 1436–1410 B.C.), while the other side bears an alphabetic inscription which Albright has brilliantly deciphered.

A "censer lid" and Lachish Bowl No. 1 bear inscriptions which are very important in the early history of alphabetic writing. These together with the inscribed Lachish "ewer" found in Fosse Temple III probably all date in the 13th century. (Miss Tufnell appears to date the first two somewhat too early.) And finally Bowl No. 3 is interesting because it bears Egyptian hieratic (moderately cursive) writing of tax receipts, all dating from the "Year 4" of an unmentioned pharaoh. Its writing is dated preferably at the end of the 13th century; and the approximately twenty-five fragments of the bowl were found scattered in a small area of the destruction of the city of Stratum VI. The implication is that the "Year 4" is that of Pharaoh Merniptah (1224–1216 B.C.) or one of his successors between 1220 and 1200 B.C.

Albright for many years has believed that this bowl provides a reasonably close date for the fall of Lachish to the invading Israelites under Joshua. Miss Tufnell on p. 37 suggests that the city may have fallen later, to the Philistines in the 12th century, because in the ruins of the destruction of Stratum VI an Egyptian scarab of Rameses III (*ca.* 1175–1144 B.C.) was found. Albright has observed, however, that the object in question bears a name used by both Rameses II (1290–1224 B.C.) and Rameses III, and there is no evidence to attribute it to the latter rather than to the former.

So little of Stratum VI was excavated on the mound that we are not provided a very good picture of what the last Canaanite city was like. To this writer it seems clear that the best *stratigraphic* evidence for the fall of the Bronze Age city is to be found in the ruins of the small Fosse Temple on the slopes of the mound (*Lachish II*, 1940). The contents of the last temple, which was violently destroyed, are clearly 13th century, when contacts with Egypt and the Aegean world were very close. Indeed, the picture is not unlike that at the great Galilean mound of Hazor, and is strong evidence for an Israelite destruction of the city during the second half of the 13th century B.C.

Part III

PROMINENT CITIES OF THE NEW TESTAMENT PERIOD

16

ANTIOCH-ON-THE-ORONTES

BRUCE M. METZGER

With the exception of Jerusalem, Antioch in Syria played a larger part in the life and fortunes of the early church than any other single city of the Greco-Roman empire. Indeed, as the home of the first Gentile Christian church and as the base of operations from which the apostle Paul went out on each of his three missionary journeys, this city could claim in a more real sense than even Jerusalem to be the mother of the churches of Asia Minor and Europe. Not only was Antioch the birthplace of foreign missions (Acts 13:2), it was memorable in at least two other respects. Here the disciples of Jesus were first given the name "Christians" (Acts 11:26), and it was among the Antiochians that the question first emerged regarding the necessity for Gentile converts to submit to the Jewish rite of circumcision (Acts 15).

In addition to Paul's presence in this city on several occasions, Peter also had a small share in the development of the church here. The confused legends as to the seven years' episcopate of Peter in Antioch are hardly worthy of consideration. The one biblical reference (Gal. 2:11-15) to his being here suggests that his views regarding social intercourse between Jewish and Gentile Christians were not altogether in harmony with those of the local church. The tradition that Luke was a native of Antioch is not older than the 3rd century, but if one admits the Lukan authorship of the Acts of the Apostles it is largely substantiated by that narrative. Indeed, a "Western" variant in Acts 11:28 which prefixes "And when *we* were assembled together" to the words, "there stood up one of them named Agabus . . . ," explicitly involves the Antiochene residence of the author (see vs. 27). Certain modern scholars also bring several other New Testament authors into connection with this city or its environs, such as the unknown compiler of the Gospel-source known as "Q," the author of the first Gospel, and even the author of the Fourth Gospel (so Goguel and Bultmann).

Subsequent to the apostolic age, Antioch was famous as the bishopric of Ignatius, the first Antiochene martyr of whom we have any record. For some unrecorded reason—perhaps the populace, seeking scapegoats for the calamitous earthquake of A.D. 115, settled on the Christians—Ignatius was condemned by the Roman authorities at Antioch and sent to Rome. There he was torn to pieces by beasts in the Flavian Colosseum, but his bones were brought back to his home city. His seven (genuine) letters were collected soon after his martyrdom and are one of the most valuable monuments of the sub-apostolic age. Later in the century, Theophilus, who was bishop of Antioch from 170–78 and a prolific writer, took a leading part in opposing the Gnostics. Besides Serapion, Babylas, Meletius, and other prominent Antiochian Christians, the most notable theologian at the turn of the 3rd century was Lucian, who met his death in the persecution of Maximinus in 312.

Lucian's chief service to biblical scholarship was a critical edition of the Septuagint,[1] compiled from a number of Greek manuscripts that represented a Hebrew text which differed slightly from the Masoretic text. He was also the founder of the first theological school at Antioch, which, in opposition to Alexandrian allegorizing, insisted upon the historico-grammatical exegesis of the Scriptures. Two outstanding products of this school were Theodore, the greatest thinker trained by Lucian, and John Chrysostom, the greatest orator of the church at Antioch. Without enlarging upon other influential Antiochian Christians—such as Nestorius, Theodoret, and a host of others—what has been outlined will be sufficient to indicate the importance of Antioch-on-the-Orontes in the life and growth of the early church. Whatever information, therefore, which can be gained from archaeology and history regarding the cultural and religious life of the people of this city will be of the utmost value in assessing the nature and strength of the crosscurrents which were bound to influence the thought and life of all its residents.

It is the purpose of the present article to describe and

[1] For a recent survey of research on the Lucianic recension of the Greek Bible, see B. M. Metzger, *Chapters in the History of New Testament Textual Criticism* (1963), pp. 1–41.

interpret some of the archaeological and historical data from Antioch and its vicinity which bear upon the presence there of pagan, Jewish, and Christian elements during the early years of the present era. First, however, it will be necessary to indicate something regarding the founding, growth, and description of ancient Antioch.

History of Antioch[2]

Antioch was founded about 300 B.C. by Seleucus I Nicator who named it either after his father or his son, both of whom bore the name Antiochus. It was situated about 300 miles north of Jerusalem where the chain of Lebanon, running northward, and the chain of Taurus, running southward, are brought to an abrupt meeting. Here the Orontes breaks through the mountains, and Antioch was placed at a bend of the river, about twenty miles from the Mediterranean on the west. In the immediate neighborhood was Daphne, the celebrated sanctuary of Apollo (see II Macc. 4:33), whence the city was sometimes called "Antioch-by-Daphne" to distinguish it from the fifteen other Asiatic cities built by Seleucus and named Antioch. Advantageously located for trade, being easily approached by caravans from the east and through its seaport, Seleucia, having maritime communications with the west, it grew under successive Seleucid kings until it became a city of great extent and of remarkable beauty. People would refer to it as "Antioch the Great," "the Queen of the East," and "the Beautiful." One feature which seems to have been characteristic of the great Syrian cities—a vast street with colonnades, intersecting the whole from end to end—was added by Antiochus Epiphanes. Among ancient cities Antioch was distinctive in being the only one known to us to possess a regular system of street lighting.[3]

During the early centuries of the Christian era the city

[2] The most recent scholarly investigation is Glanville Downey's monumental *History of Antioch in Syria from Seleucus to the Arab Conquest* (1961); this was condensed, and a chapter added on "Pagan and Christian Traditions," in Downey's *Ancient Antioch* (1963).

[3] This is known from an incidental remark made by Jerome in his *Dialogue against the Luciferians* 1, regarding the lighting of the street-lamps of Antioch.

had grown until it was the third largest city in the Roman empire, being surpassed only by Rome and Alexandria. Estimates of its population are based largely upon a statement made by Chrysostom in his *Homily on St. Ignatius* 4: "It is a hard task to govern only a hundred, or even fifty, men; but to take in hand so great a city, and a citizenry (*demos*) reaching the number of 200,000—of how great a virtue and wisdom do you consider that a demonstration?" If, as several scholars (e.g. Renan, Neubauer) have maintained, the word *demos* excludes slaves, women, and infants, the estimated population at the end of the 4th century was close to half a million. There is a question, furthermore, whether the population of the suburbs is to be understood as included in Chrysostom's figure. Some writers, taking into consideration the extensive suburbs, have estimated the total population of "greater" Antioch as high as 800,000 persons.[4]

The remaining history of Antioch must be surveyed here in but a few words.[5] In 540 the city was converted into a heap of ruins by the Persians under King Chosroes Nushirvan. It was restored by the emperor Justinian, but never quite recovered from the last blow. In the first half of the 7th century it was taken by the Saracens and remained in Moslem possession for upwards of 300 years, when it was recovered by the Greek emperor Nicephorus Phocas. In 1098 it was captured by the Crusaders. They established the principality of Antioch, which lasted until 1268, when it was taken by the Mameluke sultan of Egypt. In 1516 it passed into the hands of the Turks. The modern Antioch or Antakiyeh is a poor place of some 35,000 inhabitants.

The character of the people of Antioch was notorious in the ancient world. According to Mommsen, "In no city of antiquity was the enjoyment of life so much the main thing, and its duties so incidental, as in 'Antioch-by-Daphne,' as the city was significantly called."[6] The beautiful park or

[4] See William F. Stinespring, *The Description of Antioch in Codex Vaticanus Arabicus 286* (unpublished dissertation, Yale University, 1932), pp. 2-3 of the Commentary.

[5] For more detailed information, the reader may consult E. S. Bouchier's *Short History of Antioch* (1921).

[6] Theodore Mommsen, *The Provinces of the Roman Empire from Caesar to Diocletian*, Eng. tr., 2nd ed., II (1909), 128. See also Gibbon's zestful and glowing description of Daphne in his *Decline and Fall of the Roman Empire*, chap. xxiv.

pleasure-garden of Daphne became the hotbed of every kind of vice and depravity. Hence *Daphnici mores* became proverbial of dissolute practices, and Juvenal struck off one of his sharpest gibes against his own decadent imperial city when he said that the Orontes had flowed into the Tiber (*Sat.* iii. 62), flooding Rome with the superstition and immorality of the east.

Another characteristic fault of the citizens of Antioch appears to have been their aptitude for ridicule and scurrilous wit, and the invention of nicknames. It is related that when the emperor Julian the Apostate visited the city, he angered them by injudicious interference with their market, and they avenged themselves by shouting abuse after him in the streets. Unlike the style of most men of his day Julian wore a long beard in emulation of his revered philosophers, and the crowds made this the special object of their ridicule. They termed him "the goat" and advised him to "cut it off and weave it into ropes." They also nicknamed him "the butcher" because he was continually sacrificing oxen at the altars of his deities. In retaliation Julian stigmatized Antioch as containing more buffoons than citizens. Another serious-minded visitor of Antioch, Apollonius of Tyana, was treated in much the same way.[7] It is not surprising, therefore, that most expositors have understood the reference to the origin of the name "Christians" in Acts 11:26 as another exhibition of the same kind of derisive name-calling by the frivolous Antiochians.[8]

Excavations at Antioch-on-the-Orontes

In 1931 the Syrian government granted permission to Princeton University and the Musées Nationaux de France to excavate at Antioch over a period of six years. Four volumes have been published containing reports of the cam-

[7] For other ancient testimonies regarding the character of the Antiochians, see J. J. Wettstein's edition of the NT in Greek, II (1752), 524–25, on Acts 11:26.

[8] Eric Peterson, however, has contested this usual view of the origin of the name "Christian" as a mocking epithet, maintaining that it was an official designation of the disciples of Jesus, given by the Roman authorities at Antioch: see his essay on "Christianus" in *Miscellanea Giovanni Mercati*, I (1946), 355–72.

paigns of excavations.[9] In addition to several shorter studies of aspects of these excavations, two large volumes have appeared on the hundreds of mosaic pavements discovered at Antioch.[10] Obviously it is impossible in the space available here even to mention all of the important finds which were unearthed during the several seasons of campaigns. The selection which has been made is in accord with what is likely to be of interest to the readers of the *Biblical Archaeologist*.

The Tyche of the City

Dating from the very time of the foundation of Antioch by Nicator is the famous statue of "the Fortune" (*Tyche*) of Antioch. This symbol of the future grandeur of the city on the Orontes was devised by the Sicyonian sculptor Eutychides, a pupil of Lysippus (so Pausanius vi.2.7). The memory of it is preserved on coins, in silver ornaments, and in a small marble statuette now in the Vatican. The goddess, a graceful, gentle figure, rests negligently on a rock, while the river, a vigorous youth, seems to swim out from under her feet. The artistic type was copied for lesser cities in the East, and one of the reliefs found at Dura on the Euphrates pictures the "Tyche" of Dura, modeled precisely after the figure of Antioch, with the Euphrates instead of the Orontes serving as the attendant river god.

The Charonion

Every resident of Antioch could not help seeing a colossal bust, called the Charonion, about sixteen feet in height, carved in the living limestone cliff northeast of the city. According to a late tradition reported by Malalas (*Chronographia* p. 205), during the reign of Antiochus Epiphanes (175-163 B.C.) a destructive plague broke out and a seer,

[9] *Antioch-on-the-Orontes*, I, *The Excavations of 1932*, ed. G. W. Elderkin (1934); II, *The Excavations, 1933-1936*, ed. Richard Stillwell (1938); III, *The Excavations, 1937-1939*, ed. Richard Stillwell (1941); IV, Part I, *Ceramics and Islamic Coins*, ed. Fred O. Waage (1948); and IV, Part II, *Greek, Roman, Byzantine, and Crusaders' Coins*, ed. Dorothy B. Waage (1952).

[10] Doro Levi, *Antioch Mosaic Pavements* (2 vols., 1947). The earlier slender volume by C. R. Morey, *The Mosaics of Antioch* (1938), is still the most popular treatment of these mosaics.

Leisus by name, ordered a projecting cliff visible to the entire city to be carved with a face of Charon, the ferryman over the river Styx. Perhaps the plague came to an end before the workmen could finish the bust; at any rate, the left shoulder was never chiseled out. The head is covered with a folded veil which at its lower end on the right shoulder curves out in a way that, as G. W. Elderkin suggests, reminds one of the caps of Persians and Amazons in Greek vase-painting.[11] According to the same author, the veiled bust may have been intended to represent the Syrian goddess of Hierapolis. The *Dea Syria* had Hittite associations,[12] and the Hittite tradition of carving in living rock the figure of their nature goddess seems to have survived in the Charonion at Antioch.

Mosaic of the Phoenix

One of the best preserved of the mosaics is the so-called mosaic of the Phoenix, dating from the beginning of the 5th century.[13] Of enormous size—over forty by thirty-three feet —the impression which the regular floral pattern within a border of pairs of rams makes upon the observer is that of a carefully wrought tapestry. Something of its immensity can be appreciated when one realizes that in its original state the pattern contained more than 7500 roses. In the center of the mosaic there stands a phoenix on the top of a mountain of rocks, the over-all height being six and one-half feet. About the head of the bird is a mauve gray halo, and streaming out through the halo are five rays of light, one proceeding vertically. The phoenix is represented in profile, rearing its body and head up as though it were about to take off in flight. The neck is long, but not excessively so, bent in a double curve more energetic than graceful. The brilliant eye, encircled with black, at the center of the halo, attracts the spectator's attention. The predominant colors of the rocks are green, bister and maroon; the colors of the bird, green with brown and gray in the shadows, yellow and even white in the highlights. The plan and execution of the phoenix,

[11] *Antioch-on-the-Orontes*, I, 84.
[12] So Garstang, *The Hittite Empire* (1929), p. 306.
[13] Jean Lassus, *La mosaique du phenix, provenant des fouilles d' Antioche* (extrait des *Monuments et Mémoires* publiés par l'Académie des inscriptions et Belles-Lettres, tome XXXVI [1938]).

small in size compared with the immense tapestry of flowers, produces an impression of astonishing beauty and majesty well calculated to remind one of a glorious resurrection—for to the ancients this bird was the customary symbol of the persistence of life after death.

According to a widespread myth, this fabulous bird of great beauty, after living five or six hundred years in the Arabian wilderness, the only one of its kind, would build for itself a funeral pile of spices and aromatic gums where it would immolate itself. But from its own ashes it would again emerge in the freshness of youth.[14] Many are the ancient authors who refer to this marvelous bird; Hesiod, Herodotus, Manilius, Pliny, Tacitus, Ovid, Aelian, and Celsus may be mentioned among pagan Greco-Roman authors. According to a dramatic poem on the Exodus written by one Ezekiel, probably an Alexandrian Jew of the 3rd or 2nd century B.C., a wonderful bird (the phoenix) appeared to the Israelite host at Elim. Many Church Fathers, beginning with Clement of Rome (I Epistle, chap. 25), regarded the narrative of the phoenix as a proof of the resurrection of the Christian, some even regarding it as a type of the resurrection of Christ. Several of the Fathers, indeed, found scriptural authentication for the myth by the circumstance that the Greek word for "palm tree" in the Septuagint rendering of Psalm 92:12 is identical with the name of the bird ("the righteous shall flourish like the *phoenix*").[15]

Returning to the elaborate mosaic of the phoenix, one wonders what significance it conveyed to the owner of the house in which it was found. Unfortunately there is no evidence to indicate whether he was a pagan, Jew, or Christian, or whether he was religiously or secularly minded. If the last mentioned were the case, he probably would have explained to an admirer of his pavement that the bird was symbolic of the recurrence of the years and the eternity of the empire.[16]

[14] See Milton, *Samson Agonistes*, lines 1699–1707.

[15] Cf. R. T. Rundle Clark, *Birmingham University Historical Journal*, II (1949–50), 1–29, 105–40.

[16] It is noteworthy that the mosaics found at Antioch contain many personifications, as, for example of service, life, salvation, enjoyment, power, magnanimity, etc. See Downey, *Transactions and Proceedings of the American Philological Association*, LXIX (1938), 349–63, and *Journal of the History of Ideas*, I (1940), 112–13.

This explanation is in accord with the fact that the representation of the phoenix on coins and medals of the Roman emperors denoted eternity or renovation.

House of the Mysteries of Isis

One of the most popular of the half dozen mystery religions of antiquity was that of Isis and Osiris. Native to Egypt, the cult in somewhat modified form with chief emphasis upon the great goddess spread far beyond the Nile into almost every part of the Greco-Roman world. Hymns of praise to Isis, the beneficent Queen of Heaven, indicate the deep reverence felt by the devotees of her who granted happiness and security in this life and the next. One of the most detailed accounts of preparation for initiation into the Isiac cult is preserved in the final book of Apuleius' rollicking tales of lusty adventure (*Metamorphoses* xi). Though Apuleius is careful not to reveal any of the inner secrets which the initiates were pledged never to disclose, his description of various preparatory stages leading up to the climax of the mystical rites provides one with enough information to suggest the interpretation of a fragmentary mosaic discovered at Antioch. Unfortunately the central panel was damaged by the superposition of a pipe line, cutting obliquely across the mosaic pavement. What remains of the representation shows a man in the center with Hermes to the right and a female divinity to the left. The central figure is naked except for a red cloth on his left shoulder. Hermes is extending a rod which almost touches the man's neck. The god holds the caduceus in his left hand, its top being visible near his shoulder. The female figure on the left wears a white sleeveless tunic over which there is a dark violet mantle. Her hair is covered with a grayish white veil which is surmounted by a wreath of leaves. Her bare right arm is extended toward the central figure. Her left arm supports above her head a metallic torch, with a twofold top and central knob.

What is the significance of this fragmentary mosaic? Kurt Weitzmann[17] regards it as a scene from a Euripidean play, perhaps the lost *Protesilaus*. According to Lucian's twenty-third Dialogue of the Dead, in this play the hero, with the permission of the gods of the lower world, is released to the

[17] *Antioch-on-the-Orontes*, III, 246, n. 59.

upper world for a short time under the guidance of Hermes in order to visit his wife Laodamia. The figure at the left of the mosaic is therefore Persephone, probably giving permission for the hero's release under the surveillance of Hermes psychopompos. Hermes has just touched him with his wand to restore him again to life as a youth in heroic nakedness.

Quite a different interpretation of the same scene, however, has been suggested by Doro Levi,[18] who sees in the mosaic a representation of the *Mors Voluntaria*, the "Voluntary Death," the climax and very essence of the initiation in the mysteries of Isis. According to this interpretation the figure at the left, bearing a torch, is Isis herself. The central figure is a mortal about to undertake the symbolic trip to the underworld, being guided by Hermes psychopompos. The ritualistic nakedness of the initiate, his sober hesitation and restraint, are in accord with many artistic and literary references. He seems to turn his glance back to find a support in the goddess, who encourages him with the gesture of her outstretched hand. The symbolic content of the ritual death and the following resurrection to divine glory by the initiated are fairly clear from Apuleius' guarded description of the initiation. His account regarding the climax of the initiation is as follows: "I approached near unto Hades, even to the gates of Proserpine; and after that I was ravished throughout all the elements, I returned to my proper place: about midnight I saw the sun brightly shine, I saw likewise the gods celestial and the gods infernal, before whom I presented myself and worshiped them" (*Met.* xi. 23, Adlington's translation).

According to this interpretation the mosaic in all probability bears witness to the faith of its owner. Perhaps it served to recall to him the time when he himself had undergone a similar rite of initiation. The presence of the sacred scene in his house would consequently be a perpetual prayer for the constant protection of the powerful goddess.

The "Navigium Isidis"

In the same house with the mosaic which may represent the *Mors Voluntaria* there was found a mosaic pavement, much mutilated, which has also been interpreted in terms of

[18] *Berytus*, VII (1942), 19–55; also *Antioch Mosaic Pavements*, I, 163–64.

the Isiac cult. The broad outer border depicts a lively hunting scene, which in turn is surrounded by a narrower band of birds and flowers. The central part of the mosaic shows a curved bay of the sea where two boats, with sterns opposed, are represented against the background of the sea. One boat is apparently ready to sail, with a figure going aboard from the strand. In view of the probable interpretation of the other mosaic in this house referring to the Isiac cult, this fragmentary pavement suggests to Levi the depiction of another solemn festival belonging to the same cult.[19] This was the *Navigium Isidis,* a festival marking the opening day of navigation after the winter season, celebrated on the fifth of March all along the Mediterranean shores. From several literary references as well as from hundreds of Roman coins[20] it can be learned that there was an elaborate and gay procession in which the statue of the goddess in her most splendid attire was carried from her temple to the seaside. Here a new ship, richly adorned and bearing the name Isis, was pushed into the sea, while the priest performed certain rites and uttered propitious vows.

According to Levi's interpretation, therefore, a pious devotee of Isis had depicted on the pavements of his house at Antioch some of the representative ceremonies and festivities of his religion.

The Jewish Community at Antioch

Although the numbers of Jews at Antioch did not compare with those at Alexandria and Rome, from Josephus, the Talmuds, and the chronographer Malalas, fragments of information can be pieced together which indicate that they played a quite significant role in the history of this city.[21] From the first, Seleucus gave Jewish settlers the right to follow their own laws, and the colony, augmented by settlers, prisoners, and fugitives, steadily increased during the Seleucid dynasty. By the first century of the Christian era

[19] Doro Levi, *Berytus,* VII (1942), 32–34, and *Antioch Mosaic Pavements,* I, 164–65.

[20] These were collected by A. Alfoeldi, *A Festival of Isis in Rome under the Christian Emperors of the Fourth Century* (Dissertationes Pannonicae, 2nd series, fasc. 7 [1937]), especially pp. 46 ff.

[21] See especially Carl H. Kraeling, *JBL,* LI (1932), 130–60.

there were no fewer than three Jewish settlements in and about Antioch, one west of the city near Daphne, one in the city proper, and one east of the city in the plain of Antioch. Altogether they comprised an estimated one-seventh of the total population of greater Antioch. In addition to growth in numbers at this period, the Jewish communities increased in wealth and in prestige among non-Jews. Evidence of the former is to be found in the costly votive offerings sent by the Jews of Antioch to the temple at Jerusalem (Josephus, *War of the Jews* vii. 45). The rise in prestige can be gauged also from the testimony of Josephus (*ibid.*) that "a multitude of Greeks" came to be identified with the Jewish faith as "God-fearers" or proselytes. The name of at least one of these is known to us today, Nicolas, who later played a part in the Christian church at Jerusalem as one of the first "deacons" (Acts 6:5).

The period of Jewish prestige and prosperity, however, came to an end toward the middle of the first Christian century. Malalas records a pogrom at Antioch during Caligula's reign in which many Jews were slain. Though the Jewish community fell in the estimation of the pagan population, the synagogue continued to exert a strong influence—not to say attraction—on many Christians.[22] According to Chrysostom (*Adv. Jud. Orat.* i and viii) Christians, especially women, would visit synagogues on the Sabbath or festival days and would also observe Jewish fast days. They often took disputes to Jewish judges, finding that justice was more likely to be meted out here than elsewhere. Many would visit the mysterious underground Jewish shrine at Daphne, where nocturnal visions were supposed to be obtainable. It is significant that the first canon of the Synod of Antioch in A.D. 341 makes special provisions for the complete separation of the Easter festival from the Passover (with which it had hitherto been identified). In spite of all the prominence once enjoyed by the large Jewish community in Antioch, next to nothing has so far been found by the Princeton excavators which can be identified with certainty as Jewish. Besides a marble fragment bearing part of a seven-branched candlestick,[23] there are only a few inscriptions containing

[22] Samuel Krauss, "Antioch," in the *Jewish Encyclopedia*, I, 632, and Kraeling, *JBL*, LI (1932), 156–57.

[23] Downey in *Antioch-on-the-Orontes*, II, 150–51.

Semitic sounding names. One of these deserves mention here because it begins with what is probably a phrase borrowed from the Jewish Scriptures.

Mosaic Containing a Biblical Phrase

A mosaic floor of the 6th century in a building north of Antioch's St. Paul's Gate is particularly interesting as containing what is probably the only biblical allusion among all the inscriptions so far edited. The Greek inscription reads, "Peace be your coming in, you who gaze [on this]; joy and blessing be to those who stay here. The mosaic floor of the triclinium was made in the time of Megas and Ioannes and Anthousa, stathmouchoi, in the month of Garpiaios, in the fifth indiction." The first phrase of the inscription is paralleled by a passage of the Septuagint (I Kings 16:4), though the context there is entirely dissimilar. The word which is transliterated "stathmouchoi" is translated "innkeepers" by the first editor of the inscription.[24] Its use, however, in an inscription from Dura[25] makes it uncertain whether it means anything more than simply "landlord." The first editor of the inscription suggests that the mosaic might be the pavement of an inn.

Churches in Antioch

Through literary, epigraphic, and general archaeological remains the identity of a score of Christian churches in Antioch and its suburbs has been determined.[26] One of the most famous of these was the great Constantian edifice. Octagonal in shape, it may have served as a prototype of several other similarly designed sanctuaries in this region. Contemporary authors (e.g. Eusebius *Vita Constantini* III. 50), refer to this 4th century church as *Ecclesia Magna, Apostolica,* and *Dominum Aureum,* because of its gilded

[24] Downey in *Antioch-on-the-Orontes,* III, 83–84.
[25] *Dura-Europos, IX Report* (1935–36), Part I (1944), p. 236.
[26] For a convenient summary see Leclercq, "Antioche (archéologie)," in Cabrol, *Dictionnaire d'archéologie chrétienne et de liturgie,* tome I, partie 2, cols. 2372–91, and, more recently, Walther Eltester, *Zeitschrift für die neutestamentliche Wissenschaft,* XXXVI (1937), 251–86.

dome. It was badly injured by the great earthquake of 526 and rebuilt later with a wooden dome.[27]

At Kaoussie, one of the suburbs of Antioch, the remains of a 4th century church in the shape of a cross were discovered. From an inscription the original structure can be dated to A.D. 387, in the time of Bishop Flavianos. The mosaic pavements of the cruciform floor converge upon a burial shrine in the central square. It is almost certain that this was the final resting place of the bones of St. Babylas, the bishop of Antioch who was slain in the persecution under Decius in 250.[28] This famous ecclesiastic is credited with having refused to admit Philip the Arabian into the Church (after the latter had won the imperial title by instigating the revolt of troops in which the emperor Gordian III lost his life) during a Mesopotamian expedition against the Persians. The expression "final resting place" was used above quite designedly, because after his martyrdom the body of St. Babylas, being buried at first in the city, was later interred at Daphne. Here, however, the presence of his remains so inhibited the responses of the oracle in Apollo's temple that the emperor Julian the Apostate, at that time attempting to galvanize paganism into new life at Antioch and elsewhere, had the martyr's bones moved back to the city. A score of years later they were finally laid to rest in a martyrion or burial shrine outside the city walls and across the river at Kaoussie, where the Princeton excavators uncovered it in 1935.

The Martyrion at Seleucia

The field of activity of the expedition of the Committee for the Excavation of Antioch and its Vicinity was enlarged during the three years, 1937 through 1939, by the inclusion of the site of Seleucia Pieria, the seaport of Antioch five miles north of the mouth of the Orontes. One of the most interesting of the buildings excavated here was a martyrion or memorial church.[29] This building passed through three periods of construction, the earliest of which belongs to the late 5th century. This first building was almost totally destroyed, probably by the great earthquake in the year 526.

---

[27] See Howard Crosby Butler, *Early Churches in Syria, Fourth to Seventh Centuries* (1929), pp. 192–93.

[28] Downey, *Antioch-on-the-Orontes*, II, 45–48.

[29] W. A. Campbell, *Antioch-on-the-Orontes*, III, 35–54.

The floor plan of the earliest edifice had an inner quatrefoil formed by colonnaded, semicircular exedrae between the angles of a square. Around the quatrefoil was an ambulatory with an animal mosaic. The parts which remain contain a giraffe, peacock, zebra, deer, duck, horse, flamingo, goose, two goats, elephant, lion, sheep, ox, parrot, serpent, two gazelles, hyena, stag, lioness, cubs, eagle, as well as various kinds of trees and foliage. It is a paradise of natural wild life in which all creatures are at peace: the lioness moves slowly away from the ibexes, the hyena and the lamb walk together, and no hunter intrudes.

Adjoining the east ambulatory was a large chancel with an eastern apse, the over-all length being 175 feet. During the second period of the church the east room on the north side was used as a baptistry, for which a small semicircular pool (or piscina) was built in the apsidal end of the room. Unfortunately no evidence for the identification of the church has been found. There can be no doubt, however, that it was one of the important churches in Seleucia, as is attested by its prominent location near the main colonnaded street, and by its size. One of the most likely guesses as to its identity is that on further study it may prove to be the shrine of Saint Thekla built by the emperor Zeno (A.D. 479–91).

The Rabbula Gospels

The most important early illustrated manuscript of the gospels in a language other than Greek is the famous Syriac codex in the Laurentian Library, Florence, written in A.D. 586 by a monk named Rabbula at the monastery of Zagba in northern Mesopotamia.[30] The text of the gospels which it contains is the Peshitta Syriac, resting probably on the Byzantine Greek text, which, according to Westcott and Hort, originated in Antioch in the early part of the 4th century. The reason notice is taken here of this manuscript is that its illustrations are excellent examples of the type of art which the church at Antioch developed. Besides full page pictures there are numerous smaller paintings decorating the canon

[30] For an admirable description of the portraits of the Evangelists in this manuscript, see A. M. Friend, Jr., in *Art Studies*, VII (1929), 4–9.

tables. These tables, it may be explained, were designed to assist the reader in locating parallel passages in the gospels. Eusebius, bishop of Caesarea, divided each of the gospels into sections which he numbered consecutively, and then arranged the numbers in ten lists. The first list or canon contained those passages which are found in all four gospels; the second, third, and fourth, those common to combinations of three gospels; the fifth to the ninth comprised the passages common to every combination of two gospels (except that of Mark and John); and the tenth those passages peculiar to each gospel. In subsequent years, instead of presenting bare lists of numbers, scribes would frequently arrange them between columns of gold and red and other colors, surmounted by a highly decorated arch. In the Rabbula Gospels the canon tables are also accompanied by scenes from the Old Testament and from the life of Christ. On the page pictured on Plate 27 of this volume, presenting parallel passages in the four gospels, the two scenes at the top are identified by the Syriac script (reading from right to left) as King David and Solomon, the former depicted with his harp and the latter seated upon his throne. The other three scenes are the birth of Jesus showing the infant lying bound in swaddling clothes, the slaughter of the innocents (the artist was compelled to represent King Herod on one side of the page, giving orders to his soldiers on the other, who have seized a child), and the baptism of Jesus by John (in addition to the descending dove, observe the customary representation of the deity by a hand reaching down from heaven).

The Chalice of Antioch

No article on Antioch would be complete without at least a passing reference to the famous Chalice of Antioch. Since two contributions on this subject have appeared in past years in *The Biblical Archaeologist*,[31] a few sentences comprising a kind of appendix will be sufficient here. In 1910 the chalice was found by Arab workmen while digging a well at Antioch. The initial announcement to the public was startling enough; Gustavus A. Eisen wrote a "Preliminary Report on the Great Chalice of Antioch Containing the Earliest Portraits of Christ

[31] H. Harvard Arnason, *BA*, IV (1941), 49–64; V (1942), 10–16; Floyd V. Filson, *BA*, V (1942), 1–10.

and the Apostles."[32] The chalice consists of a plain inner cup of silver, about seven and one-half inches high, with an original widest diameter of about six inches. The outer gilded silver holder is fashioned so as to display twelve highly individualized figures divided into two groups, in each of which five apostles are placed about a central figure of Christ. Eisen dated the manufacture of the holder within the last third of the first century and suggested that the artificer was someone who had seen Jesus and his followers. In answer to the question why such an elegant holder was used to contain such a plain inner cup, the guess was hazarded that the inner cup is none other than the Holy Grail, the vessel from which Christ drank at the Last Supper. A large literature on the subject soon sprang up. Other scholars, including some of the best authorities on early Christian art, denied that the chalice belongs to the first century, assigning dates to it which range from the 2nd to the 6th centuries. Obviously its maker, therefore, could not have been acquainted with the personal appearance of Jesus and his apostles. A few scholars have even maintained that the chalice is a modern forgery. It seems likely, however, that it is an early, though by no means first century, piece of Christian art.

Conclusion

Antioch, like Vienna in Europe, was the melting pot of Eastern and Western cultures. Archaeological remains corroborate literary evidence that here met and mingled the Greek and Roman traditions on the one hand, and the traditions of Semitic Arabia, Palestine, and Mesopotamia on the other.[33] There was in addition the varying influence of Persia, considered both by itself and as a transmitter of the religious, philosophic, and artistic ideas of the extreme Orient. It is a melancholy fact, however, that this commingling of Oriental and Occidental elements resulted in the perpetuation of the worst features of both traditions. That such a city should have been destined to have so large a share in the growth of the

[32] *AJA*, XX (1916), 426–37.
[33] See especially G. Haddad, *Aspects of Social Life in Antioch in the Hellenistic-Roman Period* (1949).

Christian church was perhaps inevitable due to its location and cosmopolitan nature. At the same time its prominent role may also be regarded as another instance of the inscrutable ways of divine providence.

17

EPHESUS IN THE EARLY CHRISTIAN ERA

MERRILL M. PARVIS

In Acts 18:18 f., we read that "Paul, having tarried after this yet many days, took his leave of the brethren, and sailed thence for Syria, and with him Priscilla and Aquila . . . And they came to Ephesus . . ."

It must have been an impressive sight indeed that unfolded itself before the eyes of Paul as he approached the city from the west, entered the wide mouth of the Cayster river, and sailed into the harbor of Ephesus. The modern shore is a harborless line of sandy beach, unapproachable by ship, which gives the impression that Ephesus must have been an inland city. Such an impression, however, is a wrong one. Strabo, writing his *Geography* about A.D. 20, described Ephesus as a coastal city (xiv. 1. 24); and from this many have argued that the present coast line must have receded at least three or four miles from the position which it occupied at the beginning of the Christian era. Strabo goes on to say, however, that

> the entrance of the harbor was made narrow by order of the king Attalus Philadelphus who, together with the persons that constructed it, was disappointed at the results. The harbor was formerly shallow, on account of the embankment of earth accumulated by the Cayster; but the king, supposing that there would be deep water for the entrance of large vessels of burden, if a mole were thrown up at the mouth of the river, which was very wide, gave orders for the construction of a mole; but the contrary effect took place, for the mud, being confined within the harbor, made the whole of it shallow to the mouth. Before the construction of the mole, the flow and ebb of the sea cleared the mud away entirely by forcing it outwards.

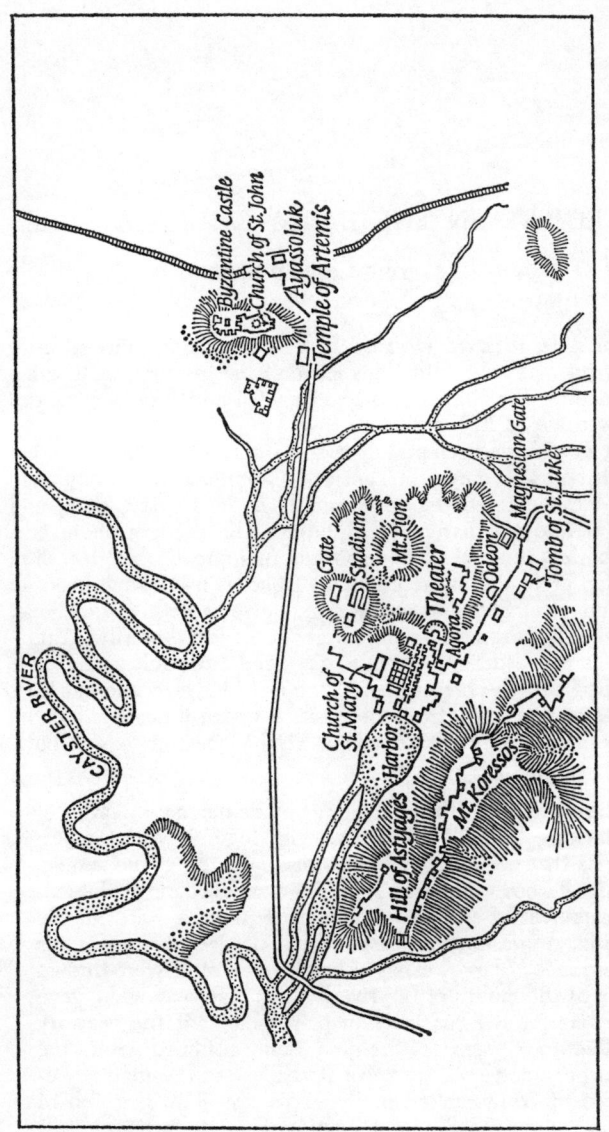

FIGURE 5. Sketch map of Ephesus and its environs.

In his *Discoveries at Ephesus* (1877), J. T. Wood says that the city port of Ephesus was fully four miles from the sea. In support of his contention, he tells of finding the extensive remains of a massive stone embankment on the north side of the river Cayster which he succeeded in tracing without difficulty to a distance within 400 yards of the present coast line. This stone embankment Wood identifies as the mole which was built by Attalus Philadelphus. If he is correct in so identifying it, it appears impossible that the sea has receded far, if at all, from the coast line as it was in the days of Paul.

By far the most impressive view of Ephesus is to be seen from the top of the twin-peaked Mt. Pion (Fig. 5). From this vantage point one's eye ranges westward over the streets of the ancient city, and on across the harbor to the hill of Astyages. To the southwest one's view is bounded by the long ridges of the Koressos mountains, along the crest of which runs the south wall of the Greek city. To the northwest, one looks across the level plain to the sea, fully six miles away. To the north lies the level plain and the steep slopes of the Gallesion mountains. The mouth of the river Cayster is hidden from sight behind the hill of Astyages. To the northeast and east, one looks over the valley to the great temple of Artemis (Diana) and to the holy hill of Ayassoluk which overhangs the temple site.

The History of Ephesus

Neither the dates nor the successive stages in the history of the Ephesian valley can be fully determined. Villages of more or less importance, however, probably had existed in the Ephesian territory for several centuries before the coming of the Greeks. About 1044 B.C., the first Greek colonists, under the leadership of Androclus, came from Athens, expelled most of the older population, and founded one of the twelve cities of the Ionian Confederation. This was a city which was composed of Greeks and of a native remnant. It occupied a tract of land along the Koressos mountains.

For four centuries that was the situation of Ephesus. There was an Ionian city bearing the name of Ephesus on the slopes of Mt. Koressos, and about a mile to the north was the temple of Artemis. When the Greek colonists arrived on the scene, they had naturally adopted the worship of the deity who presided over the land. Gradually they came to bear more respect for her than they did for their own goddess, Athena, whom they had brought with them from Athens.

During this period, the temple of Artemis became a sanctuary within a large sacred precinct on the plain. The goddess, although worshiped by the Greeks, was not transformed into a Greek deity. She remained an Anatolian deity both in character and in the ritual by which she was worshiped.

A new era began about 560 B.C. when Ephesus was conquered by Croesus, the king of Lydia who was soon to be defeated by Cyrus the Persian. The city was now attached to the temple of Artemis, and the population was moved back from the higher ground and dwelt once more beside the temple. This change marked the triumph of the Asiatic or Anatolian element over the Greek in the Ephesian population. The Ephesian goddess was henceforth the recognized deity of the city and the patroness of both family and city life.

Ephesus, however, was not entirely reduced to the pure Anatolian village system. It was not a mere union of villages with the temple as the only center. It was a city with a certain form of municipal government.

In an endeavor to maintain an equilibrium among the diverse elements which were united in the city, the population was divided into "tribes" and "thousands." Apparently, there were originally three tribes: the Epheseis, the native population; the Euonymoi, the Athenian population; and the Bembinaioi, the colonists of other Greek regions. Two more tribes, the Teioi and the Karenaioi, were introduced in order to accommodate new bodies of settlers. Ephoros, writing about 340 B.C., describes these as the five tribes of Ephesus. A sixth tribe was introduced at some later date, although the time of its formation is uncertain.

In addition to having its own organizations and municipal government, Ephesus also had its own acropolis, and struck its own coins in silver and electrum.

After 479 B.C., Ephesus was forced to join the union of Greek states which was called the Delian confederacy, but it seceded at the earliest opportunity.

With the conquest of Asia by Alexander the Great, after 335 B.C., the Greek spirit began to strengthen itself in Ephesus. This is first perceptible in the coinage. The bee, the sacred insect and the symbol of the goddess Artemis, had before this always been the principal type on Ephesian coins. About 295

B.C., however, a purely Greek type, the head of the Greek Artemis, was substituted for the bee on the silver coins.

There followed once more a change in the situation of Ephesus. The city was moved away from the neighborhood of the temple to a point not far from the location of the old Greek city. This change seems to have been resisted by the priests and a large section of the people over whom they had control. The opposition to this proposed change of location, however, was overcome by a Greek tyrant and ruler named Lysimachus. The Ephesus of 560–287 B.C. was in a low-lying situation, surrounded on three sides by higher ground, and in time of rain a great amount of water poured down through the city. Lysimachus took advantage of a heavy rain and obstructed the drains so that the city was inundated. The people were then glad to leave the site (Strabo *Geog.* xiv. 1. 21).

The new location was a good one, and the Hellenic Ephesus of this new foundation lasted for more than a thousand years. Its shape was like a bent bow, the two ends being Pion on the east and the hill of Astyages on the west. The quays, bordered by colonnades and public buildings, can still be traced amid the ruins.

The death of Lysimachus, in 281 B.C., interrupted the development of the new city which he had planned on such a great scale. Yet the new location was a favorable one, and the city soon became one of the greatest of Asia.

A period in the history of Ephesus which, seemingly, is often overlooked, is that during which there was an intimate connection between the city and Egypt. The influence of the Greco-Egyptian kings, the Ptolemies, in the eastern waters of the Aegean Sea, affected Ephesus to such an extent that she became one of the stations for the Egyptian fleet, and a recruiting center for mercenary soldiers in the Egyptian service.[1]

The Roman province of Asia was organized in 133 B.C., and Ephesus struggled with Smyrna and Pergamum for the honor of being called the first city of that province. Roman control was temporarily interrupted by the invasion of King Mithridates in 88 B.C. It was from Ephesus that Mithridates issued the order for a great massacre, in which thousands of Romans were put to death in Asia. At the time of this massacre the Ephesians did not spare the Roman suppliants at the altar of

[1] A. V. Green, *The Ephesian Canonical Writings* (1910), p. 17, citing Adolf Holm, *The History of Greece* (1894–98), IV, 276.

the goddess Artemis, disregarding the right of asylum which had hitherto been universally respected, even by invaders. Sulla soon reconquered Asia, however, and the Ephesians were eventually subdued under Antony in 41 B.C.

The luxurious life led by Antony at Ephesus, where he was joined by Cleopatra, retarded for a few years the prosperity of the city. With the peace it enjoyed in common with other cities of Asia Minor under the Roman empire, however, her commerce and her riches increased, in spite of the heavy tribute she had to pay. Augustus, in addition to restricting the limits of the sacred precincts of the temple, commenced many large public buildings which were probably finished by Tiberius. In the time of the Caesars, the majority of the public buildings, including the theater and the gymnasium, were erected. The foundations of some of the ancient Greek structures were allowed to remain wherever they could be utilized.

Under Antoninus Pius (A.D. 138–61) a great portion of the city was rebuilt. During this time, the Jews had a special quarter of the city allotted to them for their residence. About the year A.D. 262 Ephesus was sacked by the Goths, and not many years later the great temple of Diana was destroyed.

With the decline of her commerce and the destruction of the temple, Ephesus lost her historical importance, and we know but little of her history during many centuries. The city probably fell into the hands of numerous adventurers among whom is named a certain Greek pirate of the 11th century. The Turks took possession of the city in the 13th century, and built a considerable town at Ayassoluk. Both Ephesus and Ayassoluk fell into the hands of the Knights of Saint John of Jerusalem who struck some coins at Ayassoluk in A.D. 1365. Ephesus was by degrees deserted, and it remained for the archaeologist again to bring to light a once-teeming city.

After this all too brief account of the history of Ephesus, we may turn to an examination of some of the ruins of that once great metropolis.

Archaeological Investigation of the City

As we begin our visit to the ancient city, let us go first to the great temple of Artemis, as Paul himself may have done. This temple is ranked as one of the seven wonders of the ancient world, and it is alluded to by many ancient writers.

Knowledge of its exact location, however, was lost for many centuries. It remained for J. T. Wood, after exactly six years "of great anxiety and misgiving, and of almost hopeless endeavour" to bring it once again to the light of day.[2]

The temple was found northeast of the city at the foot of the hill of Ayassoluk. History shows that this was the "holy hill" although that title is never recorded in any of the documents. The sense of the holiness of this hill and of the low ground beneath its western slope was never wholly lost even amid all of the changes of religion that occurred in ancient and in medieval times.

On this hill Justinian's great church of St. John Theologos was built. Concerning this church, Procopius says,

> There chanced to be a certain place before the city of Ephesus, lying on a steep slope, hilly and bare of soil and incapable of producing crops, even should one attempt to cultivate them, but altogether hard and rough. On that site the natives had set up a church in early times to the Apostle John; this Apostle has been named "the Theologian," because the nature of God was described by him in a manner beyond the unaided power of man. This church, which was small and in a ruined condition because of its great age, the Emperor Justinian tore down to the ground and replaced it by a church so large and beautiful, that, to speak briefly, it resembles very closely in all respects, and is a rival to, the shrine which he dedicated to all the Apostles in the imperial city . . . .[3]

Tradition has said that the grave of St. John is located under this church and that a sacred dust arises from his tomb on the anniversary of his festival. This is the church that earlier writers have all too often wrongly identified as being the church in which the Council of A.D. 431 was held.

Between the church and the temple of Artemis stands the

[2] The literature which deals with the temple of Artemis may be found in abundance. Probably the best accounts of the discovery of the temple and of the work of excavation, as well as descriptions of the temple itself may be found in J. T. Wood, *Discoveries at Ephesus* (1877); D. G. Hogarth, *The Archaic Artemisia* (1908); and *Forschungen in Ephesos* (1906–37), published by the Österreichisches Archaeologisches Institut of Vienna.

[3] Procopius *Buildings* v.1.4–6.

mosque of Isa Bey. Standing by the ruins of the temple which Wood found buried more than twenty feet below the surface, one may look over the temple and the mosque to the holy hill and the church of St. John.

When we take into consideration the spirit of Anatolian religion and the persistence with which it clings to definite localities, we wonder why those who so long sought the temple of Artemis did not look for it beside the mosque, the church, and the holy hill.

The platform upon which the temple of Artemis was raised was found by Wood to be approximately 239 feet wide by 418 feet long. There was a flight of ten steps which led up to the pavement of the platform and three more steps which led up to the pavement of the peristyle. The temple itself was 163 feet 9½ inches in width and 342 feet 6½ inches in length. The 100 columns which the temple contained were six feet one-half inch in diameter at the base. At least some of these columns were sculptured to a height of about twenty feet.

The cella of the temple was seventy feet wide and it was doubtless open to the sky. The foundations for the altar were twenty feet square. It has been suggested that the statue of the goddess, which probably stood directly behind the altar, and which was said to have "fallen from Jupiter" (Acts 19:35), may have been a large meteorite which was worked by an artist to resemble a human figure.

Enough fragments have been found to prove that brilliant color as well as gold was extensively used in the decoration of the temple itself. We can well understand why this great structure, a building of exquisite beauty and proportion, the result of the united efforts of architect, of sculptor, and of painter, came to be one of the seven wonders of the ancient world.

From the temple of Artemis we may turn our steps back to the city itself. As we follow in the footsteps of the apostle we find ourselves going to the great theater which is located on the western slope of Mt. Pion. It was here that the mob gathered in a riot which was directed against Paul and where "all with one voice about the space of two hours cried out, 'Great is Diana of the Ephesians'" (Acts 19:34). This great theater was approximately 495 feet in diameter. It has been estimated that it would accommodate 24,500 persons.

The theater is connected with the harbor by the "Arkadiane," a marble paved street approximately thirty-six feet in width. On both sides, it is lined by a colonnade behind which are storerooms and shops. The length of the Arkadiane is about 1735 feet. Opposite the little square which is before the great theater, the street was closed by a great double-arch gate. At the western end of the Arkadiane is the magnificent harbor gate. At one place, the intersection of the Arkadiane and a side street is marked by a tetrapylon which reminds one of a similar intersection in Gerasa, Transjordan. This whole construction probably dates from late Roman times.

In one of the shops along the north side of the Arkadiane, there was found inscribed on a door lintel a part of the apocryphal correspondence between Christ and Abgaros of Edessa.

In this ancient city there is much that is of interest to the archaeologist and to the historian, although not of primary interest to the one who is in search of Christian monuments. The one who is interested in such monuments as the Agora, the Odeum, the wellhouse, etc., can find an abundance of material which has been published by the Österreichisches Archaeologisches Institut of Vienna under the general title *Forschungen in Ephesos* (1906–37).

One of the most interesting monuments for the historian of Christianity and one of the most striking and picturesque features of the city is the so-called prison of St. Paul. On the hill of Astyages there stands a fort which tradition has long designated as the prison in which the apostle was confined, though actually it is much later than his day. From its elevation of 450 feet it dominates the view from all Ephesus.

To the southeast of the great theater and near the street that runs to the Magnesian Gate is the so-called tomb of St. Luke. This is a circular building some fifty feet in diameter which Wood identified as the tomb of the beloved physician but which later study has identified as a Greek polyandrion (that is, the tomb of a number of men who may have died in war, or a family tomb).

On the northeastern slope of Mt. Pion lies the cave of the Seven Sleepers. The legend of these Seven Sleepers is to be found in almost all of the languages of the earth. It was embodied in the Koran in a chapter entitled, "The Cave." Tradition says that during one of the persecutions of the Christians (under Decius, A.D. 249–51 or under Diocletian, A.D.

283–304) seven young men fled to the cave for refuge. After entering the cave, they fell asleep and did not awaken until the time of the Christian emperor Theodosius II (A.D. 408–50). Their awakening was taken to be an incontestable witness to the doctrine of the resurrection of the body. They were not conscious of having slept more than one night and were greatly surprised when upon entering the city they could recognize neither people nor language nor money. Everything was changed and all the city had become Christian. The seven men, however, all died natural deaths on the day of their awakening. The emperor had them buried in their cave and he caused a church to be built on the spot. The place also became a Christian burying ground.

One of the greatest of the Christian monuments of Ephesus is the church of St. Mary. The ruins of this church have long been known to those who have visited the city. For many years it was designated as the "double-church." This name seemed to be justified by the appearance of the ruins themselves from which one gained the impression that there once had been two churches on the site. It appeared as though the two churches had been oriented in opposite directions; the so-called eastern church with its apse to the east, and the so-called western church with its apse to the west.

Excavation of the entire complex revealed the remains of at least five building periods on this site. The first period produced a long building, at the east and west ends of which were great halls, each containing an apse. Between these halls ran a colonnade which was surrounded by a porch. On the basis of an inscription which was found on the site, Josef Keil assumed that this building was the museum of the city, that is, a school of arts and learning.

During the second period, there was erected in the western part of the original building, a three-nave, pillared basilica with a narthex and an outer court. The baptistry also was erected at this time.

The third period was marked by the erection of the "dome-church" which was built in the western part of the earlier basilica. The narthex of the dome-church butted against the inside of the west wall of the earlier church of St. Mary. The outer court and the baptistry, with the exception of a few minor alterations, remained much the same as they had been before.

In the fourth period, after the dome-church had been destroyed, the area between it and the apse of the church of St. Mary was altered into a little three-nave, pillared basilica with galleries. The ruins of the dome-church thus served as an outer court from which the narthex of this latest basilica was reached by means of a door which was cut through the apse wall of the dome-church itself. A little chapel which was located along the south wall of the basilica was probably erected also during this time.

During the fifth period the basilica which had been erected in the fourth period, and which was by now in a rather bad state of disrepair, was remodeled. Among other things, the remodeling consisted of placing additional supports under the galleries and in completely changing the presbyterium.

It is the activity of the second period which holds the greatest interest for us. In the year 325 the emperor Constantine issued the edict which made Christianity a legal religion. Immediately there was a movement on the part of Christians all over the empire to build more stately houses of worship which would give adequate expression to the new importance of their faith. The Christians of Ephesus entered wholeheartedly into this movement. They obtained possession of one of the most favorable building locations in the city, then occupied only by the ruins of the once great museum. This newly acquired building lot provided an ideal spot for the erection of the proposed bishop's church and palace. Construction was begun about the year 350 or perhaps even a few years earlier. The Christian architect who designed the new bishop's church, which was to be known as the church of St. Mary, brought the new structure into relation with the extant remains of the museum with a great deal of artistic aptness as well as intelligent calculation.

The church of St. Mary, with a length of nearly 481 feet, was built in the western half of the ruins of the museum. The church complex, as finally completed, consisted of a three-nave, columnar basilica whose apse was flanked by two side rooms, a narthex, an outer court with a columnar entryway, and a baptistry.

The church of St. Mary was identified definitely by means of an inscription which was found on the site. From this inscription (a quotation from a pastoral letter of the archbishop Hypatius in the time of Justinian and preserved on a stone slab inside of the narthex) we know that the church was named for Mary the mother of Jesus ("the All-holy Mother of God and Perpetual Virgin"). It is certain, therefore, that this was the church in which the Council of 431 was held. In the official acts of this Council, the church was designated as the church of the "Holy Mary, Mary Mother of God," or simply as "the Great Church."

A long and fervent feud over the mystery of the incarnation of Christ and over the designation of Mary as Mother of God (*Theotokos*) found its culmination in the very building whose ruins we have been exploring. The champion of the party which wished Mary to be designated, not as Mother of God, but as Mother of Christ (*Christotokos*), was Nestorius who had been placed in the bishop's chair of Constantinople in the year 428 and who was patronized by the emperor and his court. Cyril of Alexandria was the champion of the opposing faction, that is, of those who favored designating Mary as Mother of God.

The emperor Theodosius II issued a call for all of the metropolitans of the empire and also for a large number of suffragan bishops to attend a universal council which would be held at the time of Pentecost, 431, in Ephesus. Because of papal instruction given the previous year, the task of presiding over the sessions of the council fell to Cyril. The council formally convened on June 22, 431. Nearly 200 bishops were present for this opening session. At this session Cyril presented his side of the argument and made a bid for the sympathy of the Ephesians. Bishop Memnon of Ephesus, together with about forty suffragan bishops, joined Cyril and carried with them the support of the whole Ephesian population. In the first session of the synod Nestorius was condemned *in absentia* after he had refused three invitations to be present at the meeting. This session lasted until late in the evening, but so great was the interest of the people in its outcome that a large crowd had surrounded the church since early morning waiting to hear the verdict. When the verdict was announced, the crowd formed a torch-light procession and amid great shouting escorted Cyril and his followers to their lodgings.

In the year 449 a second great council was held in this church. This was the so-called Robber Council of Ephesus. The last inscription found on the site has been dated as coming from the year 451.

We may safely assume, therefore, that the church of St. Mary, built just before 350, was still in use until about the last third of the 5th century. It may have been destroyed by fire.

Early Christianity was profoundly influenced by the environment in which it grew and developed. Especially was this true in the great centers of population. But the reverse is also true. For more than three-quarters of a century archaeologists have been bringing to light new materials which have illumined the history of both the city and the Christian movement.

EPHESUS AND THE NEW TESTAMENT

FLOYD V. FILSON

The apostle Paul evidently followed a deliberate missionary strategy; he chose to center his work in the important cities of the eastern Roman empire. This was not due merely to the fact that he was born and bred a city man, with his home first in Tarsus of Cilicia and then in Jerusalem. It was due mainly to his insight that by establishing himself in a key city he could not only reach a large number of residents, but could also get the gospel before the people of the surrounding area. He could either meet them when they visited the city for festivals or business, or send out helpers, such as Epaphras (according to the probable text of Col. 1:7), to preach and found churches in smaller places.

The Strategic Position of Ephesus

The city of Ephesus, a busy center of shipping and land traffic, was especially suited to be such a center of Pauline preaching. To be sure, its harbor tended to silt up; inscriptions of the first, 2nd, and 3rd centuries A.D. tell of gifts and projects to dredge out the deposits made by the Cayster river. Nevertheless, the harbor was in constant use. Here the Roman proconsul of the province of Asia first set foot on the soil of the province when he came from Rome to take up his duties. Into this port Paul sailed after his first ministry in Corinth, and made his first contact with the Jews in Ephesus (Acts

18:19). There was constant traffic between Corinth and Ephesus, and the hasty visit which Paul seems to have made to Corinth during the latter part of his stay in Ephesus (cf. II Cor. 12:14; 13:1) could be made without having to wait long for a ship.

But sea lanes leading north, west, and south were by no means the only traffic routes leading out from Ephesus. In western Asia Minor four river valleys sloped westward to reach the Aegean sea. Northernmost of these was the rather short Caicus, on the north side of which lay Pergamum. Next was the Hermus, near whose mouth lay Smyrna with its excellent harbor. Further south was the Cayster, which passed just north of Ephesus some three miles from the sea. Southernmost of the four was the Meander, near whose mouth lay Miletus. The winding course of this river gave us the verb and noun which refer to constant turning or aimless wandering.

At first sight Ephesus might seem doomed to a minor role, for both the Hermus and Meander rivers were larger and longer than the Cayster, and each might have been expected to ensure greater prosperity to the city at its mouth. Convenient passes, however, gave Ephesus access to both these larger valleys, so that in fact it held a central position. In the time of Paul it was the chief port on the Aegean for the land route which led east into central Asia Minor and the regions beyond. Thus possessed of sea trade, heavy traffic with eastern regions, and good land routes to both north and south, Ephesus was a rich and populous center. Indeed, T. R. S. Broughton considers Beloch's estimate that Ephesus had 225,000 people to be definitely too low.[1] Strabo (*Geog.* xiv. 1. 24) reported that it was the chief market or business center of Asia Minor "this side of Taurus."

The Wealth of Ephesus

Both literary records and inscriptional evidence make it clear that Ephesus was enormously wealthy. Obviously sea and land trade was the steady source of a large part of this wealth. Another source was the large territory which the city owned. How this extensive land came to be the property of Ephesus is not clear, but the coastal region to the south, in-

[1] *An Economic Survey of Ancient Rome*, ed. T. Frank (6 vols.; 1933-40), IV (1938), 813.

cluding the cities Phygela and Marathesium, and a great part of the lower Cayster valley, including the city of Larissa, belonged to Ephesus by the first century B.C.[2] The income from these cities and farming areas enriched the already prosperous city.

The Worship of Artemis

The most distinctive source of prestige and revenue, however, was the cult of the goddess Artemis (the name Diana used in English versions of Acts refers to the Roman goddess who was identified with Artemis in the days of the Roman empire). Illustrative of the deep and persistent Asiatic influence in Ephesus is the fact that, although images of Artemis in earlier times had been more of the Greek type, such images in the times of the Roman empire were covered from neck to waist with breasts. In other words, Artemis was the mother goddess, Oriental rather than Greek, and her worship was much concerned with fertility in flocks, herds, and the human family. It was akin to the earlier fertility cults in Palestine against which Elijah and other prophets of Israel had to fight.

The cult of Artemis was extremely widespread and popular. There is definite archaeological evidence of the practice of this cult in more than thirty places of the ancient world. Demetrius the silversmith had much ground for his reference to Artemis as she "whom all Asia and the world worshippeth" (Acts 19:27).

Nevertheless, the goddess was in a special sense "Artemis of the Ephesians." Her temple in Ephesus was considered one of the seven wonders of the world. It was considered so sacred and inviolable that not only the Ephesians but also foreign individuals, kings, and peoples deposited money there for safekeeping. It was the custom to loan this money, and the temple became, as Broughton says (p. 890), the "biggest bank in Asia."

Gifts to the temple and goddess were another source of wealth. An inscription, dated A.D. 104, tells of a single gift by one Vibius Salutaris of twenty-nine statuettes of silver and gold; the total weight was 111 pounds of precious metal, and expert workmanship must have made them costly objects.

[2] A. H. M. Jones, *The Cities of the Eastern Roman Provinces* (1937), p. 78.

They were to be carried in public processions during the festivals of Artemis, and so must have been of more than average impressiveness. When we read of this and similar gifts, we understand better why Demetrius was able to stir up so violent a riot among silversmiths against an apostle who taught "that gods made with hands are not gods" (Acts 19:26).

Especially dedicated to Artemis was the month Artemision (March–April). At that time tourists and especially devotees of Artemis must have thronged the city and brought great wealth to the temple and tradesmen. When Paul, writing from Ephesus about the time of Passover in the spring (I Cor. 5:7), says that he will stay there until Pentecost (I Cor. 16:8, 9), one wonders whether the great crowds of this festival season are not keeping him so busy and the conversions to Christian faith are not proving so numerous that he feels forced to postpone his departure for Macedonia and Corinth. The Book of Acts tells us that by Paul's preaching "all the residents of Asia heard the word of the Lord," and Demetrius states that "not only at Ephesus, but almost throughout all Asia, this Paul hath persuaded and turned away a considerable company of people" (19:10, 26). Festival time would be the time when the economic effects of Paul's preaching against idolatry would be most bitterly felt by craftsmen and tradesmen, and when the jealousy for the goddess could be aroused most easily to riot intensity.

Silver Shrines of Artemis?

At centers of sight-seeing and pilgrimage, trade in souvenirs and objects of remembrance is brisk. This appears to have been the case at Ephesus in connection with the worship of Artemis. Acts 19:24 states that Demetrius was "a silversmith, who made silver shrines of Artemis," and thereby "brought no little business to the craftsmen."

Although shrines made of terra cotta and marble have been found during excavations at various places, no silver shrines have come to light thus far. In view of this lack of evidence, E. L. Hicks conjectured[3] that Luke made a mistake concerning the actual position of Demetrius; he suggested that Luke

[3] *Expositor*, I (1890), 401–22. Ramsey rejected this view; see his book, *The Church in the Roman Empire* (1893), chap. vii, "St. Paul at Ephesus."

knew of a Demetrius who was a *neopoios*, i.e., "temple-warden," and that since this Greek word has the literal meaning of "temple-maker," Luke concluded erroneously that Demetrius was a maker of silver shrines or miniature temples of Artemis for sale to tourists or pilgrims.

Hicks supported his conjecture by an inscription which he dated about the time of Paul's ministry in Ephesus; this inscription refers to a Demetrius who was "temple-warden." On this view, the silversmiths mentioned in Acts made their living not by manufacturing silver shrines, but rather by skilled work on silver statuettes of the sort listed in the above-mentioned inscription of Salutaris. In any case, the silversmiths were no doubt members of a guild similar to the "guild of silversmiths and goldsmiths" referred to in an inscription from Smyrna.

It is interesting to find the name Demetrius in an inscription which must be dated in or at least near the time of Paul's ministry. Since, however, the view of Hicks involves the conclusion that Luke, an intelligent writer, did not understand a Greek word, and since shrines of terra cotta and marble have been found, it appears entirely possible that Luke was right, that silver shrines were made, and that the failure to find any thus far may be due to the limited extent of excavation. Moreover, excavations seeking light on the New Testament period have usually been more interested in temples, markets, theaters, and other public places than in the homes where such shrines might have been kept. Furthermore, the fading of the Artemis cult, conversions to Christianity, hostility to idolatry, theft, war, and plunder would all unite to decrease the number of shrines or images that survived, and any object of precious metal might thus be destroyed or melted down for other uses.

Emperor Worship in Ephesus

It must not be thought that Ephesus worshiped no deity but Artemis. Polytheism prevailed. We are told that the Roman Emperor Augustus permitted Ephesus and Nicea to dedicate sacred areas to Rome and Caesar because they were then the chief cities in Asia and Bithynia respectively. In Paul's day Ephesus was "temple-keeper" or "temple-guardian" of one temple which thus represented the early stages of emperor worship.

The title is known to readers of the Bible from Acts 19:35 in connection with the worship of Artemis. Indeed, an inscription refers to Ephesus as the "temple-keeper of the great Artemis." But the same title was used at Ephesus and elsewhere to indicate that the city was the "temple-keeper" of the imperial cult. In addition to the temple in Ephesus which served this purpose in Paul's time, the city later added a second and then a third temple for this purpose, and so finally came to be called "thrice temple-keeper" of the imperial cult. In Ephesus this cult was overshadowed by Artemis worship in the middle of the first century, but by the close of the century, as the book of Revelation and other evidence combine to show, emperor-worship had become widespread.

Jews in Ephesus

Judaism was still another religion found in Ephesus in the time of Paul. Although inscriptions do not mention Jews until the 2nd century A.D., earlier literary references are clear. Josephus tells us that the Syrian ruler Antiochus II Theos (261–247 B.C.) granted the Jews in Ionia, i.e., the region of western Asia Minor in which Ephesus is located, full citizenship. He adds that when, in the first century B.C., the Ionians sought to deprive the Jews of this right, the Roman official Marcus Agrippa refused the petition and preserved the rights of the Jews. Indeed, Josephus tells of many decrees safeguarding the right of Jews in Gentile lands to practice their ancestral faith, and several of these decrees show that both Roman officials and the Ephesians themselves acted in the first century B.C. to protect the Jews in the exercise of their religious customs of life and worship (see especially *Antiquities* xii. 3. 2; xiv. 10. 25).

It is not clear from excavations where the Jewish colony lived, but the statement of H. Leclercq[4] that it was in the northern outskirts of the city may well be correct. The need of water for ritual purposes may explain a tendency to locate synagogues near a river or seashore (cf. Acts 16:13, of Philippi; Josephus *Antiquities* xiv. 10. 23, of Halicarnassus; and the Mekilta for the general custom).[5] This should be borne

[4] *Dictionnaire d'archéologie chrétienne et de liturgie*, tome V, partie 1 (1922), article on Ephesus.

[5] See comment in Foakes Jackson and Lake, *Beginnings of Christianity*, IV (1933), 191.

in mind in any future search for the Ephesian synagogue. While the latter has never been found, its existence is put beyond all doubt by the references in Acts and Josephus.

Not all of the religious activities in Ephesus were connected with temples and synagogues. In this city with its shifting and mixed population, magic and superstition played a great role, and the reference to itinerant exorcists, sons of "Sceva, a Jew, a chief priest" (Acts 19:13, 14), may indicate that, as happened elsewhere, individual Jews sometimes slipped away from their ancestral faith and shared in the eclectic rites of the time. In any case, the use of incantations and magical formulas was so prevalent in Ephesus that books or rolls of such formulas were referred to by ancient Greek and Roman writers as "Ephesian writings." What Acts tells about exorcism and the burning of great numbers of magical formulas thus fits the situation which we know existed in Ephesus (Acts 19:13, 19).

Paul's Ministry in Ephesus

Our basic source for the study of the apostolic church in Ephesus is the book of Acts. It is worthwhile to note here the discovery in Egypt of several early papyrus manuscripts of Acts; all are quite fragmentary. They include P 45, P 48 and P 53 from the 3rd century; P 38 from the late 3rd or early 4th century;[6] and P 8 and P 50 from the 4th century. P 38 and P 48 exhibit the "Western" text, and prove that this text type was present in Egypt at a very early date.

Both I Cor. 16:9 and the account in Acts 19 indicate that Paul's ministry in Ephesus was successful and resulted in a rather large church. The reminder of praiseworthy earlier days in the later book of Revelation (2:5) supports this evidence. The violence of the outcry against Paul at the time of the riot in the theater argues for the same conclusion, although the surmise that the riot took place about the time of the Artemis festival in the month Artemision would go far to explain the strong emotional outbreak and the bitter feelings of the craftsmen concerning their loss of trade.

[6] For facsimile, reconstruction, and discussion of this fragment, by H. A. Sanders, see *Harvard Theological Review*, XX (1927); also Silva New's article in *Beginnings of Christianity*, V (1933), 262–68.

Light from Inscriptions and Papyri on Acts 19

Inscriptions, found in large numbers in Ephesus and to a lesser extent in other cities of Asia Minor, combine with papyri found in Egypt to throw much light on the language and content of the New Testament. We may therefore note a few of the words which are used in Acts, and compare the evidence from other sources as to their meaning.[7]

19:13. The expression "I adjure you by Jesus" is similar to the formula of exorcism known from papyri. The following example is from the so-called Paris magical papyrus: "I adjure you, demon, whoever you are, by this god Sabarbarbathioth Sabarbarbathiuth Sabarbarbathioneth Sabarbarbaphai, come out, demon, whoever you are, and depart from so-and-so now, now, right now. Come out, demon, for I bind you with adamantine bonds not to be loosed, and I deliver you to black chaos in utter destruction."

19:18. The word translated "deeds" in the King James Version does have that meaning in the plural; indeed, this is the word used in the title of the "Acts" of the Apostles. Here, however, the word seems to have the special sense which it has in the papyrus just quoted. There it is used in the heading of the magical formula to mean "spell." The heading reads: "An excellent spell for driving out demons." Thus we may translate the reference in Acts, not "declaring their deeds," but "revealing their magical formulas." They have been using the latter but have kept them secret, like magicians today who refuse to reveal the methods by which they accomplish their wonders. It may be noted that in the next verse the reference to "practicing" magical arts uses the same Greek root which verse 18 used for "deeds" or "spells." This supports the suggestion that in verse 18 we should follow the papyrus clue and translate "spells" rather than "deeds." (Better than "deeds" but not so good as "spells" is "practices" in the Revised Standard Version.)

19:28. The use of the title "Great" for a god or goddess

[7] The most convenient collection of such material is Moulton and Milligan, *The Vocabulary of the New Testament Illustrated from the Papyri and Other Non-Literary Sources* (1930); use of this work demands some competence in Greek. Broughton, *An Economic Survey of Ancient Rome*, IV (1938), makes skillful use of inscriptions in historical study.

was common in ancient times and thus was not limited to Artemis. It is known, however, from both literary references and numerous Ephesian inscriptions that it was customary to refer to Artemis in this way.

19:29. The great theater, seating about 25,000 persons, has been excavated. Its present form dates from a time later than Paul's ministry in Ephesus, but its essential size and plan is older than Paul's day. It was entirely natural for the crowd to rush into the theater for an informal assembly, since, as we know from inscriptions, that was the regular place for public meetings. Inscriptions in other cities show that this was common practice elsewhere; it was only natural to meet where a great crowd could find room.

19:31. The Asiarchs are mentioned frequently in inscriptions. They were chosen from families of position and means, and had leadership over the rites of the imperial cult observed by the league of cities in the Roman province of Asia. The office was held for one year, but the title was used of the individual official after he had retired from his year of service. Hence there could be several Asiarchs in Ephesus at the time of the riot, and since the position represented public honor rather than narrow religious zeal, the tolerance of the Asiarchs towards Paul is not surprising.

19:32. The Greek word used for "assembly" is *ekklesia*, which in the New Testament is usually translated "church." The term may be used of the regular legal assembly, as in verse 39, and that sense occurs frequently in Ephesian inscriptions which refer to the meeting of the assembly in the theater. We find one inscription which tells of a Roman official who gave silver and other images of Artemis to be set up on pedestals in the theater at every assembly. The New Testament student should note, however, that the use just illustrated does not convey the full meaning of the word in the New Testament. There the word "church" denotes far more than a public assembly. The word carries on the Old Testament terminology where the people of God are his congregation or assembly, and here as often the Septuagint is a better guide to New Testament meaning than the inscriptions and papyri. But the latter show how people of Hellenistic background might interpret the Christian reference.

19:35. To us the "townclerk" may not suggest an important personage, but the evidence from Ephesus makes it clear that this official was the dominant figure in the political life of the city.[8] Hence the office was held in rotation by the city's leading men. It was thus natural for the crowd to give heed to him, especially as he shrewdly timed his appearance to catch the crowd when it was tired of shouting and ready to listen to the voice of authority.

19:35. The Greek word for "temple-keeper" was widely used of individuals. In pre-Christian times we find a papyrus in Egypt using the term for a Jew who was a "temple-keeper" or attendant of a synagogue in an Egyptian village. An inscription from Priene in Asia Minor refers to a man who was "temple-keeper," i.e., a temple official, of Artemis in Ephesus. A later papyrus names a man who was "temple-keeper of the great Serapis," a famous Egyptian god. Josephus (*Wars* v. 9. 4) speaks of the people of Israel as "temple-keeper" or, better, "guardian" of the shrine of their God. This reference to a people as guardian of a temple resembles both the use in Acts, where the people of Ephesus are called "temple-keeper of the great Artemis," and the other use in which the word refers to the Ephesians as "temple-keeper" of the imperial cult.

The Ephesian inscriptions and Egyptian papyri naturally throw light on numerous other linguistic, historical and religious points throughout the New Testament. The above examples, which deal particularly with the narrative of Acts 19, show how such studies contribute to New Testament interpretation, and indicate that Luke has reflected quite faithfully the conditions in the world in which the apostles preached.

[8] A. H. M. Jones, *The Greek City* (1940), p. 239.

18

LAODICEA AND ITS NEIGHBORS

SHERMAN E. JOHNSON

Colossae, Laodicea and Hierapolis, the three cities of the Lycus valley in Asia Minor, are mentioned only occasionally in the New Testament. One of the apostle Paul's letters was addressed to the church at Colossae and in it he mentions the other cities (Col. 2:1; 4:13-16). The church of Laodicea is addressed in such scathing terms in one of the letters to the seven churches (Rev. 3:14-22) that it has been a byword ever since; yet in the 4th century Laodicea was the meeting place of an important regional council. Hierapolis, nearby, was the home of the Christian writer Papias, and here, according to tradition, the evangelist Philip (Acts 21:8f.) spent his last days. These well-known facts do not, however, tell the whole story. The full significance of the Lycus valley for the development of early Christianity emerges only when all the relevant information from archaeology and early Christian literature is brought together.

The Lycus Valley and the Roman Roads

The Meander river (now called Menderes), which has contributed a verb to the English language, rises in the Phrygian highlands and flows into the Aegean not far from the site of ancient Miletus. More than a hundred miles east of its mouth the Meander is joined by the Lycus (Çürük su), one of its principal tributaries. The junction is near the modern town of Seraiköi, about twelve miles from the site of Laodicea. From Ephesus, near the lower end of the Meander valley, it is an eight hour trip by train to Denizli, the modern successor of Laodicea. The valley presents a striking aspect, with the winding and continually shifting river, the fields marked out by mud walls topped by brush and roads and ditches between the walls at a lower level than the fields. Olives, figs, grapes and broad beans grow in profusion, and stacks of licorice root are piled everywhere.

This typical vegetation of the Mediterranean littoral is gradually left behind as one ascends the Meander. Beyond Seraiköi the railroad comes out from between two mountain ranges into the broad plain of the Lycus, which runs from southeast to northwest, a distance of about twenty-four miles. The Lycus valley has a maximum breadth of a little more than six miles, and its elevation above sea level varies from 500 to 820 feet. Highlands hem it in on the northeast; to the west is Mt. Messogis, which runs along the north side of the lower Meander; and on the south are the great mountains Salbacus (Baba-Dağ, 7590 feet) and Cadmus (Honaz-Dağ, 8250 feet), approached by gradual steppes and foothills.[1]

The Lycus valley is the meeting point of ancient Caria, Lydia and Phrygia, and it looks like the gateway that it is. On the one hand it is closely connected with the lowlands. The olive grows only as far east as Denizli. The region produces sesame, vegetables, fruits and almonds. Where water is plentiful there are groves of trees. But east of here trees are infrequent. The Lycus is on the edge of the steppe land, the lonely sheep country. The ravines of the upper Meander and Lycus lead northeast and southeast into Phrygia. At the northwest end there is an easy pass over the hills, probably not more than 2000 feet high, into the Hermus valley.

The valley was accordingly the junction point of several important roads. Two main routes—now followed by the railroads—led from the Aegean coast to the Anatolian hinterland. One ran from Ephesus up the Meander valley, past Magnesia and Tralles, to Laodicea; then it turned southeast to follow the Lycus and went to Apamea, Pisidian Antioch, Iconium, Tyana, and, through the pass in the Taurus known as the Cilician gates, to Tarsus. The south gate of Laodicea was significantly called the Syrian gate. The second route eastward followed the Hermus valley from Smyrna to

---

[1] A. Philippson, *Reisen und Forschungen im westlichen Kleinasien*, IV (*Petermanns Mitteilungen*, Ergänzungsheft Nr. 180, 1914), pp. 85 f. This work is the finest geographical description of the region and includes a magnificent map, scale 1:300,000.

Sardis and Philadelphia, then ascended the Phrygian mountains in the direction of Ancyra (the modern Ankara).

Laodicea was the first and most important junction point in the system. The two main routes were connected by a road from Laodicea and Hierapolis to Tripolis and Philadelphia. In addition roads ran south over the mountains to Attalia and Perga on the Pamphylian coast, and northeast across Phrygia to Lounda and Brouzos.[2]

The exact itinerary of St. Paul's travels in Asia Minor has often been debated and probably can never be settled. According to Acts the apostle certainly passed through Phrygia on his "second" and "third" missionary journeys. The question is whether "the region of Phrygia and Galatia" (Acts 16:6) refers to two separate localities or should be translated "the Phrygian-and-Galatic region," as Sir William Ramsay thought. In the latter case the apostle may have come through the part of Phrygia which belonged to the Roman province of Galatia and did not go into Galatia proper at all.[3] The route of the so-called "second" journey is obscure, but there is a good chance that Paul went through the Lycus valley on the "third." Acts 18:23 speaks of his going through "the Galatic region and Phrygia," and in 19:1 we read that "having gone through the upper country he came down to Ephesus." Most map-makers in England and America, following Ramsay, take this to mean that Paul came west from Pisidian Antioch, just north of Hierapolis, and followed a hill road across Mt. Messogis down to Ephesus.[4]

[2] Sir William M. Ramsay, *The Historical Geography of Asia Minor* (1890), pp. 35, 49, 59; M. Cary, *The Geographic Background of Greek and Roman History* (1949), pp. 151–64, with maps on pp. 152 and 160; W. M. Calder, *Classical Review*, XXXIX (1925), 7–11.

[3] W. M. Ramsay, *St. Paul the Traveller and the Roman Citizen* (1897), pp. 104, 180 f., 210–12; E. D. Burton, *A Critical and Exegetical Commentary on the Epistle to the Galatians* (1920), pp. xxix–xliv.

[4] G. E. Wright and F. V. Filson, eds., *The Westminster Historical Atlas to the Bible* (2nd ed., 1956), Plate XV. *Hammond's Atlas of the Bible Lands* (n. d. 1949?) gives two choices. On Plate B 26, which gives routes for all of St. Paul's journeys, the third journey goes from Laodicea to Philadelphia, Sardis and Smyrna, while on Plate B 28 the third journey goes between the Meander and Hermus valleys, as in the *Westminster Historical Atlas*. C. C. McCown does not commit himself to any route in

But this is an unnatural and unlikely route. The "upper country" is simply the whole hinterland of Ephesus and refers to "the Galatic region and Phrygia" of 18:23.[5] The most natural route for Paul to take from Syria would be from Tarsus through the Cilician gates to Derbe, Lystra, Iconium, Pisidian Antioch, Apamea, Colossae and Laodicea in the Lycus valley, and down the Meander to Ephesus. From Laodicea he may have crossed the pass to Philadelphia and so have come down the Hermus valley, but this would have been far less likely.

Ramsay and other geographers have no doubt been influenced in their choice of routes by the statement of Colossians 2:1, "For I want you to know how great a conflict I have on behalf of you and those in Laodicea and as many as have not seen my face personally" (literally "in the flesh"). The Greek does not, however, compel us to suppose that the Christians of the Lycus do not know Paul personally; and even if most of them were later converts and did not know him by sight, he may well have passed through their cities on one of the journeys.

Colossae

The site of Colossae is toward the upper end of the Lycus valley, perhaps eleven or twelve miles east and a little south of Laodicea, not far east of the Botzeli station on the railroad. The valley, less than two miles wide and walled in by great precipices, is largely covered with travertine deposits through which the river has cut its bed. The city stood on a small double hill or terrace south of the Lycus, hemmed in on two sides by streams that flowed from the snows of Mt. Cadmus.[6]

A Remapping of the Bible World (1949), Plate 40. E. G. Kraeling, *Rand McNally Bible Atlas* (1961), map XX and p. 446, brings the apostle through Colossae and Laodicea. L. H. Grollenberg, *Atlas of the Bible* (1956), endpaper map II, assumes that Paul came to Hieropolis from the northeast, missing Colossae and Laodicea, and went down the Meander valley. Cf. also S. Talip, *Le stiade romane in Anatolia* (1938).

[5] K. Lake and H. J. Cadbury, *The Beginnings of Christianity*, IV (1933), 235 f.

[6] Philippson, pp. 96 f.; Victor Schultze, *Altchristliche Städte und Landschaften, II. Kleinasien* (1922), pp. 445–49.

Little is known of the city's history. It was, according to Herodotus (vii. 30), a great city as early as the time of Xerxes, and Xenophon marched past it with the ten thousand (*Anabasis* i. 2. 6). In contrast to the newer towns, Laodicea and Hierapolis, it was ancient and autochthonous, i.e. populated by natives of Phrygia. Although it was a center for wool industry and dyeing, by New Testament times it had been eclipsed by its neighbors. Colossae must originally have been of military importance, since it commanded the road eastward toward Apamea and the Cilician gates.

Coins of the city show that in the Roman period Isis and Serapis were worshiped here, together with Helios, Demeter, Selene, Artemis the huntress and the Ephesian Artemis, and the native Phrygian god Men.[7] Paul's letter to the Colossians lifts the veil a little, and discloses a church whose members were attracted toward a curious perversion of Christianity, in which Jewish and pagan elements were mingled. The letter speaks of reverence to angels (1:16; 2:15, 18), rules or scruples about foods and holy days (2:16), and some type of asceticism (2:23; 3:5-10). If the obscure verse 2:18 refers to a pride produced by visions and revelations, it does not seem strange in a Phrygian background.

Epaphras, Paul's disciple, had been active in the evangelization of the Lycus cities (Col. 1:7 f.; 4:12 f.; Philemon 23). Buckler and Calder believed that they had found the name on a marble altar from Laodicea discovered at Denizli.[8] Epaphras is, of course, a shortened form of the not uncommon name Epaphroditus, and an inscription from Colossae mentions one T. Asinius Epaphroditus.[9]

Colossae was later the site of a bishopric, but the name of only one bishop is known—Epiphanius, whose metropolitan, Nunechius of Laodicea, signed the decrees of Chalcedon

[7] Schultze, p. 447.

[8] W. H. Buckler and W. M. Calder, *Monumenta Asiae Minoris Antiqua*, Vol. VI. *Monuments and Documents from Phrygia and Caria* (1939), p. 1. Here and in W. M. Ramsay, *The Cities and Bishoprics of Phrygia*, Vol. I (1895), is to be found most of the important inscriptional material bearing on Colossae and Laodicea.

[9] Buckler and Calder, p. 15. The authors remark (p. xi), "To archaeological research Kolossai offers attractions similar to that of Sardis: historical renown plus an accessible site completely unoccupied."

in 451. Some time about the year 700 the city was deserted, no doubt because of earthquakes, and the population moved to Chonai (the modern Honaz), which lies nearer the foot of Mt. Cadmus.

When Hamilton visited the site in 1835 he saw huge blocks of stone, foundations of buildings, and fragments of cornices, architraves, and columns.[10] These have since been quarried out and used for building operations in Honaz and elsewhere. Actual excavation might, however, yield interesting results because of the city's great antiquity.

Laodicea

The history of Laodicea is much better known than that of Colossae and has been more fully studied. Before the Seleucid period the town had borne the names of Diospolis and Rhoas. Antiochus II refounded it about 250–240 B.C. as a military stronghold on the north border of his realm, and named it for his sister-wife Laodice.[11] Not long afterward it was able to erect with its own funds a meeting hall for its *strategoi*, or magistrates.[12] After Laodicea passed into Roman hands as part of the province of Asia, it developed greatly in wealth and importance. Although suffering severe damage from earthquakes in the reigns of Tiberius and Nero, the city was able to rebuild without imperial or provincial help. Its chief source of wealth was the world-famous black glossy wool of the region.[13] It is not certain whether the color came from a special breed of black sheep, for which there is some evidence, or from dyes. The water of the Lycus was in any event well suited for dyeing. The wool was not woven into bolts of cloth, as in modern times, but directly into garments of the shapes and sizes required—dalmatics, *paragaudae* with purple borders, *chlamydes* or short cloaks, and the *paenulae* (II Tim. 4:13) or seamless overcoats with

[10] W. J. Hamilton, *Researches in Asia Minor, Pontus and Armenia* (1842), I, 509.

[11] Pauly-Wissowa, *Real-Encyclopädie*, XXIII, cols. 722–24. This article lists most of the important coins, inscriptions and literary references relating to Laodicea.

[12] Buckler and Calder, p. x.

[13] Buckler and Calder, p. 11, publish an inscription which seems to refer to a guild of graziers in Laodicea. There was a similar organization at Hierapolis.

a hole for the head, woven to resist rain, which later became popular in Rome and finally developed into the ecclesiastical chasuble. The city was also a center for banking; in fact Cicero planned to cash drafts there on his way through Asia Minor (*Ad Fam.* iii. 5).

Laodicea apparently included in its population a large colony of Jews. When the propraetor Flaccus seized the gold collected there for the Jerusalem temple in 62 or 61 B.C. he found that it amounted to more than twenty pounds in weight. Josephus tells of a letter sent by the Laodiceans a few years later to Gaius Rabirius, proconsul of Asia, informing him that in obedience to his command they will permit the Jews to keep the Sabbath and their sacred rites and that the Jews will be regarded as their friends and confederates (*Ant.* xiv. 10. 20)—this although the citizens of Tralles, farther down the Meander valley, were opposed to the decree. Thus there is evidence for oppression of the Jews in this region.

Political life in the province of Asia centered in the *koinon* or council of the province, one of the chief functions of which was maintenance of the worship of the emperor. The imperial cultus was introduced early into Laodicea, and the city proudly participated in the *koinon*. The coins bear witness to several treaties of *homonoia* or friendship between Laodicea and other cities of the province such as Smyrna, Pergamum and Ephesus. But there is no evidence that the city received the honor of *neokoros* or temple-keeper of the imperial cult, on which Ephesus prided itself (Acts 19:35), before the reign of Commodus.[14] Other gods worshiped in Laodicea were Zeus Laodicenus (perhaps a native Phrygian god later Hellenized), a goddess, who figures rather little on coins, and Asclepius. The last-named may have been identified with Men Karou, a healing deity whose temple was at Attouda, a few miles to the west. The famous medical school of Laodicea may have been under his aegis.[15]

---

[14] Acts 19:35 refers to Ephesus as *neokoros* of Artemis; the worship of the local goddess and the emperor was, however, closely intertwined.

[15] Ramsay, *Cities and Bishoprics*, pp. 51–55; *The Letters to the Seven Churches* (1904), pp. 417–19. By the year 150, joint worship of Zeus Laodicenus and the emperor had been established. For other information on this region, cf. S. E. Johnson, *JBL*, LXXVII (1958), 1–17.

The names of a number of famous Laodiceans of the period from 100 B.C. to A.D. 200 are known to us. Most of them were members of the family of Zenon, the orator who encouraged the people to defend their city when the Parthians under Labienus and Pacorus invaded Asia Minor. Zenon's son became king of Lycaonia, Pontus, and part of Cilicia in the first century B.C. M. Antonius Polemo, a noted literary figure who lived about A.D. 90–146, belonged to this family. The city produced a few intellectuals such as the skeptics Antiochus and Theiodas of the school of Zeuxis (*Diogenes Laertius* ix. 116). But Laodicea does not appear to have been particularly distinguished as a center of culture. It was rather a bustling, ambitious mercantile center, loyal to the empire, proudly situated at the road-junction, on the very edge of the barbarian highlands.

Christianity spread to Laodicea within a generation of Jesus' death, as we know from the letter to the Colossians. It is an attractive hypothesis that Paul addressed the little letter to Philemon to the Laodicean church, and intended it to be sent on to Colossae and read there also.[16] It was a natural place for a wealthy slave-owner to live. Lightfoot remarks that the name Philemon, though borne by a famous Phrygian, that husband of Baucis who offered hospitality to Zeus, is not distinctively Phrygian, and that while it is found in inscriptions of the country, it does not occur with any special frequency.[17] But Ramsay published an inscription from Laodicea, evidently erected by a freedman to one Marcus Sestius Philemon.[18] While it would be fanciful to identify this with our Philemon, it is clear that the city had at least one prominent citizen of this name who owned slaves. The Apphia of Philemon 2 is usually taken to be Philemon's wife. The masculine form of this Phrygian

[16] E. J. Goodspeed, *An Introduction to the New Testament* (1937), pp. 109–24, adopts and develops the earlier theory of K. G. Wieseler. It ought also to be remembered that the 2nd century heretic Marcion regarded the epistle to the Ephesians as a letter to the Laodiceans. Ernst Percy, *Die Probleme der Kolosser- und Epheserbriefe* (1946), pp. 451–58, identifies the "letter from Laodicea" of Col. 4:16 as Ephesians, and believes that it was originally sent to several churches in inner Asia Minor.

[17] J. B. Lightfoot, *Saint Paul's Epistles to the Colossians and to Philemon* (3rd ed., 1879), p. 302.

[18] Ramsay, *Cities and Bishoprics*, p. 72.

name, Apphios or Apphianos, is attested from Hierapolis.[19] One is even tempted to wonder if Luke the physician, who joins in the salutations (Philemon 24; Col. 4:14), and who may or may not be the author of Luke-Acts, did not at one time study medicine at the Laodicean school.[20]

In the last decade of the first century, when the book of Revelation was written, the Laodicean church was reproved by the prophet John: it was neither cold nor hot, but lukewarm; it boasted that it was rich and in need of nothing, not knowing that it was poor, blind and naked; therefore let it buy of the risen Christ gold refined by fire, white garments and salve for the blind eyes (Rev. 3:14-22). Sir William Ramsay saw local references in this—Laodicea was rich, famous for its garments, and perhaps the "Phrygian powder" for diseases of the eyes was compounded here.[21] One might go on in the same vein and suppose that the city water of Laodicea was literally lukewarm. This has been suggested by commentators,[22] and it is not impossible. One of the few remaining monuments of the city is the water tower, the terra-cotta pipes of which are completely choked by lime deposits. The water came, not from Hierapolis, but from the south, first by aqueduct and then, nearer the city, through stone barrel pipes.[23] All of this was seen by Hamilton more than a hundred years ago, but the stones have since disappeared, along with most of the other ruins of Laodicea— some of them unfortunately used by the builders of the railroad. The water may have come from hot springs, of which there are many in the neighborhood, and have been

[19] *Ibid.*, p. 88; Lightfoot, p. 305.
[20] The school was established by Zeuxis and later carried on by Alexander Philalethes of Laodicea (Strabo xii. 8. 20). I must make it clear that this suggestion, like some of Sir William Ramsay, is no more than guesswork.
[21] *Cities and Bishoprics,* pp. 39 f., 52; *Letters to the Seven Churches,* pp. 428 f.
[22] H. B. Swete, *The Apocalypse of St. John* (3rd ed., 1907), saw in the statement of Rev. 3:16 an allusion to the water of Hierapolis, which becomes lukewarm by the time it has fallen over the cliff. "The allusion is the more apposite since the letter for Laodicea was practically addressed to the other Churches of the Lycus valley." Unfortunately a later commentator speaks of these springs as becoming lukewarm by the time they reach Laodicea and form a waterfall!
[23] Hamilton, p. 515.

cooled down to lukewarmness; but even if it was originally cold, the heat of the sun no doubt warmed it until it was flat and unpalatable.

Eusebius tells of a paschal controversy in Laodicea about A.D. 164–66 (*H. E.* iv. 26. 3), and about this time its bishop Sagaris, who bore a Phrygian name, was martyred (v. 24. 5). As the seat of the metropolitan of the neighborhood, the city was important ecclesiastically. The synod of Laodicea, held in 367, though only a regional council, is highly significant for the history of the New Testament canon and for the development of church law generally.[24] The council's stringent measures against Montanist and Quartodeciman Christians, and its rules for worship, exhibit the final triumph of orthodox uniformity over local Phrygian peculiarities. It is striking that the council's list of twenty-six canonical New Testament books omits the book of Revelation, even though it had been written not far away and must have profoundly influenced Christian thought in Asia Minor. The council was evidently controlled, not by local sentiment, but by the consensus of the church in the eastern Mediterranean. Laodicea continued to be an important city until the Seljuk period; then, in the 14th century, it was abandoned, and Denizli took its place.

The site is a little hill or plateau, about a square mile in area, lying between two small tributaries of the Lycus. In almost every direction high mountains are visible, snow-capped through much of the year, and the white travertine deposits of Hierapolis are plainly to be seen, six miles away, with the broad expanse of the Lycus valley in the foreground. Two theaters, of uncertain date, are still to be seen; so are the baths (or gymnasium), and blocks of stone from the eastern gate, as well as the stadium, which was probably dedicated in A.D. 79.

Hierapolis

Hierapolis was a place well fitted to excite the imagination of the ancients. The Charonion, a cave filled with deadly

[24] Th. Zahn, *Geschichte des neutestamentliche Kanons* (1890), II, 193–202. An English translation of the canon, is given in C. J. Hefele, *A History of the Councils of the Church* (1876), II, 295–325, together with comments.

fumes, now no longer identifiable, and the hot springs—
not unlike the Mammoth Hot Springs of Yellowstone—were
no doubt from earliest times sacred to nature divinities. The
town stood on a terrace a mile and a third long and several
hundred yards wide, from which a precipitous cliff drops
down toward the Lycus plain. In the sunlight the cliff, over
which several streams flow, is blinding white, though
streaked here and there with yellow and black, and its appearance is that of a frozen waterfall.

On reaching the top of the terrace, which has an elevation of 1296 feet, as compared with 732 feet for the bridge
across the Lycus river below, one sees reddish-brown stone
buildings of the Roman period surrounded by grassy pasture,
and behind them a pool in the middle of the terrace, hemmed
about with oleander bushes, from which the streams flow to
the cliff. The temperature of the pool is 95° F. The waters
are milky from tertiary marl and contain carbonates, sulphates and chlorides of calcium and sodium. The flow has
been estimated at 10,000 gallons per minute, and about
twenty-six cubic yards of deposit is laid down daily. It is
estimated that the lower courses of the buildings are covered
to a depth of at least six feet with this deposit.[25]

Hierapolis probably took its name from a mythical Amazon
queen Hiera, and thus does not originally mean "holy city."
The name may have been given by the Pergamene kings.
The area was under Seleucid control in the 3rd century B.C.,
but after 190 B.C. it came under Pergamum and the city
may have been built up by Eumenes II as a defense against
Laodicea. Shortly after 190 an inscription, which is the first
evidence of Hierapolis' existence, calls it a city, and coins
begin to appear. It became part of the Roman empire in 133
B.C.[26] Wool, metal working and stone cutting industries
were developed.[27] The stones of the baths are beautifully cut
and joined.

We have a continuous series of coins of Hierapolis from
the time of Augustus to the early years of Nero's reign, when

[25] Philippson, pp. 68 f.; F. Akçakoca Akça, *Pamukkale Suları*
(2nd ed., 1946). The local name is Pamukkale ("cotton castle").
[26] Carl Humann, Conrad Cichorius and others, *Altertümer von Hierapolis* (*Jahrbuch des kaiserlich deutschen archaeologischen Instituts*, Ergänzungsheft IV, 1898), pp. 22–27.
[27] Schultze, p. 413.

the coins stop abruptly. The city was extensively destroyed by an earthquake in A.D. 60, and only in the middle of Trajan's reign, fifty years later, do a few types of coins again begin to appear. Thus Hierapolis was just being restored to normal life and wealth at the time when we hear of famous Christians, like Philip the evangelist and Papias, as residents of the place. Its prosperity was broken now and again by later earthquakes, but a Hierapolitan, the sophist Antipater, was secretary to Septimius Severus and tutor of his sons, Geta and Caracalla. Caracalla seems to have honored the city with the neocorate. Hierapolis was a flourishing episcopal see in Byzantine times, and finally became the seat of a metropolitan. Some time in the middle ages it was ruined and finally deserted.

When Denizli was built, Laodicea served as the principal quarry, and Hierapolis, being farther away, was spared the extensive depredation suffered by its neighbor.

Two theaters are still to be seen—the smaller one, which belongs to the Hellenistic age, and the Roman theater on the side of the hill at the east edge of the city, which is one of the most impressive archaeological remains of Asia Minor. Though not to be compared with the vast theater at Pergamum, it has a front width of more than 325 feet and an orchestra measuring about sixty-five feet in diameter; it overlooks the city and the Lycus valley. Most of the seats remain, and some stones of the scene building are still in place.

On the west side of the city, at the edge of the cliff, the baths cover a large area. Some of the great arches are still standing, with a width of as much as fifty-two feet and containing stones as large as seventy-eight inches by thirty-five inches by twenty-eight inches, laid without mortar. Next to the baths are the monolithic pillars of what appears to be a gymnasium, and to the northeast of this, and east of the present pool, is what Humann called the statuary hall because he believed that the niches in the walls had held statues of emperors.[28] Some of these buildings are dated by archaeologists about A.D. 100.

Hierapolis was apparently laid out all at one time, and in typical Hellenistic fashion, with a great street running the length of the city, from southeast to northwest, with cov-

[28] Humann, *Altertümer von Hieropolis*, pp. 12 f.

ered sidewalks on either side, and cross streets at right angles. Along this street are numerous tombs, of no particular artistic interest, and a large cemetery lies beyond the north gate.

The original colonists of Hierapolis were no doubt Greeks of Macedonian and Pergamene origin. Many Romans settled there, and in all probability native Phrygians were absorbed into the population. This is confirmed by what we know of the local religions. Apollo Archegetes, to whom one of the theaters was dedicated, and who had a temple next to the Charonion, was identified with the native god Lairbenos. Leto, or Cybele, was served by eunuch priests, who —it was believed—alone knew how to go through the fumes of the Charonion with safety. The healing deities Asclepius and Hygeia were also worshiped, along with Pluto, Men, Isis, and many others. The imperial cult is known at least from the time of Caracalla on.[29]

The next largest community was Jewish. Inscriptions speak of "the people of the Jews," "the settlement of the Jews who dwell in Hierapolis," and "the archives of the Jews." P. Aelius Glycon directs that his grave shall be decorated annually on the feast of Unleavened Bread and Pentecost.[30] In the course of time these Jews disappeared, probably by absorption into the Christian church. The Talmud preserves a memory of this in a saying which alludes to Hierapolis: "The wines and the baths of Phrygia have separated the ten tribes from Israel" (*T. Bab. Shabbath* 147b).

Perhaps the most famous man that Hierapolis ever produced was Epictetus, a younger contemporary of the Christian Onesimus, and like him a slave. Epictetus knew relatively little about Christianity, which must have come to the Lycus valley when he was a child. It is significant that at one point when he speaks of Jews he may actually mean Christians. "Whenever we see a man wavering," he says, "we are accustomed to say, 'He is not a Jew but is pretending to be one.' But when he adopts the inward disposition of the man who has been baptized and made a decision, then he is really one and is called a Jew" (ii. 9. 20). Baptism was the initiatory rite of both Jews and Christians, and some of

[29] Strabo xiii. 4. 14; Humann, *Altertümer von Hierapolis*, pp. 42–44.

[30] Humann, *Altertümer von Hierapolis*, Inscriptions 69, 212, 342.

those who were known to the Colossian Christians were certainly Jews—Mark, Barnabas, Jesus Justus, and perhaps some others.

According to the tradition handed down by Polycrates of Ephesus, Philip the evangelist spent the latter part of his life in Hierapolis. Polycrates and later tradition make no distinction between the evangelist and the apostle (Eusebius *H. E.* iii. 31. 3), although the Philip of Acts 21:8 f. who had four daughters is there called an evangelist and one of the Seven. Philip no doubt belonged to the Jewish community; on the other hand, his four daughters were prophetesses, and there were women prophets in Phrygia at a later time. An inscription refers to a church in Hierapolis built in Philip's honor: "Eugenius the least, archdeacon who is in charge of [the church of] the holy and glorious apostle and theologian Philip." At least four Christian churches can be identified in Hierapolis. Cichorius refers this inscription to a great basilica which stands outside the city in the older part of the necropolis. He suggests that the church was erected on what was believed to be the location of the saint's tomb.[31] Victor Schultze was, however, inclined to identify Eugenius' church with an octagonal building east of the city in another cemetery. This he assigned to the end of the 4th or the beginning of the 5th century. The octagonal form was usual in the 4th century for memorial churches, and the dimensions (twenty-eight and one-half feet for each of the eight sides; diameter sixty-nine feet) are comparable to those of the octagon in Constantine's church at Bethlehem.[32] If this building was not a baptistry, it was almost certainly a *martyrium*.

The most prominent and enigmatic Christian figure of the city was Papias, author of the *Exposition of the Oracles of the Lord* in five books. He commented on some of the materials of the gospels, but apparently all that he says about the gospels is for the purpose of depreciating them,[33] for he much preferred the "living and abiding voice" of oral tradi-

---

[31] Cichorius in Humann, *Altertümer von Hieropolis*, pp. 46 f.; Inscription 24. Several white lambs were penned up in one corner of the church when we visited it on March 14, 1948.

[32] Schultze, pp. 430 f.; J. W. Crowfoot, *Early Churches in Palestine* (1941), pp. 18, 22–30; André Grabar, *Archaeology*, II (1949), 95–104.

[33] I owe this suggestion to my colleague, Prof. Charles H. Buck, Jr.

tion to any written gospels. He was essentially an antiquarian, intensely interested in anything that "elders" or Christians of an older generation could tell him, and an avid collector of prophecies, the more fantastic the better. Perhaps he was a native of the old Phrygian stock. His name, well known from inscriptions and coins, was an epithet of Zeus, and when applied to a mortal might correspond to "Diogenes." Yet a contemporary rabbi, known to us from the Mishnah, bore what is apparently the same name.[34]

We have already noted that Paul in writing to the Colossians denounced the worship of angels. Papias also refers to the angels, saying, "To some of them he [i.e. God] gave charge over the affairs of the earth and he ordered them to rule well. . . . But their order ended in nothing."[35] Papias was either affected by speculations on the role of angels, or wished to warn his Christian neighbors that angels are subordinate beings who sometimes have sinned, who must not be given the reverence due to Christ alone. Canon 35 of the Council of Laodicea forbids the worship of angels. It may not be by accident that the book of Revelation, despite the immense part that angels play in it, contains a similar warning: When John fell down before the angel to worship him, the latter forbade it, saying, "I am thy fellow servant, . . . worship God" (Rev. 22:8-9).

A full study of Christianity in the Lycus valley would have to take account of later Montanism in Phrygia and the religious situation in the churches of the lower Meander valley. One point may be mentioned here in passing.

Papias' absorbing interest was in the literal coming of a messianic age, in which grain and wine would be produced in miraculous plenty.[36] A generation or less before his book was written, apocalyptic had appeared at the other end of the Meander valley; the prophet John saw the visions of the book of Revelation on the island of Patmos, not far from Miletus. These are two types of apocalyptic. A third is seen in the fourth book of the Sibylline Oracles, which must be

[34] Lightfoot, p. 48; Shekalim 4:7; Eduyoth 7:6; R. M. Grant, *Anglican Theological Review*, XXV (1943), 218-22.

[35] Andrew of Caesarea in *Apoc.* 34. 12; R. M. Grant, *Second-Century Christianity* (1946), p. 68.

[36] Irenaeus v. 33. 3 f.; Grant, *Second-Century Christianity*, pp. 66 f.

dated in A.D. 81 and was almost certainly written in the Meander valley or not far from it.[37] It is not clear whether the book is Jewish or Christian. As in Epictetus, so in this oracle, baptism is the outer mark of the convert to Judaism; not a word is said about circumcision. One is tempted to think of those disciples whom Paul met at Ephesus a generation earlier (Acts 19:1–5), who knew nothing of the gift of the Holy Spirit but had received the baptism of John. It should be remembered that Judaism and Christianity were not yet completely distinct religions. Many people must still have had a "dual membership" as late as the time of the Fourth Gospel, when believers in Christ were being excommunicated from the synagogues (John 9:22, 34; 16:1). And what are we to think of Revelation 2:9, which speaks of those in Philadelphia who say they are Jews but lie—for they belong to the synagogue of Satan? Finally, when Ignatius of Antioch writes to the church at Magnesia on the Meander, early in the 2nd century, he devotes most of his letter to the danger of relapse into Judaism. When the Council of Laodicea met in the late 4th century, there was probably not much danger that Christians would actually embrace Judaism, but there may have been some sabbath-keeping, for Canon 29 of the council reads: "Christians shall not Judaize and be idle on Saturday, but shall work on that day."

It appears, then, that the Christianity of Laodicea and its neighbors was subjected to various sorts of influences—Jewish, pagan, apocalyptic, prophetic, perhaps even Gnostic—and went through many vicissitudes in the first two centuries. Jewish and Christian preachers of different and dynamic personalities left their mark on the churches of the Lycus valley in this formative period. Since these cities were on the main highway, this is to be expected. Further archaeological discovery, it is hoped, may some day provide us with a clearer picture of Christianity in this region.

[37] Lightfoot, pp. 94 f.; S. E. Johnson, *JNES*, V (1946), 52, and literature cited there.

19

ATHENS
"City of Idol Worship"

OSCAR BRONEER

For although there may be so-called gods in heaven or on earth—as indeed there are many "gods" and many "lords"—yet for us there is one God. . . .

(I Cor. 8:5)

The story of Paul's travels and missionary work in Greece is told in the book of Acts with an economy of words that in many cases borders on obscurity. This is particularly true of his visit in Athens. From the brief account of his experiences there and from the wording of his speech to the Council of Areopagites we may, however, make some inferences regarding his stay in the city.

The writer of the Acts, whom I shall call Luke, implies that Paul's visit in Athens was comparatively brief and was perhaps not a part of his planned itinerary in Greece. He had been hustled out of Macedonia in great haste, leaving behind his two lieutenants, Silas and Timotheos. He did not travel alone, but we are told that those who accompanied him to Athens returned to Macedonia with instructions for Silas and Timotheos to come to him as quickly as they could. Perhaps there was a change of plans, otherwise why did not Paul give these instructions before he left? In any case, it seems unlikely that he remained entirely alone in Athens. Dare we suppose that Luke, or someone who made notes that were later used by the writer of Acts, was with Paul in Athens? The arrival of his helpers seems to have been delayed, and he left for Corinth before they reached him.

If he went to Athens chiefly to await his companions, and perhaps to lay plans for a longer stay in Corinth, he would not have been prepared for the type of organized work that would result in the founding of a church. He seems to have spent part of his time sight-seeing—"going about and examining objects of religious devotion."[1] The time proved to have been well spent, for while he took in the sights of the famous city he gathered material for a speech that he was later called upon to deliver before the council members of the Areopagos. He was thus able to begin his speech with references to facts well known to his hearers.

Paul was probably attracted by the fame of Athens as a center of the arts and of pagan learning. At his first sight of the city he must have come under the magic spell that Athens casts upon every visitor from afar. We would do the apostle an injustice if we assume that he passed up the opportunity to look upon the renowned monuments of Athens, or that seeing them he remained unmoved by their aesthetic appeal. But what he saw disturbed the apostle's spirit. So numerous were the shrines and altars and statues of gods and heroes that the city appeared to him to be wholly given over to the worship of idols.

Let us imagine that in his walks through the city he had engaged a local guide, perhaps one of the Jewish residents whose acquaintance he had made in the synagogue. What are the sights that his cicerone would have pointed out as especially worthy of the attention and interest of Paul and his fellow-travelers?

The Areopagos and the Acropolis

They begin their tour at the Areopagos, and the guide tells them that the hill was named after Ares, the god of war, because he stood trial here for the slaying of Halirrhotios, son of the sea-god Poseidon. A god appearing as a murderer in trial before a human court! Ever since, this rocky eminence has served as the meeting place of the most ancient court and council of Athens. On the spot where the trials are held are two stones upon which the defendant and his accuser sit

[1] Acts 17:23. The translation of the Apostle's words in *RSV*—"For as I passed along, and observed the objects of your worship" —seems to me too weak. The two participles used in the Greek imply more purposeful action than the rendering in English conveys.

as they face each other during the trial. Below the rock they see a cave with a cult of the Erinyes, dread goddesses of the underworld, whose office it is to avenge the shedding of kindred blood. Nearby are altars of other gods and a monument of Oidipous, who slew his father and married his mother. Further up the slope, below the entrance to the Acropolis, they pass by an altar of Ge Kourotrophos and a shrine of Green Demeter, the grain goddess. And closely associated with these is the cult of Aphrodite en Blaute, whom the eastern visitors recognize as akin to the Oriental goddess of love and fertility. Then on their right, as they approach the Propylaia, they look up at the exquisite little Ionic temple of Athena Nike. Its small precinct is surrounded with a parapet, sculptured with figures of Victories in varied and interesting poses. They walk up some marble steps to look closer at the temple with its altar and sculptural decoration. In the frieze above the columns there are battle scenes in one of which both men and women are engaged. As they leave the precinct to enter the Propylaia they become aware of a triple figure of Hekate, the awesome queen of the lower world. Within the Propylaia they see a bearded figure of Hermes, the messenger god, a work of the sculptor Alkamenes, who was a pupil and colleague of Pheidias. Here too is a relief of three shapely figures, the Graces, carved by Sokrates, the philosopher. In the north wing of the Propylaia they enter a small room devoted to a display of paintings by Polygnotos and other Athenian masters. As they pass through the Propylaia they look upon a statue of a dying warrior, Diitrephes, his body riddled by arrows. Nearby they see the likeness of a lioness, set up in honor of a woman said to have been tortured to death by the tyrants; to the end she refused to tell the plot of the tyrant slayers, whose statues stand in the Agora.

The impressions begin to crowd upon Paul, and he finds it difficult to keep his mind upon the information offered by the guide. Minor monuments fade into insignificance as he looks through the east colonnade of the Propylaia and sees for the first time the majestic columns of the Parthenon and the colossal figure of Athena Promachos. The latter is a dedication made out of spoils taken from the Persians at Marathon. Here is one of the famous works of Pheidias, whose name he will hear many times during his tour of Athens. And the great temple of Athena, seen in its setting on the sacred rock, leaves the impression on the visitor that the architect has here attained perfection of line and proportion beyond which it is not possible to go without making a new start in architectural form. Paul is not unmoved by this sight, and it depresses him to think that so much human skill has been wasted upon gods who do not exist. The great size and subtle refinements of the temple and the exquisite finish of its sculptural decoration must, for the moment at least, silence irrelevant remarks. The visitor will then perhaps ask questions about the pedimental groups. He learns that the seated figure in the center of the east gable is Zeus, from whose head Athena sprang fully armed, and that the accompanying figures represent other gods assembled to witness the miraculous birth of the warrior goddess. At the west end of the temple another group of gods and heroes look on as two of the major gods, Athena and Poseidon, contend for the possession of Attica. Athena displays the olive tree as her gift to the Athenians, while Poseidon shows the salt well, as a symbol of the sea, the element in which he is the ruler. Did not the Athenians establish their pre-eminence by gaining mastery of the sea? His arguments are in vain; Athena remains in power. So the Greeks make their gods quarrel about land and boundaries like the heirs in a human family. Below these major groups is the outer frieze whose metopes depict battle scenes in mythological wars, the meaning of which the otherwise well-informed guide does not explain. Looking between the columns they see above the walls of the cella a sculptured frieze with an unbroken procession of horsemen and of walking men and animals in celebration of the festival of Athena. This is the Panathenaia, in which the Athenians display their superior skills and their devotion to the maiden goddess. The party returns to the east entrance, and there, standing before the vast doors of the cult room they see, dimly at first in the reduced light of the interior, the gold and ivory image of Athena herself, rising to a height of forty feet. Here is one of Pheidias' greatest works, whose fame has reached to the remote parts of the Roman empire where Paul and his companions spent their childhood.

From the Parthenon they walk to the south wall of the Acropolis where they see a whole row of figures of warriors, both men and women, shown either dead or about to die.

These are Gauls and Amazons in defeat, dedications by King Attalos of Pergamon, who like his sons endeared himself to the Athenians by lavish gifts to the city.

On their walk across the Acropolis to the north side they pass many other statues of gods and famous men, until they reach the great altar of Athena. Then they come to another temple, dedicated to the same goddess, at the same time housing cults of lesser gods and heroes. Here are shrines of the early kings of Athens, Kekrops and Erechtheus, and here the two deities, who on the west pediment of the Parthenon appear in bitter rivalry with each other, occupy separate compartments beneath a common roof. For a moment the tourist stands speechless before this display of Athenian genius and devotion to beauty. In its graceful lines and richness of design it seems to surpass anything he has ever looked upon in his travels through the Greek world. If Paul's mind became confused by all he heard about the larger temple of Athena, the Erechtheion seems doubly difficult to comprehend. Who is Butes, whose altar stands in the cult room of Athena between altars of Erechtheus and Hephaistos (Vulcan), and whose descendants are shown in paintings on the walls of the room? What is the significance of the large bronze lamp, a work of another famous sculptor, Kallimachos, the flame of which is said never to go out? What facts lie behind the legends about Poseidon's salt water spring and trident mark in the rock, about the sacred olive tree that grew one cubit in one day after it had been burned to the ground by the Persians? Why is the tomb of Kekrops so holy that marble figures of Athenian women stand guard over the king's remains? And why is so much significance attached to the homely little wooden idol of Athena Polias? Can it be that the Athenians believe that this object, like so many other crude likenesses of gods, has fallen from heaven? All the statues of gold or silver or of ivory or of wood, the objects of idolatrous worship, do they not show the utter falsity of the Athenian claim to superior knowledge? Are they not testimonies to the ignorance of the human mind, to the need for revelation from God? Here, in the holiest of all the shrines of the Greeks, every available space within the walls is filled to crowding with proofs of superstition and fear of gods that have no existence.

Before leaving the Acropolis the guide, wishing further to

display his learning, discourses upon many of the less famous buildings and dedications. He takes them south of the Propylaia, to the court in front of the sanctuary of Artemis Brauronia, and explains the significance of bronze and marble bears dedicated in the shrine. He tells the story of the Trojan Horse, as they stand before the statue of a horse with figures of Greek heroes peeping out of the hollow interior. Statues of Athena are everywhere, often shown as engaged in activities that would do little honor to a mortal. By the Propylaia she appears in a statue by Pyrrhos as the goddess of healing. A little further up the slope she is shown as a disappointed flute player, looking in disgust upon the flutes lying on the ground, and in front of her stands an uncouth Marsyas eyeing the instrument with undisguised desire. These exquisitely wrought figures are the works of Myron, an early contemporary of Pheidias. Another statue shows the goddess with spindle and distaff in her hands, like a working woman. And again, in a figure which the guide calls the Lemnian Athena, by the hand of Pheidias himself, she appears in such divine beauty and composure as to belie the significance of the warlike armor she wears. An exquisite little relief, almost overlooked because of its small size, shows her standing with bowed head in front of a marble plaque recording the names of men killed in battle. Interspersed among these many statues of gods are portraits of men, whose valorous deeds the guide is quick to extol. He displays his knowledge of Athenian art by naming the sculptor with each statue. The names of Kritias, Myron, Kalamis, Strongylion, Lykios, and many others unknown to his listeners, roll glibly off his tongue as he discourses upon their famous works. Near the Propylaia they stop in front of a portrait of Perikles by Kresilas. Here the newcomers to Athens listen to a discourse on Athenian history and a review of the factors upon which the Athenians base their claim of superiority over the rest of the Greeks.

Other Famous Monuments

Among the monuments and great buildings from the time of Athenian pre-eminence there are not a few reminders of Roman imperial power. The most flagrant intrusion of the new among the old is a circular marble building placed directly in front of the entrance to the Parthenon. Its architectural details are clearly copied from the Erechtheion, but its inscription in large Latin letters flaunts the conquerors' cult of Roma and Augustus. Another monument, conspicuously placed at the winding ascent to the Propylaia, supports a statue of Agrippa, Augustus' dynamic minister and administrator. Standing on its lofty pedestal it dwarfs the smaller, more beautiful monuments of earlier times. Originally the high base carried a chariot group of Eumenes of Pergamon, whose statue was later removed. A similar replacement has been made on the other side of the Acropolis entrance, where an equestrian statue of Germanicus, adopted son of Tiberius and grandfather of the emperor Nero, stands on a base designed for an earlier monument. Such changes, from Greek to Roman, here seem nearer the surface than elsewhere. Athens, with its tradition of Hellenic art and letters, has resisted the impact of Rome to an extent impossible in other parts of the empire.

As they leave the Acropolis they let their eyes scan the horizon toward the south, west and north. There, straight ahead, lies Pireus, with its three harbors, where the party landed when they first set foot on Attic soil. In the distance they see the islands of Salamis and Aigina, and beyond them rise the mountains of the Peloponnesos and of Megara. To the right the low Aigaleus range stretches northward until it unites with the wooded Parnes mountain that borders the Attic plain on the north. Directly west of the Acropolis, in a quarter of the city called Melite, looms a large semicircular area supported by a massive stone wall. This is the Pnyx, where the Athenian citizens meet to be addressed by the orators and to take action on the affairs of the city. In the olden days, before the Greeks lost their political freedom to their Roman conquerors, this was the scene of many famous debates, the outcome of which set the course of events in the Greek world. The most illustrious men in the history of Athenian democracy—Antiphon, Lysias, Isokrates, Aischines, Demosthenes, Lykourgos, and others whose names mean little to the visitors—have here swayed their hearers with their forensic skill.

If Paul and his party set out to see all the famous sights of Athens, they would spend more than one day at the task. For the Acropolis, the religious and artistic center of the city, does not contain all the monuments of interest to foreign visitors.

A walk along the sun-drenched south side of the hill leads them past the tomb of Hippolytos, the tragic hero cursed by his father Theseus, and slain through the machinations and jealousy of Aphrodite, whose shrine stands close to the tomb. Next they reach a precinct dedicated to Asklepios, the god of healing. The worship of this gentle god, a contrast to the warlike maiden goddess of the Acropolis, comes perhaps nearer than any other form of pagan cult to the ideals of Jesus of Nazareth, whom Paul has come to preach among the Greeks. The Athenian Asklepieion is a branch of the cult place at Epidauros, where faith cures and practical health measures combine to give hope to the sick. It contains a temple of no great size, a colonnade with entrance to a sacred spring, a pit for the sacred snake, the *abaton*, in which the suppliants spend a night and in their dreams receive visits from the god and are healed by him. Involuntarily the thoughts of the Jewish visitors turn to the healing pool at Bethesda, where the sick lie waiting for the coming of the angel to stir the waters.

At a lower level on the slope they see the stately columns of the Stoa of Eumenes, a gift from the Pergamene king whose statue was once supported by the pedestal now carrying the figure of Agrippa. Further east they enter a very large precinct sacred to Dionysos. Here is the famous theater in which the plays of Aischylos, of Sophokles, and of Euripides were first performed. Near it is the roofed concert house, originally built by Perikles but completely rebuilt after the earlier structure had been damaged by fire during the attack of Sulla upon Athens. On days of the festival of Dionysos the Athenians gather in the theater by the thousands to see performances of the old dramas or to listen to contemporary artists competing for prizes in music, poetry, or other forms of artistic activity. The whole precinct is crowded with choregic monuments, small temple-like structures, or single columns surmounted by tripods and built to commemorate victories in such contests. So numerous are these trophies of theatrical skill, both inside and outside the precinct, that the principal approach from the east bears the name "Street of Tripods." Below the playhouse are two temples of the god, an archaic shrine containing the revered wooden statue of Dionysos and a larger temple of later date with a cult statue in gold and ivory by Alkamenes.

They mount one of the stairs in the theater to the upper

section of the auditorium, where a paved road leads eastward along the upper slope of the Acropolis. Here they gain an unobstructed view over the eastern part of the city and the mountains surrounding the Attic plain. In the near distance toward the northeast the Lykabettos thrusts its pointed top over pine-clad slopes, to a height far above that of the Acropolis, and nearly hides from view the larger Anchesmos range in its rear. In the distance rises the conical form of Pentelikon, whose green slopes are dotted with gleaming white mounds from the marble quarries. To the southeast stretches the Hymettos range, its barren west flank colored a flaming purple by the reflected rays of the setting sun. This is the picture of Athens that the poets of Greece and Rome have tried to paint in words all too inadequate.

In the cool of the evening they extend their walk toward the southeastern section of the city. There, in the valley of the Ilissos, stand the stately columns of an unfinished temple of Zeus Olympios. This gigantic structure, begun by the tyrants before the Persians invaded Attica, will wait nearly a century after Paul's visit before it is completed. Within the precinct is a small shrine of Ge Olympia, the earth goddess, and near it is a chasm through which the last waters from the great flood sank into the earth. The guide interrupts his discourse on Athenian lore to call his hearers' attention to the similarity between the Greek Deukalion and the Noah of the Hebrew story. Here, too, at no great distance, is a temple of Pythian Apollo, and an altar erected by the younger Peisistratos, as they learn from an inscription in verse on the altar coping. Farther along the slopes of the river valley are shrines of lesser divinities, whose myths are interwoven into the traditions of the Athenian people. In a district called Agrai, which originally was no part of the city, are sanctuaries of many of the gods worshiped in earlier shrines on the Acropolis and its slopes. Among these are shrines of the Eleusinian goddesses, Demeter and Persephone, of the goat-god Pan; and one of Rustic Artemis, on whose altar a hundred she-goats are sacrificed on the anniversary of the Persian defeat at Marathon. A bridge across the Ilissos unites the suburb of Agrai with Athens. Here two hills rise to an elevation of some hundred feet above the valley, and in the hollow between them is the Panathenaic stadium, where athletic contests are held on festival days. It was built a hundred years after Perikles, under the administration of Lykourgos, who became responsible for much of the civic improvement in Athens. The athletic festivals in Athens do not attract the large crowds that they once did, and the building itself shows signs of neglect.

On the following day they begin their tour with the north slope of the Acropolis, which is likewise studded with shrines of local gods and foreign deities. Here is a tract of land called "field of hunger," in which one of three sacred plowings is repeated each year, to commemorate the introduction of agriculture and to induce the gods to be benevolent toward the new crops. Higher up the slope is the spring Klepsydra, and higher still the caves of Apollo, Zeus, and Pan. These are primitive places of worship which the early settlers on the Acropolis used as shelters for themselves and later converted into places of religious devotion. Each cave has its sacred legend accounting for the beginning of the cult. In Apollo's cave the god himself is said to have lain with King Erechtheus' daughter Kreousa. The offspring of their union received the name Ion, and he is believed to be the ancestor of the Ionian Greeks, with whom the Athenians claim kinship. In the second cave the Athenians worship Zeus as god of the thunderbolt, and they watch from his altar for the lightning to strike at Harma on Mt. Parnes, before sending the sacred embassy to Delphi. Pan's cult is of more recent date. The goat-god, whose favorite haunts are in the Arcadian mountains, met the celebrated runner Pheidippides on his way to Sparta and complained that the Athenians worship all other gods but not him, although he is favorable toward their cause. Since then he has had his rocky shrine close to those of the two Olympians.

Following the path eastward along the slope the visitors come to caves with cults of Aglauros and of Aphrodite in the Gardens. The Aglaurion is situated below a large cave containing an underground stairway to the Acropolis. The guide tells this legend about the origin of the shrine. There were three sisters, Pandrosos, Herse, and Aglauros, daughters of King Kekrops. The goddess Athena brought a mysterious chest to the three girls with strict injunction not to look inside. Only Pandrosos obeyed the command; the other two, overcome with curiosity, peeked into the chest and saw the baby Erichthonios, in the shape of a reptile. They became so frightened at what they saw that they hurled themselves over the

Acropolis wall and perished. On the spot where they were killed is the shrine of Aglauros. Pandrosos, as reward for her obedience, became an associate with Athena and received honors in an outdoor sanctuary on the Acropolis, west of the Erechtheion. The sacred olive tree, gift of Athena, grows within her temenos.

Aphrodite in the Gardens shares an outdoor cult place with her son Eros farther east on the north slope. Sexual symbols and fertility rites play a part in her worship. An ancient rite, called Arrephoria, is connected with the cult. Four girls, known as Arrephoroi, who serve Athena for a year, perform the ceremony at the time of the festival. The priestess of Athena places a mystic box upon the heads of the girls, and in the darkness of night they carry the box through the underground descent at the Aglaurion to the sanctuary of Aphrodite in the Gardens and there deposit it on the altar. Then they receive other objects, which they bring to the temple of Athena on the Acropolis. Neither the girls nor the priestess are expected to know the contents of the mystic box, but it is rumored that it contains images of the sexual parts of men and women and other symbols of pagan abomination. The Aphrodite sanctuary on the Acropolis slope is the scene of very primitive rites, attended largely by the more ignorant of the citizens and by foreigners. The garden goddess Aphrodite has a newer and more spacious temple beyond the city walls in one of the eastern suburbs. The image in this temple, a work of Alkamenes, is said to be the most perfect of all the statues of the goddess of beauty.

Below these cave shrines on the upper slope are other places of primitive worship and monuments connected with the early history of the city. The Anakes, commonly called Castor and Pollux, have their shrine directly below the Aglaurion, and further down the slope stands the ancient town hall, the so-called Prytaneion, which contains the original wooden tablets inscribed with the laws of Solon. There is also an altar of Hestia, guardian of the holy fire, and statues of Hestia and of Peace have been set up inside the buildings. Two of the great Athenian heroes in the war against Persia, Miltiades and Themistokles, were honored by statues in front of the Prytaneion, but their names have been changed into those of two foreigners.

From the approach to the Acropolis a steep descent, with

steps and curbs of marble, leads northward down the slope to the Agora. As the visitors make their way down the marble pavement the guide talks steadily about places of interest along the way. Close to the fountain Klepsydra there is a paved area open to the sky, where the ship used in the Panathenaic procession lies moored. On the lower slope, to the right as they go down, they see a large precinct with two small temples and several altars. There are said to be some underground chambers of mysterious contents, but the guide can tell them little except that the Athenians regard it as a very holy place barred from the public. It is called Eleusinion en Astei and is looked upon as a city annex to the renowned sanctuary at Eleusis. Demeter, Persephone, and Pluto are worshiped here with secret rites on appointed days of the year. Vague and mysterious, too, are the legends relating to the Dionysion in the Marshes, which they reach next on their way to the Agora. Here they listen to an incredible story about a holy wedding in which King Archon's wife for one night of the year becomes the spouse of the wine god Dionysos.

In the Sanctuary of Theseus, a little to the east of the road, are the bones of Theseus, which Kimon discovered on the island of Skyros and brought to the newly-built shrine in Athens. The paintings on the walls are by Mikon, who has here depicted many of the fabulous deeds of the hero. Among all the ancestral kings of the Athenians none is held in greater honor than Theseus, who is reputed to be the son of Poseidon. His mortal father Aigeus is merely a human form of the god of the sea. It was Theseus who cleared the road to the Peloponnesos of its robbers and savage monsters, and he freed the Athenians from the tribute of human lives that Minos, king of Crete, had for many years exacted from them. Then he united Attica under one king and established a government in which the people themselves made the laws. Near the Theseion is a gymnasium which King Ptolemaios of Egypt gave to the Athenians.

The Agora

As the party enters the Agora at the southeast corner, the first building they see on the left is an ancient structure, still in use, which houses the city mint. It lies at the juncture of the Panathenaic way and an old road that skirts the lower slopes of the Areopagos and extends westward in the direction of Piraeus. South of this road the terrain rises steeply toward the Areopagos. A little beyond the mint is an ancient fountain house, with a copious supply of water.

From the square in front of the fountain the travelers descend to a small paved area bordered on the west by a colonnade. They enter this building and descend further by a flight of steps to a long narrow space lined with colonnades on three sides. Here the merchants have set up their booths and call in shrill voices to the passers-by, extolling the qualities of their wares. In one corner of this market the Jewish visitors hear their native language spoken, whenever the vendors engage in conversation among themselves. Bales of heavy woven fabric spread out on the pavement show the nature of their business. They are importers of oriental drapes, which the Greeks prize most highly for the making of tents and curtains. Paul stops to ask questions about the home towns and families of the merchants. His comments on their merchandise betray the craftsman's knowledge, for he is himself a maker of tents.

As they proceed westward they pass on the left a large building in which the Heliaia, the principal law court of Athens, holds its sessions, and beyond that is another public fountain. They have now reached the north-south road that skirts the public square on the west side. To the right of the road, as they walk toward the north is the Agora (Fig. 6)— also called Kerameikos or Potter's Quarter—with altars, statues, and minor monuments crowding the available space. On the left side a row of buildings shuts out the view toward the west. First they pass the Prytanikon, or Tholos, a circular structure entered through a small porch on the east. This is the office and dining room of the prytanies, a committee of the Boule, or city council, at whose meetings the prytanies preside. The building in which the council meets is only a few feet away, set against the steep hillside, called Kolonos Agoraios. The Bouleuterion, as it is called, has seating room for the 500 members of the council and is entered through a portico from the square in the rear of the Tholos. A fountain at the west edge of this area has cool running water to quench the thirst of the lawmakers.

They retrace their steps to the road in front of the Tholos and continue their walk toward the north. A colonnade to the left of the road gives them access to a small temple. On the wall of the stoa in front of the entrance hang marble slabs carved with the figure of a goddess holding a lion in her lap or placing her foot upon its back. This is the mother of the gods, whose cult they have learned about in their travels in Asia Minor, before crossing over to Macedonia. She is there called Kybele. Inside the temple they see a large statue of this goddess in the same general attitude as the figure on the marble reliefs. This is a famous work of art from the era of Perikles, but the guide is unable to tell them whether it was made by Pheidias or by his pupil Agorakritos. From the colonnade fronting the temple other rooms open up, one of which contains public records and official copies of the tragedies written by the great poets of Athens.

Beyond this complex of buildings there is a broad passage rising by steps and ramps fom the Agora to the top of the hill. As they look up toward the west they see the façade of a Doric temple of white marble. Its severe lines and sculptured decoration remind them of the Parthenon, and seen from be-

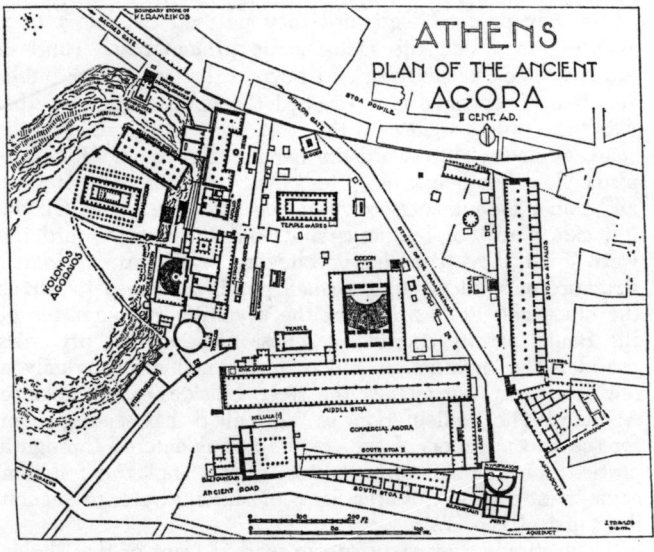

FIGURE 6. Plan of the Agora in Athens. A few of the monuments shown here, notably the Nymphaion and the library of Pantainos, were not present in the time of Paul.

low it appears almost as large, although in reality it is very much smaller. It stands surrounded by low trees and shrubs, which furnish a lovely green border around the marble colonnade. They are not surprised to learn that Athena is worshiped in this sumptuous temple too; here, however, as the companion of Hephaistos, the god of the forge. The statues within the cella show the two gods in the guise of craftspeople, Athena as the patron of the textile workers and Hephaistos as a blacksmith holding the tongs and a hammer and standing in front of an anvil. They are works of Alkamenes. But why, they ask, is the god represented as a cripple? The reply they receive is a tale so fantastic that they stand speechless at the vileness of the gods in whom the Greeks profess belief. Hephaistos, so the myth goes, is the son of Zeus and Hera—or according to another account, of Hera alone, sprung from her thigh. During one of the frequent quarrels in which Zeus and Hera engage, Hephaistos took his mother's side; Zeus, in anger at his interference, seized him by the leg and hurled him down from Olympos. For a whole day he kept falling through space and at nightfall came down on the island of Lemnos which thenceforth became sacred to Hephaistos. He made his way back to Olympos, where he was the constant butt of the divine powers. As he hobbled about, offering drinks of nectar to the gods, they would roar with laughter at his awkwardness. He was wedded to the beautiful Aphrodite, who deceived her husband and slept with the war-god Ares. In anger Hephaistos fashioned a trap, by which the two lovers were held fast until Poseidon intervened and prevailed upon Hephaistos to loose the bonds. Aphrodite, too, has a temple on the slope of Kolonos hill, not far frm the Hephaisteion.

As they return to the road along the west edge of the Agora, they pass the small temple of Apollo Patroos, reputed ancestor of the Athenians. The cult image in the temple shows the god as a musician, with long robes and holding a lyre in his hand. This is the work of Euphranor who was famous also as a painter. In the porch in front of the building stand other images of the god Apollo, one by Leochares, and another, called "averter of evil," by the hand of Kalamis. In a tiny shrine close to Apollo's temple Zeus Phratrios and Athena Phratria are worshiped as ancestral gods of Athenian family groups.

The next large building along the road is a stoa with wings projecting toward the Agora. This is called the stoa of Zeus, and in front of it stands a colossal statue of Zeus the deliverer. The walls of the colonnade are decorated with pictures painted by Euphranor. Among the subjects represented are an assembly of the twelve gods, Theseus as the founder of political equality among the Athenians, Democracy and Demos, and a battle scene in which the Athenians are shown fighting side by side with the Spartans against the Thebans at Mantineia. The last building in the northwest corner of the Agora is the stoa of the king, in which is the office of the king Archon. Here are displayed the inscribed marble slabs, which are copies of the old wooden tablets, called kyrbeis, in which the laws of Solon are recorded. These they have already seen in the Prytaneion. In the days of the Athenian democracy the philosopher Sokrates frequented the stoa and there expounded his views to his followers. The council of Areopagites have their office in the building.

The visitors have reached the point where the Panathenaic way, crossing the Agora diagonally from southeast to northwest, leaves the square through a gate in the northwest corner and continues toward the Dipylon gate. They turn back along the Panathenaic way to look briefly at other monuments within the Agora. On the right of the road they stop before an ancient altar surrounded with a sculptured parapet, a dedication to the twelve gods by the younger Peisistratos. The guide informs them that it is now popularly known as the "altar of mercy." The Athenians alone of all the Greeks worship this deity, whom they look upon as the most helpful of all the gods when men meet with misfortune. They have other altars upon which they sacrifice to Modesty, to Rumor, and to Driving Force. They are shown to be not only more humane than other Greeks, but by far the most zealous in their worship of the gods. With this characterization of the Athenians Paul readily agrees, and he recalls that as he walked from the harbor to the city he saw altars dedicated to unknown gods.[2] It appears to him that God himself has

[2] Following Jerome modern scholars have made much of the fact that Paul probably did not see an altar dedicated to an unknown god, since there is no other evidence for such a dedication to a single deity. But the Athenians had altars to unknown gods (in the plural) and Paul probably saw them, and chose for the purpose of his message to speak of an unknown god. When

prepared the hearts of the Athenians for the good message of the one true God which he has come to bring them.

Farther along the way they pass the altar of the war-god Ares, whom the Romans call Mars; and at a little distance from the road stands a marble temple of the same deity, which looks like a duplicate of the temple of Hephaistos and Athena. The contrast between these two discordant views of divinity—mercy and war—impresses the Apostle as he listens to the explanations of the guide. Formerly, the latter tells them, the Ares temple stood in another place outside the city. Under the emperor Augustus, when many new buildings were constructed in Athens, this temple was taken down to make room for a large market; it was later re-erected in the middle of the ancient Agora.

They walk about among the monuments, asking questions of the guide and now and then exclaiming with surprise at the information he offers. They are not sufficiently familiar with the history of the city to be able to take in at once all the allusions to the past that statues of famous men invoke. They pass a seated statue of Pindar, a Theban poet, whose praise of the city so pleased the Athenians that they set up his statue in the most exclusive part of the Agora, among their own great heroes of the past. A little to the north of the temple of Ares they look upon figures of two men in an attitude of combat. These are the Tyrannicides, Harmodios and Aristogeiton, who freed the city of despotic rule and made it possible for the citizens to set up a government in which the people themselves held the power. The statues were made by Antenor, considered to be the best Athenian sculptor from the period just preceding the Persian wars. Many times the Athenians have fought enemies, both from within and from without, in order to retain the freedom they had won. During one such encounter, when the king of Persia came with a huge fleet and land army, bent on enslaving the whole Greek peninsula, the Athenians abandoned their city to the enemy, who then laid it waste. Although he was finally defeated by the Greeks, fighting for their homes and gods, he had time to carry off the two statues of the liberators as a prize. The Athenians then commissioned the two sculptors Kritios and

---

Luke makes the Athenians say that he (Paul) "seems to be a preacher of foreign gods," does that imply that Paul preached polytheism? That would be taking it too literally.

Nesiotes to make copies and set them up in the same place. Five generations later the great Alexander, after his victory over the Persians, sent the original statues back to Athens. Among the great statesmen honored by statues in the Agora is Demosthenes, the orator, who tried to arouse his countrymen to resist the power of Macedon in the time of King Philip. His contemporary, Lykourgos, the distinguished administrator and orator, has a statue near that of Demosthenes. A statue of Peace by Kephisodotos shows the goddess in a benign attitude with the child Ploutos (Wealth) in her arms. Nearby is a whole row of statues, twelve in number, fenced off from the public by a guard rail. These are the ancestral heroes of the tribes of Attica. Ten are ancient; the other two are kings of Pergamon and of Egypt, standing on bases prepared for statues of other foreign benefactors. But to hear the story of all the famous men and heroes whose portraits fill the public square would require more time than the visitors can afford; they wish to gain something of a picture of the whole city without stopping at every monument, large and small.

From the southwest corner of the Agora they walk toward the south, in front of a row of administrative buildings and colonnades, until they come to the music hall which Agrippa gave to the Athenians. This fine edifice impresses the visitors with the splendor of its interior decoration and the marble statues set up in front of the entrance. Its central location in the Agora makes it the most convenient place from which to watch the processions and religious celebrations that are staged in the Agora almost daily. Looking across the Panathenaic way toward the east they see the two-storied façade of a long stoa, a gift of King Attalos of Pergamon, who as a student had enjoyed the many attractions and educational advantages of Athens. In recognition of this gift the Athenians made a portrait of the benefactor. He is shown standing in a four-horse chariot upon a lofty pedestal facing the Agora directly in front of the stoa that bears his name. The prominence of the group is enhanced by the later construction of a rostrum or speaker's stand, in front of the Attalos monument but rising to a much lower level. The colonnade in the lower story is crowded with people who have come to gaze at the line of goods displayed in front of the shops that open from the rear of the stoa. At the west end the visitors mount to the second story. Here they have an unobstructed view of the whole Agora, with its hundreds of statues, altars, marble slabs inscribed with the decrees of the democracy, public buildings, fountains, shrines of the gods. Crowds of people can be seen going to and fro among the monuments, or standing in small groups showing by their quick gestures the intensity of their discussion. Accustomed as they are to the animated gestures and gregarious habits of the east, Paul and his companions stand enthralled by the sight and sounds of these spirited crowds. They have the impression that all the residents of Athens, citizens and foreigners alike, have dedicated their lives to the art of conversation, asking questions and offering information to each other on every conceivable subject.

They descend by the northern stairway to the level of the square and walk toward the west, passing a small colonnade facing south, then cross the road that lines the Agora on the north side. Here they come to the most famous and splendid of the buildings in the Agora, a stoa commonly called Poikile, or Painted Colonnade, but also named after the donor, the stoa of Peisianax. The paintings on the walls are works of Polygnotos and Mikon, the two best painters of Athens from the era of Perikles. Some of the pictures represent battles in which the Athenians are shown as the defenders of freedom from foreign power and as the champions of law and order; others show wars of long ago—the Trojan war, the fight against the Amazons—which the Athenians like to depict in their public buildings. Bronze shields and other trophies of war hang on the walls among the paintings, making the stoa a kind of museum of Athenian history. Perhaps it is these poignant references to past glories, with their implied belittling of the deeds of later times, that made this the most favored haunt of the philosophers of Athens. The school founded by Zeno of Cyprus is known as "the Stoa" from the fact that Zeno used this building as a lecture hall. Here some adherents of Zeno are engaged in a lively dispute with another group, the Epicureans. Paul and his companions listen to their arguments and soon find themselves taking part. It gives Paul the opportunity to tell them of Jesus of Galilee who had come to save the world but was himself crucified by the Romans and on the third day rose from the grave. The philosophers find this story more unbelievable than the Athenian myths about their gods. Some merely jeer at him; others want to hear him again and make an appointment for him to appear before the council of Areopagites to be questioned about the new god he is preaching. In front of the Painted Colonnade stands a bronze statue of the great Athenian lawgiver Solon, whose laws became the foundation of Athenian justice.

Leaving the stoa and continuing westward along the north edge of the Agora they pass a row of herms, square pillars with a human head carved at the top but with no other likeness of the body except those parts which other people out of modesty seek to hide. In many cases these show signs of deliberate mutilation and later repair. The damage goes back to a time when the Athenians in an outburst of national pride sailed to Sicily bent on extending their domains to these distant parts. On the night before the departure of the fleet, Alcibiades, one of the leaders of the expedition, and a band of drunken companions amused themselves by knocking off these shameful symbols. They also made mockery of the Eleusinian mysteries, which the Greeks believe will prepare the initiated for a happy life after death. The herms themselves are war memorials from victories of the Greeks over the Persians.

The party has now made the round of the Agora and is back at the gate where the Panathenaic way leads out of the Agora toward the Dipylon gate. They have seen all the important monuments within the central section of the city. From the gate between the herms and the stoa of the king the Panathenaic way continues in a northwesterly direction for a distance of about two stades. It is lined on both sides with colonnades in front of which stand statues of famous men and of gods whom the Athenians worship. They pass by the house, formerly owned by Poulytion, who was one of the boon companions of Alcibiades, and they say that it was in this house that the outrage against the mysteries of Eleusis was staged. Later they see a statue of Poseidon on horseback, and near the further end of the road they come to a temple of Demeter. Here are images of the Eleusinian gods, Demeter, her daughter Persephone, and Inachos; they are by the hand of Praxiteles from the time of Philip of Macedon. Just inside the Dipylon gate stands a building in which the Athenians prepare the processions that pass along the Panathenaic way through the Agora to the Acropolis.

The Academy and the Lyceum

Outside the gate there is a choice of two roads, one leading past the cemeteries of private Athenians toward Eleusis, the other toward the Academy. They follow the latter, a broad, straight avenue bordered on both sides with the funeral monuments of distinguished citizens and of men who have lost their lives fighting for their homeland. Here lie buried many of the famous statesmen and military leaders of Athenian history: Kleisthenes, the father of Athenian democracy; Harmodios and Aristogeiton, the tyrant slayers; the great Perikles, under whom Athens became the foremost city of Greece; Thrasyboulos, who restored the democracy after the rule of the thirty tyrants; the great naval heroes, Konon and his son Timotheos, whose statues stand in the Agora and on the Acropolis; the orators and statesmen Ephialtes and Lykourgos; the philosophers Zeno and Chrysippos. The graves of men killed in war are so numerous that to give the list of the battles in which they fought and died is to review the whole of Athenian history. The monuments of these honored men and of scores of others are so placed that the citizens going to and from the Academy can admire them and read the epigraphs extolling the deeds of the men buried in the graves.

Near the Academy is the tomb of Plato, held to be the greatest of the Athenian philosophers, and most distinguished of the followers of Sokrates. It was Plato who founded the Academy as a corporate body, in which men are educated for service in the state. Many legends have arisen about him. While he was asleep as a baby, honey bees are said to have settled on his lips. Another story tells how Sokrates, on the night before Plato became enrolled as his pupil and follower, dreamed that a swan flew into his bosom. The swan has the reputation of being the bird most inclined toward the art of the muses. The Academy comprises a grove of olive trees, a gymnasium, and other buildings dedicated to the use of the trainees. An altar of Love stands before the entrance to the grove, and inside are altars of Prometheus, of the muses, of Hermes, of Athena, and of Herakles.

Sokrates' name is connected with another gymnasium of Athens, the Lyceum, which is located in the east section of the city. The place is sacred to Apollo Lykeios, the wolf-god. It has a covered walk, the Peripatos, from which the followers of Aristotle became known as Peripatetics, because the illustrious teacher used to give his lectures there. The names of Theophrastos and Straton, successors of Aristotle, are kept in high honor by the teachers and students in the Lyceum. The Gardens of Theophrastos are within the enclosure. A third gymnasium, whose name is connected with another philosophical school, is Kynosarges, on the left bank of the Ilissos. This is sacred to Herakles, who was an interloper among the Athenian heroes and gods. For this reason Athenians with limited citizenship rights (*nothoi*) by preference frequent the gymnasium. Antisthenes, one of the followers of Sokrates, and Diogenes of Sinope, nicknamed "the dog," chose this gymnasium as the center of their teaching activities. Antisthenes would point to Herakles as an example of the type of virtue that follows exertion and is therefore lasting and free from the harmful effects of the common pleasures. It is said that the Cynics were named "dogs" after Kynosarges, the surname of Herakles, meaning "white dog."

Paul in Athens

His walks through the city[3] gave Paul the opportunity to make contact with Athenians and foreign residents. He became acquainted with many of the Jews who congregated on Sabbath days in the synagogue, and among them were doubtless some pagan proselytes. In the Agora he talked to merchants and craftsmen and gathered from them such information as he desired. In the stoas and other public buildings he met men of science, technicians and artists, students and their teachers, members of the several philosophical schools in Athens. They were eager to hear what Paul had to say about the Messiah of the Jews. It was nothing unusual for them to

[3] It goes without saying that Paul and his party did not cover the whole of Athens to the extent suggested in this imaginary account. It is intended, as background to Paul's speech on the Areopagos, to convey the kind of information that an inquisitive visitor might have gained from a guided tour through the city. Readers who wish to pursue further the study of Athens are referred to a recent publication, *Poleodomiki Exelixis tôn Athenôn*, by John Travlos. This admirable account of the architectural development of Athens as a city from Neolithic times down to the present day will soon be available in English, in a revised edition to be published by the University of Chicago Press.

hear a religious representative from the east speak about a new god, but they were startled by his message of bodily resurrection, which seemed very foreign to their own speculations about man's existence after death. Finally they brought him before the venerable body of Areopagites,[4] who decided in cases arising from religious disputes. His speech to the council, of which Luke gives a brief summary, seems perfectly suited to the background of his hearers and the circumstances under which it was delivered.[5] Some of those who heard him made fun of him; others were sufficiently interested to ask him to speak to them again. Luke neglects to tell us whether Paul accepted this invitation.

The tone of Luke's account is such as to suggest that Paul left Athens disappointed, and this feeling is perhaps echoed in his first letter to the church at Corinth. As he looked back upon his arrival in that city, he probably recalled how he had been moved by his experience in Athens to try a new approach in his endeavor to make converts in Corinth. "When I came to you," he writes, "I did not come proclaiming to you the testimony of God in lofty words or wisdom . . . for I decided to know nothing among you, except Jesus Christ and him crucified . . . And my speech and my message were not in plausible words of wisdom, but in demonstration of the Spirit and Power" (I Cor. 1:1–3). In Athens he had made his appeal on a level of human knowledge, and he had quoted the Greek poet Aratos as authority for the statement: "For

[4] I believe that the speech was given on the Areopagos, before the council of Areopagites. The language (*epi* with the accusative —up to) favors this view (cf. Acts 17:19), but does not exclude the other interpretation. Although in the first century A.D. the council had quarters in the royal stoa, it seems to have continued to hold sessions on the hill itself. A century after Paul's visit Pausanias (I. xxvii. 5) describes the Areopagos in terms implying that trials were held on the hill in his day. According to some scholars the meeting place of the council was not on top of the hill but on the north slope, where the medieval church of Dionysios the Areopagite has been discovered. See Eugene Vanderpool, *Archaeology*, III (1950), 34–37.

[5] The account of Paul's visit in Athens seems to me to have the flavor of an eyewitness account, as much as any portion of the Acts. It was common practice among ancient historians, from Thucydides down, to give the gist of speeches in their own words, and Luke's practice in this respect does not seem to be an exception.

we are indeed his offspring" (Acts 17:23). At this kind of argument he had the disadvantage, and when he came to Corinth he was thoroughly humbled. "I was with you in weakness and in much fear, and trembling." He would never again try to impress his hearers with his learning. For God "will destroy the wisdom of the wise, and the cleverness of the clever [he] will thwart" (I Cor. 1:19). "God chose what is foolish in the world to shame the wise and God chose the weak in the world to shame the strong" (I Cor. 1:27).

If his brief visit in Athens was a disappointment the lesson he had learned stood him in good stead; in his future work he would avoid the errors that he had made there. At the next and final stop in the Greek peninsula he would settle down for a longer period and lay the foundation of a permanent and vital center of the Christian faith in the Greek world.

The apostle's stay in Athens also had some positive results. Luke mentions two converts, Dionysios, a member of the Areopagos, and a woman named Damaris; and there may have been others. On the slope below the rock where Paul preached his sermon, Greek archaeologists have uncovered the ruins of a church of Dionysios the Areopagite. As the modern visitor climbs the rock-cut steps to the top of the hill, he can stop to read engraved in bronze the immortal words of the apostle, the most extensive of the two recorded speeches that he composed for the ears of pagan hearers.

20

THE APOSTLE PAUL AND THE ISTHMIAN GAMES

OSCAR BRONEER

The Isthmian games, dedicated to Poseidon, the pagan god of the sea, and to the boy-god Palaimon—what can Paul have had to do with such celebrations? There is too obvious a contrast between his work and the gay, noisy festival designed to appeal to human emotions and desires of the flesh that the apostle would have labeled as sinful. Yet, when we look more closely at the picture we come to realize that the pagan festival may have been a factor in determining Paul's itinerary in Greece. Can it be that the Isthmian games influenced him in his choice of Corinth, in preference to Athens or any other large city, as the pilot plant for his work on Greek soil? The answer is a qualified yes.

The writer of the Acts, who was probably the author of the third gospel, does not say anything about the motivation for the choice of site. In an earlier passage of the Acts (16:9–10) he tells us that a vision in a dream moved Paul to cross the north Aegean into the Roman province of Macedonia; while in Corinth he had another vision (Acts 18:9) urging him to use more aggressive methods to win converts. No such motivation is recorded for his departure for the south of Greece. At each place in the north where he stayed for any length of time he encountered enmity from the Jews, who were suspicious and jealous of his success (cf. Acts 13:45), and restrictions from officials of the Roman administration, whose business it was to prevent disorder in the province. Harassed by such opposition Paul and his party appear to have altered their plans in each place where they tried to establish beachheads in their campaign to Christianize the Grecian peninsula. At Philippi (Acts 16:12–40), where they remained "some days," they were stripped of their clothes, then publicly flogged and thrown into jail; but, after a miraculous intervention in the form of an earthquake, they were released and urged to leave the city. At Thessalonica, where they remained three weeks, they were set upon by a mob and had to flee by night to Beroea. Their reception among the Jews in that city was cordial, but troublemakers soon arrived from Thessalonica and forced Paul to flee in haste, to escape further harassment. His two companions, Silas and Timothy, remained to settle affairs among the converts. Paul's clandestine departure brought him first to the shore, somewhere near the mouth of the Haliakmon river or a little to the south of it at the city of Pydna, and then, presumably by ship, to Athens.

If Paul's visits in the Macedonian cities had been less auspicious than his vision in the night at Troas might have led him to expect, his brief Athenian venture was no more encouraging.[1] Perhaps it was not a part of the original travel plan. The narrator (Acts 17:16) leaves the impression that Paul's chief reason for stopping at Athens was to await the arrival of his companions. The account (Acts 18:1-5) is so abbreviated that the reader is led to believe that Paul had already left for Corinth when Silas and Timothy arrived from Macedonia. But in the letter written from Corinth to the Thessalonians (I Thess. 2:17-3:6) it appears that Timothy had been sent by Paul from Athens to Thessalonica to bring his message to the church and to report to him about the situation there. Silas must have gone with Timothy or met him in Thessalonica, since they seem to have arrived in Corinth together, where Paul had already established himself by the time of their return. Did Luke remain with Paul during all this time? He reports in great detail and in language befitting an eyewitness about Paul's appearance in Athens and his departure for Corinth but has not a word to say about Timothy's or Silas' arrival in Athens or about their subsequent departure for Macedonia.

The account of Paul's travels from the time that he left Asia Minor until he departed from Athens creates an impression of constant improvisation. He seems to have been in a hurry to reach Corinth. The fame of the city as a thriving metropolis, crowded with foreigners from all the Mediterranean lands, probably attracted him from the beginning of his journey in

[1] On Paul's visit in Athens see "Athens, 'City of Idol Worship,'" chap. 19, in this volume, reprinted from *BA*, XXI (1958), 1-28.

Greece. Corinth was the most advantageously located city in Greece for Paul's purposes.[2] At frequent intervals ships from the east and west would arrive and unload their cargoes and passengers in the two harbors, Kenchreai and Lechaion, later to return to their home base or leave for other parts of the Mediterranean. Once every two years the city played host to a multitude of delegates, athletes, visitors and merchants who arrived for the celebration of the Isthmian games. Here in Corinth, especially at such occasions, Paul would find means of communicating with the newly established churches throughout Asia Minor and in the north of Greece. This was of the greatest importance, for at this time he was ready to put into operation a plan that had gradually matured in his mind. He could no longer permit his mission to be interrupted or his headquarters moved each time that he ran into opposition. He would now settle down, earning his livelihood with others as a skilled maker of tents and tapestries—a type of work that had for centuries been a specialty, if not a monopoly, of craftsmen from the east. He would have ample opportunity and leisure to meet with the Jews in the synagogue on Sabbath days, but he did not restrict his association to people of Jewish faith. Being in business as a tentmaker would bring him into contact with other foreigners and with the Corinthians, who met in the Agora and in the public centers in the city. Corinth doubtless offered better business opportunities to a man in his trade than did most Greek cities because of its wealth and business activities and, in particular, because of the Isthmian games. At such occasions large numbers of tents would be needed to provide shelter for the crowds of visitors.[3] He may have expected that such an unobtrusive approach would be less likely to arouse suspicions against him and his message. If this was the case, his calculations proved wrong; his speeches in the synagogue eventually brought him into conflict with the strict adherents to the law of Moses. In the past such opposition had led him to break camp and to depart for some other place. In Corinth he had come to stay.

[2] See *BA*, XIV (1951), 77–96.

[3] Later, in the 2nd century A.D., an extensive building program was initiated by the high priest of Poseidon, P. Licinius Priscus Iuventianus, to erect public buildings, including quarters for athletes and visitors to the games. See *Inscriptiones Graecae*, IV, No. 203; and O. Broneer, *Hesperia, Journal of the American School of Classical Studies at Athens*, VIII (1939), 181–90.

But his patience was stretched to its limit by his own people, whom he threatened to abandon in their hostility toward his mission. "He shook out his garments and said to them: 'Your blood be upon your heads! I am innocent. From now on I will go to the Gentiles'" (Acts 18:6; and cf. Acts 13:46).

We may reasonably assume that Paul made use of the opportunity to deliver his message to the many visitors at Isthmia and to make contact with the places that he had visited earlier in his travels. He and his group of co-workers probably joined the festive crowds who set out on foot from the city to the Isthmus, where they met thousands of visitors coming by land and sea for the biennial celebrations. A description of the site of the games as revealed in the excavation, with its temples and public monuments and athletic buildings, will help us create the background for the visit of Paul and his followers.

The Isthmian Sanctuary

The sanctuary is situated near the east end of the Corinth canal, some ten miles from Ancient Corinth by the shortest route. The general location has been known since ancient times; and two of the monuments, the later stadium and the theater, were always visible above the ground. But prior to 1952 the location of the sanctuary proper, containing temples of Poseidon and Palaimon, was unknown. In the 1880's the French archaeologist Monceaux made investigations at the site and came to the conclusion that the two temples lay within a massive enclosure surrounding the modern church of St. John the Forerunner.[4] The enclosure itself came to be regarded as the precinct wall, although it is provided with massive towers and fortified gates that indicate its defensive character. It was later proved by two English scholars[5] that this enclosure was constructed as a fortress in the time of the emperor Justinian and consequently had nothing to do with the ancient sanctuary. The construction of the fortress has since been shown to have been the cause of demolition of the ancient buildings. The two temples were definitely located

[4] On the early explorations of the site see Fimmen, *Pauly Wiss. Real-Encyclopädie*, IX, 2, columns 2256 ff.; and Harold N. Fowler, *Corinth I* (1932), pp. 51 ff., and the literature cited in these works.

[5] R. J. H. Jenkins and H. Megaw, *British School Annual*, XXXII (1931–32), 69 ff.

and excavated by the University of Chicago expedition, which began its work at Isthmia in 1952. Over a period of nine years the site has been under investigation, and the major monuments connected with the Isthmian games have now been exposed.[6]

The Temple of Poseidon

Chief among the buildings is the temple of Poseidon, which occupied a conspicuous position in the center of a large quadrangular area artificially leveled for this purpose. The first temple whose existence we can trace was constructed here in the first half of the 7th century B.C. It was a long narrow building of archaic type, probably divided by a central row of columns into two aisles. It is this temple to which Aeschylus refers as the "house of the earthshaking god of the sea" in a fragment of a satyr play, *The Theoroi*, or *Isthmiastai*, the scene of which was laid at Isthmia.[7] The building itself was a modest structure, but at the time of its destruction by fire about 470 B.C. its interior was crowded with votive objects: metal armor, especially helmets, but also shields, spears, and daggers. Archaic coins of gold and silver had been brought by worshipers as gifts to the god, along with pottery, bronze figurines, architectural implements, and other objects deemed worthy of the god's attention. Most conspicuous among the furniture of the temple is a large marble basin supported by four female figures standing on the backs of lions, each holding a leash and the animal's tail in her hand. This masterpiece of early Greek art is to be dated about the middle of the 7th century B.C. It was one of several basins set up for the convenience of priests and worshipers who washed their hands ceremonially as they approached the god's presence. The practice continued down to Roman imperial times, for we have an inscription from the late first or early 2nd century A.D. which mentions the "clean hands and cleansing streams of water" at the entrance to the temple.

After the destruction of the archaic building, a new and

[6] For a year by year account of the excavations see *Hesperia*, XXII (1953), 182–95; XXIV (1955), 110–41; XXVII (1958), 1–37; XXVIII (1959), 298–343; and *Archaeology*, VIII (1955), 56–62; IX (1956), 134–37, and 268–72; XIII (1960), 105–9.

[7] The literature on this important document can be found in an article by Bruno Snell in *Hermes*, LXXXIV (1956), 1–11.

much larger temple was erected, probably during the decade 470–460 B.C. This was a Doric building with six columns at either end and thirteen on the flanks. Walls and columns were made of the kind of common stone called poros, covered with a thin stucco of marble dust, and marble sculptures probably adorned the two gables and the metopes in the front and rear of the temple proper. We know nothing of the cult statue from the 5th century; but it is likely that two deities, Poseidon and Amphitrite, were jointly worshiped under the same roof. This we may conclude from the existence of a single row of columns in the interior dividing the room into two equal parts. Later the central row of columns was replaced with a double colonnade, whereby the interior received the normal triple division of a Greek temple. The two deities were probably then moved from their separate pedestals and made to occupy a single base.[8] This building too was heavily damaged from a fire that broke out in the year 390 B.C., but part of the building remained standing and could be restored in its original form. What changes it underwent between this restoration and the time of Paul's visit we do not know. All that we can determine for certain from the meager remains is that other repairs were made in Roman times, in one of which the lower part of the walls and the floor were revetted with marble. The temple remained standing until the middle of the 6th century A.D.

A necessary adjunct to the temple was an altar to Poseidon. From the archaic period we have no altar proper, but the ground to the east of the temple has been identified as a sacrificial area because of the ash and burnt animal bones found in the fill. In the 5th century B.C. an altar, 130 feet in length, was constructed in front of the temple. This was demolished, probably at the time of the destruction of Corinth under Mummius in 146 B.C.; and for the following two centuries we can find no trace of an altar. During that time the Isthmian sanctuary, like the city itself, seems to have been, if not wholly abandoned, at least in a state of disrepair. The Isthmian games continued to be held; they were managed by the Sikyonians, but whether at Isthmia or at Sikyon

[8] The torso of a colossal female statue, probably a goddess, was found in the rear part of the temple during the first campaign of excavation. It is a Roman copy of an original from the 5th century B.C.

we do not know. A second altar was constructed some time in the first century A.D., not much earlier than the time of Paul's visit. The Roman colony of Corinth had then been in existence for over a century, but the settlers had been fully occupied with rebuilding Corinth and turning it into a Roman city.

The Athletic Buildings

In addition to this chief temple the most conspicuous remains from pre-Roman times are those of the two stadia and the theater. The first stadium at Isthmia, as at Olympia, encroached closely upon the god's domain. This early stadium, at the southeast corner of the sanctuary, has very intricate starting gates, called balbides, unlike those found in other athletic buildings of this kind. At the curved end of this stadium there was an underground reservoir which supplied water for the channels that line the race track. Somewhere near the reservoir there may have been a cult place in which the Isthmian hero, Melikertes-Palaimon, received honors.

The site chosen for the stadium may have served the needs of that early period, but it soon became evident that it would interfere with the processions and the religious exercises centered in front of the temple. The embankment that provided space for the spectators, i.e. the spectatory, was small and could not be raised to greater height because of the nearness of the temple and long altar. More space was soon required to accommodate the growing crowds at the festivals. For whatever reason, the stadium was moved—probably as early as the 4th century B.C.—to a conspicuous hollow some 300 yards to the southeast. The later stadium incorporated all the new features common to such buildings in Greece. It continued to function for seven or eight centuries with but few changes introduced in Roman imperial times. It was here that the apostle Paul and his entourage saw the Isthmian games—if our conjecture is correct—in the year A.D. 51.

The Palaimonion

The site of the old stadium near the sanctuary had in the meantime become buried under an accumulation of earth and debris. But the shrine of Palaimon may have continued in use, for as early as the beginning of the first century A.D. we find traces of a cult to the hero in the area once occupied by the stadium. At first the cult functioned without a temple. A sacrificial pit lined with stones and surrounded by a low temenos wall seems to have been all that existed at that time. Later a second pit was added and the enclosure was enlarged. Finally a complex of buildings was erected surrounding a very much larger sacrificial pit, and a circular temple on a square base was constructed over the spot reputed to contain the bodily remains of the drowned boy. This final development probably postdates Paul's visit. In this area, devoted to the worship of Palaimon, we discovered hundreds of lamps of two very distinct categories. One kind consists of large open bowls, with a wick holder in the center of each and with no handles. This type, found nowhere else in Greece, was designed to be placed on the ground or on pedestals during the nightly celebrations of the mystery rites in honor of Palaimon. Together with these lamps we have found a large number of ordinary types, small lamps to be carried in the hands of the worshipers. We know something about the animals sacrificed in the pits and the manner of their sacrifices. Among the ashes that filled the pits there were no bones of smaller animals, only bones of cattle, probably of young bulls. A black bull was the prescribed victim in a sacrifice to Palaimon; and the bones indicated that the animals had not been cut up, as was customary during sacrifices to the Olympian gods,[9] but had been offered as holocausts, i.e. they were consumed whole.

The Theater

Another building closely related to the sanctuary is the theater, situated on a hillside sloping toward the north, some fifty yards to the northeast of the sanctuary of Poseidon. The theater was constructed either in the 5th century B.C. or in the first half of the 4th. Not much of it remains today, but enough to trace its successive reconstructions from classical times down to the time of Nero. It was in this building that T. Quinctius Flaminius appeared before the assembled Greeks

[9] Paul (I Cor. 8:1–13) alludes to the common practice of eating the meat of sacrificial victims or offering it for sale to the public.

in the year 196 B.C. to declare the freedom of the Greeks. Fifty years later another Roman general, Lucius Mummius, conveyed a different message to the hapless inhabitants of Corinth, then the capital of the Achaean league. After capturing the city he put the men to the sword and sold the women and children into slavery. For 100 years Corinth lay vacant, or nearly so, for a few settlers appear to have been left to administer the religious needs of the city. Among these, we may assume, were the functionaries of the Isthmian cult of Poseidon. But the shrine had lost its luster and the Isthmian games their power to attract visitors from afar. Who would now come to Isthmia when all the allurements of the city of business and of pleasure had ceased to exist? Even if the games were not actually transferred to Sikyon but continued to be held at Isthmia, they would have retained only a sorry reflection of their former splendor.

Once more during Roman times, the Greeks would gather in this theater to hear a proclamation of freedom from a Roman emperor. This was in the year A.D. 66 when Nero made his famous journey to Greece.[10] It was then that he broke ground for the Corinth canal that remained unfinished until the 1880's of our own era. In the Isthmian theater he competed for the prize in musical composition and in heralding; here, as elsewhere in Greece, he was awarded the first prize. He probably escaped the ordeal of taking an oath in that crypt of Palaimon, for he was lavish with gifts that he offered to secure his victory. One competitor from Epirus, who was well equipped by nature to compete with the emperor in vocal competition, refused to withdraw unless he received ten talents in compensation. This was more than Nero was willing to grant. Realizing his limitations as a singer, he sent his henchmen to beat up his competitor until he was unable to appear in the theater. After this exhibition of his generosity and sportsmanship, he made his famous proclamation to the Greeks.

The Cult Caves

In earlier times, before such venalities were employed to pick the victor among the contestants, the theatrical per-

[10] See Suetonius *Nero* 23, 24; and *Inscriptiones Graecae*, VII, 2713, which contains the text of the emperor's speech to the Greeks delivered at Isthmia.

formers were organized into guilds with strict laws governing their conduct. We may have material traces connecting the excavations with the activities of these organizations. At the upper edge of the auditorium we found a cave with two chambers, each entered separately from an outdoor court. The chambers were provided with couches, a cult niche, and other paraphernalia of religious nature; and in each court we found a kitchen, stone table, and cooking vessels dating from the late 4th century B.C. The chambers had been used as dining rooms, certainly of a religious nature, and we may conjecture that they served the needs of the artists of Dionysos.[11] The two chambers had eleven couches, five in one, six in the other. Another double cave, located at the northeast corner of the precinct of Poseidon, had the same number of couches and was also divided into two separate chambers. Possibly the two double caves had served the same organization at different times. It is not clear whether they were directly connected with the theater, but we cannot go wrong in assuming that all these subterranean dining rooms were closely related to the cults of the Isthmian sanctuary.[12]

Our excavations have uncovered other buildings, mostly of secular character, at some distance from the twin temples of Poseidon and Palaimon. The identification of these scattered monuments is less certain, and their relation to the cults of Isthmia is not clear.

The Later History of the Site

For a hundred years after Paul's visit the sanctuary continued to attract visitors to the Corinthian isthmus. But the decline of athletics and the trend toward professionalism, which Dio Chrysostom (see below, pp. 404–408) marked with derisive scorn, continued until they had drained the

[11] On these guilds of actors see Pickard-Cambridge, *Dramatic Festivals of Athens* (1953), pp. 286–315; J. A. O. Larsen in *An Economic Survey of Ancient Rome*, ed. T. Frank (6 vols.; 1933–40), IV (1938), 306 f. For a more detailed description of the caves and their functions see my article in *Hesperia*, XXXI (1962), 1–25.

[12] In the Dionysiac mysteries meals were sometimes served in caves, and certain functionaries were called *antrophylakes* 'guardians of the grotto.' See M. P. Nilsson, *The Dionysiac Mysteries of the Hellenistic and Roman Age, Acta Instituti Atheniensis Regni Sueciae*, V (1957), 61–63.

games of the cultural value that they had once possessed. The stadium yielded its place to the amphitheater; with the brutal shows of the Roman arena Greek athletics could not compete. The effect is apparent in the Isthmia excavations. There is little that can be dated after the 2nd century A.D. The festival continued to be held as late as the emperor Julian,[13] but the nature of the contests was less suited to the stadium than to the amphitheater, where they may have been held. In 493 the Olympic games were abolished by imperial decree, and the Isthmian sanctuary may have been closed at the same time. The ancient buildings remained standing for 150 years more and were then demolished to provide material for a fortress and trans-Isthmian wall. Two inscriptions[14] built into the fortress contain a prayer for the emperor Justinian and for "his faithful slave Victorinus"; the latter was probably the engineer in charge of the work. By the irony of history the name of the architect who built the great temple of Poseidon is unknown; the name of the man who razed it is securely recorded—albeit in grammar of questionable form. The stones from the demolished temples made excellent building material; marble sculpture and epigraphical records were melted down to make lime. Little regret would have been felt at the time for the demolition of the pagan structures. It did not seem too great a sacrifice to secure the safety of the empire. But that safety was short-lived; the Isthmian wall did not stop the Avar invasion[15] of the Peloponnesos in the eighties of the 6th century. Little now was left above ground to mark the site of the Isthmian games; for more than a millennium the very location of the temple remained unknown.

The Isthmian Crown

The crown of victory, which Paul characterized as a perishable wreath, was the chief reward given by the umpire at the games. A palm branch also became a badge of victory. Winners at Isthmia, as at the other Panhellenic games, frequently received prizes of material value from their own cities; but these were less highly prized than the wreath

[13] Julian, *Epist.* 28 (408 B). Cf. R. S. Robinson, *Sources for the History of Greek Athletics* (1955), p. 205.

[14] *Inscriptiones Graecae*, IV, 204, 205.

[15] On the Avar invasion, see G. R. Davidson, *Hesperia*, VI (1937), 227–39.

placed upon the successful contestant. The Olympic crown was made of wild olive, the Pythian of laurel, the Nemean of wild celery. At Isthmia two types of crown, pine and wild celery, were awarded. The earliest Isthmian crown was made of pine; but in the 5th century, when Pindar wrote his odes, and throughout the 4th and 3rd centuries the Isthmian crown, like those at Nemea, was made of celery. The Nemean crown was green, that at Isthmia was withered. The pine crown was reintroduced at Isthmia and was certainly the common kind in the 2nd century A.D. There is some evidence to show that the celery crown was still used in the first century A.D., at the time of Paul's stay in Corinth.[16] It is tempting to see in his reference to the perishable wreath (corruptible crown) a reference to the crown of celery which, when bestowed at the Isthmian games, was already withered (I Cor. 9:25).

An Ancient Description of the Isthmian Festival

Such are the material remains that have come to light, and with their help we can form some conception about the Isthmian games, whose beginnings are but dimly revealed in the myths relating to their founding. Early in the 6th century, 582 or 580 B.C., the games were reorganized as a Panhellenic festival, which became famous for the large crowds it attracted and for the gaiety and splendor of its celebrations. We have an eyewitness account of the Isthmian festival from a writer who is almost a contemporary of Paul, Dio Chrysostom of Prusa. He describes a visit to the Isthmian games by the cynic philosopher Diogenes, in the 4th century B.C., but the details of his account are drawn from the writer's own time. To help picture the events at the festival I quote the pertinent passages from Dio's imaginary account of the philosopher's visit.[17]

From Dio Chrysostom VIII *Concerning Virtue:*

6   When the time came for the Isthmian games and all were at the Isthmus, he [Diogenes] too went down . . .

[16] See the author's recent article, *AJA*, LXXI (1962), 259–63.
[17] *Oration* VIII:6, 9, 11, 12, 13, 14; IX:10, 11, 12, 13, 14, 15, 16, 18, 22. With this compare Dio's description of the Olympic festival in *Oration* 28.

9   And at that time it was that you could hear in the area around the Temple of Poseidon any number of luckless sophists shouting and abusing each other, and their notorious students wrangling among themselves, and many authors reciting their silly compositions, poets declaiming their verses to the applause of their colleagues, magicians showing off their marvels, soothsayers interpreting omens, tens of thousands of lawyers twisting lawsuits, and no small number of hucksters peddling whatever goods each one happened to have for sale . . .

11 When someone asked him if he too had come to look at the games, "No," he said. "I am going to enter the contests." The man laughed and asked who would be his opponents. Diogenes gave him a wry
12 look, as he likes to do. "The toughest," he said, "and hardest to fight against, whom no one among the Greeks dares to face, not the ordinary kind of competitors who race or wrestle or jump, not even those who box and hurl the javelin and throw the discus, but opponents who chasten you." "Who
13 would that be?" the man asked. "Hardships," he said. "They are powerful and unconquerable to men who are stuffed with food and dulled in their senses, men who eat all day long and snore at night; but they can be overcome by men who are thin and scrawny, whose waists are pinched
14 more than those of wasps. Or do you think these pot-bellies are good for anything, men who ought to be led around and be purified, and driven out like scapegoats; or, rather, to be used as sacrificial victims, cut into pieces and eaten, by men of sense? You know, as they do with the meat of whales, boiling it in salt and sea water, so as to melt off the fat, just as at home in Pontus they use the lard of pigs [or dolphins] when they wish to grease themselves. I think these people have no more soul than swine.

And from the same, IX *The Isthmian Discourse*

10 Altogether the directors of the Isthmian games and those among the others, who were men held in esteem and exercising power, were very much at a

loss and withdrew whenever they chanced upon him, and all of them passed him by in silence casting sidewise glances at him. But when he went further and crowned himself with the [Isthmian] pine crown, the Corinthians sent some of their servants and ordered him to take off the wreath
11 and do nothing against the rules. But he asked them why it was against the rules for him to wear the pine crown and not for the others. Someone then told him: "Because you are not a victor in the games, Diogenes." But he said: "I have won over many and mighty antagonists, not like these slaves who are now wrestling here and throwing the dis-
12 cus and running races, but more difficult, anyway you look at them: poverty and exile and ill repute; and, furthermore, anger and pain and desire and fear; and, of all the wild beasts the most invincible [and at the same time] treacherous and cringing, I mean pleasure, which no one, either among the Greeks or the barbarians, can claim to fight and prevail by the strength of his soul. All have been vanquished and failed in that contest— Persians and Medes and Syrians and Macedonians
13 and Athenians and Spartans—all but me alone. Do you think then that I am worthy of the pine, or will you take it and give it to one who is stuffed with the most meat? This, then, is what I would have you tell those who sent you, and tell them too that they are the ones who break the rules. For without winning a single contest they walk about wearing crowns. I have made the Isthmian games more illustrious by seizing the crown myself, something goats, not men, ought to fight for.
14 Afterwards he saw someone leaving the stadium with a great throng, and not even walking on the ground but carried aloft by the mob; others following and shouting, some leaping for joy and stretching their hands toward the sky, some others decking him with wreaths and ribbons. When he was able to come near he asked what the uproar
15 meant around the man and what had happened. He replied. "I am the first in the stadium race [200

yards] for men." "And what of it?" he said. "You are not a bit wiser than you were before, just because you ran ahead of your competitors, nor are you any more moderate now than before, nor less cowardly; nor will you suffer less pain, nor will your needs be fewer in the future, nor will your
16 life be less full of grief." "No, by god," he said, "but I am the swiftest Greek afoot." "Yes, but not swifter than rabbits," said Diogenes, "nor swifter than deer; and yet these wild animals, swiftest of all, as they are, are also the most cowardly. They are afraid of people and dogs and eagles, and they live a miserable life. Don't you know," he said, "that speed is a sign of cowardice? For it so happens that the same animals who can run the fastest are
18 the most easily frightened. . . . Are you not ashamed," he said, "to give yourself airs in a matter in which you are outdone by the meanest of animals? I don't think you could outrun even a fox. . . ."
22 Once during this festival he saw two horses that were hitched up in the same place, fighting and kicking each other and a large crowd standing around watching; until one of the horses, not being able to stand anymore of it, broke loose and ran away. Then Diogenes walked up to the horse that remained standing; and, putting a wreath on him, he proclaimed him an Isthmian victor because he had won the kicking contest. At this juncture everybody started laughing and shouting, and many of them admired Diogenes while they made fun of the athletes. And they say that some went away without seeing the contests of the athletes, such, that is [of the visitors] who had poor sleeping quarters or none at all.

Exaggerated as this account is, it helps us to fill out the picture of Isthmia and its celebrations which we can form on the basis of the monuments and the objects unearthed in the excavations. With these aids to our imagination let us return to the story of Paul and the Isthmian games which he, with his lieutenants, may have attended during those decisive eighteen months of his first, and more prolonged, stay in the Corinthia.

Paul at Isthmia

Paul arrived in Corinth probably before the end of A.D. 50 and had already spent some months there in the spring of A.D. 51[18] when the Isthmian games were celebrated. The aim of his mission was to preach the new religion to as large a group of people as possible and to make his missionary work self-perpetuating; he conceived of his mission as encompassing the ancient world. With the transportation at his disposal he could not visit every Mediterranean port, much less find the time to establish churches everywhere. It was important that he make converts who could carry the work further. In Corinth he established close relations with Jews from Rome, from the Black sea area, and from Asia Minor. When the time for the Isthmian games approached, we can imagine Paul and his lieutenants going into conference for the purpose of laying effective plans to reach the visitors from other parts. We cannot conceive of them sitting in Corinth working on their tents while crowds of people from all the world met at Isthmia ten miles away. Their very craft would give them entree to the foreign delegations at the festival. In April, or early May, when the Isthmian games were held, the air is chilly enough to require shelter; and frequent showers and violent gusts of wind that buffet the Isthmian region make such shelter imperative. Paul and his companions would find plenty of customers for the goods they had produced during the preceding months. We recall the new resolve of

[18] The question of the dates of Paul's residence in Corinth is too complicated to discuss here. Its solution depends primarily on the restoration and interpretation of a fragmentary inscription from Delphi. There is a formidable amount of literature on the subject. The interested reader is referred to Adolf Deissmann, *Paul, A Study in Social and Religious History* (2nd ed., 1957), Appendix I, p. 270, n. 1. The letter of the emperor Claudius to the Delphians was written some time between the end of 51 and August 52, during Gallio's office as proconsul of Achaea. He probably entered upon his office in July 51. Paul, who had already spent more than a year in Corinth when he was called to appear before Gallio, would have been there during the celebration of the Isthmian games in the Spring of 51.

the apostle to sell the work of his hands and the gospel in the same bargain. Paul's associates accompanying him to Isthmia might have included his faithful lieutenants in the ministry, Timothy, Silas, and Luke; his companions in the tent business, Priscilla and Aquila; some of his new converts, Crispus and members of his family, and Stephanas and his household who were the first converts to Christianity in the Achaea, and especially Erastus, the high city official, who as a citizen of rank acquainted with the games could have served as guide and interpreter.[19]

They set out on a road that leads eastward across the gently rolling hills and plains between Corinth and the Isthmian sanctuary. Along the way they stop to read the signs on the monuments and on the tombs of famous men on the roadside. They pass a number of minor shrines, one of Black Aphrodite, another of Bellerophon just outside the city; then the road goes through the village of Kromnoi at the halfway point, and soon they reach the hippodrome a short distance from the Isthmian sanctuary and functionally part of it. In the distance they can now see the white marble roof of the temple of Poseidon, and the tops of other monuments that formed the sanctuary complex. Before they reach the temple, they pass a well-watered area above a deep ravine, the sacred glen, in which several of the lesser sanctuaries of Isthmia are located. Here are temples to the twin goddesses of fertility, Demeter and Kore (Ceres and Proserpina), of the wine god Dionysos, of Artemis, of Eueteria (goddess of good seasons). These are modest shrines subordinated to the two major cults of Poseidon and Palaimon whose sanctuaries lie further east. As they approach this center of religious life, they become aware of people approaching in groups from all directions. Some are followed by slaves and servants carrying equipment for camping; they come on donkeys and horses, festooned with baskets and bundles containing the necessities for the occasion. In the distance toward the east are the blue waters of the Saronic gulf, now dotted with sailboats and with long galleys propelled by rowers, all headed toward the

[19] On the identification of Erastus of the New Testament with the Corinthian aedile whose name occurs on an inscription in Corinth, see *BA*, XIV (1951), 94. The identification is not universally accepted. Cf. Henry J. Cadbury, *The Book of Acts in History* (1955), pp. 44, 55, and n. 26.

harbor, where their passengers disembark and then wind their way up to the festival grounds.

Paul and his party enter the sanctuary of Poseidon from the west through a narrow gateway in the precinct wall recently constructed around the temple. The imposing building shows its age and the ravages of time. Here and there its walls are patched where they have crumbled from damage by fire, the effects of which have not been wholly obliterated by repairs. They enter the rear chamber (*opisthodomos*), which is crowded with statuary representing gods and heroes and with all kinds of religious gifts and mementos. Then re-entering the colonnade they walk along the south side to the principal entrance from the east. There they see visitors dipping their hands for ceremonial ablution in the marble basin placed there for the convenience of priests and and worshipers. In the forechamber (*pronaos*) are other statues, some of bronze, others of marble, dedications to Poseidon or to his wife Amphitrite. They stop to read the names of the dedicators and to admire the skill of the artists who produced them. Then, the doors having been thrown open to admit visitors to the games, they enter the inner hall of worship where a flood of light from the open door illumines the colossal statues of the deities. Poseidon, lord of the sea, is enthroned, holding his trident in his right hand, and at his side sits the goddess Amphitrite, joint ruler of the sea. The statues are set on a high base on which are depicted in marble reliefs the twin sons of Tyndarus, Castor and Pollux, whom the Greeks worship as saviors from the terrors of the sea. The cult group dominates the interior of the temple, and by contrast, reduces to proper proportion the many other statues and monuments that crowd the cult room. On another statue base a marble frieze shows the agonies of Niobe and her children being laid low by the darts of Apollo and his sister Artemis. Niobe, a mere mortal blessed with many children, had dared to compare herself boastfully with Leto, mother of the two deities. Such arrogance could not go unpunished; the pagan gods require humility from their human worshipers. The floor of the room and even the lower parts of the walls are covered with marble slabs in white and blue colors. As they leave the temple they notice on their right an enclosure which, as they judge by the large crowds, is to play a decisive part in the celebration. Here they intend to return to witness the nocturnal rites for which preparations are in progress. Farther east there is a large altar recently constructed, and in front of it the main gateway to the sanctuary. From here an avenue stretches southeastward toward the stadium. Tall pine trees planted in a row line the road on the left, a row of statues of victorious athletes on the right.

Before descending to the lower level where the stadium is located they turn left in the direction of the theater. Here, at the northeast corner of the sanctuary, there is a small enclosure whose anomalous orientation attracts their attention. It encloses an altar on which sacrifices are made to the Cyclops, one-eyed monsters of an early era who became famous as builders of mighty citadels throughout Greece.[20] Below the altar appears the entrance to a cave, and as they stop to inquire about it, a temple servant informs them that in the old days the cave housed the members of a sacred guild who reclined on couches as they participated in their fraternal meals. All this has long since passed; the cave, like its counterpart further east, has become a convenient place for storing away equipment used during the celebration.

From here they descend on the gently sloping ground toward the theater, whose walls and temporary seating arrangement show clearly that the building has not yet been finished. There are eight rows of stone seats surrounding the orchestra; the rest of the auditorium has just been fitted out with wooden seats to accommodate the festival crowds. The orchestra has been newly covered with tamped earth and a wooden scaffold has been erected in front of the scene building for the speakers and actors who will participate in the celebrations. From the lofty spot where they enter the auditorium, they see before them a picture of shifting colors that surpasses in beauty all the magnificence of the festal preparations. The fields have donned their new garments in yellow, blue and green and in all the varying hues of the spring vegetation. A thick forest of pine covering the slopes of the ravine adds a tasseled border at the edge of the plateau;

---

[20] Pausanias II. 2. 1, who mentions the altar of the Cyclops, which he calls an ancient shrine, gives no hint regarding its location. The altar terrace in the northeast corner of the precinct of Poseidon is not earlier than the 4th century B.C., and the suggestion made here that it may have supported the altar of the Cyclops is no more than a conjecture.

and the Geranion mountain ridge limiting the view toward the north, descends in easy ripples toward the shore.

Preparations for the celebrations are in full swing. In the orchestra a group of actors stage a preview of a performance of Euripides' *Medea*, which has been advertised as one of the events in the dramatic contests. Sounds of the flute and the lyre come from a room in the rear, where a poet from Miletus, Themison by name,[21] is training musicians in a musical composition of his own accompanying the Euripidean lyrics. Above the measured sounds of actors and musicians are heard the strident shouts of mule drivers and the clatter of merchants unloading their wares in the rear of the theater and preparing booths for their displays. They have come a long distance, on foot, on mule-back, or by boat. They are tired and hot and dusty, and their weariness and hardship seek expression in the shrill voices that nearly drown out the notes made by performers. Around the fountain to the east of the court people have lined up in a long queue waiting to refresh themselves and their beasts of burden.

From the theater they walk south in the direction of the stadium past a number of monuments, statues, and decrees erected in honor of former directors of the Isthmian games (*agonothetai*) and illustrious athletes and their families. The stadium is a beehive of activity. On the stepped embankments on either side spectators come and go, watching the tryouts of the athletes whose participation in the games has already been announced. Near the end of the race course runners practice the take-off, all their muscles tense and their gaze fixed on the rope in front of them, waiting for the attendant to pull it back. Farther on some athletes are engaged in throwing the discus, now and then stopping to receive instruction from the trainers, whose excellence will be judged on the morrow by the performances of the pupils. In another part of the race course four pairs of muscular giants roll on the ground jabbing, pounding, twisting, and bending each other's limbs until the bones seem to crack under the merciless treatment. A pair of boxers with leather straps around their knuckles parry blows with each other. By word-

[21] An inscription recording the achievements of this productive artist was found in 1952, built into the wall of Justinian. See *Hesperia*, XXII (1953), 192 f. His career must have covered several decades and probably went back to the time of Paul's visit.

less agreement they stop short of inflicting bodily harm on each other, conscious of the fact that any injury received in the training will disqualify them and their competitors for the final performance. Boys and girls carrying small baskets filled with fruit and sweets scurry among the crowds calling the visitors' attention to their products.

Over to the left a small group of onlookers have gathered in a cluster engaged in excitable conversation: "Have you heard the latest? A Jewish visitor from Tarsos is urging the people to believe in a new god. This surpasses anything that has come from the east. Paul, a tent-maker now living in Corinth, is telling people that a man by the name of Jesus, a carpenter's son from Palestine, who was killed by the Roman authorities as a criminal, came back to life after he had been dead for three days. And he does not stop at that. He tells the people that those who believe this incredible story will themselves rise from the grave and live with the resurrected Jesus, whom they also call the Christ. This man Paul has already converted many Jews in this area to his religious beliefs, and he is now turning Greeks away from their ancient gods to join the followers of the resurrected Jewish criminal."

One of Paul's helpers overhears this conversation and tells the apostle about it. Although perhaps disturbed at the form in which his message is being cast, he is happy to hear that the fame of his mission has already spread among the crowd. This is the purpose of his visit. He has not come, like the rest of the visitors, to admire the monuments or to thrill to the athletes' performances. He is a salesman—a seller, yes, of oriental tapestries; but his chief mission is to carry out the behest laid on him by God. Toward the end of the day, as the sun sinks low, the clouds and mountains merge to form a dark curtain in the west; then suddenly the clouds part and the sun's rays, pouring out from below the curtain, wreath the solitary hill of Acrocorinth in a halo of light. To the ancient Corinthians Acrocorinth was the property of Helios the sun god; a sunset such as this would give meaning to their belief. Paul and his small group of followers are not insensitive to such displays of nature's beauty, and every manifestation of this kind speaks to them the glory of the maker. It gladdens their hearts as they face the tasks before them, turning over in their minds the plans for the rest of their visit. On the morrow the games will begin. Paul and his friends are keenly aware of their part in the program; they know how much depends on their success on these festival days. As he watches the athletes, relentlessly torturing their bodies to prepare them for the events in the stadium, Paul sees himself in the role of contestant for a crown which does not wither.

The athletes are about to end their final rehearsal in the stadium when the apostle and his group of friends depart for the main sanctuary. As they ascend from the hollow of the race course toward the upper level, they hear a murmur of many voices and see smoke arising from an enclosed pit. Their guide and informant, who has attended similar celebrations in the past, tells them that they are approaching the precinct of Palaimon, which encloses the fiery pit. None of the visitors from the east know who Palaimon is, nor have they ever heard his name before; and the guide is prompted to tell them the story of the boy-god whose death led to the founding of the Isthmian games.

The sanctuary where the fire has been lit is a new one; but formerly Palaimon, under a different name, Melikertes, received sacrifices on a small altar that stood on the edge of an early stadium. Melikertes was the reputed son of Ino, whose father was Kadmos, king of Thebes. Ino's husband, Athamas, king of Orchomenos, had been punished for impiety by the gods who deprived him of his reason. In his madness he set out to kill all the members of his family. He seized his older son Learchos and crushed him to death against the wall of his palace. Ino, in terror, holding in her arms the younger son, Melikertes, fled from the pursuing madman. He caught up with them as they were headed for Corinth along the rocky north shore of the Saronic gulf. Before he had time to lay his hands on the fleeing woman, she leaped with the baby in her arms into the waves of the gulf.

Here the story, as told by the guide, becomes confused. Ino, he explains, was not drowned but became changed into a goddess of the sea and took on a new name, Leukothea (white goddess). She receives worship from the Greeks as queen of the sea, but she is not alone in this capacity; Amphitrite, Thetis, and other female divinities also claim dominion over the watery deep.

And the baby, which she carried in her arms, what happened to him? Did he too become a sea divinity? Melikertes was drowned and his dead body was carried on the back of a dolphin to the Isthmus and deposited on the shore. On the spot where he was found an altar has been erected, and ever since the Corinthians have offered sacrifices to the dead boy. He too received a new name, Palaimon (the wrestler). The king of Corinth at that time was Sisyphos, whom the Greeks, in their mythology, picture as a sinner against the gods, suffering eternal torment in hell.

The mention of punishment for sins stirs the interest of Paul, who is unaware that the heathen believe in the eternal punishment of the damned.

The guide then tells them the story of Zeus' amours with Aigina, daughter of the river Asopos. Sisyphos, who knew about the scandalous behavior of the god, told the girl's father about it. It was this that aroused the anger of Zeus, who then confined Sisyphos to eternal punishment by forever rolling a heavy stone up a steep slope; and each time, as he neared the edge and began to see the end of his labor, the stone slipped out of his hands and rolled to the bottom of the hill.

They discuss the moral of this tale and to them it seems that Sisyphos, for informing the girl's father about the immorality of the god, should have been rewarded instead of punished.

The guide continues his recitation of the myth. Sisyphos, by chance, happened to be near the Isthmus when the dolphin brought the dead boy ashore. He did not believe that the dolphin, who was a sacred animal accompanying Poseidon, accomplished this feat without divine intervention. Sisyphos brought the boy's body to the sanctuary of Poseidon and buried him with royal honors. The funeral of a distinguished person then called for loud lamentations over the dead and merriment for the comfort of the living. On the day that the boy was buried, the king ordered athletic contests to be held near the grave. This was the beginning of the Isthmian games.

A member of the party recalls that it was Theseus who was responsible for the founding of the games and notices the discrepancy with the guide's story. It is true, he admits, that the story which the Athenians believe is at variance with the one he has just recited. According to the Athenian myth Theseus, son of King Aigeus of Athens, had been brought up by his uncle in Troizen; and when he reached manhood, he made a memorable journey along the shore from Troizen to Athens. The road was infested with robbers and monsters of many kinds. He does not recite the rest of the tale concerning Theseus' fight with those mythological creatures but tells only as much as relates to the founding of the games. Here at the Isthmus, he continues, a cruel giant by the name of Sinis held sway. He would seize travelers passing through the Isthmus and tie their limbs to two pine trees which he bent down to the ground. As he let go of the trees, they would spring back and tear the victim's body apart. Theseus, of course with the aid of the gods, as the Greeks believe, seized the robber and dispatched him in a similar way. After his victory over Sinis, he celebrated the Isthmian games for the first time.

A member of the group then observes that this would make the Isthmian games Athenian. How is it then that they are held on Corinthian territory and under Corinthian management?

The story about Theseus' founding of the games, the guide tells them, is not accepted by the Corinthians. And yet the Athenians are more directly concerned with the Isthmian games than any of the other foreign delegations. Here the guide reminds them of the large vessel with a square, striped sail, which they saw as they approached the stadium. This is one of the sacred boats of the Athenians bringing their delegations to the games. They have a standing agreement with the Corinthians for reserved seats in the stadium, and the space assigned them must be at least as large as the sail on their galley. Tomorrow the Athenians will be seen in a group occupying the best seats in the stadium.

They have now reached the enclosure surrounding the fiery pit, and follow the crowds through the gates. Their guide leads them to the far edge of the area where a small wicket opens into an underground reservoir. Several athletes stand in front of the entrance; and a priest, fingering some amulets, stands in their midst. The participants in the games must here descend into the underground tank to take an oath to Palaimon promising that they have followed all the rules in their preliminary training and that they will not try to cheat in order to win the Isthmian crown.[22] The priest now opens the gate, and with bowed head he walks into the underground chamber followed by the young men. After the last one has left, someone closes the gate, and the crowd stands around the entrance in excited expectation. Two of the visitors are overheard in muffled conversation. They know that one of the athletes during his training omitted to sacrifice to Theseus because, as he said, he was a foreign hero who had no jurisdiction at the Isthmia. The gods are jealous; Palaimon will punish those who swear falsely in his crypt.

They wait a long time before the gates are opened again and the group of young men emerge, led by the priest. They look deathly pale as they come into the light from the flames rising out of the pit. The exact ritual is not divulged, but all believe that to break an oath sworn in the crypt of Palaimon is to invite vengeance from the offended god.

The sun has long since set behind Acrocorinth, and by now the area in front of the shrine is illuminated by large lamps set out on the ground, and by the fire in the pit. Many of the worshipers carry small portable lamps in their left hands and in their right a jug containing olive oil. The level area in front of the shrine is crowded with people, moving toward the pit in the northeast corner, where the fire from the logs is in full blaze. As they come up, they cast their jugs of oil together with the containers into the fire. The flames, fed by the oil from hundreds of vessels, rise higher and higher until they seem to reach the very clouds. Here the temple servant (*neochoros*) approaches with a large lamp in his hands[23] and pushes the crowd aside so as to form a wide avenue leading directly to the pit. Other servants of the altar file by in solemn procession carrying censers and sacred vessels, and leading a young black bull with gilded

[22] "An athlete is not crowned unless he competes according to the rules" (II Tim. 2:5).

[23] An inscription on a marble fragment representing the reflector of a lamp gives the name of a neochoros, G. Julius Eutyches, whose statue stood somewhere in the sanctuary. The support, on which the inscription is carved, was in the form of a lamp, probably as an allusion to the office of the temple caretaker; *Hesperia*, XXVII (1958), 23, No. 4.

horns and hoofs and with garlands hanging from his neck. At the edge of the pit the priest, sweating profusely from the heat of the fire and the voluminous robes that he wears, takes from his garments a large sharp knife with which he cuts the forelock of the victim, then throws it into the fire. There follows the recitation of a prayer, in which the blessings of Palaimon are invoked upon the proceedings, on the city of Corinth and its citizens, the visitors to the games, the athletes, their trainers, and upon all the officials connected with the Isthmian festival. Finally with a quick stroke of the knife the priest slashes the throat of the animal, whose blood spurts on the ground and flows into the pit. The frantic struggle of the wounded bull is checked by attendants who have already tied his legs together. When at last he sinks to the ground, they tighten the ropes around his feet and heave the struggling animal into the fire. The mixed smell of oil, burning hair, roast meat, and melting fat fills the whole area surrounding the pit.

This, their guide explains to them, is the biennial sacrifice to Palaimon. Since he is a hero who was once mortal but has become a god, dwelling with Persephone and Pluto of the netherworld, none of the meat sacrificed to him may be sold or eaten.

The administration of the oath within the crypt and the solemn sacrifice around the pit have occupied several hours,[24] and now the celebrants begin to depart, each to his improvised lodging for the night. Paul and his companions retire to the court behind the theater where servants in their company have been left in charge of the tents erected earlier in the day.

* * *

To help the reader visualize the games and the buildings connected with them I have composed this description of a visit by Paul and a group of his friends on the eve of the Isthmian festival. So far as it is possible I have based my

[24] The athletes at Isthmia took an oath at the altar of Poseidon (E. N. Gardiner, *Greek Athletic Sports and Festivals* [1910], p. 220); but it is likely that they also had to swear to Palaimon in the crypt of his temple, specifically used for the administration of oaths. We do not know at what point in the celebration the sacrifice to Palaimon took place.

description on the actual remains, briefly described above, and on the testimonies of ancient authors regarding the games and their preparations. We do not know how many days were devoted to athletic contests, how the sacrifices to the gods were meshed into the athletic celebrations, or at what stage the winners received their prizes. To attempt a description of the actual games and the other ceremonies throughout the several days that the festival lasted would be to draw upon the imagination further than can be justified in an article of this kind.

The writer of the Acts, who condensed the account of Paul's work of eighteen months in Corinth to only eighteen verses of the eighteenth chapter of his book, gives us no hint about any visit that Paul and his lieutenants may have made to the Isthmian games. There must have been many episodes during this time that were equally important to his missionary work, yet the writer cloaks them in silence. The conversion of Erastus, a man of high position in the city government, would have been a decisive event in the life of a newly founded church; but Luke says nothing about it. Although in the next chapter he mentions Erastus and Timothy as two of Paul's assistants who followed him to Asia Minor, we should not have known who this Erastus was but for a more specific identification in Paul's Epistle to the Romans, written from Corinth (Rom. 16:23).

What would Paul have accomplished with such a visit to the Isthmia? Surely he would have found the means to send personal messages and perhaps letters to the Christian communities in the north of Greece and in Asia Minor. In his epistles his great concern for the churches is an ever recurrent theme, and he was constantly seeking means to communicate with them. He and his companions may have been successful in making converts among the visitors to the games. The contests made a lasting impression on Paul's mind. Five years later, when he wrote from Ephesus to the Christians at Corinth, he recalls the athletes' training for the foot race and the boxing match to illustrate the severe self-control to which he subjected himself. And again at Rome, near the end of his life, the same imagery of the athletic contests comes to his mind as he writes to Timothy, in whose company he may have watched the games in the Isthmian stadium. "I have fought the good fight, I have finished the race, I have kept the faith. Henceforth there is laid up for me the crown of righteousness which the Lord, the righteous judge will award to me on that day."[25]

FIGURE 7. "Do you not know that in a race all the runners compete, but only one receives the prize? So run that you may obtain it." This drawing from a Panathenaic amphora, found at Isthmia, recalls Paul's words in I Corinthians.

[25] II Tim. 4:7–8. The words in the Greek have a more distinctly athletic flavor. To bring this out the passage might be rendered: "I have competed in the good athletic games; I have finished the foot race, I have kept the pledge [i.e. to compete honestly, with reference to the athletic oath]. What remains to me is to receive the crown of righteousness, which has been put aside for me; it will be awarded to me by the Lord, the just umpire, on that day" (an allusion to the last day of the games when, presumably, the prizes were handed out to the winners). Although biblical scholars assign the writing of the pastoral letters—including the two addressed to Timothy—to a period after the time of Paul, they concede that these letters may incorporate genuine fragments of Pauline writing. Cf. Arthur D. Nock, *St. Paul* (1938), p. 232; and Adolf Deissmann, *Paul*, p. 16.